Becoming a Citizen

Becoming a Citizen

*Incorporating Immigrants and Refugees
in the United States and Canada*

IRENE BLOEMRAAD

University of California Press

BERKELEY   LOS ANGELES   LONDON

Parts of chapter 5 originally appeared in Irene Bloemraad, "The Limits of de Tocqueville: How Government Facilitates Organisational Capacity in Newcomer Communities," *Journal of Ethnic and Migration Studies* 31, no. 5 (2005): 865–87. Reprinted by permission of Taylor and Francis, http://www.tandf.co.uk.

University of California Press, one of the most distinguished university presses in the United States, enriches lives around the world by advancing scholarship in the humanities, social sciences, and natural sciences. Its activities are supported by the UC Press Foundation and by philanthropic contributions from individuals and institutions. For more information, visit www.ucpress.edu.

University of California Press
Berkeley and Los Angeles, California

University of California Press, Ltd.
London, England

Library of Congress Cataloging-in-Publication Data

Bloemraad, Irene, 1972–.
    Becoming a citizen : incorporating immigrants and refugees in the United States and Canada / Irene Bloemraad.
        p.   cm.
    Includes bibliographical references and index.
    ISBN-13: 978-0-520-24898-4 (cloth : alk. paper), ISBN-10: 0-520-24898-8 (cloth : alk. paper) – ISBN-13: 978-0-520-24899-1 (pbk. : alk. paper), ISBN-10: 0-520-24899-6 (pbk. : alk. paper)
        1. Citizenship—United States.   2. Citizenship—Canada.   I. Title.

JK1759.B65   2006
323.60973—dc22   2005031017

Manufactured in the United States of America

15   14   13   12   11   10   09   08   07   06
10   9   8   7   6   5   4   3   2   1

This book is printed on New Leaf EcoBook 50, a 100% recycled fiber of which 50% is de-inked post-consumer waste, processed chlorine-free. EcoBook 50 is acid-free and meets the minimum requirements of ANSI/ASTM D5634–01 (*Permanence of Paper*).

For my mother, Gerda R. Bloemraad, an immigrant who ran for elected office and who taught me that foreign birth is no obstacle to full civic and political engagement in one's adopted country.

And in memory of my father, Jan Bloemraad, who taught me how much you can accomplish with perseverance, strength, and sheer stubbornness.

There is no notion more central in politics than citizenship, and none more variable in history, or contested in theory.

JUDITH SHKLAR, *American Citizenship: The Quest for Inclusion*

You don't become a full citizen in a sense of—I'm not talking citizenship now, but in a sense of a citizen in your community— until you have all the rights, privileges, and obligations that being a citizen of your community means.

AGOSTINHO, Portuguese immigrant, Toronto

Contents

Illustrations

Acknowledgments

Writing a book is a lot like having a child. You conceive of an idea, you nurture it so that it grows and develops, and then you labor to transform the idea into words. Having had two children over the course of researching and writing this book, I am not sure which is more difficult. A book does not wake you up at 2 A.M., crying and running a fever of 103°F, but if the gestation and labor involved in producing a child were as long as it is for a book, there would be many fewer parents in the world.

Nonetheless, books get written, largely due to the support and encouragement of others. The genesis of this book reaches back to 1995, from conversations I had with Jerome Black at McGill University. While at McGill, I also benefited from the advice of Suzanne Staggenborg, Maurice Pinard, and Tony Masi. At Harvard University, many people read material that found its way into the final product. Thanks to Andy Andrews and everyone at the social movements workshop, Larry Bobo, Marc Busch and the graduate student program at the Weatherhead Center for International Affairs, Bayliss Camp, Kathleen Coll, Susan Dumais, Tomas Jimenez, Andy Karch, Peggy Levitt, Stan Lieberson, Ted Miguel, Mark Moore and the people at the Hauser Center for Nonprofit Organizations, Monica McDermott, Ziad Munson, Danny Scholzman, Theda Skocpol, Mike Tomz, Mary Waters, and Christopher Winship. At the University of California, Berkeley, my writing and thinking benefited from the generous feedback of Michael Buroway, Claude Fischer, Marion Foucade-Gourinchas, Jenna Johnson-Hanks, John Lie, Dawne Moon, Dylan Riley, Sandra Smith, Ann Swidler, Cihan Tugal, Margaret Weir, and the participants of the Interdisciplinary Immigration Workshop. I also benefited from suggestions and advice given by Alex Alienikoff, Frank Bean, Jim Hollifield, Christian Joppke, Anthony Matthews, Reed Ueda, and Ari Zolberg.

Four individuals at the University of Toronto deserve special mention for their generosity of spirit and time. Thanks to Jeff Reitz for reading everything I sent so carefully and insightfully, to John Myles and Monica Boyd for helping secure access to resources at Statistics Canada, and to Raymond Breton for good conversation, regular lunches, and help with my initial entrée into the Toronto Portuguese community. In Ottawa, Doug Norris, Jane Badets, and especially Derrick Thomas provided invaluable assistance in accessing and understanding Canadian census data, while Denise Ledoux of the Library of Parliament helped provide access to the Library's dataset of Canadian parliamentarians.

The project would have been impossible without the research assistance of the following people: Hung Chau, Naomi Couto, Tuyet Le, Duong Nguyen, and Fernando Nunes in Toronto; Mai Le, Duong Nguyen, Hao Nguyen, Daniel Schlozman, and Jessica Valente in Boston; and Els de Graauw, Shannon Gleeson, Rebecca Hamlin, and Naomi Hsu in Berkeley. My fingers and sanity were also saved by the rapid and accurate transcription done by Jerry Nunes, Patrick Gardner, and Cherie Potts and the computer support provided by Cheri Minton and Nancy Williamson at Harvard.

I was fortunate that many organizations gave financial backing to this project. I gratefully acknowledge support from the National Science Foundation (SES-0000310); the Canadian Social Science and Humanities Research Council; the Quebec Fonds FCAR; the Social Science Research Council; Statistics Canada (Division of Housing, Family and Social Statistics); the Center for American Political Studies, the Weatherhead Center for International Affairs, and the Hauser Center for Nonprofit Organizations, all at Harvard University; and the Institute of Industrial Relations, the Institute of Governmental Studies, the Survey Research Center, the Portuguese Studies Program, the Canadian Studies Program, and the Committee on Research, all at the University of California, Berkeley.

Finally, my deepest debts are to those I interviewed and to my family. The people quoted in these pages gave me hours of their time. They certainly had no obligation to do so, and sometimes they barely had the time to spare. I learned something from each, and I am sorry that these pages cannot do justice to the sacrifices some of them made in trying to build a new future in North America. As for my family, finding the right words is impossible. I dedicate this book to my parents, who brought their young family to North America years ago. While my father never saw the final product, he was there for most of the labor. Finally, to David, thank you for holding my hand during all three births.

Abbreviations

CAP	Citizenship Assistance Program
CDC	community development corporation
CIC	Citizenship and Immigration Canada
ESL	English as a Second Language
HOs	Vietnamese admitted to the United States under the Humanitarian Operation Program
IAFT	Interagency Task Force for Indochina Refugees
ICE	U.S. Immigration and Customs Enforcement
INS	Immigration and Naturalization Service
IRAP	Indochinese Refugee Assistance Program
ISAP	Immigrant Settlement and Adaptation Program
LINC	Language Instruction for Newcomers to Canada
MAA	Mutual Assistance Association
MAPS	Massachusetts Alliance of Portuguese Speakers
MIRA	Massachusetts Immigrant and Refugee Advocacy Coalition
NDP	New Democratic Party
OCASI	Ontario Council of Agencies Serving Immigrants
ODP	Orderly Departure Program
ORR	Office of Refugee Resettlement
PIN	Portuguese Interagency Network
USCIS	U.S. Citizenship and Immigration Services
VACA	Vietnamese-American Civic Association
VAT	Vietnamese Association of Toronto
VOLAGs	American voluntary agencies

Introduction

The Challenge of Immigrant Political Incorporation

If you don't work, if you can't, you can't live. It is tough. But they [the government] don't know how it is. . . . You can't say, "Sir, sir, send people that care about the immigrants, because they are the people who can't speak up." There is nowhere to complain to, and we can't complain.

MANUELA, *Portuguese immigrant, Cambridge, Massachusetts*

Oh, I want to vote, I want to vote. . . . [It is] very difficult because my income is not much and my husband's income not very much. Manuel, he's the one who taught us to get [citizenship] papers. And he applied for a supplement from [the] government to pay him to teach us about the politics to become a citizen.

TILLA, *Portuguese immigrant, Toronto*

Many debates around immigration and ethnic pluralism originate from a fundamental question of whether unity or community can develop out of diversity. Is *e pluribus unum* possible? In countries with significant ethno-racial diversity such as the United States and Canada, the glue that binds strangers is citizenship in the political body. Citizenship is not only a legal status that accords rights and benefits, but it is also an invitation to partici-pate in a system of mutual governance, and it can be an identity that pro-vides a sense of belonging. When residents of a country do not acquire citi-zenship or fail to participate in the political system, not only is the sense of shared enterprise undermined, but so, too, are the institutions of democra-tic government.

Recent trends in immigrants' acquisition of U.S. citizenship consequently set off alarm bells. In 1950 almost four out of every five foreign-born resi-dents in the United States held American citizenship, but in 2004 fewer than two out of five were citizens. The decline occurred as the number of migrants coming to the United States increased significantly and the origins of these newcomers shifted from Europe to Latin America, the Caribbean, South America, and Asia. Given the United States' long tradition as a land of immigration and the country's largely successful integration of past European immigrants, some wonder what is wrong with today's new-

comers. Do they have less loyalty and civic spirit than previous generations? Are they uninterested in participating? Do they lack the ability to
participate? Do modern communication and transportation technologies
keep migrants tied to their old home, preventing them from putting down
roots in their new country?

These explanations, each plausible in its own right, all assume that the decline in immigrant citizenship or the problem of political incorporation
stems primarily from the characteristics of immigrants. If foreigners are not
becoming full citizens, the problem must lie with them. This book argues
that while the characteristics of immigrants and newcomer communities
matter—some have a harder time with political incorporation than others—the story of citizenship is not just about the immigrants we receive, but
also fundamentally about the reception we give them. In the United States,
immigration policy largely starts and ends at the border. Government attention and resources revolve around border control; later processes of immigrant integration are considered outside the purview of state action. As
Nathan Glazer puts it, "the settlement, adaptation, and progress, or lack of it,
of immigrants is largely, in the U.S. context, up to them" (1998: 60).

Relative to the United States, Canada has taken a more interventionist
stance toward immigrant incorporation. First, the Canadian bureaucracy
overseeing immigration and citizenship supports integration and has a normative bias in favor of citizenship. Second, federal, provincial, and municipal governments in Canada tend to offer more public assistance with the
practical business of settlement and integration, subsidizing, for example,
classes to learn English or programs to find a job. Finally, an official policy
of multiculturalism, espoused by the federal government and with provincial or local equivalents, promotes integration through public recognition—
and funding—of ethnic diversity. In the United States, the bureaucracy
dealing with immigration and citizenship engages in little outreach, and the
federal government provides sustained settlement support only to legally
recognized refugees. It has no official multiculturalism policy akin to
Canada's, although U.S. governments at various levels enforce laws and run
programs that aim to protect and assist racial minorities. These laws, regulations, and programs constitute a diversity policy that can help nonwhite
immigrants, but because such initiatives were primarily conceived with the
native born in mind, they deal poorly with the particular concerns of foreign-born newcomers.

These differences in the context of reception produce quantifiable differences in political incorporation. The 2001 Canadian census reported that
the overwhelming majority of foreign-born residents in Canada, 72 percent,

had acquired Canadian citizenship, almost double the proportion in the United States. The divergence with American patterns is all the more surprising since citizenship levels in Canada and the United States looked quite similar over much of the twentieth century. Only since the 1970s—at exactly the point that Canada established a policy of multiculturalism and expanded government intervention in newcomer settlement—have trends in the two countries diverged. Whereas U.S. citizenship levels declined over the final three decades of the twentieth century, the proportion of naturalized Canadian citizens in 2001 represented a sizeable increase over the 60 percent of foreign-born residents who were Canadian in 1971. The increase occurred despite large-scale migration that also became globalized and diversified during this period.

The U.S.-Canada gap is also remarkable since the benefits of citizenship in the United States far outweigh the benefits of mere U.S. permanent residency: having American citizenship makes it easier to sponsor family members into the country and provides greater access to social welfare benefits. Canada, by contrast, does not link citizenship to sponsorship or social benefits. There are fewer reasons for a permanent resident to acquire citizenship in Canada.

The difference in U.S.-Canada citizenship levels varies depending on the immigrant group, and it changes after controlling for individual attributes such as length of residence or education, but even after we take such factors into account, today levels of citizenship are consistently higher in Canada than in the United States.

Diverging patterns of political incorporation also show up elsewhere. In 2000, 11 percent of the U.S. population was foreign born, but less than 2 percent of the members of the 107th U.S. Congress were born outside the United States. In 2002, 15 percent of the members sitting in Canada's House of Commons were foreign born, a proportion not far off the 19 percent of the population that was foreign born. The immigrant face of Canada finds better reflection in that country's legislature than is the case south of the border.

The statistics are also reflected in the stories that immigrants tell. Manuela and Tilla, two women who came to North America in the 1960s, have lived very similar lives. Both were born in the Portuguese Azores, islands in the Atlantic Ocean about eight hundred miles west of Lisbon. Life in the Azores was not easy. Families were large—both Tilla and Manuela have eight siblings—and economic opportunities were limited. Manuela's father worked in fishing, and Tilla's father found odd jobs as a farm laborer. Facing a bleak future on the islands, Manuela moved to Cambridge, Massachusetts, with her husband and young son after her sister-in-law sponsored the family's immigration. Tilla and her parents were sponsored by an aunt living in Toronto, Ontario. Limited educational opportunities in the Azores left both women with only primary schooling. To put food on the table and a roof over their families' heads, both found factory work immediately after arriving in North America.

Manuela has spent a bit more than half of her life in the United States. She rents a home close to the Portuguese church that she attends weekly, she works long hours as a cleaner, and she has raised three children to adulthood. Manuela has become a U.S. citizen and plans to live out her days in her adopted country, close to her children and grandchildren, but despite her passport and her years in the United States, she feels shut out of the American political system. According to Manuela, immigrants are "the people who can't speak up," and political decision makers do not know or care about people like her. Without some link to government, through "people that care about the immigrants," she feels silenced.

Tilla, who has also raised three children in her adopted country and carries a similar devotion to her Catholic faith, shares with Manuela the view that the migrant's life is a hard one: things are better in North America, but the price in sweat and tears is significant. Long hours in factories and as a cleaner have taken a toll. However, Tilla holds a more positive view of politics: politicians sometimes overlook people like her, but there are others who will listen. Politics matters, and immigrants can have a voice. "I want to vote," she declares adamantly. Critically, government shows an interest in immigrants. In her case, a small government grant paid a stipend to a fellow Portuguese immigrant to teach her and others about Canadian citizenship: how to apply for it and how to exercise a citizen's political rights.

Tilla and Manuela come from similar backgrounds and face comparable obstacles to political participation, but they have quite different views of their importance in the political system and their sense of political efficacy. As we will see, the way governments react to immigration exerts a powerful influence on understandings of citizenship and the ability to be politically active. This book argues that the difference between Tilla's and Manuela's political perceptions and behavior lies in large part in the distinct American and Canadian policies of settlement and diversity. These policies offer immigrants symbolic and material resources, which produce two interrelated dynamics affecting political incorporation. One is *interpretative*, affecting understandings of citizenship, especially of immigrants' legitimate political standing as citizens and of their ability to participate in the political process. The second is *instrumental*, enhancing the ability of newcomer communities to mobilize and participate politically. Government policies both inform understandings of citizenship and directly affect the ability to participate.

At its core, this book shows that the seeds of civic involvement and political engagement lie as much in public decisions as in private actions. Indeed, there is a certain irony in realizing that Canadian multiculturalism— attacked by some in Canada and the United States as divisive—promotes political integration. In contrast, the government's laissez-faire attitude in the United States, nurtured by the belief that integration will arise through millions of immigrants' individual decisions, appears to produce political apathy and alienation rather than incorporation.

THEORIZING POLITICAL INCORPORATION

The United Nations estimates that the number of migrants in the world has doubled since 1970, with about 175 million people living outside their country of birth in 2000 (United Nations, Department of Economic and Social Affairs 2002). In North America alone, the number of migrants increased 48 percent from 1990 to 2000. In 1960 only one in twenty people in the United States was foreign born, but at the dawn of the twenty-first century more than one in ten U.S. residents had been born outside the United States. The number exceeds one in four in California and stands at about one in eight in Massachusetts. In Canada, nearly one in five residents is foreign born, as are more than a quarter of those living in Ontario. Despite increased control of migration following the terrorist attacks of September 11, 2001, there are few signs that the upward trend in migration will stop anytime soon.

Immigrants' political behavior will therefore increasingly determine the outcome of political contests and the policies that governments pursue. Indeed, as soon as they arrive, migrants' physical presence changes the apportionment of political seats in national and subnational legislative bodies.[1] The political incorporation of today's immigrants also carries long-term consequences for participation among future generations of Americans and Canadians, since parents' political behavior shapes that of their children.[2]

This book investigates how immigrants achieve *full citizenship*: acquisition of legal or formal citizenship, known as naturalization, and engagement in the political system of the adopted country, what we might call *participatory* or *substantive citizenship*. Achieving both constitutes political incorporation. The term *political* must be understood broadly, but I concentrate on three indicators: acquisition of citizenship, community advocacy (that is, mobilization endeavors by community organizations and leaders), and immigrants' success in getting elected to political office.[3] *Incorporation* refers to the process of becoming a part of mainstream political debates, practices, and decision making.[4] The end point of the process is difficult to identify, but incorporation is generally achieved when patterns of immigrant participation are comparable to those among the native born, although different individuals and groups might privilege certain forms of participation over others.

What factors facilitate or hinder political incorporation? Why do the United States and Canada exhibit divergent trajectories of political incorporation? Surprisingly, we know little about the determinants of immigrants' political integration. Students of immigration have developed a sophisticated literature on economic, social, and cultural integration, but they have largely overlooked the political sphere.[5] Students of politics have produced voluminous research on voting and political behavior, but most studies fail to distinguish between persons born abroad and those born and raised in North America. In Canada, immigrant political behavior, when examined, is largely incorporated into the study of mass politics by adding immigrant status as another variable in a regression equation (Stasiulis 1997). In the United States, immigrant participation tends to be subsumed under minority politics, making it impossible to know whether findings for Asian Americans or Latinos apply equally to immigrants and the U.S. born, or whether place of birth makes a difference in outcomes.[6]

Both tendencies are problematic. Economic, social, and cultural integration is structured by laws, policies, and regulations passed by government. Poor educational outcomes for immigrant children might arise in part from public decisions to cut funding to schools or to eliminate programs for students with limited English-language skills. Immigrant incomes can be affected by minimum wage laws. Since public decisions shape immigrants' lives, we need to know how much say immigrants have in these decisions.

There is also good reason to believe that immigrants' political experiences differ significantly from those of the general population. Initial political socialization often takes place in an entirely different context. Arriving in North America, immigrants must go through political (re-)learning, a process aided by informal networks to those "in the know" and by organizations or associations that educate and mobilize community members. Language differences also make the immigrant experience unique. Those who do not speak the host society language well must rely on ethnic organizations and informal networks, and they also consume ethnic, rather than mainstream, media for political information. Furthermore, being an immigrant provides alternative identities and self-understandings. Nonwhite migrants in North America might be perceived or act as immigrant "ethnics" in some political contexts but as native-born racial minorities in others.[7]

Approaches to the study of immigrant political incorporation vary substantially depending on whether we consider traditional immigrant-receiving countries, such as Australia, Canada, and the United States, or more recent migrant destinations, like those in Europe. Research about North America largely uses theoretical and methodological frameworks that are behavioral and employ statistical data to measure the effect of individual attributes on outcomes such as naturalization, registering to vote, casting a ballot, partisanship, and participation in electoral campaigns.[8] Would-be citizens are conceptualized as rational decision makers who must weigh the benefits of naturalization, like family reunification (Jasso and Rosenzweig 1986), against costs, such as giving up one's former citizenship (Jones-Correa 1998a). Characteristics like gender, age, educational attainment, income, marital status, and home ownership become indicators of how people perceive the relative costs and benefits of citizenship and political involvement or tools that allow an immigrant to naturalize and participate in the political system. The micro-level approach is repeated in immigrant-receiving countries such as Canada.[9] Political incorporation boils down to resources, skills, and interests.

We can, of course, find variants to this approach. Some researchers emphasize the effect of contextual factors such as the characteristics of the sending country (Jasso and Rosenzweig 1986, 1990; Yang 1994), immigrants' perceptions of discrimination in the host society (Portes and Curtis 1987; Uhlaner 1996), or the availability of dual citizenship (Jones-Correa 2001b). In doing so, they offer more refined models of immigrants' decision-making environments. Other researchers consider the effects of inter-ethnic social networks (Liang 1994) or shared cultural understandings of political behavior (Greeley and McCready 1975). This work focuses on group traits. In general, however, much of the North American scholarship concurs that the characteristics of immigrants—whether personal, such as education and language ability, or by origin group, such as social capital—hold the key to understanding naturalization and participation.[10]

The major weakness of the behavioral tradition is its inattention to institutional contexts. Most research on traditional immigrant-receiving countries considers one host country at a time and assumes that results in one country are equally applicable in another. In other words, Australian findings inform dynamics in the United States, and American conclusions apply to Canada. But for such research to be truly transferable, one must assume that institutional factors such as political systems and government structures play no role in immigrant political incorporation and that they do not interact with individuals' attributes and preferences. This assumption is largely untested, and it is challenged by contemporary American and Canadian incorporation trends.

An extensive European literature instead concentrates on institutional contexts. Adopting terminology from the literature on social movements, Koopmans and Statham (1999) suggest that states' unique political opportunity structures direct immigrant protest behavior.[11] Students of citizenship find that the relevance of immigrants' attributes fades after we consider the characteristics of reception countries.[12] The average naturalization rate in the core European Union and European Free Trade Area countries—calculated as the annual number of naturalizations over the noncitizen foreign "stock"— varies widely. On the low end, countries such as Germany, Ireland, Italy, and Switzerland recorded an annual naturalization rate of less than 1 percent in the early 1990s, compared to a rate of about 6.5 percent in the Netherlands and Sweden in 1994 (Clarke, van Dam, and Gooster 1998). Reproducing the calculation in North America for the same period, we find a naturalization rate of about 3 percent in the United States and 10 percent in Canada.[13]

Given these figures, the central puzzle shifts from "Why do certain immigrants naturalize while other do not?" to "What causes large cross-national variations in political incorporation?" Scholars point out that differences in laws and bureaucratic procedures generate greater hurdles for immigrants in one country compared to another. Legal differences are in turn explained by variations in national ideologies and philosophies.[14]

The comparative institutional viewpoint, widespread in Europe, has not been applied to North America, mostly because, according to current theorizing, Canada-U.S. differences in immigrant political incorporation should not exist. Relative to other countries in the world, Canada and the United States are largely seen as interchangeable. Both fall into the category of liberal welfare states (Esping-Andersen 1990) and are considered classic countries of immigration, embracing expansive citizenship regimes (Brubaker 1989; Joppke 1999). Citizenship acquisition is promoted through easy naturalization policies, and the new citizen is legally indistinguishable from the native born.[15] According to Laczko (1994), the two countries are among the few in the world that successfully combine heterogeneous populations and a high standard of living.[16] Both countries also share a darker side to their immigration history. Canada and the United States engaged in comparable policies of exclusion in the late nineteenth and early twentieth century, penalizing and barring Asian immigration, interning perceived enemies such as those of Japanese origin during World War II—even when some internees were born in North America—and promoting immigration systems that favored white Europeans until the 1960s.

This book makes the case that an institutional approach *can* illuminate North American incorporation patterns. Although people's individual interests, skills, and resources help explain dynamics of political integration, such a lens only provides a narrow view of overall incorporation processes. Contexts of reception channel the beliefs and behaviors of immigrants through a nested process of *structured mobilization*. Immigrants, as outsiders, must mobilize themselves to become politically incorporated. This process of political learning and mobilization is nested in the social organization of the ethnic and mainstream communities. Locally, social networks, community organizations, and ethnic leadership play critical roles in helping newcomers. This local infrastructure is in turn shaped by government policies. Migrants acquire resources and support for political participation through the actions—or inactions—of government, and government actions shape immigrants' very impressions and understandings of citizenship.

My argument finds inspiration in European scholarship on political incorporation, but it also flows into a nascent research trend among scholars of immigration that suggests that institutions shape newcomers' political mobilization, economic success, and language learning.[17] The institutional approach runs the risk at times of understating immigrants' agency, implying that individuals can do little once they are locked in the iron cage of national ideologies and political opportunity structures.[18] Here I push this research agenda by identifying *how* government policies affect newcomers' interest and ability to pursue full citizenship. I specify mechanisms that link individuals and immigrant communities to the political system. In particular, I draw attention to the ways in which U.S. and Canadian policies toward newcomer settlement and ethno-racial diversity shape the building blocks of political mobilization: organizations, community leadership, and effective political discourses. They do so by providing material and symbolic resources that assist in political incorporation and affecting conceptions of participatory citizenship.

The United States and Canada are both nations of civic citizenship: they allow foreigners membership.[19] All civic nationalisms contain cultural elements of who can be civic and what counts as civic behavior, but citizenship status is predicated on political belonging rather than blood or background. There are, however, nuanced differences between immigrants' perceptions of American and Canadian citizenship, and these are consequential. In the United States, migrants understand citizenship as offering rights and legal protections, such as protection from deportation, as well as economic opportunity, notably the freedom to achieve economic success. Such rights and freedoms do not lead to a strong conception of political belonging but rather to legal or economic citizenship. In Canada, migrants link citizenship to economic opportunities and rights—especially since the 1982 Charter of Rights and Freedoms increased the salience of rights appeals in Canada. But immigrants in Canada also link citizenship to government protection and support. The result is a greater sense of political citizenship. In addition, the greater ethnic focus of Canadian multiculturalism generates a sense of recognition as an immigrant, with a unique cultural, linguistic, and historical background. American multiculturalism, couched largely in categories of race, requires immigrants to move away from specific cultural and identity backgrounds. In doing so, American citizenship appears to imply membership as part of a pan-racial group, creating ambiguities about one's place in the nation.

Different understandings of citizenship arise from a host of policies and government actions in the two countries. The policies of the welfare state—social assistance, health care, unemployment insurance, and so forth—play a role in forming understandings of citizenship and providing instrumental means to participate. The strands of this influence come up in the conversations with immigrants reported in this book. The focus here, however, is on the two policy arenas most fundamentally related to newcomers' incorporation: settlement and diversity policies.

THE CENTRALITY OF POLITICAL INCORPORATION

The stakes in better understanding political integration are significant. Demographic trends will force politicians, academics, and public observers to think much more about political incorporation than they have previously. The arrival of newcomers also raises important philosophical and normative questions about the nature of democracy and equality in liberal nation-states. Across the Western world noncitizens enjoy increased rights as citizenship restrictions on employment, social services, and licensing requirements gradually disappear.[20] These changes have led some to wonder whether the foundations of political membership and belonging are moving beyond traditional notions of citizenship to a new normative and legal framework based on human rights and personhood.[21]

Yet political rights such as voting and running for office have remained, for the most part, linked to citizenship.[22] There are some proposals in the United States to allow noncitizens voting rights, and a handful of jurisdictions permit alien suffrage (Harper-Ho 2000). However, few in North America challenge the link between citizenship and the vote. It seems unlikely that Canada or the United States will follow the example of some

European countries, such as Sweden and the Netherlands, which increasingly give noncitizens access to the ballot box. Membership matters, because, as Joseph Carens puts it, citizenship in Western liberal democracies is "the modern equivalent of feudal privilege—an inherited status that greatly enhances one's life chances" (1987: 252). From the immigrant's perspective, political exclusion undermines newcomers' control over their own destinies: noncitizens cannot represent their interests as easily, nor do they enjoy the same rights as citizens. The absolute importance of citizenship might be diminishing, but citizenship remains "a powerful instrument of social closure" (Brubaker 1992: x).

Immigrants' political incorporation thus carries significant repercussions for states that derive their legitimacy from notions of equality and democratic involvement. If a sizeable proportion of a country's population remains outside the political system—as when immigrants fail to naturalize or participate—the moral and political legitimacy of the nation-state is challenged. My work is predicated on the belief that immigrants' political incorporation matters to immigrants, host countries, and by extension, the native-born population of such societies.[23]

Immigrants might also tell us much about more general processes of politics and nation building in North America (Gerstle and Mollenkopf 2001). Declining levels of citizenship in the United States correspond to an apparent decline in civic and political engagement among the general American population as well as a qualitative change in the form of such participation.[24] Starting sometime between 1960 and 1975, Americans have become less likely to vote, to attend a political meeting, or to be a member of a civic association. An understanding of immigrant political incorporation, particularly through a cross-national comparison like the one developed here, can teach us about broader processes of change in American politics. If immigrants similar in so many ways, like Tilla and Manuela, experience divergent political outcomes depending on whether they migrate to Canada or the United States, we learn that something about the context of reception matters to participation. In this way, immigrants act as a lens on the political system, magnifying our ability to see the effect of institutional configurations on all members of a polity.[25]

RESEARCH DESIGN, DATA, AND METHODOLOGY

The concept of citizenship has animated an enormous body of philosophical and theoretical scholarship over the past twenty years. Usually written by political theorists or legal scholars, debates revolve around the moral and social foundations of citizenship and participation, the content of rights, the role of membership categories in a complex, global world, and the challenges of multiculturalism.[26] While stimulating, little of this literature is grounded in empirical research. Do these abstract discussions reflect or inform the lives of ordinary immigrants?

I concentrate on the empirical process of political incorporation. The arguments presented here build on evidence from census and survey statistics, documentary materials, and in-depth interviews with 151 individuals. The book engages in a series of comparisons: a cross-national U.S.-Canada comparison and a comparison of Portuguese immigrants and Vietnamese refugees in metropolitan Boston and Toronto.

Surprisingly, few students of politics or immigration compare Canada and the United States, although such a comparison is ideal for immigration research.[27] The many similarities between the United States and Canada control for extraneous variability inherent in U.S.-Europe comparisons.[28] As Seymour Martin Lipset, a longtime advocate of U.S.-Canada comparisons, argues, "the more similar the units being compared, the more possible it should be to isolate the factors responsible for differences between them" (1990: xiii).

Cross-national differences exist, of course. Due to geography, history, and immigration policies, the United States attracts a large percentage of immigrants from Mexico and Latin America. Canada receives few immigrants from these areas but draws heavily from Asia, especially the Indian subcontinent and East Asia. We know that immigrant groups differ in their propensity to naturalize and participate; thus variations in the two countries' immigration streams could produce aggregate differences in citizenship and participation unrelated to government integration and diversity policies or dynamics of community mobilization. To mitigate this problem, I conducted an in-depth investigation of two newcomer communities, the Portuguese and the Vietnamese.

The Portuguese, because of their nearly identical migration patterns to both the United States and Canada, provide a unique "quasi-experiment." In a laboratory experiment, the effect of a particular intervention, such as a new teaching technique or a new drug, can be tested by varying its administration between a treatment and a control group which are otherwise the same. In a like manner, because Portuguese migrants arriving in North America share similar cultural, socioeconomic, and political backgrounds, differences in political incorporation can be attributed to their different "treatment," that is, the different impact of the host society's institutions. Almeida (2000) claims that Portuguese immigrants in North America share so many sociocultural features that the two populations are largely inter-changeable. In my own interviews, many respondents told of a sibling, cousin, or friend who lives on the other side of the border.

The Portuguese in the United States are also of interest since they represent a negative case: Portuguese immigrants have not naturalized quickly, and they have been practically invisible on the political scene, despite high concentrations in New England and California.[29] This invisibility stems in part from Portuguese immigrants' relatively impoverished socioeconomic background. Portuguese immigrants' levels of education—a strong predictor of political incorporation—average about grade eight, one of the lowest levels of educational attainment of any immigrant group in North America (Reitz 1998; Borjas 1999). Given the more supportive policy environment in Canada, we would expect immigrants such as the Portuguese to incorporate more quickly and easily into the Canadian political system than compatriots in the United States.

The Vietnamese community offers a further evaluation of structured mobilization. Vietnamese migration, although not as uniformly similar in the United States and Canada, originates in comparable refugee flows. Like the Portuguese, the Vietnamese community contains a significant proportion of individuals with limited schooling, significant language problems, and a distrust of politics—all barriers to full citizenship. We can also compare the effect of race-based obstacles to political incorporation. Unlike the Portuguese, who are considered part of the white majority in North America, the Vietnamese are seen as a racial minority. Most important, the Vietnamese, as an official refugee group, have received substantial assistance, individually in the form of social benefits and settlement services and as a community through technical assistance and funding to community organizations, in both Canada and the United States. U.S. governments do not provide similar support to those who immigrate for economic or family reunification reasons such as the Portuguese.[30] Because refugees in the United States face a policy environment more similar to the one in Canada, cross-country differences should be attenuated for refugees, while refugee/nonrefugee differences should be more pronounced in the United States. That is, if everything else is equal, Vietnamese experiences should be more alike in Canada and the United States, and Vietnamese Americans should be more politically integrated than Portuguese Americans.[31]

I situate my study of these two groups in the Boston and Toronto metropolitan areas. Toronto is home to an extremely large and diverse migrant population. Boston boasts a smaller foreign-born population, but it shares significant similarities with Toronto. Both are eastern financial centers, both have large service economies, and both house the state/provincial capital.[32] The two cities also have weathered similar demographic revolutions. The Boston area went from being a white ethnocentric community in the 1960s—with a tiny minority island, mostly black, at its core—to a multicultural metropolis by the 1990s (Bloemraad 2003; Bluestone and Stevenson 2000). In a similar manner, Toronto evolved from a historic guardian of Anglo-Protestantism to claiming that the United Nations had designated it the most multicultural city in the world (Siemiatycki et al. 2003; Troper 2003).[33]

I use a variety of evidence in support of my argument. The analysis of immigrants' citizenship status employs census data and statistical modeling to artificially control for variations within migration streams—such as differing demographic and socioeconomic characteristics—in order to identify cross-national and intergroup variations. Census data do not, however, provide information on aspects of political incorporation beyond citizenship, and they fail to reveal the mechanisms through which political incorporation takes place.[34] We cannot learn what people think about citizenship or the sequence of events leading to naturalization and participation.

I thus turn to in-depth interviews and documentary materials to understand conceptions of citizenship and the processes behind political integration. The bulk of my data comes from 151 open-ended interviews with first- and second-generation immigrants, individuals associated with newcomer settlement, and government officials. The immigrant interviews were divided into two roughly equal sets. For the first set, I used referrals to seek out "ordinary" migrants with personal backgrounds, migration histories, and sociodemographic characteristics reflective of the average Portuguese or Vietnamese migrant. The second set of interviews involved local community leaders active in organizations serving the Portuguese or Vietnamese communities or who were identified by others as spokespersons or advocates. I also interviewed twenty-one non-Vietnamese and non-Portuguese who worked with newcomers or in government as elected officials or public employees.[35]

Interview data are supplemented by documentary evidence from organizations serving Portuguese and Vietnamese migrants. I tried to enumerate all the key organizations and associations in each community through my interviews and by using ethnic telephone directories, municipal referral lists, or compilations from social service networks. Where possible, I used annual reports or internal documents to construct a history of the organization and to trace funding relationships and organizational ties to government agencies. For the government perspective, I accessed public and internal papers documenting funding, philosophies, and bureaucratic practices. Interviews with individuals active in the various agencies and organizations provided additional information and placed the written material in context.[36]

LOOKING AHEAD

Chapter 1 provides an in-depth look at diverging patterns of political incorporation in the United States and Canada, focusing on the acquisition of formal citizenship and election of foreign-born individuals to national legislatures. To account for cross-national differences, I take seriously the lessons of past scholarship, examining the policies that bring migrants to North America, the laws governing citizenship, and the characteristics of each country's newcomers.

Chapter 2 moves away from these established frameworks to argue for the social nature of immigrants' political incorporation: newcomers rely on personal networks, community organizations, and mobilization by ethnic leaders to learn about citizenship and participation. Using the examples of Portuguese immigrants and Vietnamese refugees, I show that regardless of whether they live in Canada or the United States, newcomers' political learning is a social process.

However, U.S. and Canadian policy environments provide very different contexts for political mobilization and learning. In chapter 3 I examine three sorts of government intervention: the bureaucratic administration of citizenship acquisition, each country's policies of settlement, and approaches to managing diversity. Localized, community-based political incorporation must be understood as nested in these larger institutional and policy structures.

Chapters 4 through 6 investigate the consequences of structured mobilization. I explore migrants' understanding of citizenship and beliefs about their political standing in chapter 4. Chapter 5 examines the impact of government support on the organizational landscape of newcomer communities, showing that groups that receive more resources establish more numerous and diverse community organizations. Chapter 6 highlights similar dynamics for patterns of leadership in migrant communities: symbolic and material resources affect opportunities for leadership among immigrant advocates, while policies combine with other political institutions—such as party systems, union presence, and finance regulations—to shape immigrants' ability to run for and win political office.

The conclusion revisits the question of how multiculturalism can enhance or imperil the ability of states to generate unity from diversity, a critical question given various countries' apparent retreat from multicultural citizenship. The final chapter also speculates on what might change or remain the same for immigrant citizenship in the post–September 11 environment.

1. Diverging Trajectories of Political Incorporation

> I swear (or affirm) that I will be faithful and bear true allegiance to Her Majesty Queen Elizabeth the Second, Queen of Canada, Her Heirs and Successors, and that I will faithfully observe the laws of Canada and fulfill my duties as a Canadian citizen.
>
> OATH OF AFFIRMATION OF CITIZENSHIP, *Canada*

> I hereby declare, on oath . . . that I will support and defend the Constitution and laws of the United States of America against all enemies, foreign and domestic; that I will bear true faith and allegiance to the same . . . and that I take this obligation freely without any mental reservation or purpose of evasion; so help me God.
>
> OATH OF ALLEGIANCE, *United States*

The passage of the U.S. Personal Responsibility and Work Opportunity Reconciliation Act, commonly known as the Welfare Reform Act, suddenly and dramatically highlighted the importance of citizenship in the United States. Signed into law on August 22, 1996, the act introduced sweeping revisions to the distribution of public benefits for all residents of the United States. Immigrants faced arguably the harshest change: within a year of the law's passage, most noncitizens, including longtime legal permanent residents, would be denied Supplemental Security Income and food stamps. States could also refuse Medicaid and welfare to those who were not U.S. citizens.[1]

The act reversed a long trend blurring distinctions between citizens and legal permanent residents. In the 1960s and 1970s courts and legislatures had rolled back citizenship requirements for certain professions, licenses, and public benefits. Welfare reform redrew a sharp divide between citizens and "aliens."[2] Statistics from the U.S. Census Bureau showed that of approximately 25.8 million foreign-born residents living in the United States in March 1997, barely 35 percent had acquired citizenship (Schmidley and Gibson 1999). Millions of people would be unable to turn to the government if they fell on hard times.

The Census Bureau statistics also sparked concern over immigrants' political incorporation. Citizenship among the foreign born hit an all-time low in 1997, standing at less than half the midcentury percentage, 79 percent. Since political rights such as the right to vote in state and federal elections or the ability to stand for elected office are tied to American citizenship, declining naturalization means declines in immigrants' ability to participate in electoral politics.

The fall in naturalization in the United States is all the more startling if we consider America's neighbor to the north. In 1996, 70 percent of foreign-born residents in Canada were naturalized citizens (Statistics Canada 2001). For the level of naturalization in the United States to mirror that in Canada, more than nine million noncitizen residents would need to acquire American citizenship overnight. Both countries share a liberal approach to immigrant naturalization predicated on a historic belief in immigration as a tool for population growth and economic expansion. American and Canadian citizenship laws draw from common English roots. Given such similarities, it is not surprising that immigrant naturalization in the United States and Canada looked remarkably alike for most of the twentieth century. However, beginning in the 1970s, naturalization trajectories part course dramatically.

A similar phenomenon can be seen in the percentage of foreign-born individuals in each country's legislature. Successfully electing a foreign-born politician to national office is a highly symbolic, and potentially influential, indicator of immigrants' political incorporation. As with citizenship, over the first half of the twentieth century, similar proportions of foreign-born legislators sat in the U.S. Congress and Canadian Parliament, relative to the percentage of the foreign born in the overall population. Since the 1960s, however, immigrants in Canada have moved much closer and more rapidly to representational parity than immigrants in the United States.

These differences are surprising given the many similarities between the two countries. The direction of divergence also flies in the face of conventional wisdom. Many would predict that the United States, with a longer history of independence and an arguably stronger assimilationist impulse, would encourage political integration more than Canada. The United States promotes a unifying civic nationalism based on the ideals of the American Revolution; Canada weathers recurrent separation attempts by Quebec (Lipset 1986, 1990). Further, in the eyes of some, Canada espouses a potentially divisive policy of official multiculturalism that encourages difference rather than common "Canadianness" (Bissoondath 1994; Gwyn 1995). Even those sympathetic to the recognition of difference assume that government promotion of multiculturalism retards immigrant integration: "The more the social and political institutions of the host society accept and recognize ethnic differences, the less likely are immigrants to experience pressure, either formally or informally, to file for citizenship. In the case of landed immigrants, the multiculturalist context of Canadian society has contributed toward prolonging their decisions to apply for citizenship. . . . The situation should be different in the United States, where ethnicity has officially received a low profile" (Legendre and Shaffir 1984: 257). Yet the opposite is true. Why have trajectories of political integration diverged so sharply in North America? Why does incorporation happen more quickly in Canada, despite worries over the country's political future and its sense of national identity?

The most obvious answer, prevalent in many comparative accounts of immigration and citizenship, suggests that legal codes make political incorporation easier and more attractive in Canada, or more costly and less beneficial in the United States. Alternatively, scholars of politics suggest that the immigrants, rather than the legal codes, likely differ. General models of voting consistently show that people with greater skills, resources, and interest in politics are more likely to participate. It is easier to naturalize, vote, or run for office if you have good communication skills, as measured by years of education or English proficiency. Differences in political incorporation might consequently stem from differences in the type of immigrants who move to the United States or Canada. As we will see in this chapter, both explanations have merit, but—surprisingly—neither explains away the gap in political incorporation.

CITIZENSHIP AND NATION BUILDING IN NORTH AMERICA

Working within—and sometimes against—their common British history, the United States and Canada formulated similar systems of liberal naturalization. Individuals can acquire U.S. citizenship at birth if they are born on American soil *(jus soli)* or, if born in a foreign country, based on their parents' American citizenship *(jus sanguinis)*.[3] *Naturalization* is the legal process that enables those not born with U.S. citizenship to become American citizens. Canada similarly grants citizenship based on birth, blood, and naturalization. Despite earlier restrictions based on race and gender, citizenship policies in the two countries have been among the most open in the world (Brubaker 1989; Ueda 2001).

Inclusive citizenship policies reflect a desire to integrate immigrants into the polity and to forge identities as independent countries. Once naturalized, foreign-born citizens in the United States and Canada enjoy equality with the native born. For countries of immigration, naturalization plays a particularly important role in nation building: it increases the number of citizens, and by specifying the conditions of membership, it defines how the citizenry is constituted.

British Roots

British colonists to North America, whether they went to the thirteen colonies or farther north, imported a common law tradition based on feudal notions of subjectship. A 1608 judicial dispute in Britain, Calvin's Case, established a theory of political membership based on natural law: like parent to child, so was the king to his subjects (Schuck and Smith 1985). The king provided protection to anyone born on his lands in return for the subject's service, allegiance, and obedience. As part of the British Empire, those born in the North American colonies became British subjects.[4] A native-born British subject enjoyed free movement and rights throughout the British Empire, including the right to own property or run commercial establishments. Foreigners, denied such rights, had a clear interest in acquiring the benefits of subjecthood.

In response to migration and imperial conquest, English law developed alternative statuses and procedures for obtaining subjecthood, including naturalization. The Crown, English Parliament, and colonial assemblies and proprietors engaged in fierce jurisdictional competition; each claimed authority to naturalize aliens. The colonies wished to lure settlers and usually embraced a liberal policy of naturalization.[5] Parliament, in London, favored limited naturalization to restrict trading rights and because of religious intolerance.[6] A two-tiered system developed in which the colonies could naturalize aliens locally, granting local legal status, but England controlled the empire-wide status of British subjecthood.[7]

America's Revolutionary Citizenship

Shifting power dynamics between the Crown and Parliament, as well as among parties within Parliament, created frequent changes in England's policies. A crisis point was reached in 1773 when London banned colonial naturalization. At this juncture, American and Canadian citizenship parted course. Among the grievances outlined in the Declaration of Independence, the colonists charged that King George III "has endeavoured to prevent the Population of these States; for that Purpose obstructing the Laws for Naturalization of Foreigners." Article IV of the Articles of Confederation introduced the idea of citizenship rather than subjecthood, and it left determination of citizenship to the individual states. This arrangement soon proved unworkable, since it was not clear whether someone naturalized in one state possessed reciprocal rights in another.[8] The U.S. Constitution consequently gives Congress the power "to establish a uniform Rule of Naturalization" (Article 1, Section 8). Congress acted on this authority quickly, passing the first U.S. naturalization law on March 26, 1790.

Defining the criteria for membership in the new nation provoked heated debate and frequent legal changes. By 1802 the proponents of liberal naturalization had triumphed: applicants could file for citizenship in any court of record after five years of residence in the United States and a prior declaration of their intention to become a citizen. Would-be citizens had to swear an oath to uphold the Constitution and renounce allegiance to foreign sovereigns. These criteria would define naturalization throughout the nineteenth century.[9]

The idea that citizenship could be an individual choice was radical for the period. The concept of voluntary adherence to an adopted country, as embodied in naturalization, predated the American War of Independence, but by calling people "citizens" rather than "subjects," Americans signaled a view of membership predicated on Lockean notions of social contract and consent (Kettner 1978). The revolutionary period made the act of naturalization not just a question of legal status, but also an affirmation of the new state's legitimacy (Schuck and Smith 1985; Ueda 1982).[10]

At the same time, American citizenship contained important limits to its inclusive vision. The first law on naturalization restricted its application to "free white persons." Black immigrants gained access to naturalization under legislation passed in 1870, but twelve years later the Chinese Exclusion Act of 1882 prohibited any Chinese immigrant from acquiring U.S. citizenship through naturalization.[11] Using a narrow interpretation of the Fourteenth Amendment, subsequent court decisions made it difficult for any East or South Asian immigrant to naturalize (Gualtieri 2001; Haney López 1996). Rogers Smith argues that despite lofty ideals, citizenship in the United States had a strong tendency to "ascriptive Americanism": legal statutes, judicial decisions, and legislative debates "manifested passionate beliefs that America was by rights a white nation, a Protestant nation, a nation in which true Americans were native-born men with Anglo-Saxon ancestors" (1997: 2). Racial restrictions on naturalization ended only in the middle of twentieth century. Chinese immigrants gained access to citizenship in 1943, Filipinos and Asian Indians in 1946. The 1952 McCarran-Walter Act definitively removed race or national origin as a criterion for American citizenship.

Citizenship regulations also varied by gender. Naturalization was open to white women, but an 1855 legislative act decreed that a married immigrant woman automatically became a citizen upon her husband's naturalization or, if he were a U.S. citizen prior to marriage, upon their marriage, regardless of her wishes (Bredbrenner 1998). The 1907 Expatriation Act extended the logic of linking a woman's citizenship to her spouse: under the act, a naturalized or U.S.-born American citizen *lost* her U.S. citizenship upon marriage to an alien and could gain it back only if her husband naturalized (Bredbrenner 1998). Only when women's suffrage appeared imminent— and concern built that thousands of immigrant women would have the right to vote without having proven their suitability for citizenship—did politicians and the public push for gender-neutral naturalization. The 1922 Cable Act gave most women control over their nationality, ushering in the current practice that men and women must apply for citizenship independently, regardless of marital status (Sapiro 1984).[12]

Naturalization procedures and the benefits of citizenship also varied by locality in nineteenth- and early-twentieth-century America. Although the Constitution assigned jurisdiction over naturalization to Congress, local courts could bestow citizenship, and judges enjoyed great latitude in their decisions (Erie 1988; Gavit 1922). The penalties of not being a citizen varied widely: in some states certain professions and privileges were restricted to citizens; in other states immigrants who had merely declared their intention to naturalize could vote in elections.[13]

Partly because of gross geographic variation in immigrant citizenship, Congress passed the comprehensive Naturalization Act in 1906, which codified and standardized the requirements for citizenship. The act established a new federal bureaucracy, the Bureau of Immigration and Naturalization (later, the Immigration and Naturalization Service, or INS), to oversee and systematize naturalization procedures.[14] The act also required applicants to demonstrate a rudimentary knowledge of American history and civics, and it mandated a basic ability to speak and understand English. These changes made greater demands on immigrants, but they also led to fairer and more equal treatment of all would-be citizens (Bloemraad and Ueda 2006).

The only major change to U.S. naturalization procedure in the post–World War II period came with the 1952 Immigration and Nationality Act, also known as the McCarran-Walter Act. Applicants henceforth needed to read and write a simple sentence in English. There have been only minor modifications to naturalization regulations since then. Today, special cases aside, someone wishing to become a U.S. citizen must prove five years of residence as a legal immigrant, pay a fee of $330, prove basic oral and written ability in English, and demonstrate knowledge of U.S. government and history. A judge or immigration and naturalization official can refuse to grant citizenship for a variety of reasons, including past criminal convictions, long visits outside the country, or a failure to demonstrate "good moral character." Immigrant children can derive citizenship when their parents naturalize, but all adults must apply for citizenship independently.[15]

Incremental Canadian Citizenship

If American citizenship was born in revolution, Canadian citizenship evolved in polite revolts against British tutelage. In Canada, British influence lasted longer, since Canada's break with Great Britain was more incremental. Passage of the British North America Act (Constitution Act, 1867) created an autonomous Dominion of Canada through a confederation of four British colonies. Under confederation, residents preserved their status as British subjects, the primary citizenship category in the new dominion.[16] The Canadian government gained the right to make most laws in the dominion, but Britain retained residual power over key aspects of sovereignty, including amending the Constitution and British subjecthood. Britain sought control over subjecthood because this status gave rights throughout the British Empire.[17] At the same time, Section 91 of the Constitution Act accorded exclusive legislative authority over "naturalization and aliens" within the dominion to Canadian Parliament.[18] The eighteenth-century tug-of-war between London and the colonies continued into the nineteenth century.

In an 1868 act of Parliament, the new Canadian government guaranteed that those who had naturalized in the confederating colonies before 1867 would continue to hold equal rights in the new country. The act also established liberal guidelines for future naturalization: three years of residence, good character, and an oath of loyalty to the Crown (Kaplan 1991: 10–11).[19] Two years later the British Parliament approved an imperial statute (Naturalization Act, 1870) stipulating that an individual naturalized in one of the colonies enjoyed equal rights with native-born subjects but that such rights were exclusive to that colony (Hancock 1937). Dissatisfaction with the lack of a uniform rule led Britain and the dominion governments to agree, during the Imperial Conference of 1911, to a uniform procedure of naturalization and recognition of local naturalization throughout the British Empire (Brown 1996).[20] These negotiations were enshrined in the Canadian Naturalization Act, 1914, which instituted a five-year residence requirement and also specified that applicants must be of good character, not be under any disability ("infant, lunatic, idiot, or married woman"), and possess adequate knowledge of English or French (Hancock 1937).[21] The law largely governed membership in Canada for the next three decades.

Under the 1914 act, judges oversaw verification of the law, but unlike in the United States, the ultimate authority to grant naturalization rested with the secretary of state, a cabinet position held by a member of Parliament from the governing party. Hancock underlines that "the Secretary of State may, in his own absolute discretion, grant the certificate [of naturalization]. . . . So far as I know, no one has attempted to challenge his action . . . in the courts of justice" (1937: 92, 95). This difference—of strong judicial authority in the United States and strong government oversight in Canada—would have repercussions in the years to come.[22] The Canadian structure of authority and responsibility permits greater latitude, and arbitrariness, by allowing orders-in-council and ministerial decisions to modify legal codes or administrative regulations (Kelley and Trebilcock 1998). The American system, heavily reliant on legal interpretation and judicial oversight, promotes transparency but also rigid and narrow interpretation of congressional legislation.

A patchwork of membership classes thus characterized Canadian residents in the early twentieth century. *Aliens* designated people born outside the British Empire and living in Canada. They had no right of admittance and could only gain standing as a British subject or Canadian citizen through naturalization. *Native British subjects,* either born in Canada or elsewhere in the British Empire, needed no special status to enter Canada. They could also become Canadian nationals, a "rather hollow distinction," by simply residing in Canada for five years (Hancock 1937: 98). Aliens who naturalized in Canada were variously called *British subjects of Canada, Canadian citizens,* or *Canadian nationals.*[23] These individuals enjoyed right of entry into Canada, but their status elsewhere in the British Empire depended on prevailing laws. At the close of World War II, Canada's citizenry consisted of native-born Canadians, naturalized Canadians who had affirmatively sought political membership along the lines of U.S. volitional citizenship, and a third class of individuals who were foreign born but, because of their status as British subjects, were not required to take any confirmatory action for permanent status.

A series of political and legislative acts eliminated this third category of legal membership as Canada further asserted its sovereignty and national identity in the post–World War II era. The first step in this process was the passage of the Canadian Citizenship Act. The act went into effect on January 1, 1947, and it established for the first time clear, legal Canadian citizenship, accompanied by the first Canadian passport.[24] As in the United States, the impetus to assert independent nationality arose from war and a desire to integrate individuals of various backgrounds into one political member-ship.[25] Under the new act, immigrants could naturalize after attaining twenty-one years of age, five years of residence, demonstrating adequate knowledge of English or French, and showing understanding of the respon-sibilities and privileges of Canadian citizenship. Language requirements were waived for those with more than twenty years of residence.

The government took great pains to underscore the symbolic unification accorded by the new citizenship, a bond that crossed ethnic lines. During the inaugural ceremony organized in January 1947, the first certificate of Canadian citizenship was given to the prime minister, but the second went to "Wasyl Elnyiak, one of the first Ukrainians to farm in western Canada. . . . We had discovered him after a long search through the immi-gration department's records" (Martin 1993: 76). Other recipients were of Danish, Italian, and Jewish background. According to Kaplan, "The *Act* was designed in such a way as to extend the opportunity of citizenship to as many people as possible, to impress upon all Canadians the value of citizen-ship status and to promote nationality unity. The *Act* was an immediate success" (1991: 20).

At the same time, British connections remained. Canadian citizenship was primary, but all Canadians continued to be British subjects. Immigrants who were already British subjects enjoyed special rights in Canada: after a year of residence, they could vote in Canadian elections without naturaliz-ing, and they could gain Canadian citizenship after five years of residence without seeing a citizenship judge.[26] These provisions were eliminated in Canada's second major piece of citizenship legislation, the 1977 Citizenship Act and accompanying Citizenship Regulations. Henceforth all immi-grants, regardless of origin, would be treated the same.[27] Various technical changes made naturalization easier—the age of majority was reduced to eighteen, residence requirements were dropped to three years, and dual cit-izenship was implicitly allowed—but most important was a change in phi-losophy heralded by the 1977 act. According to Kaplan, "The 1947 *Act* operated on the principle that the granting of citizenship was a privilege. This was viewed by many as negative and restrictive. The 1977 *Act* made citizenship a right which could be enjoyed by anyone once the require-ments . . . were met" (1991: 24). As we will see later, the shift in attitude—transmitted to the bureaucracy administering naturalization—stands in contrast to the stance taken by the American immigration and naturaliza-tion bureaucracies.

THE PUZZLE OF THE NORTH AMERICAN
NATURALIZATION GAP

How do these laws translate into citizenship outcomes? To answer that question, we need a measure of immigrant naturalization.

Naturalization can be calculated as a *level* or a *rate*. A naturalization level counts how many individuals in an immigrant group or cohort hold citizenship on a certain date. Thus Current Population Survey figures from 2004 indicate that out of a foreign-born population of over 34.2 million, just over 13.1 million individuals, or 38 percent, hold U.S. citizenship.

Aggregate levels are deceptive, however, since they vary greatly with migration flows and immigrants' length of residence, which is one of the strongest and most consistent predictors of citizenship. A more accurate statistic is the naturalization rate. It measures the time elapsed between arrival in a country and naturalization. U.S. census data from 1920 suggest that Irish immigrants were quicker to take up U.S. citizenship than French Canadians: on average, 9.7 years elapsed between immigration and naturalization for adult Irish immigrants, while French Canadians waited 13 years.[28]

The rate and level of naturalization are linked but not equivalent. An immigrant group that acquires citizenship slowly can have a high level of citizenship if the group has lived in the adopted country for decades. A recent immigrant group might have a low level of citizenship but be naturalizing quickly.[29]

Citizenship Levels in the United States

Figure 1 tracks the level of citizenship among foreign-born residents in the United States from 1890 to 2000. For the decades prior to 1920, the data reflect only adult male naturalization; enumerators did not systematically collect information on women and minors, since their status largely depended on their husband or father.[30] A trend line in figure 1 shows the percentage of the U.S. population that is foreign born in a given census year.

The United States witnessed two great immigration waves during the twentieth century, the first from 1880 to 1924 and the second from 1965 to the present. During the first, the INS records more than 26 million admissions (U.S. Immigration and Naturalization Service 2002). This influx doubled the foreign-born resident population from just under 6.7 million in 1880 to a bit over 13.9 million in 1920 (Gibson and Lennon 1999).[31] During periods of massive immigration, new arrivals increase the number of foreign born living in the United States—the denominator for calculations—

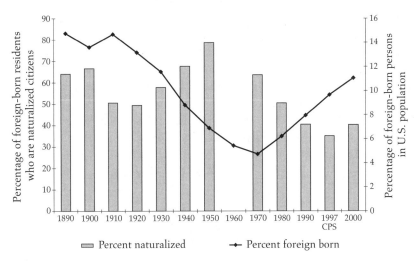

Figure 1. Foreign-born residents of the United States, 1890–2000. The line represents the percentage of the overall U.S. population that was foreign born; the bars represent the percentage of foreign-born residents who were naturalized. Figures for 1890 to 1910 are for adult men only. The U.S. Census Bureau did not collect citizenship data in 1960. SOURCES: Gibson and Lennon (1999); Schmidley and Gibson (1999); U.S. Census Bureau (2002).

but because the newcomers cannot become citizens immediately, their presence drives down aggregate naturalization levels. Not surprisingly, the levels of naturalization decline during this first period of massive immigration.

The more years an immigrant lives in his or her new home, the more likely he or she is to naturalize. Researchers debate why time is important: perhaps it reduces the costs of citizenship and makes the benefits more apparent (Jasso and Rosenzweig 1986; Yang 1994), or it may mark assimilation and growing attachment to the receiving society (Evans 1988; Liang 1994). Regardless of the reason, when few new immigrants arrive in the United States, naturalization levels rise as average length of residence increases. Immigration restrictions in 1921 and the implementation of permanent immigration quotas under the 1924 National Origins Act reduced the flood of newcomers to a trickle. In response, citizenship levels rose steadily from 1920 to 1950, peaking at 79 percent (Gibson and Lennon 1999).

U.S. immigration only liberalized with the 1965 Immigration Act, or Hart-Cellar Act. Congress eliminated national origin quotas and raised the overall ceiling on immigrant admissions. The effect was dramatic: in 1960, 265,000 individuals became legal permanent residents of the United States;

two decades later immigrant admissions doubled to 530,000; and by 2000 they stood at 850,000 (U.S. Immigration and Naturalization Service 2002).[32] As a result, citizenship levels fell over this period so that by 1980, they stood at 1920 levels. The level of naturalization hit an all-time low of 35 percent in 1997 and then rose slightly to 40 percent in 2000. The rapid increase in the number of recent noncitizen arrivals during the post-1965 period accounts for about a third of the drop in the naturalization level from 1970 to 1996 (Schmidley and Gibson 1999). That is, some of the post-1965 decline merely reflects substantial new migration, like in the 1880 to 1924 period, not a decrease in immigrants' propensity to acquire U.S. citizenship.

Citizenship Levels in Canada

The gradual evolution of Canadian citizenship makes historic comparison with the United States a bit complicated. Determining levels of naturalization in the United States is relatively simple: identify the foreign-born population, eliminate those who acquired U.S. citizenship at birth through their parents, and then calculate the percentage of the resident foreign born who have naturalized.[33] Identical calculations are less evident in the Canadian case. Prior to 1947, any immigrant from the British Empire who was a British subject—whether from Great Britain, the Caribbean, or the Indian subcontinent—had legal standing akin to citizenship. A fair comparison with the United States must therefore be based on the citizenship status of those born outside the British Empire. In 1901, 40 percent of immigrants fit this description; by 1941 it was 50 percent. In the second half of the century, a calculation similar to the one used in the American case becomes appropriate.[34] Figure 2 depicts changes in the level of Canadian naturalization from 1901 to 2001 based on Canadian census data. The figures prior to 1951 are calculated using the non-British immigrant population; those in 1951 and later include individuals born in the United Kingdom and British dependencies.

Figure 2 also includes a trend line tracing the proportion of the Canadian population that is foreign born. Compared to the United States, Canada has experienced less dramatic fluctuations in immigrant admissions, due to a largely open-door policy throughout much of the twentieth century.[35] During the American closed-door period, from 1924 to 1965, Canada remained open to immigration, except during the Depression and World War II.[36] Like in the United States, new Canadian immigration regulations in 1962 and 1967 removed discriminatory policies favoring European migrants, but the actual number of migrants admitted in any year remained relatively stable, only creeping up late in the century. From 1960 to 1990, admissions gradually doubled, from 104,000 to 216,000 (Citizenship and Immigration Canada

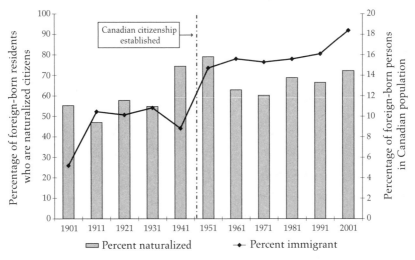

Figure 2. Foreign-born residents of Canada, 1901–2001. The line represents the percentage of the overall Canadian population that was foreign born; the bars represent the percentage of foreign-born residents who were naturalized. Figures for 1901 to 1941 do not include British immigrants, since they did not need to naturalize until Canadian citizenship was established in 1947. SOURCES: Leacy (1983); Statistics Canada (1995, 2004).

2002). In the 1990s and into the new century, about a fifth to a quarter of a million people migrated to Canada each year.

The relationship between the immigrant population and naturalization in Canada is similar to the one in the United States in the first half of the century and from 1951 to 1961: as the number of newcomers increases, the percentage of naturalized citizens decreases. Surprisingly, from 1971 to 2001 naturalization levels tend to *rise* as the proportion of foreign born in the Canadian population increases.[37] We would expect the opposite: residency requirements and immediate adjustment pressures should produce a delay between arrival and naturalization. For naturalization to rise over this period of growing immigration—a modest increase in the foreign-born population from 15 percent to 19 percent—naturalization applications had to be increasing more rapidly, in contrast to the pattern in the United States.

Indeed, juxtaposing Canadian and American citizenship trends reveals a growing naturalization gap over the last decades of the twentieth century. As seen in figure 3, levels of citizenship for adult immigrants in the two countries largely parallel each other up to 1971. In the first half of the century the largest difference in naturalization occurs in 1900–01, a time of particularly

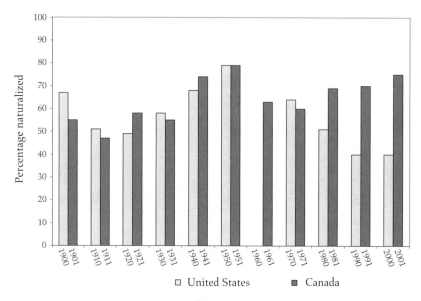

Figure 3. Percentages of foreign-born adults naturalized in the United States and Canada, 1900–2001. The U.S. figures for 1900 and 1910 are for men only. The Canadian figures for 1901 to 1941 do not include British immigrants. The U.S. Census Bureau did not collect citizenship data in 1960. SOURCES: Gibson and Lennon (1999); Leacy (1983); Schmidley and Gibson (1999); U.S. 2000 Census of Population and Housing; Statistics Canada (1995, 2004).

robust citizenship acquisition in the United States. In the ensuing decades, Canadian levels of citizenship are slightly higher around the two world wars, while American levels are a little higher in 1910 and 1930. Given Canada's early engagement and long involvement in both wars, it is not surprising that immigrants acquired Canadian citizenship during these periods or at least reported citizenship on the census. U.S.-Canada similarities end in the 1970s. We see a sharp divergence in levels of citizenship. Why, during a period of sustained immigration in both countries, does U.S. citizenship acquisition fall so dramatically while Canadian levels actually increase?

SEARCHING FOR AN EXPLANATION:
CURRENT THEORIZING

It is possible that this puzzle stems from a comparison of apples and oranges. Perhaps the people who move to Canada are not at all like those who move to the United States. Or perhaps the legal structure of citizenship—the naturalization laws and the costs and benefits of citizenship—differs radically between the two countries.

Size and Composition of Immigrant Streams to North America

Is the North American naturalization gap an artifact of differences in Canadian and American immigration policies? As we have seen, when the absolute number of newcomers rises, citizenship levels usually fall due to length-of-residence effects. The proportion of foreign-born residents has changed less in Canada than in the United States. From 1971 to 2001, the percentage of foreign born in Canada increased by about a quarter, from 15.3 percent to 19.1 percent, whereas in the United States the percentage more than doubled, from 4.7 percent in 1970 to 11.1 percent in 2000. Is the U.S.-Canada difference merely a function of the rapidly growing immigrant population in the United States?

The short answer is no. The increase in the Canadian foreign-born population, although modest, should have resulted in a slight decrease in naturalization if naturalization rates were constant. Instead we observe a small increase in Canadian citizenship levels. The anomaly hints that changes in the relative size of the immigrant stream cannot account for the bulk of the North American naturalization gap. Indeed, a comparison of migrant cohorts suggests that the rate of naturalization slowed significantly in the United States since 1970 but increased in Canada. At the start of the 1970s, foreign-born individuals with eleven to fifteen years of residence in Canada or the United States had nearly identical levels of citizenship, just over 61 percent. In 1980 the level of naturalization among those with eleven to fifteen years of residence decreased by almost a third in the United States to 43 percent, but it rose in Canada to 68 percent. The Canadian figure increased again in 1991 to stand at almost 78 percent, while only 42 percent of immigrants in the United States with eleven to fifteen years of residence reported naturalized citizenship in 1990. Cohorts with fewer or more years of residence exhibit similar patterns.[38] The North American naturalization gap is not merely a function of changes in the magnitude of immigrant admissions.

But what about the composition of the migrant streams? There is overwhelming evidence that immigrants from different countries naturalize at varying rates.[39] Little consensus exists as to why country of origin matters. Some believe that shared cultural traits influence incorporation patterns. According to this line of reasoning, immigrants bring their home country's civic or political culture with them when they migrate, influencing the group's attitudes toward citizenship and political participation (Greeley and

McCready 1975). Others contend that immigrants from the same country act in a like manner because they face similar decision-making contexts over the costs and benefits of naturalization. For example, the "reversibility" thesis posits that the smaller the distance between the sending and receiving country, the less likely immigrants are to naturalize because chances for return seem high (Portes and Mozo 1985). Developed to explain low Canadian and Mexican naturalization in the United States, the argument can be extended to understand high rates of naturalization among refugees: refugees take out citizenship since they see little chance of returning home, or "reversing" their migration. Other factors relevant to immigrants' calculations include the relative economic development of their country of origin, or its orientation toward capitalism or socialism.[40]

These considerations are important because migration streams to Canada and the United States come from different parts of the globe. Before 1965 immigration policy in the United States favored permanent immigration from Europe and Canada and temporary migration from Mexico. Individuals from Asia and Africa found it almost impossible to move to the United States. In the 1950s, 53 percent of those granted permanent residency in the United States came from Europe while only 6 percent and 0.6 percent came from Asia or Africa, respectively. The 1965 Hart-Cellar Act removed restrictions that blocked non-European migration. In the 1990s Europeans accounted for only 15 percent of legal immigrants in the United States, while the figures for Asians and Africans were 31 and 4 percent, respectively (U.S. Immigration and Naturalization Service 2002: 16, 200). The United States continues to draw large numbers of Hispanic migrants, primarily from Mexico but also from Central and South America and the Spanish-speaking Caribbean. Indeed, Hispanic immigration makes up the majority of the contemporary immigration flow.

In comparison, Canada is home to relatively few Hispanic immigrants and historically has been more dependent on European immigration. Following World War II, Canada absorbed hundred of thousands of Europeans displaced by war or seeking better economic opportunities. As late as 1966, two-thirds of all immigrants to Canada came from just five countries: the United Kingdom, Italy, the United States, Germany, or Portugal (Canada. Department of Manpower and Immigration 1967). New immigration policies introduced in 1962 and 1967 opened the door to the rest of the world so that, by 2000, Europeans made up just 19 percent of immigrant admissions. The majority of immigrants, 53 percent, came from Asia and the Pacific (Citizenship and Immigration Canada 2002: 8). About 18 percent of immigrants hailed from Africa and the Middle East, and only 7 percent came from Central and South America (Citizenship and Immigration Canada 2002: 8).

Table 1 details the thirty most prevalent birthplaces among the foreign-born population living in the United States and Canada in 2000 and 2001. Table 2 lists the top ten countries of origin for immigrants admitted in 2000. Canada has a greater proportion of European immigrants, mostly of older migrant stock, and it draws newer migrants primarily from Asia, the Middle East, and the English-speaking Caribbean. The United States also receives sizeable Asian migration, but unlike its northern neighbor, Hispanics make up a large proportion of the total, and Mexicans clearly dominate.

These differences can have important effects on aggregate naturalization levels. For example, the very large Mexican-born population in the United States—almost 30 percent of all foreign-born residents in 2000—dwarfs the community in Canada, which constitutes less than a percentage point in 2001. Mexicans have some of the lowest naturalization levels of any immigrant group in the United States, so this population drives down aggregate U.S. citizenship levels.

A second issue is illegal migration. Unauthorized migration, by individuals either crossing the border clandestinely or overstaying temporary visas, became a significant political issue in the United States during the 1980s and 1990s. Calculations of the unauthorized population are extremely difficult to make with precision; reasonable estimates range from seven to eleven million undocumented residents living in the United States in 2000 (Bean and Stevens 2003: 25). Of those, approximately 55 percent are thought to originate from Mexico, and another 15 percent come from the next four biggest sources of illegal migration combined: El Salvador, Guatemala, Canada, and Haiti (U.S. Immigration and Naturalization Service 2002: 271). Canada is also home to illegal immigrants, most of whom overstay tourist visas. Recent news reports put the number at about two hundred thousand, but lacking any reliable estimates from government or the academic community, this figure is purely speculative (Jimenez 2003). It is certain, however, that illegal migrants in Canada constitute a smaller percentage of the overall foreign-born population than in the United States.

The difference in Hispanic migration, especially from Mexico, affects comparisons between Canada and the United States. Mexicans are less likely to naturalize than many other groups but are numerous in the United States, and they constitute a larger proportion of the illegal population, a group barred from citizenship. If we calculate the naturalization level in the United States including only non-Mexican migrants who fulfill residency requirements, the proportion of citizens increases to 48 percent in 2000.[41]

TABLE 1. TOP THIRTY COUNTRIES OF BIRTH FOR IMMIGRANTS
IN THE UNITED STATES (2000) AND CANADA (2001)

	United States (2000)				Canada (2001)		
Rank	Country of Birth	Population	Percentage of Immigrant Population	Rank	Country of Birth	Population	Percentage of Immigrant Population
1	Mexico	9,177,487	29.5	1	United Kingdom	614,610	10.9
2	Philippines	1,369,070	4.4	2	People's Republic of China	345,520	6.1
3	India	1,022,552	3.3	3	India	322,215	5.7
4	People's Republic of China	988,857	3.2	4	Italy	318,095	5.6
5	Vietnam	988,174	3.2	5	United States	258,420	4.6
6	Cuba	872,716	2.8	6	Hong Kong	240,045	4.3
7	Korea (North and South)	864,125	2.8	7	Philippines	239,160	4.2
8	Canada	820,771	2.6	8	Poland	181,810	3.2
9	El Salvador	817,336	2.6	9	Germany	177,675	3.1
10	Germany	706,704	2.3	10	Portugal	155,770	2.8
11	Dominican Republic	687,677	2.2	11	Vietnam	150,135	2.7
12	United Kingdom	677,751	2.2	12	Yugoslavia (former)	147,830	2.6
13	Jamaica	553,827	1.8	13	Soviet Union (former)	137,680	2.4
14	Colombia	509,872	1.6	14	Jamaica	121,795	2.2

	Country	Population	%
15	Guatemala	480,665	1.5
16	Italy	473,338	1.5
17	Poland	466,742	1.5
18	Haiti	419,317	1.3
19	Japan	347,539	1.1
20	Russia	340,177	1.1
21	Taiwan	326,215	1.0
22	Ecuador	298,626	1.0
23	Iran	283,226	0.9
24	Honduras	282,852	0.9
25	Peru	278,186	0.9
26	Ukraine	275,153	0.9
27	Pakistan	223,477	0.7
28	Nicaragua	220,335	0.7
29	Brazil	212,428	0.7
30	Guyana	211,189	0.7
	Total	25,196,384	81.0
	Total foreign-born population	31,107,889	

	Country	Population	%
15	Netherlands	118,460	2.1
16	Sri Lanka	91,670	1.6
17	Guyana	84,160	1.5
18	Pakistan	83,235	1.5
19	Korea (North and South)	82,855	1.5
20	Greece	76,525	1.4
21	France	75,820	1.3
22	Iran	75,000	1.3
23	Taiwan	70,615	1.3
24	Lebanon	68,510	1.2
25	Trinidad and Tobago	65,145	1.2
26	Romania	61,330	1.1
27	Haiti	53,905	1.0
28	Hungary	50,720	0.9
29	Mexico	42,740	0.8
30	Czech and Slovak Republic	40,570	0.7
	Total	4,551,910	80.6
	Total foreign-born population	5,647,125	

SOURCES: U.S. Census Bureau (2002); Statistics Canada (2004).

TABLE 2. TOP TEN COUNTRIES OF ORIGIN FOR IMMIGRANTS ADMITTED
TO THE UNITED STATES AND CANADA, 2000

	United States				Canada		
Rank	Country of Origin	No. Admitted	Percentage of Total No. Admitted	Rank	Country of Origin	No. Admitted	Percentage of Total No. Admitted
1	Mexico	171,748	20.2	1	People's Republic of China	36,718	16.2
2	People's Republic of China	41,861	4.9	2	India	26,064	11.5
3	Philippines	40,587	4.8	3	Pakistan	14,173	6.2
4	India	39,072	4.6	4	Philippines	10,077	4.4
5	Vietnam	25,340	3.0	5	Korea, South	7,630	3.4
6	Nicaragua	24,029	2.8	6	Sri Lanka	5,832	2.6
7	El Salvador	22,332	2.6	7	United States	5,809	2.6
8	Haiti	22,004	2.6	8	Iran	5,606	2.5
9	Cuba	19,322	2.3	9	Yugoslavia	4,719	2.1
10	Dominican Republic	17,441	2.1	10	United Kingdom	4,648	2.0
	Total	423,736	49.9		Total	121,276	53.4
	Total admissions	849,807			Total admissions	227,209	

SOURCES: U.S. Immigration and Naturalization Service (2002: 21); Citizenship and Immigration Canada (2001: 8).

However, if we adjust the Canadian figures in a similar fashion to only include those who satisfy the length of residence requirement, aggregate naturalization increases even more, to 84 percent in 2001.[42]

Taking the analysis a step further, we can disaggregate citizenship statistics by country of origin. Table 3 contrasts citizenship levels in the United States and Canada for twenty-five migrant groups based on 1990 and 1991 census data.[43] I use older census data to minimize the effect that heavy illegal migration in the 1990s could have on the cross-national comparison. The first column of the table reports the percentage naturalized of those who meet minimum residency requirements for citizenship. In each case, the proportion of naturalized Canadian citizens exceeds that of the United States, although the magnitude of the gap varies, depending on the group. Differences range from six percentage points or less for traditional European source countries such as Germany, Italy, and Ireland to over fifty percentage points for countries such as Haiti and Mexico. Only when we compare the naturalization of Canadian or American nationals living in the other country do we find apparently higher citizenship acquisition among those in the United States. Overall, 55 percent of Americans residing in Canada have naturalized, compared to 60 percent of Canadians living in the United States.

Aggregate figures are deceptive, however, since they hide variation in the size of migrant cohorts over time. The next three columns in table 3 present naturalization statistics for those with six to eight, eleven to fifteen, and twenty-one to twenty-five years of residence.[44] The apparent anomaly represented by Canadian and American nationals disappears when we control for length of residence. In each cohort, Americans living in Canada are more likely to be naturalized citizens than Canadians living in the United States. The aggregate difference stems from the fact that Canadian immigrants in the United States tend to be of older migrant stock than the average American in Canada. In a similar manner, controlling for length of residence makes the German, Italian, and Irish differences much larger, hovering around thirty percentage points for those who arrived in North America in the later half of the 1970s.

The cohort of immigrants with eleven to fifteen years of residence provides a strong comparative baseline. These immigrants have had sufficient time to adjust to their new homes, learn about citizenship procedures, and undertake the naturalization process if they are so inclined. In no case is the U.S.-Canada naturalization gap for this cohort less than seventeen percentage points, and it can be as high as sixty-three percentage points.[45] Migrants born in the former Soviet Union and Lebanon show the least difference,

TABLE 3. ADULT IMMIGRANTS NATURALIZED IN THE UNITED STATES (1990) AND CANADA (1991)

In percentages

Place of Birth	United States (1990 Census)					Canada (1991 Census)				
	All Eligible Immigrants	6–8 Years of Residence (1982–84)	11–15 Years of Residence (1975–79)	21–25 Years of Residence (1965–69)	Adult Immigrant Population Estimate	All Eligible Immigrants	6–8 Years of Residence (1983–85)	11–15 Years of Residence (1976–80)	21–25 Years of Residence (1966–70)	Adult Immigrant Population Estimate
Canada/ United States*	60.3	8.5	21.4	36.7	706,525	55.0	30.9	39.7	54.8	225,635
El Salvador	22.0	11.6	22.6	47.1	387,995	63.8	69.3	81.2	93.8	20,400
France	65.8	12.6	32.2	58.6	111,891	88.0	73.9	86.7	88.4	51,885
Germany	77.2	15.5	31.7	57.7	698,425	83.1	41.6	60.9	73.2	175,575
Greece	75.4	21.7	51.1	76.2	170,204	88.0	72.5	81.0	87.5	82,320
Guyana	53.3	23.9	58.9	78.9	101,458	86.1	78.7	90.0	95.1	61,245
Haiti	33.3	12.3	30.9	53.7	193,844	89.3	92.1	93.5	86.4	34,805
Hong Kong	73.5	30.5	73.6	87.0	128,894	87.9	86.6	92.4	95.6	124,370
India	50.4	18.6	51.8	72.2	409,157	73.1	53.4	72.2	90.7	164,570
Iran	37.9	12.7	32.6	73.6	187,109	79.0	85.4	89.0	93.8	25,340
Ireland	78.2	14.9	38.4	60.0	164,752	79.3	45.7	69.7	76.6	26,495

Italy	78.3	26.1	37.0	61.0	564,986	82.2	59.2	68.7	74.1	349,705
Jamaica	48.3	20.2	41.7	64.6	292,478	81.1	58.8	81.2	91.1	94,100
Korea (North and South)	58.5	21.0	62.8	88.5	496,730	80.4	59.3	86.1	96.5	28,230
Lebanon	68.5	29.1	71.0	83.3	80,725	85.4	86.0	88.0	91.7	45,785
Mexico	29.0	17.1	23.2	34.0	3,616,564	81.4	72.1	79.3	86.9	14,845
Netherlands	69.2	7.8	24.3	48.5	91,715	87.0	32.1	49.6	76.0	127,515
Pakistan	52.5	20.9	62.0	80.4	75,253	85.5	75.1	87.3	95.6	22,840
People's Republic of China	64.0	27.2	59.9	82.0	494,653	88.5	84.0	89.8	95.8	152,210
Philippines	71.0	38.2	72.9	86.9	831,302	87.1	81.4	91.3	95.6	111,115
Poland	74.5	31.6	45.3	65.6	371,851	90.7	82.5	84.7	88.9	166,560
Portugal	48.4	15.0	31.7	50.5	199,765	65.6	44.7	57.5	71.1	150,645
Soviet Union	83.7	44.8	77.1	69.1	355,813	95.6	85.7	93.9	87.5	97,255
United Kingdom	58.2	7.3	23.6	47.3	609,182	81.9	56.4	69.3	78.5	693,690
Vietnam	58.5	31.8	69.9	86.7	439,252	84.6	83.0	88.3	92.8	94,545

*Born in Canada for residence in the United States, and born in the United States for residence in Canada.

SOURCES: Author's calculations from 1990 U.S. census 5 percent Public Use Microdata Sample (Ruggles et al. 2004) and from 1991 Canadian census 20 percent sample data.

while those from Haiti have citizenship levels three times higher in Canada than in the United States. Because significant gaps, always with a lower U.S. naturalization level, hold across all groups, we can be confident that cross-national differences do not stem merely from the size and birthplace origins of migration streams to Canada and the United States.

Micro-Level Explanations of Naturalization

Most research on naturalization in North America explains immigrants' citizenship as an outcome of personal attributes. Some scholars adopt a rational choice framework that postulates a world of autonomous actors making decisions based on rational calculations. Depending on an immigrant's particular hierarchy of preferences, acquiring citizenship becomes rational when the benefits outweigh the costs.[46] Others adopt a resource or skill framework. Political participation depends on interest and ability to be involved, so attributes such as education, income, and familiarity with politics affects immigrants' motivation for citizenship and capacity to naturalize. Resource and rational choice explanations overlap: individual traits not only supply resources for naturalizing but also alter decision-making contexts.[47]

Cross-national variation in immigrants' attributes can arise from the screening function of immigration policy and from self-selection by migrants who choose to go to the United States or Canada. The impact of immigration policy has received particular attention from those concerned with immigrants' economic success.[48] Researchers and policy makers debate whether a particular method of choosing migrants correlates with their "quality"—usually expressed in terms of human capital attributes—and whether differences in prior human capital subsequently affect incorporation. The effect of policy on *political* incorporation is rarely considered, but a similar logic applies: to the extent that human capital correlates with both economic outcomes and interest in politics, highly skilled immigrants might achieve better economic *and* political integration.

Both Canada and the United States administer mixed immigration systems that accord entry based on skills and economic contribution, family ties, or the need for asylum. The relative proportion of these three categories varies. In the late 1990s, between two-thirds and three-quarters of legal immigrants to the United States acquired their status through family ties: a relative already living in the United States sponsored their application to migrate (U.S. Immigration and Naturalization Service 2002: 17). Under the current U.S. preference system, only about 20 percent of numerically limited visas are given based on employment (Usdansky and Espenshade 2001).

This percentage has remained relatively constant since 1965 and drops lower if we consider all immigrant admissions.[49] Refugees accounted for 6 to 16 percent of admission in the 1990s (U.S. Immigration and Naturalization Service 2002: 17).

Canada has depended more heavily on "independent" migrants, those with no family ties to Canada but who can show that their skills or resources (such as investment capital) are needed in the Canadian economy. Since the mid-1970s, selection as an independent migrant is based on a point system, which gives potential migrants points according to job skills, language ability, age, and other personal characteristics.[50] If an applicant's total points surpass the government-set threshold, that person can be granted an immigrant visa. In the second half of the 1990s, a bit over 50 to 60 percent of all immigrants arrived as independent migrants (a figure which includes the dependents of the principal applicant), 26 to 36 percent entered under family reunification provisions, and about 13 percent came as refugees or special admissions (Citizenship and Immigration Canada 2005).[51]

Scholars such as George Borjas (1999) contend that a point system screens out individuals with low human capital, resulting in better outcomes for immigrants and the host society. To the extent that Canada's immigration policy selects individuals with better language skills and more years of schooling, we might expect these immigrants to have a greater propensity to naturalize and to be active politically.[52] Borjas's conclusions are not without critics. Jeffrey Reitz (1998) argues that the impact of the Canadian point system is exaggerated. For example, Canada's "skill" selection mostly sought to fill employment shortages. As a result, depending on economic conditions, people with experience as cooks or welders might receive more points than a foreign lawyer, despite significant differences in education.[53]

We must also consider supply-side selection. Do immigrants' motivations for choosing one country over another correlate with political outcomes? Most migrants would ideally move to the United States. I found this to be the case in both the Portuguese and Vietnamese communities. Canada is frequently viewed as a second-best option. According to Reitz (1998), the United States consistently attracts better-educated immigrants from most sending countries.[54] We might expect that those who realize their first choice of destination would be more interested in developing a permanent relationship to the country through naturalization. On the other hand, the attraction of the United States might be purely economic: people move there to make money, only to return home after a few years. It is not clear whether selection biases attract more politically "assimilable" immigrants to Canada or to the United States.

Evaluating Micro-Level Explanations   Do immigration policy and immigrants' destination preferences explain the North American naturalization gap? Census data provide information on various attributes used to select immigrants under the Canadian point system, such as years of schooling, age, and language ability. Such data do not provide information on the reasons people migrate, but to the extent that motivations correlate with personal attributes, we can use statistical data to probe for self-selection effects.

Let us first consider material resources. Historically, immigrants in Canada do better than those in the United States, even without superior human capital attributes (Reitz 1998). In 2000 and 2001, however, immigrants' median income was nearly identical in the two countries, about $21,000, as was labor force participation, at 61 percent.[55] Rates of business ownership are also similar, though more immigrants in Canada own homes than in the United States. If home ownership, or historic income differences, correlates with citizenship acquisition, such differences might explain the naturalization gap.[56]

Turning to skills, census data offer limited support for the contention that Canada's point system produces an immigrant population with greater human capital than in the United States. A higher percentage of the foreign born in the United States report only an elementary education or no schooling compared to those in Canada, and of all foreign born, 37 percent in the United States but only 30 percent in Canada do not hold a high school diploma. On the other hand, more foreign-born residents in the United States, 24 percent, hold a university degree, compared to 21 percent in Canada. Thus immigrants to the United States tend to two extremes—poorly educated or highly educated. In terms of language, a smaller percentage of foreign-born adults in Canada report being unable to conduct a conversation in English or French compared to the proportion in the United States who report no English ability. The difference is perhaps a function of substantial migration to Canada from English-speaking countries such as the United Kingdom, India, and Jamaica; it might be a product of the point system that screens for language skills; or it could be the result of sustained government intervention in newcomer language acquisition in Canada.[57] Since language ability is a requirement for naturalization, language differences could affect citizenship levels.

In both countries we find a high correlation between linguistic ability in the host society's language(s), education, and length of residence on the one hand and naturalization on the other. Importantly, the relationship between these variables is more attenuated in the Canadian case. That is, in both countries higher levels of education are associated with a greater chance of being a citizen, but the relationship is stronger in the United States. Years of residence and citizenship are likewise highly correlated in both countries, but again the relationship is stronger in the United States than in Canada. These differences suggest that the barrier to becoming a citizen in Canada might be lower than in the United States, or that those with less schooling or fewer years of residence have a greater motivation to acquire Canadian citizenship than their counterparts in the United States. Although skills matter in explaining immigrants' citizenship in both countries, they matter more south of the forty-ninth parallel. Given that immigrants' attributes cluster—or correlate—such that those with more education also have higher incomes, better language abilities, and a greater chance of home ownership, a true evaluation of micro-level explanations requires statistical techniques that control for intercorrelations.

The Portuguese in North America: A Quasi-Experimental Group   The ideal way to evaluate individual-level explanations of integration outcomes would involve experimental manipulation: to eliminate the bias of state- and self-selection, we would randomly assign a group of individuals to migrate either to Canada or to the United States. If we subsequently found differences in political behavior, we could be certain that such variation stemmed from the different experimental treatment—living in one country versus the other—rather than from a nonrandom distribution of personal attributes.

Practical and ethical considerations bar such a course of action. Instead, we can turn to "quasi-experiments" by considering groups with very similar migration patterns to Canada or the United States. One such group is the Portuguese. In both the United States and Canada, approximately 60–70 percent hail from the Azores, while another 20–30 percent come from mainland Portugal, often from the Lisbon area or northern Portugal. Smaller groups come from Madeira or Portugal's former African colonies. Most arrived in North America in the late 1960s or early 1970s.[58]

Interregional differences exist between Portuguese immigrants, but the overall picture is of broad similarities. Portuguese immigration is largely ethnically homogeneous, and almost all are Roman Catholic.[59] Before moving to North America, the majority of Portuguese engaged in subsistence farming, fishing, or manual labor. Many have low levels of education since free schooling only extended to grade four under the Portuguese dictatorship, in place until 1974.[60] Nonetheless, Portuguese workforce participation rates in North America resemble those of the native born. Many are employed in manual and semiskilled jobs, such as cleaning, factory work, and construction.[61]

Almeida (2000) concludes that Portuguese communities in Canada and the United States are largely interchangeable, and census data support this observation (Bloemraad 2002). We find that for most individual characteristics, including education, age, marital status, length of residence, and business ownership, little distinguishes those living in the United States from their compatriots north of the border. Only three differences stand out. First, Portuguese-born adults in Canada are more likely to be citizens than their American counterparts. Second, more people in Canada report being unable to speak English.[62] Finally, median income in Canada is higher than in the United States, though the gap is less than for the entire foreign-born population. Income differentials might partially stem from different rates of unionization in Canada and the United States (Reitz 1998). In Canada's urban centers, many Portuguese men have found employment in the construction trades, often in unionized positions, generating a decent income despite low levels of education. In the United States, fewer Portuguese work nonresidential construction, and they appear less likely to be members of a union. The difference in income probably also drives the higher level of home ownership in Canada, although this difference is characteristic of the total immigrant population in the two countries.

If we cannot use experimental methods, we can use statistical modeling to rule out some of the possible effects of the immigration system and migrant self-selection. Statistical modeling artificially attempts to replicate random assignment in experiments by comparing individuals who are alike on a range of potential explanatory factors and assessing whether differences on one specific variable correlate with variation in the outcome.

Census data allow such analysis of Portuguese immigrants. As suggested by research on other immigrant groups, people who have spent more years in the host country and who have better English skills are more likely to have naturalized. We also find that Portuguese immigrants with more education are more likely to acquire citizenship and that income is positively correlated with citizenship.[63] When it comes to age, we see a curvilinear relationship: those who are middle aged are more likely to be citizens than young adults or the very old. As Portes and Curtis (1987) found in the case of Mexican immigrants, home ownership is positively correlated with naturalization, as is business ownership. There is a positive relationship between marital status and citizenship, but we find no significant statistical relationship between sex and naturalization. Men do not appear any more likely than women to have naturalized. All of these relationships hold, regardless of whether an immigrant lives in Canada or the United States (Bloemraad 2002).

Yet even after holding all these factors constant—individual attributes that might be distributed unequally in North America because of immigration policy and destination choices—living in Canada exerts a strong, positive effect on the likelihood of being a naturalized citizen. Statistically predicted probabilities of naturalization can vary from 1 (absolute certainty of citizenship) to 0 (absolute certainty of no citizenship). The likelihood of citizenship for an average Portuguese immigrant living in the United States is .47. Living in Canada raises the estimated probability to .70, an increase of 47 percent.[64]

A similar analysis with similar results can be done for the Portuguese communities of Massachusetts and Ontario, the sites of the in-depth community studies I detail in coming chapters. Table 4 provides examples of how key individual attributes change the probability that a Portuguese immigrant has naturalized. The first column describes the type of change; the second reports the increase in the estimated probability of citizenship. The final column provides a 95 percent confidence interval around the probability estimate.[65] Education is critical in explaining citizenship: holding a high school diploma increases the probability of being a citizen .16 compared to only possessing primary schooling, and being a university graduate further increases the probability of citizenship by .19. Years of residence and English proficiency also show noteworthy increases in the likelihood of naturalization. In comparison, home ownership only increases the probability of citizenship by .04. These results support the contention that immigrants' characteristics influence naturalization, as the bulk of North American research suggests.

However, personal characteristics fail to explain the cross-national citizenship gap. Even controlling for individual characteristics, living in Ontario boosts the probability of citizenship .22, virtually the same advantage we find at the national level. The effect of residence is comparable to the strongest and most consistent individual-level predictors.

Indeed, we find that the impact of personal characteristics *varies* depending on whether an immigrant lives in Ontario or Massachusetts. The bottom of table 4 reports changes in expected citizenship probabilities by place of residence for different explanatory variables—education, English proficiency, and years of residence. Residing in Ontario increases the probability of being a citizen much more for someone with an elementary school edu-

TABLE 4. EFFECTS OF A CHANGE IN THE EXPLANATORY VARIABLE
ON THE PROBABILITY OF BEING A CITIZEN

Portuguese-born adults in Massachusetts and Ontario, 1990 and 1991

Variable Change*	Probability Increase	95 Percent Confidence Interval
Individual Attribute Effects		
Years of Residence		
From 12 years to 20 years	0.20	(0.18, 0.22)
English Language Ability		
From unable to able to speak English	0.30	(0.26, 0.34)
Education		
From grade 8 or less to high school graduate	0.16	(0.12, 0.20)
From high school to university graduate	0.19	(0.12, 0.25)
Home Ownership		
From being a renter to a home owner	0.04	(0.01, 0.07)
Place of Residence Effect (MA to ON)		
Moving from MA to ON (average effect)	0.22	(0.18, 0.24)
Someone with a grade 8 education or less	0.23	(0.20, 0.26)
A university graduate	0.14	(0.10, 0.17)
An English speaker	0.20	(0.17, 0.22)
Someone unable to speak English	0.22	(0.19, 0.25)
Someone with 10 years of residence	0.22	(0.19, 0.25)
Someone with 25 years of residence	0.17	(0.15, 0.19)

* First difference results are calculated using median income and median years of residence,
level of education at high school completion, and putting all other variables at their mean.

SOURCES: Author's calculations from 1990 U.S. census 5 percent Public Use Microdata
Sample (Ruggles et al. 2004) and 1991 Canadian census Public Use Microdata (Statistics
Canada 1995).

cation compared to someone with a university degree (.23 versus .14). This
effect makes sense when we consider the stronger correlation between education and citizenship in the United States discussed earlier. The finding
hints that something in the Canadian context facilitates naturalization
among those with less education to a greater extent than in the U.S. context.
The same observation holds when we compare more recent migrants to
longtime residents. The advantage of living in Ontario decreases over time,
but it remains surprisingly high—more than four times the increase in

probability from owning a home—even after twenty-five years in North America. Not only does place of residence matter for naturalization, but living in Canada appears to facilitate political incorporation, as measured by citizenship, more for those who have the least amount of education and have spent less time in North America.

In contrast, living in Ontario or Massachusetts makes little difference when we compare those unable to converse in English with those able to do so; the change in the probability of being a citizen is .22 versus .20, respectively. We can infer that barriers for those unable to speak English—notably the legal language requirement for citizenship in both countries—have a similar effect in Canada and the United States.

Another way to understand the effect of residence on citizenship is to imagine a "typical" Portuguese immigrant: a person who migrated to North America in 1970 or 1971 at the age of twenty-four, who speaks English but only has completed elementary school, and who earns the median income of any Portuguese immigrant. Statistical simulation predicts that there is a 68 percent chance that this immigrant, living in Ontario, has acquired Canadian citizenship. The likelihood that the same person, living in Massachusetts, possesses American citizenship is 46 percent. While personal characteristics affect citizenship status, where an immigrant lives matters as much or even more.

The Portuguese represent a unique opportunity to probe cross-national integration differences since the migration history and background of Portuguese immigrants to Canada and the United States are so similar. The migration experiences of other immigrant groups differ more. We can still employ statistical modeling in these cases, but the potential for bias from omitted variables is higher.[66] With this caveat in mind, we can compare four groups with a significant presence on either side of the forty-ninth parallel: Chinese from the People's Republic of China, Haitians, Jamaicans, and individuals born in the former Soviet Union. These groups are noteworthy because of their large numbers and because they entered North America under different migration statuses. These different statuses provide varying degrees of government support. A model of structured mobilization predicts that the effect of place of residence will vary with the degree of government support received.

In each case, residing in Canada has a significant, positive effect on the odds of being naturalized. The residence advantage varies among the groups. It is highest for Haitians, increasing the probability of citizenship by .62 (from .26 in the United States to .88 in Canada), and lowest for those born in the Soviet Union, only augmenting the predicted probability by .04 (from a very high .93 in the United States to .97 in Canada). This corresponds to varying governmental responses. Haitian migrants to Canada were generally accorded a warm welcome out of sympathy with political instability in their homeland and a sense of language commonality with French-speaking Canada. Many received some settlement assistance once in Canada. In the United States, most Haitians were denied status as asylum seekers prior to the early 1990s and received little help from the American government.[67] In contrast, people born in the former Soviet Union are mostly cold war migrants. They benefited from assistance in both Canada and the United States.[68] Jamaicans and Chinese migrants sit between these extremes. Individuals from Jamaica and China tend to enter both countries as regular immigrants, a status that generates some government assistance in Canada but little support in the United States, since immigrants there are expected to make their own way or rely on family, friends, and private organizations. For these groups, the advantage of Canadian residence is seen in an increase in the probability of citizenship of .34 for Jamaicans (from .49 to .83) and .41 for the Chinese (from .48 to .89). The recurrent significance of place of residence suggests that something about living in Canada promotes citizenship acquisition. The variation in this effect hints that the reception governments accord to particular groups might be behind such differences.

Existing Macro-Level Explanations:
The Legal Structure of Citizenship

Various researchers point out that laws channel individuals' interest in citizenship and their ability to naturalize. From the point of view of rational choice theory, the benefits of Canadian citizenship and/or costs of naturalizing in the United States must make Canadian citizenship more attractive.[69] Alternatively, a political opportunity approach suggests that American citizenship regulations must be more onerous than Canadian ones, making it harder to naturalize.[70] The first argument suggests that laws related to citizenship influence immigrants' motivations to naturalize; the second highlights how legal structures can hinder immigrants' ability to acquire citizenship.

It is difficult to sustain the argument that the advantages of citizenship are higher in Canada. In the five decades following World War II, individuals increasingly accessed state-controlled rights and benefits through "personhood," not citizenship.[71] By the mid-1990s, the principal benefits of citizenship were the same in both countries: access to certain public sector jobs, absolute right of entry (and thus protection from deportation in the event of a criminal conviction), the ability to travel with an American or

Canadian passport, and the right to vote or run for elected office. Although noncitizen immigrants in the United States face new restrictions with the passage of the 1996 Welfare Reform Act, prior to this legislation both countries made few distinctions for public benefits based on citizenship, especially for those with legal permanent residence status.[72]

If anything, the benefits of citizenship appear greater in the United States, and not only because access to certain means-tested programs is now denied to noncitizens. American citizens may petition for a wider range of relatives to immigrate to the United States than resident aliens (Jasso and Rosenzweig 1990). Only citizens can sponsor brothers and sisters, and the petitions of citizens sponsoring spouses and children get approved more quickly than those of permanent residents. In Canada, a permanent resident's ability to sponsor relatives is not affected by citizenship status. In fact, a proposal to link sponsorship and citizenship put forward in the 1966 White Paper on Canadian Immigration Policy received significant criticism from the Special Joint Committee of the Senate and House of Commons, in part for attaching "a utilitarian value" to citizenship (Hawkins 1988: 161). The proposal quickly died.[73] Since family reunification is an important goal for many immigrant families, a pure cost-benefit analysis would predict higher citizenship levels in the United States.

It is also difficult to argue that the laws and regulations governing naturalization are more onerous in the United States than in Canada. Historically, both countries have adopted liberal citizenship policies and, as table 5 demonstrates, contemporary naturalization regulations are similar: costs are relatively low, required residency periods are short, and both nations administer language and knowledge exams. The main discrepancies are a slightly longer residency requirement in the United States and Canada's acceptance of dual citizenship.

Since 1977 immigrants in Canada need to wait only three years before applying for citizenship. The United States generally requires five years of residence, although the spouses of American citizens can apply after three years, and those who see active military service face only a year or even no residence requirement. The residency difference can explain gaps in citizenship acquisition among very recent cohorts, but it fails to explain the persistence of such gaps. If residency requirements were the only barrier to naturalization, we would expect U.S. citizenship levels to quickly catch up to those in Canada for later cohorts. Instead, it takes over thirty years for the gap to narrow substantially.

A second regulatory difference concerns dual citizenship. The original legislation establishing Canadian citizenship in 1947 did not require a

TABLE 5. REQUIREMENTS FOR NATURALIZATION
IN THE UNITED STATES AND CANADA, JANUARY 2006

United States	
Minimum age	Eighteen years
Status	Must be a legal permanent resident
Residency requirement	Must have lived in the United States for at least five years, with absences totaling no more than one year, and have residence in one state for at least three months*
Language requirement	Must show ability to read, write, speak, and understand "ordinary" English (exceptions: those older than fifty-five living in the United States fifteen years or more, or those older than fifty living in the United States twenty years or more)
Knowledge requirement	Must demonstrate knowledge and understanding of fundamentals of U.S. history and government ("special consideration" is given to those with impairments or older than sixty-five with at least twenty years of residence)
Grounds for refusal	Certain criminal offenses, and/or a failure by the candidate to show that he or she is of "good moral character"
Oath of allegiance	Required
Cost	U.S.$330 per application (does not include U.S.$70 fingerprint fee)**
Dual citizenship	The oath of allegiance includes a phrase renouncing "foreign allegiances"

* A number of exceptions exist. The most common is for the spouses of U.S. citizens, who may apply after three years of residence. Those who saw active military service in the U.S. armed forces have no residence requirement.

** Fee information is accurate as of January 1, 2006. The current U.S. fee is more than triple the amount it was when I started my fieldwork in 1996. Then immigrants paid U.S.$95 to file the N-400 form.

renunciation of previous nationalities, but it did stipulate that individuals who adopted another citizenship once they were Canadian lost their Canadian status (Galloway 2000). Thus, immigrants to Canada could theoretically hold dual nationality upon naturalization, but Canadians who migrated elsewhere would lose Canadian citizenship if they acquired another citizenship. The 1977 Citizenship Act eliminated this provision—apparently without any debate in Parliament—ushering in "a wholly permissive stance

TABLE 5. *(continued)*

Canada	
Minimum age	Eighteen years
Status	Must be a legal permanent resident
Residency requirement	Must have lived in Canada for at least three of the previous four years before application (before February 15, 1977, the requirement was five years)
Language requirement	Must show adequate knowledge of English or French, which requires oral ability and possibly some reading and writing ability
Knowledge requirement	If between the ages of eighteen and fifty-nine, must show basic knowledge of Canada (history, geography, political institutions)
Grounds for refusal	Certain criminal offenses, as well as being deemed a security danger
Oath of allegiance	Required
Cost	C$200 per adult; C$100 per child; if citizenship is refused, C$100 of the adult fee is reimbursed
Dual citizenship	Allowed since February 15, 1977

SOURCES: Author's compilation; Citizenship and Immigration Canada website: www.cic.gc.ca/english/citizen/menu-howto.html (last accessed January 5, 2006); U.S. Citizenship and Immigration Services website: http://uscis.gov/graphics/services/natz (last accessed January 5, 2006).

on the issue of multiple nationality" (Galloway 2000: 99). In contrast, the American oath of allegiance requires all adult would-be citizens to swear the following: "I absolutely and entirely renounce and abjure all allegiance and fidelity to any foreign prince, potentate, state, or sovereignty of whom or which I have heretofore been a subject or citizen." Some contend that the absence of legal dual citizenship prevents immigrants from naturalizing (Hammar 1990; Jones-Correa 1998a). For some immigrants, it is argued, the attractions of the new country's citizenship cannot compensate for the lost benefits or psychic costs associated with giving up the old nationality.

Dual citizenship is important to some immigrants, but the American oath of allegiance, by itself, only explains a small amount of the variation in Canadian and American naturalization patterns. There are at least three reasons why this is so.[74] First, although American law formally demands that the naturalizing immigrant renounce his or her former citizenship, in practice the immigration service and State Department almost never take action if a new American uses his or her former passport outside the United States. As one INS official explained, "Dual citizenship from our point of view is not really a problem. We're in the business of saying who's a U.S. citizen or not. And whether some other country also recognizes that person, we basically think that it's an issue of that country's domestic law. And so, it's really not a big concern for us."[75] The State Department denationalized some Americans who took another country's citizenship in the 1950s and 1960s (Finifter and Finifter 1995), but court rulings such as *Afroyim v. Rusk* and *Vance v. Terrazas* made dual citizenship legal for the American born. The legal position of naturalized citizens is less clear, but in practice they can keep a former nationality.[76]

Second, foreign governments are not required to recognize would-be Americans' renunciation of former nationalities, and in many cases they do not recognize it. Many immigrants consequently find themselves dual citizens without any affirmative action on their part. For example, if a Portuguese immigrant today swears the oath of allegiance and becomes an American citizen, the state of Portugal continues to consider that person a Portuguese national. Indeed, countries increasingly promote dual citizenship to keep emigrants tied to the homeland (Basch, Glick Schiller, and Szanton Blanc 1994; Jones-Correa 2001a; Levitt 2001). The former president of Portugal, Dr. Mário Soares, is widely quoted by Portuguese American activists as having said, "The best way to be a good Portuguese citizen in the United States is to be a good American citizen."[77] U.S. officials recognize this phenomenon and, to some extent, embrace it, since it allows them to avoid the politically sensitive issue of multiple nationalities. Reflecting on her time as INS commissioner, Doris Meissner explained, "[Dual citizenship] was unlikely to change as a matter of U.S. policy, and we really didn't need to raise it because other countries were changing their policies rather rapidly."[78]

Finally, for most immigrants who plan to remain in the United States or Canada, the critical issue is not whether the host country recognizes dual citizenship, but whether the home country does. The benefits of naturalization are assured in the adopted country. In contrast, an immigrant might be very worried about property rights and other benefits tied to citizenship in the country of origin. From a purely practical standpoint, the immigrants' concern is whether the sending country recognizes dual nationality, not the United States or Canada.[79]

The stories of two Portuguese immigrants illustrate this calculation. In 1981 Portugal allowed dual nationality and permitted former Portuguese nationals to regain Portuguese citizenship if they had lost it after naturalization. Joaquim, who acquired American citizenship in the 1990s, explained why he had not naturalized in the 1970s: "I didn't want to trade in my Portuguese citizenship. [Now] I won't lose anything, so I decided to go ahead and apply for [U.S.] citizenship." Martin was in the process of naturalizing when I interviewed him, and he offered a similar logic: "Another thing that has made me decide with no hesitation is the fact that becoming a U.S. citizen, I can still be Portuguese. And that influences me a lot. . . . Right now I know that for as long as I live in the United States, I am a U.S. citizen, once I become naturalized. But if I retire and go to Portugal, I am Portuguese. Which I think is great. We don't lose anything." Clearly both men do not consider the oath of allegiance a major obstacle to naturalization. Rather, they worry about the laws of their home country. Since I compare the same immigrant groups in Canada and the United States, I control for the influence of homeland nationality laws. It is unlikely that legal differences in the American and Canadian approach to dual citizenship explain the naturalization gap. The puzzle remains.

WINNING ELECTIONS

I have spent considerable time on citizenship because it is such a basic step in immigrants' political incorporation. Those interested in politics can also participate as noncitizens, writing to officials, speaking out on political issues, joining in demonstrations, or otherwise trying to influence the political process. Nevertheless, core political activities—such as voting and running for office—are almost exclusively tied to citizenship.[80] Although immigrants can acquire citizenship for reasons unrelated to political participation, such as wanting the security of guaranteed residence or access to certain jobs, political actors tend to treat the foreign-born citizen differently from the noncitizen, encouraging the use of new political rights. The new citizen suddenly becomes a target of electoral or fund-raising campaigns and can participate in referenda or local ballot initiatives.

Unfortunately, at this juncture it is almost impossible to compare immigrants' voting behavior in Canada and the United States. Most voting surveys contain too few foreign-born respondents to allow for statistical comparison, especially of subgroups identified by country of origin, and most fail to ask critical immigration-related questions such as country of birth or length of residence.

We can, however, compare another indicator of immigrants' political integration: the number of foreign-born politicians elected to national legislature. Holding elected office is an extreme form of political participation—only a minute proportion of the general population ever runs for election, much less sits in office—but it is a revealing one. The election of foreign-born individuals can signal immigrant voting strength, at least in the candidate's riding or district, and it can indicate ordinary citizens' acceptance of the foreign born in the political process. Foreign-born politicians often become a symbol that a certain community has "arrived" in politics, not only for the immigrant community but also for those in the mainstream. They can serve as role models and spokespeople for immigrants or as a lightning rod for criticism.

The United States and Canada figure among only a handful of countries where the presence of foreign-born individuals in national legislative bodies is not considered abnormal or dangerous. While the writers of the U.S. Constitution were sufficiently suspicious of foreigners to make the office of president the only position in the United States closed to naturalized citizens, foreign-born citizens are welcome in all other political positions. In Canada, given its longer membership in a multinational empire, native birth has never been a requirement for office holding. Indeed, Canada's first prime minister, Sir John A. Macdonald, was born in Scotland, and a number of subsequent prime ministers also claimed birthplaces outside Canada.[81]

Asking whether immigrants succeed in gaining national office carries with it the assumption that a politician's biography matters. This is not necessarily an obvious proposition. In the American and Canadian political systems, one person is chosen from a particular area to speak for its residents. Such representation can take a variety of forms. Two common types are statistical and substantive representation.[82] Under statistical representation, the membership of a municipal council or legislative body should mirror central lines of diversity in the general population: if women constitute half the population, they should hold half of all seats; if an ethnic minority makes up 10 percent of the population, this percentage should be reflected in the elected body. If a system is fair and all groups have equal interest in office holding, the legislature's composition should roughly mirror that of the general population. Support for "mirror" representation is in part predicated on the belief that someone from inside the group better understands community concerns than someone outside it.

Substantive representation instead suggests that an elected official can represent diverse individuals' policy interests regardless of personal characteristics. Since no one person can reflect the statistical makeup of an area's voters, the most a politician can do is reflect the dominant views and opinions of those who elected him or her. From the point of view of substantive representation, an elected official does not need to be an immigrant in order to support or promote issues of concern to immigrant communities.

The latter has certainly been true in a variety of times and places in Canada and the United States. Nonimmigrant politicians listen to immigrant concerns, take up those concerns in a variety of arenas, and succeed in passing legislation that might be of particular benefit to foreign-born residents. A comparative historical analysis of substantive representation is, however, extremely difficult, because it demands a definition of what an "immigrant" issue is. Immigrants, like the general population, are a heterogeneous group. Just like Americans or Canadians who live in the same society but hold very different political views, immigrants from the same origins differ in their views on the economy, the role of government, social issues, and even the appropriate level and composition of future immigration streams.

Instead of trying to navigate such contentious terrain, I focus on statistical representation. The vast majority of Portuguese and Vietnamese immigrants with whom I spoke look favorably on the idea of having one or more people from the community serve as an elected representative. While a few qualify their views by commenting on incompetent coethnic politicians, almost all see value in statistical representation. Newcomers believe that coethnic politicians better understand the interests of the community and take these interests to heart; that ethnic representation offers immigrants a point of access into the political system; and that coethnic representatives serve an important symbolic function.[83]

Furthermore, one would expect that in a political system in which all individuals have equal access to office, those elected *should* look more or less like the general population. Although only a small proportion of any group of people might be sufficiently passionate about public affairs to campaign for office, there is no reason to believe that the distribution of political passion is found only in some groups (e.g., men, the native born) and not in others.[84] Of course politics, like most social institutions, does not provide equal access to all types of people—wealth and education are two characteristics overrepresented in elected bodies. But theoretically, beyond an initial adjustment and socialization period, there is reason to expect immigrants to become interested and engaged in politics, including running for office. Ideally, the proportion of foreign-born individuals in the U.S. Congress or Canadian Parliament should mirror the proportion in the general population. Do patterns of office holding reinforce the picture already painted by citizenship data?

Continued Divergence: Immigrant Politicians in National Office

Both the United States and Canada have bicameral systems at the federal level: the national legislature is made up of two bodies, the House and the Senate. The structure of the two houses is similar: each country is divided into constituencies (districts in the United States; ridings in Canada), and one person is elected by the residents of each constituency to be the area's representative. The two senates differ. The Canadian Senate is an appointed body. The prime minister nominates a senator to the sovereign (in reality to the Queen's representative, the governor general) for approval.[85] In the United States, the Constitution originally gave state legislatures the power to select senators, but with the passage of the Seventeenth Amendment in 1913, this power was transferred to the voters of a state.[86] Given senate differences, I focus on the proportion of foreign-born individuals sitting in the U.S. House of Representatives and the Canadian House of Commons in the twentieth century.

We find a pattern largely analogous to the one for citizenship. If election to the legislature were equally accessible, the proportion of foreign-born members of each house should reflect the proportion of the foreign born in the general population. Dividing the first proportion by the second allows us to calculate an index of representation. For example, in 2001, there were forty-five members of the House of Commons born outside Canada, a number that represented 15 percent of the total seats in the House. Since the percentage of foreign-born individuals in the population that year stood at 19 percent, the ratio of representation in the House to the general population is 15 to 19, for a representation index of .78. In comparison, the U.S. House of Representatives only included 8 foreign-born individuals in 2000, out of a total of 435 seats. The percentage of foreign-born individuals in the House, 1.8, stood much lower than the 11 percent of the population born outside the United States, for an index of representation of .17. An index of one signals parity between the composition of the population and the House. A lower number indicates underrepresentation and a higher number suggests more representation than we would expect.[87]

As with citizenship, the current discrepancy in representation between Canada and the United States did not always exist. In 1911, 16 sitting members of the 261-seat House of Commons were foreign born (7.2 percent), compared to 21 of 391 representatives in the U.S. House (5.4 percent) in 1910. While the proportion of foreigners was higher in Canada, it represented a lower percentage than the proportion of foreign born in the general population, which stood at 22 percent and 15 percent, respectively, in Canada and the United States. Thus the index of representation was higher in the United States, at .37, than in Canada, at .33, in the early part of the twentieth century.

The comparison of statistical representation carries a number of interpretative issues. The first and most important issue is determining whether a foreign-born representative can be considered an immigrant. Both Canada and the United States allow citizen parents living overseas to register their foreign-born children as citizens. From a legal perspective, these foreign-born citizens are *not* immigrants if they return to their parents' home country. Socially and culturally, we might consider these children to be more like other Canadians and Americans or more like other immigrants, depending on the amount of time they spend abroad and their family's roots in North America. For instance, the only foreign-born senator sitting in the U.S. Congress in 2000 was John McCain of Arizona. McCain was born in the Panama Canal Zone while his father was serving in the U.S. Navy. The son and grandson of decorated U.S. admirals, few would classify McCain as an immigrant, and because he received American citizenship at birth, McCain is eligible for the presidency. Analogous stories are found among Canadian foreign-born members of Parliament (MPs).

Unfortunately, we lack detailed personal histories for many of the hundreds of foreign-born individuals who served in national legislatures. Beyond the most prominent politicians, there are surprisingly few records that detail the citizenship of politicians' parents or the age at which they came to North America. We must therefore treat foreign birth as an imperfect proxy for immigration status. This means that we overestimate immigrant representation in Congress and Parliament since we include some individuals who are, for all intents and purposes, similar to the native born. Since the presence of individuals like McCain does not seem to be more prevalent in the United States or Canada, we can consider differences in the two countries' representation ratios as indicators of political incorporation.

We must also deal with a second issue, Canada's former use of British subjecthood. Given that Canada did not adopt a separate citizenship until 1947, should we consider British migrants from England, Scotland, Wales, and, prior to its independence, Ireland to be immigrants upon their arrival in Canada? Legally, these people were British subjects, like those born in Canada, and they enjoyed full political rights immediately after entering the country.[88] Socially and culturally, they might not have been brought up like those born in Canada. Still, strong strains of British imperialism in some segments of Canadian society might have led these individuals to be treated like native-born residents. It is unclear whether migrating British subjects should be considered akin to non-British immigrants or native-born Canadians.

We can recalculate the index of foreign-born representation in the House of Commons to count only non-British immigrants prior to 1947, as we did with the citizenship statistics. Most ratios change slightly after we compare the proportion of non-British foreign-born MPs to the proportion of the non-British foreign born in the general population. The index of representation for all foreign-born individuals, regardless of British origin, is .33 in 1911, .29 in 1921, and .53 in 1931. The recalculated ratios, excluding those born in the United Kingdom (defined as those born in England, Wales, Scotland, and Ireland), are .22, .17, and .34, respectively. The values are lower—suggesting that British migrants had an advantage in gaining access to the House of Commons—but they are not so different as to suggest that non-British immigrants were entirely shut out of national Parliament.[89]

A final issue is determining which population should serve as the base line for comparison. Above, we compared the proportion of elected representatives to the foreign-born composition of the general population. Is the general population the appropriate yardstick? It might be better to compare those elected to the naturalized foreign-born population, since only citizens can vote or stand for office.[90] Not surprisingly, indices of representation improve. While the foreign-born presence in the U.S. House of Representatives in 2000 was only about a sixth (.17) of what we would expect given the proportion of foreign born in the general population, the index more than doubles to .41 if we consider the *citizen* foreign-born population. The lack of immigrant representation in Congress stems in part from low naturalization among the foreign born.

Naturalization does not explain the whole story, however, since a sizeable deficit remains between actual representation and what we would expect for perfect mirror representation. The use of the same base comparison group in Canada—that is, the foreign-born citizen population—reveals that the foreign born appear somewhat *over*represented in the House of Commons in 2001. The recalculated index of representation is 1.19. The cross-national gap in political incorporation, apparent in citizenship acquisition, also holds for elected representation.

Table 6 consequently reports three different indices of representation for the Canadian House of Commons and two for the U.S. House of Representatives. For both countries, I compare the proportion of the foreign born in the House to the proportion in the general population and to the proportion of the naturalized foreign born in the population. In the American case, some years cannot be calculated because full naturalization information is not available for 1900, 1910, or 1960. For Canada, I also calculate an index that only counts the foreign born not born in the United Kingdom.

Not surprisingly, the numbers change depending on the point of comparison, but the overall trends—over time and cross-nationally—largely remain the same. In the United States, incorporation appears stronger in the pre–World War II period than in the years since 1965. In Canada, integration patterns before and after World War II resemble each other, although political incorporation appears to pick up speed at the end of the twentieth century. Thus Canada and the United States appear roughly analogous in the 1920–40 period, but statistical representation of immigrants in the United States did not keep pace with Canada from 1970 to 2000.

A visual representation makes the patterns clearer. Figure 4 compares indices of representation in Canada and the United States over the twentieth century, using the proportion of foreign-born residents in the general population as the point of comparison. Given British subjects' unique status in Canada prior to 1947, the Canadian ratio includes only those not born in the United Kingdom from 1901 to 1941. The sharp peak in the 1951 Canadian data stems in part from the change in way the ratios are calculated.

Between 1900 and 1931 political incorporation was, on average, more successful in the United States than in Canada. Although representation in the U.S. House was only about a third or two-fifths of what we might expect, the proportion of foreign-born residents sitting in Congress was closer to the percentage in the general population than for the non-British in Canada's House of Commons. Interestingly, both countries saw an increase in foreign-born representation in 1940–41. We might not expect the foreign born to have been welcome in national legislatures with the Second World War raging. The increase in representation is dramatic in Canada and continues to 1951, although the spike is in part due to the different calculation of foreign-born residents.

Both countries see a dip in foreign-born representation in the immediate postwar period, but the Canadian figures do not fall as far as those in the United States. Unlike in the case of citizenship, U.S. foreign-born representation rises slightly in 1990, but the increase might be an anomaly. In 2000 few foreign-born individuals sat in the House of Representatives, while in

TABLE 6. REPRESENTATION OF THE FOREIGN BORN IN THE U.S. HOUSE OF REPRESENTATIVES
AND THE CANADIAN HOUSE OF COMMONS, 1900–2001

Year (United States)	1900	1910	1920	1930	1940	1950	1960	1970	1980	1991	2000
No. seats in House of Representatives	357	391	435	435	435	435	435	435	435	435	435
No. foreign born elected to House	18	21	19	16	17	10	7	1	1	8	8
Percentage of foreign born in House	5.0	5.4	4.4	3.7	3.9	2.3	1.6	0.2	0.2	1.8	1.8
Percentage of foreign born in population	13.6	14.7	13.2	11.6	8.8	6.9	5.4	4.7	6.2	7.9	11.1
Index of representation[a]	0.37	0.37	0.33	0.32	0.44	0.33	0.30	0.05	0.04	0.23	0.17
Percentage of foreign-born citizens in population[b]	—	—	6.1	6.5	5.5	5.0	—	3.1	3.1	3.2	4.5
Index of representation[c]	—	—	0.71	0.57	0.71	0.46	—	0.08	0.07	0.57	0.41

Year (Canada)	1901	1911	1921	1931	1941	1951	1961	1971	1981	1991	2000
No. seats in House of Commons	213	221	235	245	245	262	264	264	282	295	301
No. sitting foreign-born MPs	24	16	15	29	33	34	21	18	24	29	45
Percentage of foreign born in House	11.3	7.2	6.4	11.8	13.5	13.0	8.0	6.8	8.5	9.8	15.0
No. sitting U.K.-born MPs	20	11	11	20	17	17	9	6	8	5	7
Percentage of non-U.K. foreign born in House	1.9	2.3	1.7	3.7	6.5	6.5	4.5	4.5	5.7	8.1	12.6
Percentage of foreign born in population[a]	13.0	22.0	22.3	22.2	17.5	14.7	15.6	15.3	16.0	17.0	19.1
Index of representation[a]	0.87	0.33	0.29	0.53	0.77	0.88	0.51	0.45	0.53	0.58	0.78
Percentage of non-U.K. foreign born in population[d]	5.2	10.4	10.1	10.8	8.8	8.0	10.0	10.2	11.7	13.7	15.1
Index of representation[d]	0.36	0.22	0.17	0.34	0.74	0.81	0.45	0.45	0.48	0.59	0.83
Percentage of foreign-born citizens in population	10.7	16.5	18.0	17.3	15.3	11.6	9.8	9.2	11.0	11.3	12.6
Index of representation[c]	1.05	0.44	0.36	0.68	0.88	1.12	0.81	0.74	0.78	0.87	1.19

[a] Proportion of foreign born in House divided by proportion of foreign born in population.

[b] The census did not collect information on immigrant citizenship before 1920, and did not collect this information in 1960.

[c] Proportion of foreign-born citizens in House divided by proportion of foreign-born citizens in population.

[d] Proportion of non-U.K. foreign born in House divided by proportion of non-U.K. foreign born in population.

SOURCES: Author's calculations, using data compiled by author and from data provided by the Canadian Parliamentary Library and the Inter-university Consortium for Political and Social Research datafile "Roster of United States Congressional Officeholders" (1997).

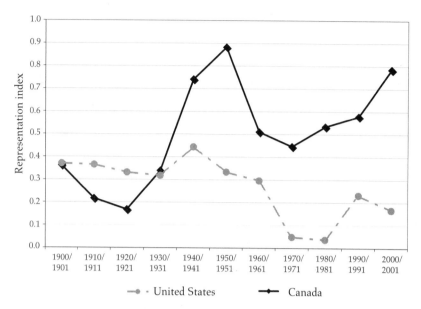

Figure 4. Representation index of foreign-born national legislators to foreign-born residents of the United States (even-numbered years) **and Canada** (odd-numbered years), **1900–2001**. Before 1951, Canadian data include only non-British foreign-born residents. SOURCES: ICPSR and Carroll McKibbin (1997); Parliamentary Library of Canada database of Canadian Parliamentarians and author's compilation.

Canada foreign-born legislators continued to enter the House of Commons. The data on elected representatives confirm the pattern of diverging incorporation trajectories that we saw with citizenship.

It is also worth noting the changing origins of these foreign-born politicians. Before 1951 the overwhelming majority of non-U.K. foreign-born politicians serving in the Canadian House of Commons reported an American birthplace. The next most common birthplace was France, but judging from last names, perhaps two of the four French-born MPs were actually of British origins, at least on their father's side. The most culturally "foreign" immigrants serving in the House prior to 1951 include two men born in Germany, two in Russia, one in Switzerland, one in Poland, one in Sweden, and one in Iceland. These origins reflect, in part, major sources of non-British immigration, though the relationship is not perfect, since Switzerland and Iceland were not especially significant migrant-sending countries.

People born in the United Kingdom and Canada also dominated the foreign-born contingent in the U.S. House of Representatives in the early part of the century. In the Fifty-sixth and Sixty-first Congresses, sitting in 1900 and 1910, respectively, more than half of the foreign-born representatives claimed birthplaces in England, Wales, Scotland, or Ireland and another fifth to a quarter had been born in Canada. The next most prominent birthplace was Germany, with four elected representatives. In 1900 the foreign-born contingent was rounded off by a man born in Norway and another born in Luxembourg, while in 1910 the remainder hailed from Sweden (two), Norway (one), and Czechoslovakia (one). By 1940 those born in the United Kingdom and Canada only accounted for 45 percent of the twenty foreign-born representatives. The remainder were from Scandinavia, Germany, and Eastern Europe (Czechoslovakia, Hungary, Poland, and Romania).[91]

At the end of the twentieth century, foreign-born Canadian MPs came from around the globe. A bit more than the majority of the forty-five sitting MPs still reported a birthplace in Europe or the United States in 2001, but three members of Parliament were born in India, two in China, two in the Middle East (Lebanon and Syria), five in the Caribbean or Latin America, four in Africa, and one in the Philippines.[92] In the United States, only eight representatives were foreign born in 1990 and 2000. More than half hailed from Europe in 1990, but in 2000 the European born were in the minority. In 1990 the three non-European foreign-born representatives were from Cuba, the West Indies, and Central America. In 2000 two representatives had Asian birthplaces, though we must be cautious about ascribing ethnicity or immigrant background based on birth. David Wu, born in Taiwan, is the first and only Chinese American to serve in Congress. Diane DeGette, born in Tachikawa, Japan, is not of Japanese background and proudly presents herself as a fourth-generation Coloradoan. The limited number of foreign-born representatives in the United States makes the group less globally diverse than in Canada, but as in Canada, origins go beyond the pre–World War II reliance on European-born individuals.

Thus, up until the 1960s, the political incorporation of immigrants looked quite similar in Canada and the United States. This is the case whether we consider citizenship or election to national office. Patterns diverge in the final decades of the twentieth century, with greater signs of political integration in Canada than in the United States. More foreign-born individuals serve as representatives in the Canadian House of Commons, and a much greater proportion of immigrants residing in Canada take out citizenship. Variation in naturalization regulations or the costs and benefits of citizenship are not substantial enough to account for these differences. The sorting of immigrants to the two countries—by country of origin and by personal characteristics—explains some of the difference, but a large gap remains even after we control for such variation.

We need to go beyond immigrants' skills, interests, and resources to understand the social nature of political incorporation and the role of institutional arrangements and government policies in shaping incorporation experiences. Citizenship seems to vary by migrant group in a manner consistent with the level of government support a group receives. Indeed, researchers from the Urban Institute have estimated that refugees in the United States are one and a half times more likely to take up American citizenship than eligible nonrefugee legal immigrants with similar personal characteristics (Fix, Passel, and Sucher 2003: 6). We also find a weaker correlation in Canada between citizenship and education, implying that something in the Canadian context attenuates the barriers faced by those with less schooling or encourages them to naturalize more. This leveling of citizenship probabilities stands in sharp contrast to Louis DeSipio's analysis of the United States, where "the contemporary process of immigrant political adaptation has not only shifted from a group focus to an individual focus, but it has also incorporated the class and education bias that shapes political participation more generally in American society" (2001: 69). Government intervention might level some of these biases.

2. The Social Nature of Citizenship and Participation

I have no time, and because I just came to the U.S. I don't know who is good or who is bad. Since I don't know much about politics, I am afraid that I [might] vote for the wrong person.

VIETNAMESE REFUGEE IN BOSTON,
*explaining why he has not voted
since acquiring citizenship four years earlier*

We try to provide much information: what this election is, why should you vote, how do you vote. That type of information. What responsibilities are. "These are feds, this is the province, this is the city." What questions you should be asking your own politicians as they knock at your door and ask for your vote. . . . So, [we] try to help them analyze the situation.

PORTUGUESE CANADIAN STAFF MEMBER,
*St. Christopher House, Toronto,
community-based organization*

If we were to distill a complex phenomenon such as democracy to a single image, we might picture an individual voter before a ballot box, making a private choice for his or her preferred representative. We see such photos regularly in magazine articles on authoritarian countries' transition to democracy or in television images of election day in established Western democracies.

While powerful, these portrayals are deceptive. They imply that politics is driven by purely individual action centered on a (distant) relationship between the voter and the candidate. Yet mobilization occurs most readily through personal contact and social interaction, that is, through social ties and organizations rather than through impersonal appeals or spontaneous engagement. Involvement with voluntary associations, workplaces, and religious institutions can teach civic and political skills, build interpersonal trust, and foster feelings of citizenship.[1] This holds true whether political activity is routinized or contentious.[2] Political incorporation is a social process.

Historically, academics viewed immigrant social cohesion as a problem, believing that ethnic ties and organizations isolate immigrants from the mainstream, hindering assimilation. More recently, students of immigration have documented the importance of interethnic ties, and the social capital that results from such networks, for migration, educational outcomes, and success in the labor market.[3] It seems logical that such benefits carry over into politics, especially since the political system demands aggregation of interests to exert influence. Indeed, given the collective nature of political activity, we would expect mobilization to be a central concern in the explanation of immigrant political incorporation. Surprisingly, such is not the case. Models of citizenship and political integration tend to focus on the formal laws regulating access to citizenship or on the individual characteristics of migrants. Missing from such accounts is the social nature of political learning and mobilization as well as an analysis of the mechanisms that link individuals with political systems.

In this chapter I show how friends, family, ethnic businesses, immigrant organizations, and community leaders facilitate political involvement. They teach newcomers how politics work in the adopted country; they offer concrete assistance during naturalization; and they encourage political engagement. Taking a social approach shows how immigrants' political incorporation starts within communities and personal networks, involving processes of mobilization that go beyond how well an immigrant speaks English or how much education she received. First, however, I outline the barriers that Portuguese and Vietnamese migrants face in achieving full political citizenship.

SEARCHING FOR A BETTER LIFE IN NORTH AMERICA: PORTUGUESE AND VIETNAMESE MIGRATION

Political incorporation in North America should be easy. Expansive democratic rights allow widespread participation. There are no onerous naturalization requirements as in other countries around the world. Yet members of the Vietnamese and Portuguese communities of Boston and Toronto consistently lament their group's lack of political voice. Many attribute political failings to the limitations of the community itself: a lack of resources, interest, skills, or understanding of politics. In the words of one Vietnamese American, "Basically, I think [voting] is the people's responsibility. I mean, back in the early 1900s, people fight for their rights to vote. And then in the '60's, the civil rights movement fights for the black people to vote. We are not there anymore. I mean, you [are] entitled to vote. Therefore it really becomes [the] responsibility of the people to do their part."[4]

Such reasoning echoes the assumptions behind many academic models of citizenship acquisition and electoral participation. These focus on the effect of immigrants' personal or group characteristics in explaining political outcomes, given that the regulatory barriers to legal and participatory citizenship are relatively low. Such accounts tell us something important. Skills, resources, and interests matter. Relatively low levels of education, linguistic barriers, antipathy toward politics, and limited exposure to the North American political process make political incorporation a challenge for Portuguese and Vietnamese migrants.

The origins of these two migrant groups differ. The majority of Portuguese in North America migrated for economic reasons, arriving under family reunification provisions or as laborers, both legal and illegal.[5] Vietnamese migration has stronger political motivations, with the majority arriving in North America as refugees. Both communities contain political and economic migrants who fled authoritarian regimes. Many see migration as a permanent move; others believe they will return to their homeland once they have made enough money or after the old regime is overthrown.

Portuguese Migration

Portuguese immigration to Canada began in the 1950s after the Canadian and Portuguese governments negotiated an agreement for the migration of agricultural laborers and skilled tradesmen.[6] The arrangement represented a radical shift from previous practice. The Portuguese state had historically discouraged emigration because of its need for labor and its desire to promote settlement in Portuguese colonies (Halpern Pereira 1980). People could be jailed for unauthorized emigration or for helping others leave the country illegally.[7] On the Canadian side, Canadian governments discouraged Portuguese farmers from immigrating in the 1920s because, as the deputy minister of immigration put it, "it has been the experience of this Department that Portuguese in general are not particularly adaptable to farming conditions in Canada" (Marques and Marujo 1993: 2).

By the 1950s, however, the Canadian economy was facing manpower shortages, and Canadian immigration officials held recruiting sessions in Portugal, where they searched for men with "hardened hands" to work as laborers on Canadian farms, railroads, and lumber camps. These initial recruits sponsored family members and told friends about the economic opportunities in Canada. By the 1960s and early '70s about six thousand Portuguese migrants were arriving yearly (Teixeira and Lavigne 1992: 5). According to the 2001 Canadian census, individuals born in Portugal formed the tenth-largest immigrant group in Canada (155,770 individuals, or 2.8 percent of all foreign-born residents). They were the eighth-largest immigrant group in the province of Ontario (112,510, or 3.6 percent of all foreign-born residents) and in metropolitan Toronto (80,195, or 3.8 percent of all foreign-born residents).

The story of Dan's father, one of the original Canadian recruits, is typical. He has often told his son how immigration authorities inspected the men like cattle, checking for physical vigor and the absence of disability. Dan's father, like most of his compatriots, tolerated such treatment because economic conditions in the Azores were so poor that he could barely provide for his young family. Limited industrialization and an archaic landowning system concentrated ownership in the hands of a few, relegating many Portuguese men to an insecure existence as agricultural laborers, fishermen, or, occasionally, factory workers.[8] Women often worked at home or helped out with farming. More than one person told me that Sundays meant the addition of a prized egg to the regular staples of bread, cabbage, and potatoes or that military service provided them with their first pair of boots.

Dan's father initially planned to return to Portugal once he had saved up enough money. The belief that moving to North America is only a short sojourn, the "myth of return," is pervasive in the Portuguese overseas community and dates back as far as the early nineteenth century, when poor migrants sought their fortune in Brazil. Even after decades in North America, some immigrants continue to tell friends and family that they will return "home" next year, a nostalgia for past lifestyles and relationships summed up by the Portuguese word *saudade*. Community leaders often cite the belief in eventual return as a reason why Portuguese immigrants fail to naturalize or evince much interest in politics. In reality, most remain in North America because of family or superior wages. Dan's father sponsored the rest of his family to immigrate to Canada a few years later, after his wife's letters reported little economic improvement in the islands.[9]

In the United States, the first substantial postwar influx of Portuguese arrived in 1959 as a special refugee class, escaping earthquakes and volcanic activity on the island of Faial in the Azores.[10] The passage in 1965 of the new U.S. Immigration Act removed the old quota of 500 Portuguese visas and opened the door to a wave of newcomers. Like Dan's father, most left their homeland for economic reasons. Some entered the United States on a work visa. Most used family connections to acquire immigrant status under the second (spouse or unmarried children of resident aliens and citizens) or fifth (siblings of citizens) preference categories of the new U.S. immigration system (Ito-Alder 1980 [1972, 1978]).[11] Pap claims that "more than half the population of the Azores had some personal ties, some relatives or friends, in the United States" (1981: 96). Almost 10,000 Portuguese arrived yearly from 1966 to the late 1970s so that by 2000, there were 203,120 individuals of Portuguese birth living in the United States, 66,627 of them in Massachusetts. The Portuguese constituted the largest immigrant group in the state (8.6 percent of the total foreign-born population), and the eighth-largest group in metro Boston (3.9 percent of all foreign-born residents).

The majority of Portuguese in North America identify economics as the prime reason they left. Nonetheless, some Portuguese view their move to North America as a political act, even if they arrived under family sponsorship or with a work visa. In a number of cases, young men sought to escape service in the Portuguese army. From 1961 to 1975 the Portuguese state was embroiled in conflict with its African colonies. Many Portuguese saw little point in fighting for the preservation of the empire. For some, migration was an act of self-preservation; for others, it was a rejection of the state's political goals. Often a family would attempt to move to North America before the eldest son was called for military service. An even smaller minority of those I interviewed, all living in Toronto, left Portugal after facing persecution for their political activities.[12] A military coup in 1926 and the establishment in 1933 of the fascist-inspired Estado Novo led by Dr. António de Oliveira Salazar eliminated free expression and democratic opposition for almost fifty years.[13] These dissidents left Portugal after being jailed or denied job opportunities, although none formally entered Canada as refugees.[14]

Vietnamese Migration

The designation of some Portuguese as refugees highlights the difficulty of making a distinction between political and economic migrants. According to the 1951 UN Convention Relating to the Status of Refugees, amended in 1967 by the Protocol Relating to the Status of Refugees, a "convention refugee" is someone "owing to well-founded fear of being persecuted for reasons of race, religion, nationality, membership of a particular social group or political opinion, is outside the country of his nationality and is unable or, owing to such fear, is unwilling to avail himself of the protection of that country" (article 1, A [2]).[15] In practice, countries such as the United States often follow foreign policy goals in their designation of refugees, applying the label to those who flee unfriendly regimes but denying the status to the nationals of allies.[16]

Most Vietnamese label themselves as refugees, even if they entered Canada or the United States under nonrefugee immigration categories. Motivations for flight, however, span a continuum from entirely political—a fear of persecution and ideological opposition to the communist regime—to largely economic. Almost all arrived in North America following the fall of South Vietnam to communist forces in 1975.[17] Twenty-five years after the fall of Saigon, the almost one million Vietnamese-born individuals living in the United States comprise the fifth-largest immigrant group in the country, after Mexicans, Filipinos, Indians, and Chinese but ahead of Cubans and Koreans.[18] In Canada, those born in Vietnam constitute the eleventh-largest immigrant group (150,135 people) in the country in 2001. The numbers in Massachusetts and Ontario are 30,457 (3.9 percent of all foreign-born residents) and 72,845 (2.3 percent), respectively. In Boston, the 19,788 Vietnamese counted in the 2000 census make the community the seventh largest in the metropolitan region (3.9 percent of all foreign-born residents), while in Toronto it ranked thirteenth in 2001 (2.5 percent of all foreign born, or 53,220 individuals).

Vietnamese migration can be roughly characterized by three waves. The first began in the spring of 1975 and cumulated with the fall of Saigon on April 30. Many who left—government officials, members of the military, and people who had worked for the U.S. government or American companies—feared retribution by the invading communist forces. About 65,000 were directly evacuated by the United States, while others commandeered naval ships, fishing boats, and planes in their bid to escape (Kelly 1977). In all, about 130,000 individuals settled in the United States under the Indochinese Refugee Act. Hein calls these individuals *allied aliens*, "foreigners who are the responsibility of an interventionist state as a result of foreign policy defeats" (1993: xi). As such, the United States felt a certain sense of obligation to the refugees, and they in turn looked to the United States for assistance. Canada, not directly involved in the Vietnam conflict, welcomed about 7,800 individuals, including 3,926 who were resettled to Canada from reception camps in the United States (Dorais 2000; Kelly 1977: 130). Most of these people had relatives already living in Canada.

Many refugees in the first wave came from relatively privileged backgrounds, and a significant proportion had held important positions in their homeland. Only about 1 percent of the South Vietnamese population had a university education, but 19.5 percent of the 1975 refugees had attended university (Kelly 1977: 49–50). Many had held white-collar occupations in urban centers back in Vietnam.[19] In the North American economy, however, most refugees faced substantial downward mobility, in part due to limited English-language skills.[20] Rose, the daughter of an important businessman in Vietnam, remembers that the speed of her family's departure as well as the cost of flight, including bribes and the purchase of a leaking boat, left the family with little money to start a new life in America:

My father lost everything that he ever owned, the land, and the house, and then his businesses because he owned quite a few investments there. But, he was willing to leave all that behind in the name of freedom. . . . It was everything that he had. And he was in his late forties, so it was hard for him to learn English and try to start a new life again. . . .

[In the United States] he was given a bike, as a form of transportation to go from home to work and to grocery shop. And you can imagine in the wintertime. Having had everything, the wealth, and then riding a bike to the office in the wintertime, as a maintenance guy. . . . You can imagine that was an insult to him.

Linguistic isolation, economic marginalization, and the loss of their country led most Vietnamese to turn to their ethnic community for support. For a significant number in the first refugee wave, this inward turn included sustained activity around homeland politics. For people such as Rose's father, political activity within the immigrant community—where one's former position was recognized and, to a certain degree, respected—increased a sense of self-worth, especially among men.[21]

The second refugee wave, beginning in 1977 and continuing into the mid-1980s, is often referred to as the "boat people" exodus because of the hundreds of thousands who left Vietnam by sea.[22] Following North Vietnam's victory and the consolidation of the country under communist rule, many freedoms were suppressed, and former combatants from the South were sent to prison and reeducation camps. Suspected enemies of the regime had little chance of economic or social advancement. They and their family were relegated to menial jobs or barred from attending university. Those not designated as political enemies also faced a bleak future. Vietnam's economy, already hurt by war, further deteriorated as paper money lost all value and the government nationalized much of the economy. New Economic Zones were set up in remote parts of the country to get people back to the land after war-related migration depopulated rural areas, but often those sent to work in the New Economic Zones were small businesspeople with no skills and no interest in farming. Natural disasters aggravated economic woes, and the state faced problems with feeding the population. Many of those who left during this second wave tell a complex tale of political and economic motivations.

Vietnamese migrants in the second wave came from more diverse backgrounds than the first. The boat people exodus began with the departure of Sino-Vietnamese. Many ethnic Chinese, whose families had in some cases lived in Vietnam for generations, owned commercial interests in South Vietnam. Ideology and pragmatism lead the new regime to confiscate much of their wealth, take over their businesses, and send entire families to work in the New Economic Zones. In 1977 Sino-Vietnamese began fleeing across Vietnam's northern border into China, and in 1978 ethnic Chinese from the South started leaving, some with government approval, facilitated by corrupt minor officials. These early departures were reasonably orderly. One woman in Toronto remembers, "The Vietnamese communists, they wanted to get rid of the Chinese. We boarded on a boat—we left legally, so the boat I think was pretty well built, built for the purpose of going to the sea." In return for their expedited departure, "we left all our lands and left everything to the government. We had to pay practically all our wealth to the government. We had to pay [in] gold." When fighting broke out briefly between Vietnam and China in February 1979, flight became more chaotic as Sino-Vietnamese became even more unwelcome.

In contrast, ethnic Vietnamese faced imprisonment if they attempted to emigrate. Most of those I interviewed made multiple attempts to escape, with some making a dozen attempts or more. These attempts were followed by jail time when police thwarted their departure. Nonetheless, starting in 1977 and then rapidly accelerating after, more and more Vietnamese embarked on clandestine flight, taking to the sea in fishing or cargo boats or walking through the jungle into neighboring Cambodia and from there to Thailand. The means of escape partially determined who left: fishing families who had a boat; rural villagers living on the coast; and city dwellers with enough money to buy their way onto a vessel. By June of 1979 the UN High Commissioner for Refugees reported over 350,000 Indochinese in refugee camps throughout Southeast Asia (Hawkins 1991: 180). Given the rising urgency of the refugee plight—thousands were dying on the seas in decrepit boats and at the hands of pirates while neighboring countries felt overwhelmed by the exodus—the United Nations called a conference in Geneva in July 1979 at which numerous Western countries agreed to resettle the displaced Indochinese. Between 1979 and 1982 about 60,000 individuals went to Canada and more than 450,000 were admitted to the United States (Hawkins 1991: 184; Hein 1993: 90). Clandestine flight from Vietnam continued throughout the 1980s.[23]

The third wave of Vietnamese migration dates from the mid-1980s to the present. This movement tends to be more orderly, as tens of thousands of individuals continue to arrive in North American under a variety of immigration categories. Many enter Canada using family reunification provisions, sponsored from refugee camps or sometimes arriving directly from

Vietnam (Richard and Dorais 2003). Family sponsorship also occurs in the United States, but three additional programs provide alternative access. The Orderly Departure Program (ODP), created in May 1979 through an agreement between the United Nations High Commissioner for Refugees and the Hanoi government, allowed former South Vietnamese officers and soldiers who were in prison or reeducation camps to be interviewed by U.S. officials and, if approved, resettled with their families in the United States. Over 200,000 Vietnamese were admitted to the United States under ODP provisions (Zhou and Bankston 1998). A complementary agreement struck in 1989, the Humanitarian Operation Program, allowed current and former detainees to be resettled in the United States. Over 70,000 entered the United States and are sometimes referred to as "HOs" in Vietnamese communities. Like those in the first wave, many ODP and HO migrants militate for the overthrow of the communist regime. Ideological opposition is intensified by painful experiences in jails and reeducation camps, including torture and psychological abuse.

A final group of Vietnamese arrived in the United States under the Amerasian Homecoming Act of 1987, which targeted the offspring of Vietnamese women and U.S. servicemen. The act eliminates most of the requirements faced by other refugees and immigrants, and it directs the U.S. government to bring as many of these children to the United States as possible. These individuals were often ostracized in Vietnamese society as "half-breeds." Ha, a friendly woman with large, almond-shaped eyes and thick, kinked black hair, recalls, "when I went out [in Vietnam], people often showed their hate to me and shouted at me '*con lai*' [half-breed]. . . . I felt bad about myself because I don't look Vietnamese. I wanted to go to America because my father was American." According to INS statistics, 73,854 people entered the United States under this act between 1989 and 2003. Between 20,000 and 25,000 are Amerasians, and the remainder are accompanying relatives.[24]

THE CHALLENGES OF POLITICAL INCORPORATION

Although they come to North America from opposite ends of the earth and with different degrees of political or economic motivations, Portuguese and Vietnamese migrants have a surprising amount in common. In particular, they face similar hurdles to political incorporation. The Portuguese community is consistently described as politically "invisible" in the United States and Canada.[25] Portuguese political apathy is variously attributed to low levels of education (Pap 1981), socialization under a dictatorship that actively discouraged civic and political participation (Anderson and Higgs 1976), factionalism within the community (Wolforth 1978), or ingrained cultural traits that discourage political involvement (Almeida 1999).[26]

Many of these same themes crop up in discussions of Vietnamese political behavior, with the added obstacle of recent arrival in North America. A 1994 poll by the *Los Angeles Times* of 861 Vietnamese in Southern California found that only 29 percent were registered voters and an even smaller percentage actually turned out to vote (Lien 2001). Recent migration and a concomitant lack of citizenship account in part for the low percentage, but a survey conducted seven years later with Vietnamese respondents in five major U.S. cities found that only 40 percent voted in the November 2000 presidential election (Lien et al. 2001).[27]

Whether in Toronto or Boston, Portuguese and Vietnamese migrants largely share these political liabilities. When looking at political incorporation from the perspective of a traditional voting behavior model, it is clear that Vietnamese and Portuguese immigrants are particularly likely to lack political efficacy, opt out of formal electoral participation, and be adverse to other forms of political involvement. All have migration histories that discourage involvement in Canadian or American politics, low levels of schooling, and internal fissures dividing the community.[28]

A Lack of Interest: The Effects of Previous Political Socialization

Most immigrant activists feel that homeland experiences feed into political silence in the adopted country.[29] Putting the community's political apathy in context, one Portuguese Canadian explained, "In the Portugal that they knew, you fended for yourself. You didn't expect anything from the state, except for the expectation that Salazar was going to take more and more away from you. You were not to trust the state; you were not to get involved. The further away you are, the farther removed, the better off." Another person elaborated, "Not only were they not allowed to vote, but they were not supposed to participate either. They are not used to using the vote to get into the decision-making circles."

For the Vietnamese, the opposite problem—excessive politicization in the homeland—produces similar reports of political antipathy. Those hit hardest by political turbulence in Vietnam fear and distrust politics. One Vietnamese Canadian explained that in Vietnam, "When you're [the] bottom of the ladder, it did not make any difference if you go and cast your vote or not. It would not lift you higher than that. So why bother? . . . In Vietnam, it used to [be] that you HAVE to go to vote. . . . So that's why at election time always 99 percent get on the list. . . . But it did not mean a thing." Others feel they are guests in their new home and should remain silent out of gratitude to their hosts (Zhou and Bankston 1998). More than once, in interviews with Vietnamese or Portuguese immigrants, my questions about political participation would be dismissed with a wave of the hand.

To a certain degree, Portuguese and Vietnamese attitudes mirror the feelings of native-born Canadians and Americans. Levels of trust and confidence in government have declined in the last four to five decades (Putnam 2000; Rosenstone and Hansen 1993). It is thus difficult to separate out a generalized distaste of politics, held by many residents of the United States and Canada, from a particular abhorrence of politics on the part of Portuguese and Vietnamese migrants.

Still, the Vietnamese and Portuguese appear to hold more reservations about politics than other groups.[30] Statistical surveys of ethnic groups in Toronto find that Portuguese respondents express relatively little faith in the use of organized action or political parties to resolve problems, and while they are on average quite satisfied with life in Toronto, they are less likely than most other groups to feel that they have access to local politicians (Breton et al. 1990; Goldfarb Consultants 1999).[31] A survey of Asian Americans in five major U.S. cities found Vietnamese to be the least interested in politics. A bit over half, 52 percent, said that they were very or somewhat interested in politics and government, compared to 61 percent of all Asian Americans polled (Lien et al. 2001).[32] The relative difference becomes more important when we realize that, on average, Asian Americans are more reluctant to engage the political system than African Americans, Latinos, or whites (Uhlaner, Cain, and Kiewiet 1989).

In many interviews, Vietnamese and Portuguese migrants expressed disinterest and distrust in politics, elected officials, the effectiveness of electoral contests, and the ability of the media to fairly and accurately portray political choices. Adjectives such as "dirty" or phrases such as "can't be trusted" cropped up frequently: "A politician has to be a self-centered individual that will sacrifice friends, will sacrifice anything for the sake of achieving that end." Being in office makes elected officials "dilute the things they stand for." Grumbling about his failed efforts at getting fellow Portuguese Canadians to run for office, one man lamented, "Too often I have seen the connotation being that getting involved in politics is just not as ethical as it should be." Or as one Portuguese American explained, "politics for a lot of Azoreans was considered what is called the 'realm of the witches.'" Although North America is poles apart from pre-1974 Portugal or communist Vietnam, it takes significant convincing to change a lifetime of distrust and disinterest.

The Skill Deficit: Education and Language Ability

Skills matter in explaining political behavior. Familiarity with the host society's predominant language facilitates citizenship acquisition and participation in mainstream political activities such as voting (Bloemraad 2002; Cho 1999). According to the 2000 U.S. census, 70 percent of those born in Vietnam say that they cannot speak English well, while more than half of Portuguese immigrants report the same, despite the fact that many have lived in the United States for over twenty-five years. Language questions on the Canadian census are not directly comparable to those in the United States, but we find similar linguistic barriers. Of all Toronto residents, Vietnamese are three times more likely and Portuguese three and half times more likely than other Toronto residents to report an inability to carry out a conversation in French or English (Ornstein 2000).[33]

Education also plays a crucial role. A long history of scholarship in political science shows that low levels of education depress electoral participation. Education generates political interest, provides information, and develops civic skills, all of which correlate with political involvement. Education also indirectly affects voting and campaign activity by increasing income and chances for recruitment. In studies of citizenship acquisition, education shows a significant, positive relationship with the propensity to naturalize.[34]

The link between education and participation hurts the Portuguese and Vietnamese communities in particular. In Toronto, Portuguese have by far the lowest levels of educational attainment of any ethno-racial group. In 1996 over 51 percent of Portuguese between the ages of twenty-four and sixty-four had only primary schooling or none at all, compared to 14 percent of the general population, and almost 70 percent had not completed high school, more than double the 31 percent among all Toronto residents (Ornstein 2000: 38). At the other end of the educational ladder, fewer than 4 percent held a university degree. Numbers in the United States are similar: in 2000, 45 percent of Portuguese immigrants in Massachusetts never attended high school; only 37 percent held a high school diploma; and less than 6 percent possessed a university degree.[35] These numbers compare to 6 percent, 85 percent, and 33 percent, respectively, among the general population in the state.

The Vietnamese fare better, but only marginally. In Toronto 24 percent never attended high school and 54 percent do not possess a high school diploma, the lowest level of high school completion after the Portuguese and

Italians (Ornstein 2000: 37). The community boasts relatively more university graduates than the Portuguese, about 8 percent, but this proportion falls far below the 23 percent of Torontonians with university degrees. Comparable figures for Vietnamese living in Massachusetts are 25 percent with primary schooling or less, 47 percent without a high school diploma, and 15 percent with a university degree. The Boston Vietnamese community thus counts a relatively larger proportion of highly educated individuals than the Toronto one, but the community as a whole is characterized by low levels of schooling very similar to the Toronto Vietnamese community.

Those with limited schooling express fear of the political system and blame a lack of knowledge for their reluctance to become involved. Maria, a Portuguese American who migrated in the 1960s, is typical of many. In the Azores, she completed four years of schooling and helped on the family farm. In the United States, she works as a cleaner and found time to attend evening classes and achieve a high school equivalency diploma (GED). But despite decades in Boston, she has never voted: "I'm afraid to vote for the wrong person; I am not confident in myself. . . . I always feel that I am going to do a mistake or something." A Vietnamese American in Dorchester who has six year of schooling tells a similar tale. He has not voted since he acquired citizenship four years earlier: "I have no time and because I just came to the U.S. I don't know who is good or who is bad. Since I don't know much about politics I am afraid that I [might] vote for the wrong person." Political activists recognize the difficulty of mobilizing a community with limited education, although lack of schooling can be a very sensitive, if not taboo, topic.[36]

Internal Divisions and Community Solidarity

Community leaders consistently cite internal divisions as a major reason for lack of political success. Because of community infighting, leaders explain, the community cannot pool its material resources or the political leverage that comes from the power of numbers through bloc voting. This refrain is slightly more prevalent among the Portuguese, where regional prejudices between mainlanders and Azoreans, and between Azoreans from different islands, divide the community into distinct social networks and organizations. Describing the cultural differences between mainlanders and Azoreans apparent in her American classroom, one woman explained:

> When we were in grammar school, there were maybe twenty kids . . .
> of Portuguese background. Some came from the Azores, and some
> were from the continent, and they really didn't understand much about
> each other. . . . There was always this certain competition that the main-
> landers always seemed to think that they were better than islanders.

And then the people from the islands would think the girls from the mainland were really racy, because they could go out at night, and they could not go out at night. And islanders are very religious. . . . Where we came from [the mainland] . . . we went to church, we listened to the sermon, but it wasn't that blind.

Such divisions, which revolve around perceptions of superiority and relative backwardness, also characterize the Vietnamese. Among Vietnamese Canadians, "The southerners always think that we're much more sophisticate than the northerner. Because the northerner tend to be under the communist rule for so long . . . [and] because we always get involved with the West and [were] influenced by old French culture and Americans." Those in Toronto are especially apt to blame regionalism between south, center, and north for internal tensions (Pfeifer 1999), more so than in the United States, where the bulk of Vietnamese come from the south.[37]

Class differences provide the second line of significant tensions in all four communities, although the strain is often latent rather than explicit.[38] In most cases, difference in class, income, and education do not produce outright clashes but rather detachment between community subcultures organized around different occupation paths and social organizations. Ordinary immigrants allude to the gap between their own issues and the activities of prominent community members by using a shrug of the shoulder and a reference to "those guys" when discussing coethnic elites. Prominent first-generation Portuguese often had access to education denied to the vast majority of their compatriots. Among Vietnamese, ordinary farmers and fishermen do not always have warm memories of the former elite of South Vietnam. One refugee spoke bitterly about the death of two siblings in Vietnam for want of medicine while "The rich kids," the children of high-ranking military officers, businessmen, and government officials, "talk about parties; they compare their wealth. And so I felt the injustice." The North American environment equalizes such differences somewhat—working-class Portuguese buy houses and purchase the material possessions of the middle class; Vietnamese refugees see their children pursue higher education—but some continue to harbor resentment over class inequalities.

A Lack of Understanding: The Liability of "Newness"

Finally, limited experience in North America crops up repeatedly as an obstacle to political participation in all four communities. Research on native-born citizens finds that those who move to a new town or neighborhood are less likely to participate in politics than those with established ties, since "New arrivals face the many demands of relocation. . . . They must reestablish themselves politically . . . [and] they must wait for new channels of political information and encouragement to develop" (Rosenstone and Hansen 1993: 157).

For immigrants and refugees, such costs are multiplied. Immediate settlement concerns overwhelm thoughts of politics, as for this Vietnamese American: "You basically have no time to [be] involve[d] with anything else. . . . Not that we didn't care about race or [being] politically active with [the] mainstream community or anything like that. It is more of a time issue because as [a] minority community, as refugee and immigrant communities, you have so many issues that you have to work on. . . . You [are] trying to basically take care of more immediate needs."[39] It is the rare migrant who feels knowledgeable, comfortable, and established enough in his first few years in North America to immediately become active in a local political issue or volunteer during the first election campaign he experiences.

Immediate needs, such as finding housing and work, placing children in childcare or school, and building a certain level of comfort and familiarity with a new sociocultural environment, gradually diminish with time. Then, as newcomers learn some language skills, begin to understand the political system, and feel more settled, they might become more interested in political issues and participation. Not surprisingly, the number of years an immigrant has resided in North America is consistently one of the strongest predictors of electoral participation and naturalization.

The liabilities associated with newness affect the Vietnamese more than the Portuguese, though the latter remain largely an immigrant group and hence "newer" than most white, native-born ethnic groups with whom they are compared. The majority of Portuguese immigrants in Toronto and Boston left Portugal before that country's transition to democracy in the mid-1970s, and less than one in ten migrated after 1986. In contrast, almost all Vietnamese migrants arrived in North America after 1974. In Boston we find a slightly higher proportion of first-wave Vietnamese arrivals than in Toronto, but the bulk of newcomers in both communities came in the 1980s and 1990s. Thus, on average, the Portuguese have lived in North America about fifteen to twenty-five years longer than the Vietnamese.

WITH A LITTLE HELP FROM MY FRIENDS: THE SOCIAL NATURE OF CITIZENSHIP AND PARTICIPATION

Most immigrants in North America are interested in becoming citizens. Mexicans in the United States are among the least likely to naturalize of any immigrant group, yet in a survey conducted by de la Garza and associates (1992), only 14.7 percent of Mexican-born residents had no plans to apply for citizenship. The problem lies in moving from an interest in citizenship to actually taking the steps necessary to naturalize. For those who are college educated, proficient in English, and comfortable with bureaucracy, the process is annoying but manageable. To the average Portuguese or Vietnamese immigrant, who has limited schooling, poor English, and a distrust of politics, naturalization appears formidable.[40] Community activists and political scholars are right in saying that limited skills, resources, and interest slow down political incorporation.

Yet a focus on individuals' attributes ignores the social origins of political incorporation. Outside support can help overcome participatory barriers when personal skills and resources are lacking. Immigrants especially derive benefit from ethnic ties and mobilization around group membership.[41] New to a country and often speaking a different language, newcomers naturally seek out compatriots in religious congregations, business associations, social clubs, and cultural organizations. Politicians often view such groups as an easy and efficient way to reach a large number of voters.[42] Shared language, culture, and integration challenges provide a "glue" that encourages community bonds.

A model of immigrant political incorporation consequently needs to acknowledge the social, localized nature of acquiring and practicing political citizenship. In particular, I highlight three sources of support: interpersonal networks of family and friends; immigrant organizations, including coethnic businesses and nonprofit or public agencies; and mobilization efforts directed by community leaders. In the remainder of the chapter, I show how these three types of support facilitate the acquisition of citizenship, encourage participation in the electoral process, and foster involvement in public debates.

Friends and Family: Using Personal Networks

Interpersonal social ties help immigrants learn about citizenship, encourage them to naturalize, and provide assistance for completing the process. Maria became a citizen after someone at her brother's school approached her and convinced her that citizenship was important for her and her family.[43] Maria was reluctant. With only four years of schooling in the Azores and little chance to practice English at the shoe factory where she worked, she did not feel capable of filling out the necessary paperwork. The prospect of being tested by an INS examiner was daunting. The school employee nevertheless urged her to try, providing advice about what to do and offering to act as a character reference.[44] Coethnic friends directed her to a local travel agency, which would complete naturalization applications for a fee. Maria had the forms filled out, and then she asked her nine-year-old daughter to teach her to read some basic sentences in English and to quiz her with civics questions. Reflecting back, Maria recalls, "I thought that it would be hard; [Portuguese friends] told me it was hard." However, when she actually went in for her interview, "I find it was very easy." The examiner did not ask many questions, and both she and her husband became American citizens.

It is unlikely that Maria would have naturalized when she did were it not for the support and encouragement she received. Tina, a woman about the same age as Maria, still has not become an American citizen, even though she has lived in the Boston area for almost thirty years. Like Maria, Tina had little schooling on her home island of Santa Maria. She can speak and understand simple English but prefers to conduct her affairs in Portuguese. When I ask whether she is a citizen, Tina shakes her head, "Maybe next year." She has heard that her pension benefits might be better if she were a citizen, but she confides with an embarrassed laugh that she finds the process a bit scary.

The Vietnamese tend to seek out naturalization more frequently than the Portuguese, since American or Canadian citizenship offers safety. For those who fled their country as refugees, citizenship provides guaranteed residence, a passport for travel, and permanent access to North American society and economy. A few Vietnamese see naturalization as a betrayal of their Vietnamese nationality, but in general the community views it as a good thing. Occasionally a successful applicant in Boston or Toronto will throw a party to celebrate his or her new status. As one man in Boston explained, "My friends would also ask me if I have citizenship, and they will say 'Good' if I have it." There is no penalty to not acquiring citizenship—"they never treat me badly or differently if I don't [become an American]"—but naturalization is considered normal and desirable.

Even then, help from family and friends makes things easier. For Duc, there was little doubt that he should apply for Canadian citizenship. He left Vietnam in 1985, mostly to secure a better future for his three children. As he explained, "I live in Canada, so I want to be a citizen of Canada. As soon as I left Vietnam, they erased my citizenship right away. I am no longer a Vietnamese citizen. I wanted to be a Canadian citizen because by having that, I can go anywhere and wherever I want to. I have the freedom." The process of acquiring citizenship came with certain challenges. Duc only completed five years of schooling in Vietnam because he was needed to work on the family farm, and educational opportunities were limited. Arriving in

Canada, he spoke virtually no English. After a six-month English as a Second Language (ESL) class offered by the Canadian government, Duc went to work in a factory.

When Duc applied for citizenship, an official at Citizenship and Immigration Canada (CIC) gave him a book about Canada that contained the information he had to learn for the naturalization exam. He explained, "I can read a little bit of English. My friends guided me throughout the learning process, and I studied according to the guidelines. I asked my friends whenever I have a problem or encountered difficult words." Friends can also provide Vietnamese translations of the citizenship guide and tapes with practice questions. Bilingual practice questions, on paper and on cassette, float through the Canadian and American Vietnamese communities, passed on from one person to another as kin and acquaintances successively apply for citizenship. Although the advantages of citizenship do not need to be promoted to the same degree with the Vietnamese as with the Portuguese, social networks play a similar role in transferring knowledge and providing assistance.

We should not be surprised that social networks matter in the naturalization process, given their importance in migration more generally. Early theories of migration, like some accounts of naturalization, postulated atomistic rational actors who calculate their optimal place of residence based on various "push" and "pull" factors such as relative earning potential (Borowski et al. 1994; Massey et al. 1998). More precise examinations of who migrates, where they come from, and where they go show that migration is not a flow of atomized individuals but rather a process filtered by "sets of interpersonal ties that link together migrants, former migrants, and non-migrants . . . through bonds of kinship, friendship, and shared community origin" (Massey 1990: 69). Extended to citizenship acquisition, quantitative analyses show that living in areas with high concentrations of coethnics increases an immigrant's propensity to naturalize (Liang 1994; Yang 1994).

There are, however, limitations to social networks.[45] We are often friends with or related to people like ourselves. If an immigrant is semiliterate, speaks little English, and has not acquired citizenship, there is a strong chance that friends and family also share these characteristics and face the same problems. Sometimes a person can get lucky, and a chance remark at church or to a next-door neighbor generates an offer of assistance. Martin, for example, learned that his elderly Portuguese neighbor was having trouble finding someone to help him with his naturalization application, so Martin offered to take the neighbor to the INS office on his day off. Within seven months, Martin's neighbor was sworn in as an American citizen.

"This guy was thrilled," Martin reports. Others, however, slip through the cracks: "Sometimes we find gaps in the process that if you don't have the right person to help, you get stuck. And people sometimes [don't] move on, because they get disappointed." Pride often stops people from imposing on others for help, especially if asking for help reveals one's limitations. In many Portuguese and Vietnamese families, it falls on the shoulders of children—who often have a better grasp of the language and more familiarity with North American culture—to deal with mainstream institutions, including citizenship officials. When children refuse or are unable to help, or when parents are too proud to ask for assistance, potential citizens must turn to other options.

The Organization of Political Incorporation

Formal organizations offer an important alternative when social ties fail. Organizations generally have greater ability to assist large groups of people because they pool resources. Resources can be financial, material (such as photocopiers, fax machines, and physical space for meetings), or intangible, such as accumulated collective knowledge. Organizations also offer temporal stability. Although they can undergo "life cycles" of birth, growth, stability, and death, organizations tend not to be dependent on any one person. They can pursue multiple projects and offer various forms of assistance through an internal division of labor and formalization of roles that is difficult to accomplish through an informal social network. In immigrant communities, we find both for-profit businesses and nonprofit organizations active in newcomer settlement. These organizations tend to promote newcomers' political incorporation by (1) gathering and disseminating information; (2) representing and advocating for a group; (3) mobilizing individuals to participate; and (4) teaching people skills that promote political participation.

Ethnic Media A critical first step on the road to political incorporation is the acquisition of information: information about citizenship, voting, the party system, norms of protest, the key political issues of the day, and a host of other issues that are often taken for granted by the native born. Information frequently defuses through informal social networks—over a glass of wine or during a break at the water cooler—but informal ties are often grounded in, and can be expanded by, formal institutions.[46] Organizations consequently serve as a key source of political information in the immigrant community. Because information barriers stand higher for newcomers than the native born, immigrants are especially apt to rely on community organizations.

A central source of information is the ethnic media. Most ethnic media devote the bulk of their newsprint or airtime to entertainment and advertisements, although newspapers also provide regular coverage of political events at the international, national, and local levels. Much of the news is translated from the mainstream press into Vietnamese or Portuguese, although occasionally journalists or volunteers will write up or produce original content.[47] The Boston-area *Asian Times,* printed in Vietnamese, is typical in its content, which can be broken down into four categories: news, general information (lifestyle, health, advice columns, etc.), community news (mostly announcements of coming events from local groups), and entertainment (including fashion, music, and film, both Western and Vietnamese).[48]

Almost all ethnic media seek to make a profit, but media outlets also believe they are service-oriented community institutions, a role they take seriously. One journalist at a Vietnamese American newspaper explained: "Most [refugees] have very little English and can't follow what is going on [in English media], so they need a newspaper in the Vietnamese language. It has news and some information about community news. It is free; you can get it at Vietnamese stores, the supermarket. To keep us alive, we sell advertisements. . . . [But] we are not focused on making a profit; our intent is to serve the community."[49] Similarly, a woman who appears on Portuguese-language television in Toronto sees her role as that of a liaison between the community and mainstream society: "For the past two years I have been doing a current affairs commentary . . . I have been covering the larger broader [national] social, social economic, political news that I feel affect equally the members of my community. . . . I felt that there wasn't enough of that information in their language, going to them, about current affairs, about current news. . . . Because it affects them and because it's an opportunity to bring forth an idea or opinion and it's an opportunity to bring the issue to their minds and to their awareness." The ethnic media thus try to transmit, and at times comment on, mainstream political issues, increasing immigrants' information about domestic affairs.

It is difficult to know the extent to which ethnic media facilitate political incorporation. Among those I interviewed, Vietnamese immigrants appear particularly inclined to read community newspapers on a regular basis and use these as a source of information.[50] Most Portuguese listen to local radio stations or watch Portuguese-language TV. Consumption of ethnic media is consequently widespread. However, for a great number in both communities, political news and current events do not rank high in their reading, listening, or viewing preferences. The producer of a Portuguese-language call-in show in the Boston area prefers to concentrate on what he considers "important" issues, ones that teach viewers about topics such as health care, money management, or local politics. He nonetheless regularly includes a show on soccer: "I want people to be more glued into my program, so I am going to give them the trash that they love." A show devoted to Portuguese-language instruction in local schools might elicit only two calls, while a show on sports generates hundreds of calls.

Even so, exposure to ethnic media matters. One Vietnamese Canadian who expressed distrust of the local ethnic papers because of their stance toward homeland issues nevertheless reported learning about Canadian political parties from these papers. He trusted this information more because he knew it was translated from the English-language press. When asked why they voted for a particular candidate or party, a number of older immigrants pointed to newspaper articles or media reports outlining candidates' or parties' political platforms. Second and 1.5 generation Portuguese and Vietnamese ("1.5 generation" refers to individuals who migrated to North America at a young age) regularly report that their parents keep up with current events through the ethnic media. Based on a survey of immigrants in Toronto, Black and Leithner (1988) found that newcomers report a substantial amount of coverage of domestic politics in the ethnic media and that consumption of ethnic newspapers correlates with greater politicization among respondents.

The ethnic media can also facilitate political participation by providing information on naturalization campaigns, voting drives, or ESL classes. Almost all ethnic media provide some free advertising to community organizations and local social service agencies to promote classes, clinics, or other community events. Immigrants and refugees with whom I spoke consistently said that they heard about a particular class or event from the ethnic media or from a friend who had read or heard about it in the ethnic media. A middle-aged Vietnamese woman in Boston explained that she learned about ESL courses and a special employment-training program through the Vietnamese newspapers. Both classes facilitated her political incorporation. The language class helped her to become a naturalized citizen. The job program brought her into contact with a local community organization that has since encouraged her political participation. When the organization invited the mayor of Boston to a town-hall-style meeting, she went to the meeting and voiced concern about high rents in the city.

The Naturalization Business: Paying for Assistance　For-profit organizations also offer direct assistance to facilitate political incorporation, mostly around citizenship. Both Boston and Toronto boast a rich network of travel agencies, insurance brokers, notaries, and self-proclaimed immigration consultants who help immigrants fill out paperwork for a fee. Although she was assisted by friends and her daughter, Maria resorted to using a travel agency for the naturalization application as well as other immigration paperwork: "When I came to this country, I didn't [hear] about anybody to help me. We just had to go to the [travel] agency; we had to pay for everything, every little thing." Beatriz, who immigrated to Toronto from Portugal when she was six, also remembers the travel agencies, "if you had to deal with a government agency, for any reason—passport, whatever—you go to your travel agency. . . . The travel agencies do a really good business because one of the first things immigrants want to do is to go back. . . . But I would wager that they make more money making phone calls and filling in the simplest forms than they do in anything else."[51] Portuguese and Vietnamese community newspapers regularly contain ads for notary publics or immigration consultants who offer a range of migration-related services.

Friends also recommend businesses when they are unable to offer assistance themselves. Tung, who came to the United States in 1989, wanted to apply for citizenship in 1997. With rudimentary English and limited schooling—six years of primary school before working on his parents' rice farm—he needed help studying for the citizenship exam. His friends, of similar backgrounds, did not feel able to teach him the civics material, and in any case, they worked long hours at various factory and flooring jobs. Instead, "I studied from the book and I also took a course in Chinatown. I had to pay. There were a mix of people in the class. . . . My friends who had already took the course told me about it." Other Vietnamese Americans also mentioned such businesses. For example, Thien paid someone in Boston's Chinatown to fill out the application for him. Instead of taking a class, he bought a booklet that listed the standard one hundred citizenship questions asked by the INS in English and Vietnamese.

Private businesses consequently offer an alternative pathway to citizenship, but it can be costly, a fact that prevents some immigrants from taking this route. Businesses may charge significant fees for very simple services or readily accessible materials. Individuals such as Thien are regularly charged for citizenship guides or bilingual photocopies of the standard naturalization questions, although such materials are available free of charge from government agencies, the public library, or community organizations. The sale of otherwise free material is also found among Portuguese. One Portuguese American remembers that in the 1970s [businesses] were charging $25 for mimeographed sheets of questions. They would copy the questions for the citizenship exam and the free pamphlet put out by the INS, and they would charge people. And remember, this was a lot of money twenty-five years ago, with some of these people making nothing. And the more questions they gave, the more people thought they were getting their money's worth. These agencies would fill out the paperwork, and they would promise to go to the citizenship exam to help, but then they sometimes wouldn't show up. I remember one woman crying downstairs. . . . When I asked her what was wrong, she told me that story, that no one had showed up.

Businesses can also practice outright fraud. Unscrupulous individuals can take advantage of immigrants' ignorance and, especially in the United States, fear of the INS. According to Manuela, "Years ago you can just pay some fee for the [citizenship] papers," an option that she wanted to take because she preferred buying the papers to the stress of applying and studying for the exam. Her husband refused. In the end, Manuela had the satisfaction of acquiring citizenship on her own, but others were less fortunate, believing false promises that bribes and connections could circumvent the regular process. One Portuguese American who volunteers as a citizenship teacher recounts: "There is this one fellow . . . he's had people who go to him because he would lie and say he has connections with immigration. I have actual proof here that he would ask for hundreds of dollars. . . . I've seen him over at immigration, when I'm waiting for someone, taking people—I call them victims—people who he has charged. . . . I tell people that you don't have to pay anything to anybody to get citizenship papers." Such stories are exceptional, but they highlight the potential for abuse.[52]

Community Groups and Nonprofit Organizations   A third source of assistance for those who cannot or will not rely on social networks or private businesses are community groups and nonprofit organizations. Because these organizations operate on a not-for-profit basis, immigrants can avoid problems associated with some for-profit businesses.[53] Staff in community-based organizations also argue that they tend to be more attentive to newcomers' needs, since their primary purpose is settlement and related social or advocacy services. Many such organizations actively or implicitly promote civic and political involvement. Over the past thirty years, the growth of nonprofit service organizations catering to newcomers has made immigrants less dependent on for-profit businesses.

Such was the case for Ngoc, who asked the Boston Vietnamese-American

Civic Association (VACA) for help in filling out her naturalization application. Ngoc migrated with her husband under American ODP provisions but left him after marital problems intensified once they were in the United States. After a brief move to California, she relocated to Boston on the advice of a friend. Apart from the friend and her current boyfriend, Ngoc has few social ties on which to rely: there are no relatives in the area and few close friends. It is also hard to make ends meet, foreclosing recourse to private businesses. After her daughter was born, Ngoc collected social assistance benefits. Today she works in an electronics factory, but scraping together $850 for her monthly rent is difficult, leaving little for other expenses. Thankfully, Ngoc explains, the services at VACA were free.

Beyond direct service provision, community organizations help diffuse information to immigrants and mainstream political actors; they represent their constituencies; they mobilize newcomers; and they teach political skills. Social, religious, or recreation groups, which have no explicit political goal, can facilitate the flow of information by providing a regular meeting place or time that allows people to come together and share news and opinions. While much of the conversation in a Portuguese social club might revolve around the latest soccer scores or the weather, people also talk about the state of the economy or complain about high taxes. Such discussions lead naturally to judgments about who can best address such problems or what constitutes the best course of action. A number of politically active Portuguese Canadians, including two people who served on the Toronto municipal council, explained that they first met friends with whom they later campaigned during meetings of their local church youth group.

Community organizations, especially community-based social service agencies, also organize formal events that explicitly seek to educate newcomers about current policy issues or teach them about the political system. Consumption of the ethnic media tends to be a passive process, and given the lack of personal contact, it engenders a certain distance from political contests. In contrast, a formal event such as a "meet the candidates" night can bring newcomers into direct contact with politicians. The seniors' program at St. Christopher House, a nonsectarian community center that serves Portuguese and Vietnamese newcomers in Toronto, organizes a series of special events when there is an election. As one staff member explains: "We try to provide much information: what this election is, why should you vote, how do you vote. That type of information. What responsibilities are. 'These are feds, this is the province, this is the city.' What questions you should be asking your own politicians as they knock at your door and ask for your vote. . . . So, [we] try to help them analyze the situation. So if it is the city, it's not long-term [health] care. It is garbage [collection]." Such meetings have increased seniors' interest in Canadian politics. Following one meeting, regulars at the senior center asked staff for periodic updates on how politicians in their area voted on issues of concern.

Information exchanges can also be more practical, showing newcomers the nuts and bolts of the electoral system. Cai, a fifty-six-year-old Vietnamese American who works as a teacher's aide, attended an event hosted by a local church to understand the mechanics of voting, "I heard that the election is counted by a machine. I didn't want to have any trouble so I decided to come and learn how to vote." Boston's VACA has offered similar workshops, inviting city officials to explain to Vietnamese community members how to cast a ballot.

It is a short step for organizations to go from gathering and diffusing information to being representatives and advocates for their community. As information flows change direction, moving from the immigrant community to the mainstream, those who provide information about the community become de facto representatives. Many organizations make the transition from serving as sources of information to acting as representatives or advocates for the community when government agencies and politicians seek constituents' opinions on a particular public policy. The Toronto-based Portuguese Interagency Network (PIN) was set up to help Portuguese organizations share information with each other. As part of its mandate, the agency conducted several needs assessments of the Portuguese community. The original purpose of these surveys was to provide information to member organizations applying for funding from government, foundations, or private groups such as the United Way. The information also proved valuable, however, when governments solicited public response on proposed legislation. When the province of Ontario considered closing a hospital heavily frequented by Portuguese immigrants, PIN made a deputation, a presentation to a legislative committee on behalf of the community, outlining how the proposed hospital closure would affect the community.

Governments often prefer to deal with organized groups when they seek to communicate with newcomer communities. Other actors with influence on the political process, such as the mainstream media, also find it easier to deal with organized communities. Sometimes mainstream actors' desire for a single or unified community voice creates problems, especially when an organization represents only a portion of immigrants or pursues an agenda that is out-of-touch with the desires of the majority. However, the alternative is often no voice and no place at the policy table.[54]

Community organizations also command more legitimacy than their shoestring budgets might suggest. The information and recommendations offered by nonprofit organizations can be perceived as more valuable than professional presentations by established lobbying groups because of ethnic organizations' roots in their communities. A former executive director of one Portuguese Canadian agency explains:

> It is very hard to put together a deputation. But, you know, a lot of times we have done it. It has been a process not very scientific, not very comprehensive, not very filled with research quality. You know, it has been very difficult to pull things together. So when we go to a lot of these deputations, we always feel a little bit . . . We are always a little bit humbled, I guess that is the word, because you have large institutions or organizations that will go with three panelists. And they've hired three consultants to do all of this incredible research which will throw all these numbers in their faces, and we'll go "wow."
>
> And a lot of times, all we have to say, the only thing that we can safely argue, is "There will be a lot of pain and suffering. There will be a lot of disruption to our community, to our people, if you do this or if you do that. We have spoken to people, to community workers and family workers, and we know that this is going to create a lot of hardships." And what I've come to know is that governments are equally interested in hearing that as well. That it is equally important to them.

In cases where government asks for input or where the community mobilizes to make sure that its voice is heard, the task of communicating information is often left to community-based organizations. Because of language and cultural barriers, many immigrants feel uncomfortable dealing directly with public officials and government representatives.

An organization's efforts to represent the community can naturally evolve into the political mobilization of community members. The passage of the 1996 U.S. Welfare Reform Act and the subsequent creation of a citizenship assistance program in Massachusetts provide a good example of this dynamic. Under the Welfare Reform Act, noncitizen residents were denied Supplemental Security Income and food stamps, benefits formerly available to legal residents, and states could henceforth use their discretion in providing legal permanent residents with Medicaid and welfare benefits under Temporary Assistance for Needy Families. Some states, including Massachusetts, supplemented the loss of federal dollars with state monies, but since access to federal benefits could only be guaranteed with citizenship, nonprofit organizations and the Commonwealth of Massachusetts placed a high priority on encouraging immigrants to take out citizenship.

The state of Massachusetts had a particular interest in moving individuals off state-funded public assistance to programs financed by the federal government. The state legislature consequently appropriated funds for a new initiative, the Citizenship Assistance Program (CAP), which began in July 1997. Administered by the Massachusetts Office for Refugees and Immigrants, the program provided funds on a competitive basis to community organizations for ESL/civics classes, native-language citizenship instruction, and application assistance.[55] The original appropriation allocated $2 million to CAP and specified an intention, subject to renewal, to fund the program for three years. In 1999 the new governor, Paul Cellucci, used a line item veto to halve the program's budget. The Massachusetts Immigrant and Refugee Advocacy Coalition (MIRA), an umbrella organization of immigrant and refugee groups, subsequently urged members to mobilize their communities in support of CAP by contacting legislators and speaking to the media. After heavy lobbying, the legislature overrode the governor's veto, restoring most of the program's funding. In subsequent years, community groups have engaged in similar advocacy efforts each budget period, as CAP regularly comes under threat.[56]

Both the Massachusetts Alliance of Portuguese Speakers (MAPS) and VACA are members of MIRA, and both responded to the call for action. In VACA's case, staff brought Vietnamese refugees who had taken part in the association's citizenship classes to testify before legislative hearings, and staff also contacted state representatives and senators to communicate the Vietnamese community's concern with the impending cuts.[57] MAPS encouraged similar activities. During a citizenship class, MAPS' citizenship coordinator made a presentation about CAP and the potential cuts, asking students to write letters to their state senator in support of CAP. The whole class did so, and the volunteer teacher took the opportunity to remind the students of the names of their elected representatives, a question that is sometimes asked during the INS interview for naturalization.[58]

Groups can also mobilize immigrants around more general participatory notions of citizenship. In Boston, VACA and Viet-AID, the country's first Vietnamese American community development corporation, have organized a number of successful voter registration drives in conjunction with the city of Boston's Office of New Bostonians. The executive director of VACA estimates that prior to the 2000 election, a one-month drive aimed at registering Vietnamese Americans in Dorchester added eighty people of Vietnamese origin to the voters' list for the first time. Efforts like theirs are credited with raising registration and participation rates in Boston since 1997.[59]

Finally, community organizations can act as political schools, teaching people skills that they can use to make their voice heard in the political system. Political training may be explicit, or it can be an unforeseen by-product of regular participation in a civic group or community-based organization. Verba, Scholzman, and Brady (1995) contend that civic skills—the ability to communicate and organize effectively—can be transferred from a workplace, voluntary association, or church to the political arena. Because they are better able to communicate their wishes and organize on behalf of a particular cause, those who are "institutionally connected" enjoy an advantage in the political system.

The experience of Toan, a Vietnamese Canadian senior and former soldier, illustrates the way organizations facilitate political incorporation through explicit programs that promote participatory citizenship and through informal skill development. Toan's children, who fled Vietnam during the boat people exodus, sponsored Toan and his wife to migrate to Canada in the early 1990s. Toan faced many barriers to political involvement when he arrived, "It's very hard for the elders like us to fully understand and adapt." He had only eight years of education, virtually no knowledge of Canada, and no understanding of English. Yet today Toan votes regularly in Canadian elections and understands enough about the political system to identify the party he feels best represents immigrants.[60] Toan also regularly attends public hearings, a political activity in which few native-born citizens engage. As he explains: "I read the information in the [English] newspapers, and I go to the place. It might be at City Hall, or a community organization. There will be a speaker talking about this or that thing. I usually listen to the election organizations [parties] or about social benefits, taxes, housing, T.T.C. [public transit] fares increasing or decreasing." The transition from uninformed newcomer to participatory citizen occurred in large part because of the political and civic training he received from various immigrant and mainstream institutions.

The immigrant community initially helped Toan to get settled and establish a new social network. A friend told him about a local Vietnamese veterans' group, which he joined, and he also became part of the Hung Vuong association, a group that honors the first Vietnamese king. It was through conversations with members of these associations that he began to understand the Canadian political system: "I'd learn from a lot of people to know who cares for the immigrants, or who are well liked by the majority." Friends also referred Toan to the Vietnamese Association of Toronto (VAT), where he attended an ESL class that VAT runs with money from the federal government. Toan tried his hand at agricultural work, but at the age of sixty he found manual labor too difficult and instead decided to concentrate on improving his English. Toan transferred to another ESL program run out of a local public school and found that it not only taught basic English skills, but also, "we were taught about Canadian culture. There were field trips like visiting the courts, the Hydro company, about Canadian cultures, including entertainment." This knowledge, combined with his growing English skills, sparked an interest in reading Canadian newspapers, albeit slowly and imperfectly. He and his wife became Canadian citizens.

During this period, Toan participated in events organized by the veterans' group, including the annual April 30 commemoration of the fall of Saigon, Canadian Remembrance Day (November 11), and Vietnamese Armed Forces Day (June 19), and he participated in a few protests over human rights abuses in Vietnam, including a trip to Ottawa to demonstrate in front of the Canadian Parliament buildings.[61] Toan considers himself only a "regular member" of the veterans' group, not a leader, but his participation has evolved over time: "I used to just join the crowd in the events. But since I've been here for awhile, I have participated in organizing the events." He also started volunteering at St. Christopher's House, helping the staff who run the seniors' program. By most measures, Toan has become an active citizen, not only in his immigrant community but also in Canadian society.

Not all immigrants move so far on the path to political incorporation, but among those who are active, many tell similar stories. Informal ties—usually fostered by an organized group or association—combine with more formalized activities to assist newcomers with the process of political integration. A number of Portuguese in Toronto and Boston who migrated at a young age developed civic and political skills through local Portuguese-language youth theater groups. One former participant fondly recalls:

> That little youth group, we used to go all over Ontario, wherever there was a Portuguese community where a priest went to say mass on Sunday at the local church. What we would do is rent a bus; we would take the props and the costumes and all. . . . They would pay [for] lunch, we would have lunch, then do the play after lunch; and then once the play was over we had a little rock group that would go up on the stage and start playing for a dance for the rest of the afternoon. So that was my first community activity here in Canada.

Putting together a play required that the teenagers practice public speaking and reinforced their Portuguese language skills, which helped them to communicate with older first-generation immigrants. They learned to coordinate a relatively complex event, and they developed close friendships with others in their ethnic community. In at least three cases, initial links to a theater group led to further involvement in the Portuguese community and eventually to active participation in mainstream politics.

Cultural and social activities consequently carry important indirect consequences for political incorporation. Some commentators criticize early Canadian multiculturalism for what they perceive as the policy's superficial celebration of folklore and ethnic cuisine (Brotz 1981; Kallen 1982). The recognition and promotion of ethnic diversity may not address problems of stratified access to public resources or differential socioeconomic outcomes, but organized activities that foster community pride—or which are just plain fun—can serve as "schools," teaching newcomers the requisite skills for civic and political involvement.

The same process can occur within transnational organizations. The first established political organizations in an immigrant community often concentrate on homeland concerns. Some worry that groups focused on homeland concerns divert newcomers' attention from the host country's civic and political life. For the Vietnamese, the focus is invariably ending communism in Vietnam. For the Portuguese, a few organizations in Toronto debated Portugal's military engagement with its African colonies and its regime change during the 1970s. At some point, however, interests widen or shift to domestic politics, usually under the guidance of 1.5 or second-generation community members. Then transnational groups become conduits to domestic involvement.

For example, a Vietnamese Canadian woman in Toronto involved in protests over human rights abuses in Vietnam developed contacts with nonethnic organizations such as Amnesty International and PEN Canada through her activism.[62] Involvement with such mainstream organizations taught her about the Canadian political system, "because [these organizations] have been here longer and they know the system a lot better than us and they have their own connections." The mainstream organizations explained how to bypass secretaries who screen the calls of members of Parliament and provided access to bureaucrats in various government ministries. Immigrant advocates such as this woman can then use this information and experience later to influence domestic issues affecting their community.

Homeland politics have not mobilized Portuguese immigrants in the same way as Vietnamese refugees.[63] Contemporary involvement in Portuguese homeland politics remains an arena of elite activism. Since Portugal's extension of dual citizenship in 1981, overseas Portuguese may vote for special parliamentarians who represent the overseas communities in

Portugal's national legislature. There are also regular meetings with the Lisbon government and the Azorean regional government, to which emigrant communities send representatives. Individuals in both metro Boston and Toronto have used such opportunities to become involved in Portuguese politics, but these activities rarely involve more than a small percentage of the community.[64] Many of these elites are also involved in domestic politics, and interestingly, Portuguese officials and politicians encourage the North American focus because they use Portuguese immigrants as conduits to American and Canadian decision makers. Indeed, one Portuguese American, active in U.S. politics, complained that he is frequently "used" by Portuguese officials. They have found that migrants sometimes have more political contacts than diplomatic staff in the local consulate.

Thus the presence of a rich organizational infrastructure—even if recreational or oriented toward homeland concerns—can support political incorporation in the new home. In Boston, refugee status also provides many Vietnamese with access to agencies outside the community. Organizations such as the International Institute of Boston or Catholic Charities assist refugees during the early settlement phase, helping people to apply for a Social Security number, access medical services, and settle into a first apartment. This early contact builds a relationship, so that years later, when a refugee seeks to sponsor relatives or wishes to apply for U.S. citizenship, he or she might return to the original settlement agency for help.

The services and options available to Vietnamese in Toronto resemble those in Boston, though monies directed at citizenship or ESL classes might come from a general government program for immigrant integration, not specifically refugee resettlement. A number of Vietnamese remember with fondness a Vietnamese Canadian who worked for Ontario House, a government-run agency charged with newcomer settlement. Ontario House was closed in the 1990s during a period of government cutbacks, but while it was open the Vietnamese liaison would assist community members with government-related paperwork, such as applications for citizenship or subsidized housing. Other Vietnamese Canadians attended free citizenship classes offered at local community centers and public libraries sponsored by CIC. As one former attendee remembers, "Not only did I not have to pay, but I received 2 T.T.C. [transit] tickets for every class I attended!" In this way, program organizers offered transportation assistance so that those on restricted incomes could still come to class. Because such programs tend to be geared to all newcomers, Portuguese immigrants in Toronto enjoy a wider range of options than those in Boston, where some services are targeted specifically to refugees.

Nonprofit organizations, especially those offering settlement services and direct outreach programs, play a similar role whether they serve the Portuguese or the Vietnamese (or a multiethnic constituency) and whether they are located in Boston or Toronto. The communities differ, however, in the number and diversity of such organizations. The Portuguese in Boston appear to have the fewest such organizations, especially compared to the services offered to Vietnamese Americans, a much smaller community if we consider the number of foreign-born people in each community. In Toronto, a range of ethnic-specific and more general multiethnic groups serves both Vietnamese and Portuguese.[65]

Community Leaders and Mobilization

The least consistent source of assistance, but one that can mobilize thousands of individuals over a short period, comes in the form of citizenship, registration, and "get out the vote" drives organized by community leaders.[66] In 1998 both the Boston and Toronto Portuguese communities launched, with fanfare and great enthusiasm, Citizenship 2000 campaigns.[67] Conceived and planned by community leaders, the goal was to get two thousand Portuguese immigrants to become citizens for the year 2000.[68] Estimates of the numbers eventually naturalized run from two hundred to four hundred in Boston and between two thousand and twenty-five hundred in Toronto.[69] Neither effort was linked to a particular organization or public agency; each was instead billed as a spontaneous, grassroots effort of concerned private citizens. Nonetheless, both relied on a core group of organizers who were employed or had been employed in for-profit, nonprofit, or public organizations working with immigrants, such as the businesses and community groups described above.

In Boston, Fatima Martins launched Citizenship 2000 following legislative changes in 1996 that made access to public benefits more problematic for noncitizens and increased their chances of deportation. Martins's interest in citizenship stemmed from her experience as a volunteer citizenship teacher and, according to some in the community, her failed bid for elected office a decade earlier. Informal discussions with friends and acquaintances in the fall of 1997 led to the establishment of a working group that included an employee at the nonprofit Massachusetts Immigrant and Refugee Advocacy Coalition, an employee from the state's Office for Refugees and Immigrants, an employee at the local Portuguese Credit Union, a local businessman, a priest at the local Catholic church, and the principal of the neighborhood public school, which runs an extensive bilingual program for Portuguese-speaking students.

After a series of Sunday afternoon meetings, the group created an advertising campaign that was launched on March 8, 1998, in the hall of St. Anthony's Catholic Church in Cambridge, in the heart of the metro Boston Portuguese community. On hand were about two hundred fifty people, including representatives of many local nonprofit organizations, various politicians, recognized community leaders, and ordinary immigrants drawn from across eastern Massachusetts. The campaign aimed to complement existing citizenship programs by disseminating naturalization and referral information. It had two prongs: first, to spread the word in the media regarding the importance of citizenship and, second, to advertise sources of Portuguese-language citizenship assistance through bumper stickers and posters put up in Portuguese businesses. Bumper stickers carried a toll-free telephone number, run by the state Office for Refugees and Immigrants, which provided citizenship information in Portuguese. The posters referred people to local agencies that offered naturalization services, such as MAPS in Cambridge and Somerville.

Given that the campaign aimed to provide referrals rather than direct services, it is difficult to estimate its impact. It is extremely doubtful that the campaign achieved the twenty-five thousand statewide naturalizations it set as its goal. According to one participant, hundreds of people filed an application in the Boston area because of Citizenship 2000. Other observers, including a non-Portuguese who helped with some of the campaign logistics, express reservations regarding the estimate, but all agree that the effort raised the profile of citizenship within the Portuguese community. It also served an important symbolic function in showing that prominent Portuguese who are proud of their heritage, such as the priest and local school principal (the latter a past representative to Portugal's council of overseas communities), support American citizenship.[70]

In Toronto, Citizenship 2000 began at the initiative of Armindo Silva, the owner of an insurance company located in the heart of the Portuguese business community and a former president of the Federation of Portuguese Canadian Businessmen and Professionals. Silva is an active member of the Liberal Party of Canada and made an unsuccessful bid to be a candidate in the 1988 federal election.[71] In February 1998 Silva called a meeting of more than two dozen politically active Portuguese Canadians from across the political spectrum in the hope of devising a plan to increase Portuguese representation and presence at the polls. The group identified lack of citizenship as a major obstacle to political voice. Subsequent meetings brought the group down to about ten members, who organized four naturalization "processing days" in the fall and winter of 1998–99. This core group included a former executive director of PIN, the owner of the ethnic-language station CIRV-Radio, a municipal politician, a union organizer, members of the Alliance of Portuguese Clubs and Associations, a representative from a local Portuguese bank, a prominent Portuguese-language TV producer, and various business owners.

The processing days aimed to provide A to Z naturalization services, including filling in the application form, photocopying and notarizing the required documents, taking photographs, processing the administrative fee, offering applicants a Portuguese translation of the citizenship booklet, *A Look at Canada,* and providing audio tapes of volunteers asking two hundred common citizenship questions in both English and Portuguese. As one participant put it, "People could go to citizenship schools to learn, but what if they didn't have the time? So we thought . . . if they're driving to and from work in a car, they can put something in their car, like a cassette, where they can listen to this stuff till they're blue in the face." Organizers hoped to encourage about two hundred people to take out citizenship, but at the first event over two thousand Portuguese showed up, of whom only eight hundred could be processed. Subsequent events provided assistance to roughly sixteen hundred other immigrants. While efforts like Citizenship 2000 do not happen on a regular basis, community leaders can foster naturalization en masse by generating communitywide interest in citizenship and providing organized assistance with the process. Similar initiatives occur around voting and, in the United States, voter registration.

The Social Nature of Participatory Citizenship

Community leaders play a special role in political incorporation, but the way in which they become activists mirrors the social processes we see among less involved members of the community. Almost everyone who reported high levels of participation in electoral campaigns, party politics, or community advocacy explained that their initial involvement occurred through personal or organizational ties. Vivaldo's explanation was typical: "I had a friend who was involved, and I was curious. I wanted to see what it was all about." Most had an interest in politics prior to being invited to participate, but interest did not usually transfer to behavior without personal contact.[72]

The only significant difference between the experiences of activists and ordinary immigrants is that initial contact with the political system for community leaders often involves politically active individuals *outside* the ethnic community whom would-be leaders met through school or, less frequently, at the workplace. In Rosemary's case, a non-Portuguese friend at her Toronto high school asked her to help out with a political campaign. In

Boston, Lily was invited to join a political meeting of the Democratic Party by someone at work. Initial participation leads to further involvement, since "once they have you by the finger, you get taken by the hand, and then the whole arm, and then politics takes all of you." Not everyone gets bitten by the political bug, but as one active Portuguese Canadian put it, "I think that politics is very addictive, once you get into it. . . . If you really love it, which I did, it's just an amazing feeling."

Community leaders thus rely more on community "outsiders" to educate and train them in civic and political engagement. Often they access politically involved nonethnics through colleges, universities, and mainstream, professional jobs. Ordinary immigrants usually enjoy fewer chances to build relationships with people outside their community; they might not attend school in their adopted country or they might work mostly with fellow immigrants. They consequently depend more on contacts with community leaders and participation in ethnic organizations to facilitate involvement with the mainstream political system. Community leaders become "insider" bridges to coethnics, passing on information, mobilizing fellow immigrants, or serving as representatives to mainstream institutions.

These building blocks of political incorporation—personal ties, community organizations, and coethnic leaders—come together in the story of Tilla. Tilla has been bitten by the "political bug" more than most ordinary immigrants. She arrived in Toronto as a teenager in the early 1960s. She immediately started to work in a factory, since the primary education she received in the Azores put most jobs out of her reach. About ten years later, she took a job as a cleaner in a downtown office tower. She remembers her supervisor, a Portuguese man, with disgust, "He's a devil. He's evil. He treat the Portuguese people, he treat us dirty. Like we are a piece of garbage. . . . In my brain, I think it's not right, and I think I should push something in there." When she complained to another cleaner and suggested that working conditions would improve if they had a union, she was fired for being a troublemaker. Tilla decided to fight her dismissal.

Tilla first tried to take matters into her own hands. She remembers: "I went myself with my poor English to the Labour Department on University [Avenue]. I never forget. I cry, I cry so much there when I made my complaint. When I discussed with them what happened there. They seem to not care about [it]; they seem to avoid my case. They seem to take care more with the owner, the company, the cleaner company." Tilla then turned to someone within the Portuguese community for help, a lawyer named Jorge. Jorge had written a Portuguese-language endorsement for a local politician, Tony Silipo, which Tilla found on her doorstep. Silipo, an Italian Canadian and member of Canada's left-wing New Democratic Party (NDP), was Tilla's member of Provincial Parliament at the time. After reading the pamphlet, Tilla thought that those connected with the NDP might be sympathetic to her situation, "because they fight for the working-class people." Given her limited English, she contacted Jorge and asked him to discuss her situation with Silipo to see if his intervention might help.

Tilla's decision to ask for help from an elected politician broke with her family's distrust of politics. In Portugal, Tilla's parents were "afraid to talk," and in Canada, she says, "I don't think they care" about politics. But with Jorge as the initial contact person and intermediary, she built a link with the local politician. The two men helped Tilla take her former employer to court, and she won damages. The experience led to further activism: "So, then they pay me [damages], as I say before, and then I start to [get] involved: Jorge involve me with Fran. Fran, she's the one who always work with working-class cleaners to fight for the woman's rights, the union's rights. . . . And me and Fran and the other Portuguese woman who work for Portuguese television at that time . . . we go to the doors, to the woman's work [downtown] to see if we can do something to put [in] the union." Fran was associated with St. Christopher House. This community organization provided meeting space and money to pay Tilla and the women helping her to educate cleaners about their rights. The women were not successful in unionizing the cleaners, but Tilla directed other women to Jorge for legal advice. Although Tilla stopped doing union organizing, she stayed involved with the NDP and became a member of the party. She worked on election campaigns as a Portuguese-language canvasser, and today she continues to make donations to the party and volunteers at election time.

When a supportive network of community activists and organizations is missing, it is hard for ordinary immigrants to translate political concerns into action. Manuela moved to the United States in 1968. Making ends meet can be a challenge: today Manuela works as a cashier in a Portuguese-owned business and her husband does manual labor. Manuela, like Tilla, holds strong views about socioeconomic hardships, though in her case she rails against high rents: "Now, the rents can't be paid. . . . The poor don't have the means for that. They are immigrants that buy little. How are they going to pay $700 in rent, dear? . . . If you don't work, if you can't, you can't live. It is tough. But they [the government] don't know how it is there. . . . You can't say, 'Sir, sir, send people that care about the immigrants, because they are the people who can't speak up.' There is nowhere to complain to, and we can't complain." Manuela cannot identify many people or organizations to help her protest what she considers to be exorbitantly high rents. After a

"Jewish man" came to her door, Manuela attended a meeting at City Hall to voice disapproval over the end of rent control in Cambridge, but her participation was a one-time event. There was no follow up by a political party, little involvement by Portuguese organizations in her area, and no Portuguese community leader that she could identify as a spokesperson for the community or her individual concerns. Unlike Tilla's experience, Manuela's participation did not develop into other activism.

The differing experiences of Tilla and Manuela are not just two stories among many. Instead, their stories point to important differences in how localized mobilization processes in Toronto and Boston arise from and feed back into larger policy and institutional environments. These environments differ among immigrants and refugees in Canada and the United States. For example, although organizations matter in similar ways to all four migrant communities, they are less present among Portuguese in Boston than in the other three communities. This is not because the Portuguese in Boston are especially lacking in the skills or resources needed to establish community organizations. As we have seen, Portuguese Americans in Boston face problems similar to those of members of the other three communities. Rather, they do not receive the same sort of settlement support—support that helps build community organizations—as most newcomers in Canada or official refugees in the United States. The localized mobilization of newcomers, as describe here, is nested in a larger context of reception. Critical to this context of reception is differential access to government policies of multiculturalism and settlement, a topic I take up in the following chapter.

3. Structured Mobilization

The Role of Government

> The Citizenship Act ensures the facilitation of citizenship, so that immigrants can exercise their voting capacity. That is the main policy thrust.
>
> SENIOR CIVIL SERVANT, *Citizenship and Immigration Canada,* June 2001

> The dominant culture of the agency . . . [is] rooted in a view of immigration as a source of security and law enforcement vulnerability more than of continuing nation building.
>
> DORIS MEISSNER, *former commissioner of the U.S. Immigration and Naturalization Service,* November 2001

In the United States, immigrants are considered autonomous individuals capable of making their own choices about citizenship and involvement in the political system. Why then, if newcomers in the United States are equally free to naturalize and participate as compatriots in Canada, are citizenship levels and measures of political success consistently lower in the United States than in Canada? This chapter suggests that the dynamics of political mobilization are nested in a larger context of reception shaped by government policy toward newcomers.

In particular, we need to consider the degree of material and symbolic public support offered to newcomer communities. With the exception of legally recognized refugees, U.S. governments do not engage in active promotion of settlement, citizenship, and political participation. The large influx of immigrants that arrived in the United States after 1965 has received little public assistance with political integration. Over the same period, Canadian governments have expanded immigrant settlement programs and established a diversity policy that celebrates multiculturalism and Canadian citizenship. These government programs, combined with diverging approaches to interventionist public policy, have made the institutional landscape in Canada more favorable to immigrants' political incorporation than the environment in the United States, helping to explain incorporation differences and their timing.

The roots of these policy divergences stem less from careful thought about immigrant integration than each country's attempt to deal with long-standing ethnoracial conflicts. As we will see, public opinion toward newcomers and ethnoracial diversity is comparable in the two countries. However, each nation faced somewhat different crises of citizenship and cohesion in the 1960s and 1970s, in the United States between blacks and whites, and in Canada between French and English speakers. Government intervention around diversity in the United States would center on race and civil rights. In Canada it would be grounded in ethnicity, culture, and language, with a strong state interest in integration. These different responses carried important repercussions for foreign-born newcomers.

FROM POLITICAL OPPORTUNITY STRUCTURE TO POLICY

When considering institutional contexts, social movement scholars speak of a country's political opportunity structure, generally understood as persistent dimensions of the political environment that affect people's willingness to undertake collective action (Tarrow 1994). For immigration scholars, the salient features of a country's political opportunity structure include citizenship laws (Clarke, van Dam, and Gooster 1998; Weil 2001), immigration policies (Portes and Rumbaut 1996), national political cultures (Brubaker 1992; Lipset 1990), and the presence of anti-immigrant parties or politicians (Koopmans 2004; Ramakrishnan and Espenshade 2001).

We have already seen that variations in immigration policy and citizenship law do not account for the magnitude of the U.S.-Canada gap in political incorporation. Consideration of political culture moves us closer, but such accounts lack specificity. According to Seymour Martin Lipset (1990), the American Revolution created two distinct political cultures on the North American continent. Revolutionary radicals in the United States generated norms of individualism, universalism, and distrust of the state, while the Loyalists who fled north to Canada established a statist, group-oriented political culture that defers to authority.[1] According to this view, immigrants to the United States are either attracted by or, once in the United States, assimilate to an anti-statist stance that depresses political participation. Conversely, Canada attracts or socializes immigrants to engage in collective participation in the political process.

Two major problems with the political culture argument are identifying which societal values matter and how, exactly, they influence people. Many countries contain competing ideological traditions that hold legitimacy among some segment of the population.[2] Canadians' supposed deference to authority could theoretically depress political activity, while Americans' love of democracy and freedom could encourage participation. Accounts of political culture also often lack a clear causal mechanism explaining how societal beliefs arise and how they produce specific outcomes. Much of the political culture literature assumes historical continuity over very long periods, about one hundred fifty to two hundred years in the case of Lipset's analysis of Canada-U.S. differences. Yet the citizenship and representation data in chapter 1 show that immigrants followed similar trajectories of political integration in Canada and the United States prior to the 1960s; trends only diverge in recent decades. If political culture plays a role, this culture changed over the past forty years. The question then becomes identifying those changes and showing how they affect incorporation patterns.

One possible change could be the attitudes of established residents toward immigrants, that is, their relative openness and acceptance of immigration. If a population welcomes immigration, it will be easier for newcomers to participate, whereas a hostile reception might make political incorporation more difficult.[3] Do Americans and Canadians hold widely divergent opinions on immigration and immigrant-generated diversity?

The evidence offers no clear indication that Canadians hold consistently more favorable opinions of immigrants than Americans. In a series of national surveys conducted between 1996 and 1998, an average of only 8 percent of Canadians believed that there were too few immigrants entering the country, while 42 percent thought there were too many (Palmer 1999). A slightly different question, posed to Americans in 1996, found that only 5 percent favored an increase in the number of immigrants entering the United States, while 58 percent favored a decrease in the number. In surveys conducted between 1977 and 1996, the proportion of Americans wanting a decrease in immigrant admissions fluctuated from two-fifths to two-thirds, but with no apparent trend over time toward a more or less restrictionist stance (Tichenor 2002: 19). Interestingly, since 2001 Gallup polls show a slight increase in the percent of Americans favoring more immigration, from 8 percent in 2001—a level on par with Gallup surveys from 1965 to 1995—to 16 percent in June 2005.[4] This increase has apparently occurred despite increased emphasis in the United States on border security following the terrorist attacks of 2001.

If we instead consider the impact of immigration, an Ipsos–Public Affairs poll, conducted for the Associated Press in 2004, found that similar proportions of Canadians and Americans, 18 percent and 14 percent, respectively, thought that immigrants were having a "very good influence" on the way things were going in their country.[5] A significantly higher number of Canadians, 55 percent, thought that immigrants had a "somewhat" good influence, compared to 28 percent in the United States.[6] Conversely, 40 percent of Canadians agreed that it is better for a country if almost everyone shares the same customs and traditions, while in the United States only 27 percent agreed with the statement. A similar question, asked in the two countries in 1989, also found greater tolerance of diversity among Americans, with 47 percent of Americans but only 34 percent of Canadians supporting maintenance of "distinct cultures and ways" (Reitz and Breton 1994: 28). Canadians consequently seem more convinced of the need for migration—perhaps to compensate for a declining birth rate and attendant problems in paying for social welfare programs in the future—but they are less optimistic about the effects of immigration on the sociocultural makeup of their country.[7]

The lack of systematic difference in public opinion suggests that differences in political incorporation cannot be accounted for by differences in established residents' attitudes. More generally, a study conducted for the Canadian government in 2002 found that focus group participants had very low awareness of immigration and refugee policies and that views were strongly influenced by media coverage of the issue (Aubry 2002). Similarly, it is not clear that Americans' opinions on immigration are deeply held or extremely salient in making political decisions (Tichenor 2002). Public opinion might not matter much when creating policy for newcomers.

Similarly, explanations centered on party politics fail to provide greater insight on the problem. American politics appears slightly more open to strong restrictionist discourse, although criticism is largely centered on illegal migration rather than immigration generally. As Daniel Tichenor (2002) observes, one of the most noteworthy features of American immigration policy in the 1980s and 1990s was its expansionist character, despite strident restrictionist voices.[8] In Canada, the rise of the new Reform Party in the late 1980s added a stronger restrictionist discourse into Canadian politics, but as the party evolved and sought to replace the Progressive Conservatives as the national party of the Canadian Right, leaders quieted the loudest anti-immigrant voices.[9] In the Canadian case, the harshest criticism of immigration has centered on refugee and asylum policy, in some respects the Canadian equivalent of the United States' contentious debate around illegal migration. Most important, divergences in incorporation have occurred regardless of the party in power in Canada or the United States.

Instead of political culture, public opinion, or party politics, we need to examine differences in the two countries' policies toward immigrants after they enter North America, in particular, the level of government support for immigrant settlement, including citizenship activities, and the official promo-

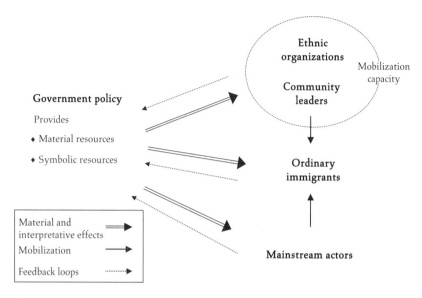

Figure 5. Immigrant political incorporation through structured mobilization.

tion of multiple identities and attachments as reflected in support for multiculturalism. A policy orientation does not fit neatly into a political opportunity structure model, though it is clearly influenced by the general attention to institutional contexts. Policy is a less fixed or stable part of a country's political system than party systems or national cultures, though once policies are enacted, they can prove to be quite "sticky" and difficult to reverse.[10] This means that a policy orientation provides a more dynamic and fluid account of political incorporation than standard structural arguments: since policies can be established, changed, or ended, so can patterns of political integration.[11]

A policy approach also helps to identify the mechanisms of political integration. I focus on three sets of policies and practices that affect citizenship and political involvement: the bureaucracies that deal directly with naturalization; government programs directed at newcomer settlement; and government-sponsored diversity policies. Government policies can facilitate incorporation by providing immigrant communities with material resources to engage in political mobilization, by increasing access to political decision makers, and by shaping understandings of immigrants' symbolic place within the polity. Figure 5 provides a visual representation of immigrant political incorporation, bringing together an attention to local mobilization dynamics, as outlined in the previous chapter, with the contextual mechanisms that structure integration through government policy.

THE ADMINISTRATION OF CITIZENSHIP: ENFORCEMENT OR PROMOTION?

In Canada, the administration of citizenship falls to Citizenship and Immigration Canada (CIC), a stand-alone federal department. In the United States, the Immigration and Naturalization Service (INS), a part of the federal Department of Justice, oversaw naturalization until March 1, 2003. Now immigration services and citizenship adjudication fall under the purview of the Bureau of U.S. Citizenship and Immigration Services (USCIS), housed in the new federal Department of Homeland Security.

Comparing the two countries' administrative bureaucracies, we find that citizenship, and immigrant integration more broadly, tends to be promoted in Canada. In the United States, an ethos of law enforcement loomed large over the INS and imbues the overall mission of Homeland Security.[12] According to Canadian officials, immigrants are free to make their own choices regarding citizenship, but government seeks to sway such decisions by offering assistance to potential citizens and influencing community leaders and ethnic organizations. In the United States, the prevailing concern is policing the country's borders and administering immigration adjudications, including naturalization, in a fair manner. The state favors a more distant, neutral relationship with would-be citizens, ethnic organizations, and community advocates, believing that the individual should make an independent and autonomous choice to become an American.

Political and bureaucratic decisions regarding policy and priorities drive these decisions, not legal structures. The two countries share similar laws: nowhere in the Canadian Citizenship Act is the state required to promote citizenship, and in the United States the "promotion of naturalization programs . . . is clearly permitted, if not actually mandated" under the U.S. Immigration and Nationality Act (North 1985: 58). Instead, once immigration is viewed as primarily about integration or security—including the prevention of illegal immigration—the resulting programs and bureaucratic structures institutionalize these attitudes, perpetuating both policies and outlooks. Organizational cultures develop that treat immigrants with suspicion, in a neutral fashion, or as a needed and welcome addition to the country.

The Former INS: Enforcement and Administration

Robert Alvarez, in his study of recently naturalized Hispanic immigrants, notes that regardless of an individual's personal experience with the INS, horror stories are legendary, creating substantial trepidation among would-be citizens. People hear about "long waits in I.N.S. offices [and] being treated rudely and unfairly by I.N.S. clerks and employees," so that "there was a pervading sentiment that the I.N.S. was generally an institution to avoid" (1987: 339). Many of the immigrants and refugees I spoke with voiced similar fears, although reality often contradicted the stories—most of my respondents reported that they were treated with respect and had a good experience during the naturalization process.[13] Yet positive interactions with specific INS officials did little to change newcomers' overall perception that the Immigration and Naturalization Service was first and foremost an enforcement agency. With relatively few symbolic or material resources directed to naturalization, the INS sent the message that citizenship is simply an administrative matter that the INS oversaw.

Early in the twentieth century, U.S. government and society promoted naturalization much more. The Americanization movement of the 1910s and 1920s brought together private voluntary organizations, local school boards, businesses, and government agencies to encourage immigrants' assimilation through naturalization, learning English, and cultural adjustment to the "American" way of life. In 1913 Congress detached oversight of naturalization services from immigration, establishing an autonomous Bureau of Naturalization that would focus on citizenship promotion.[14] To this end, the secretary of labor approved a plan of cooperation between the bureau and public schools so that by 1915 a formal arrangement, detailed in the Fiscal Regulations of the Department of Labor, specified that the Bureau of Naturalization "furnishes [public school authorities] the names and addresses of the declarants for citizenship and petitioners for naturalization for the purpose of bringing these prospective citizens into contact at the earliest moment with the Americanizing influences of the public school system and thereby contributing to the elevation of citizenship standards. By insuring the comprehension of the true spirit of our institutions on the part of aliens admitted to citizenship the Bureau may hope to make their acquisition serve as a strengthening influence upon the moral, social, political, and industrial qualities of those institutions" (cited in Smith 1926: 11–12). The bureau also worked with schools to assemble and publish the first *Federal Textbook on Citizenship* in 1918 and distributed the textbooks to schools offering citizenship classes. Such cooperative activities continued until 1925, when fiscal pressures forced reorganization. In 1933 the Bureaus of Naturalization and Immigration were reunited as one agency within the Department of Labor.

Following the outbreak of war in Europe, then-president Franklin D. Roosevelt's 1940 Reorganization Plan (Number V) transferred the now-named Immigration and Naturalization Service from the Department of Labor to the Department of Justice. The move reflected the changing perception of immigration as a national security issue rather than an economic one. War responsibilities included recording and fingerprinting every alien in the United States through the Alien Registration Program, organizing and operating internment camps and detention facilities for enemy aliens, and guarding national borders with the Border Patrol (Smith 1998).[15] The location of the INS in the Department of Justice shaped the actions and priorities of the agency and played into the INS's image as an enforcement agency. Sixty years later former INS commissioner Doris Meissner still finds that "the dominant culture of the agency . . . [is] rooted in a view of immigration as a source of security and law enforcement vulnerability more than of continuing nation building" (2001: 2). The move to place immigration and naturalization services under the new Department of Homeland Security continues this tradition.

By the 1950s, few organizations or programs directed at immigrant naturalization remained, in large part due to low levels of immigration following the 1924 National Origins Act, which set restrictive quotas on many countries with large numbers of would-be immigrants. Furthermore, with the growth of the civil rights movement in the 1960s, "Americanization" largely lost favor. The earlier focus on assimilation—including implicit renunciation of homeland cultures and languages—gave way to new discourses of diversity (Gleason 2001).

Even after immigration levels rose in the mid-1960s, government promotion of citizenship has been largely absent. Rather, the agency stuck largely to the administration of petitions and border control, as represented by its mission statement: "The U.S. Immigration and Naturalization Service . . . is responsible for enforcing the laws [of entry] and for administering various immigration benefits, including the naturalization of qualified applicants for U.S. citizenship."

The most significant contemporary attempt to change the post–World War II pattern came with the Citizenship USA program, which took place between August 1995 and September 1996. With the goal of facilitating naturalization, the INS tried to speed up the citizenship process; contract out certain services, such as administration of the citizenship exam; and interact more with community groups. As one INS official commented, "I think that [it was] sort of a high-water mark in terms of where INS has ever been in terms of affirmatively inviting people to step forward and naturalize." The program quickly came under fire, however, after some applicants with criminal records were given citizenship. Further, a number of Republicans in

Congress accused the INS of partisan behavior, since they felt that naturalization promotion was done to build Democratic support during the 1996 presidential election. The political uproar pushed the agency back to a stance of neutral administration, since "given the political accusations about the motivations behind Citizenship USA, INS is a little bit loath at this point to actually get too far out in the promotion realm."

The failed attempt to facilitate naturalization came at the same time that INS saw a remarkable expansion in its border control activities. During her tenure as commissioner of INS (1993 to 2000), Doris Meissner's stated desire was to put the "N" back in INS—to increase the prominence of citizenship—and to reemphasize the "S" for Service. Yet the border control budget grew by more than $1.5 billion over fiscal years 1993 to 1999 while citizenship and other immigration services saw an increase of only about $270 million (U.S. Immigration and Naturalization Service 2000). According to Peter Andreas (2000), the dominance of policing functions, especially in the 1990s, was actively promoted by politicians and certain INS officials. By emphasizing border control, the latter gained unprecedented standing and resources, while for the former, "the overwhelming political focus on curbing the influx of . . . immigrants has drawn attention away from the more complex and politically divisive challenge of dealing with the enormous domestic demand for . . . cheap migrant labor" (Andreas 2000: 8). In 2000 the INS was the largest law enforcement agency of the federal government.

Given the policing image generated by the direction, resource allocation, and culture of the INS, the agency's image did little to encourage citizenship and probably served to dissuade some from naturalization. The pattern has largely stayed the same after the INS became part of the new Department of Homeland Security. Despite some moves to increase integration and citizenship outreach services and a commitment to reduce processing times, border control and policing capture much greater proportions of the department's financial and personnel resources.

Promotion of Citizenship in Canada

Citizenship and Immigration Canada, as well as its earlier incarnations, has favored more active citizenship promotion.[16] A senior official at CIC explains: "The Canadian policy is that we are a country of immigration. The only way an immigrant can influence how the country is run, to do that, you need to vote. And you can only vote if you become a citizen. The Citizenship Act ensures the facilitation of citizenship, so that immigrants can exercise their voting capacity. That is the main policy thrust." Another official linked naturalization to a history of immigrant integration, "We want immigrants to be full participants in Canadian society. All of us, except for a few people, are immigrants to this country, if not us or our parents, our grandparents." Citizenship is consequently a central part of CIC's mission. This emphasis stands in contrast to the dominant ethos in the INS, where naturalization has often been pushed to the back of workload priorities. Former INS commissioner Doris Meissner remembers:

> "In the early 1970s, when I first had an opportunity to meet people in the agency at the working level who are responsible for managing these programs, like naturalization . . . I was always quite interested to hear the institutional view that in many ways naturalization could be put at the end of the queue or toward the end of the queue in setting priorities because, after all, the people who were eligible for naturalization already had a green card. . . . There was just less of a sense of urgency about it."[17]

Such differences in attitude and priorities subsequently affect organizational culture and naturalization programs.

The procitizenship stance of CIC has been a feature of Canadian policy since the establishment of Canadian citizenship in 1947, but the strength of this commitment has grown over the post–World War II era. As in the United States, World War II raised concern over enemy aliens and led to domestic internment camps and a general suspicion of foreigners. Strikingly, however, the forerunner of the Bureau of Citizenship, the Nationalities Branch of the Department of National War Services, was established in 1941 to promote a sense of Canadian identity among ethnic minorities (Kelley and Trebilcock 1998: 272). The Department of National War Services began a propaganda campaign which argued that Canada's ethnic diversity did not threaten unity or security. The Nationalities Branch promoted this message in the ethnic press, signaling a new government interest in ethnic outreach and citizenship promotion.

Wartime suspicions were further tempered in the postwar period by the perception that immigration was needed to populate Canada's vast territory, fuel its economy, and fulfill humanitarian obligations, notably the resettlement of European displaced persons. Prime Minister Mackenzie King's famous statement on immigration in May 1947 adopted a cautiously expansionist stance: "The policy of the government is to foster the growth of the population . . . [and] to ensure the careful selection and permanent settlement of such numbers of immigrants as can be advantageously absorbed in our national economy" (Knowles 2000: 67).[18] Reports from the Senate Committee on Immigration and Labour, published in 1946, 1947, and 1948, pushed for an open immigration policy and the strengthening of the Citizenship Branch, including endorsement of closer cooperation between government departments on matters of citizenship education and promotion (Hawkins 1988: 85). In 1950 the government established the new Citizenship and Immigration Department, elevating both policy areas from their previous status as branches within the Department of the Secretary of State and the Department of Mines and Resources, respectively, to full departmental standing.

The ethos among civil servants in the new department was decidedly proimmigration. From 1950 onward: "A strong conviction about the benefits of immigration grew among the younger post-war recruits to the service, and by the late fifties it was very strong. It derived first from the Department's simple possession of the field: from their management of this area of public policy, their sense of responsibility for it, and their awareness of it as a national asset. Secondly, it derived from their contact with immigrants" (Hawkins 1988: 72). Those in the Citizenship Branch were also strongly invested in their work. According to Hawkins, employees had mostly "been trained in the social sciences, with experience in and a strong orientation towards, community development," or as a former staff member described it, they "came out of Canadian adult education, community organization and the Y" (1988: 97). The contrast with the INS is striking. Up to the 1990s, most adjudicator positions in the INS—the individuals who make decisions on immigration visas and naturalization requests—were filled by staff moving up the internal INS career ladder from border enforcement.[19] Whereas broad public opinion toward immigration probably had limited effect on diverging U.S.-Canada integration outcomes, the stances of those working in these agencies likely did make a difference.

Political interest in the Citizenship and Immigration Department waned, however, during the Conservative Party's tenure in office from 1957 to 1963.[20] An internal review in the mid-1960s concluded, "one receives the distinct impression that successive administrations had considered the [Citizenship] Branch too small to merit their attention and yet doing work that was too important to be discontinued" (cited in Hawkins 1988: 97). Some of this work included fielding "liaison" officers in key immigration areas, overseeing a relatively large language-training program with some citizenship classes, and offering small grants to nonprofit voluntary organizations seeking to help immigrants and ethnic minorities. There was no equivalent institutionalized office within the INS providing such services.

Promotion of Canadian citizenship and community development was hampered by limited resources and a tendency to provide advisory services rather than self-standing programs. The social scientists and community activists "always seemed reluctant to engage in the hard fighting for the resources and support which its [the branch's] responsibilities really required" (Hawkins 1988: 98). In fiscal year 1951–52, the Citizenship Branch of the Department of the Secretary of State gave out $20,000 to four community groups working on settlement and citizenship; a decade and a half later, in the 1966–67 fiscal year, the branch had increased its outreach marginally, disbursing $88,150 to twelve groups concerned with settlement and ethnoracial citizenship (Pal 1993: 85, 108).[21]

The type of groups receiving funding was, however, slowly shifting to finance immigrant communities rather than mainstream organizations serving immigrants. In the early 1950s, monies went to established mainstream groups such as the Canadian Association for Adult Education, or la Société canadienne d'enseignement, which provided training and language instruction to newcomers. In the mid-1960s these adult education associations still received funding, but so too did COSTI, an organization established in 1962 by members of Italian Canadian community to provide settlement assistance to Italian immigrants.[22] Staff interest in community development was very slowly being matched with material support for such efforts.

Political interest in immigration and citizenship resurfaced in the late 1960s and quickly led to an expanded and revitalized Citizenship Branch.[23] The cabinet approved a new program on citizenship with five policy objectives: to reinforce Canadian identity and unity; to encourage cultural diversity within a bilingual framework; to preserve human rights; to increase and improve citizenship participation; and to develop meaningful symbols of Canadian sovereignty (Hawkins 1988: 365). As was the case earlier, this project targeted native-born Canadians and newcomers alike. Fears over Quebec nationalism and a strong desire among high-ranking Liberal politicians to define a unique Canadian identity undoubtedly fed the citizenship push.

The programmatic overhaul of the Citizenship Branch was accompanied by an astonishing expansion in the branch's budget. In 1970 more than 100 new staff members and consultants were hired to work for a unit that employed just 110 employees the year before (Hawkins 1988: 311, 365). The next year, after the announcement of a new multiculturalism policy, more funding followed. By fiscal year 1974–75, the branch was disbursing $2,650,000 to 648 groups (Pal 1993: 189, 192). The overwhelming bulk of these monies, more than $2.3 million, went to Multiculturalism Project grants. The remainder went to multiculturalism centers, language assistance centers, and citizenship orientation programs.

It is important to underscore the date of these changes. As shown earlier, naturalization levels in Canada and the United States were virtually identical up to the early 1970s. A decade later, Canadian citizenship acquisition rose slightly despite large numbers of new immigrants while U.S. levels fell dramatically. It was at this same juncture that Canadian citizenship promotion, already somewhat more interventionist than U.S. citizenship promotion after World War II, developed greater organizational capacity and received increased resources.

Attitudes and Bureaucratic Practice Compared

Differences in attitudes and bureaucratic practice shape immigrants' perception of citizenship and their evaluation of how onerous naturalization will be. In the United States, "the process of becoming a citizen includes a number of well defined steps," but the actual experience of naturalization is "embedded in the quagmire and inconsistency of the I.N.S. bureaucracy" (Alvarez 1987: 333). According to David North, American policy and practice can be summed up as a "long gray welcome": "Documents are needlessly cold, and potentially alarming to some. The language is often needlessly ponderous and above the average education level of most of the applicants. The graphics range from the uninspired and cramped to messy and illegible" (1987: 325). In Canada, in contrast, "the offices are pleasant, but not opulent; the lines are not long; the printed material is brighter and more abundant than in the U.S. The predominant color is not gray" (North 1985: 55). Such bureaucratic differences are not apparent from a country's formal citizenship code, but they likely influence naturalization rates.

Many of those I interviewed in Boston reported that INS officials were fairer and more approachable than the picture painted by compatriots, but I nonetheless heard more frequent stories of intimidation or unfriendly behavior among my U.S. informants. One Vietnamese applicant in Boston remembers: "The officer I had to face was very hard. He noticed that my English was not very good. So he asked how much I paid for the written test. I stood up and answered that I myself took it, not paid for it. Then he asked why I did not change my name to an American name. I explained to him that . . . I cannot change my name."[24] The only complaint I heard in Toronto was a similar problem with foreign names. A woman of Portuguese birth wished to have her full name, including her father's surname, written on her citizenship document, but the government employee "told me that I didn't need my Dad's name or anybody else's name because I was married. That was the only nasty person." Michael Jones-Correa is probably correct to caution that "fear of the INS and the impact of bureaucratic hurdles may be overstated," since I found many respondents reporting a relatively good experience of naturalization (1998a: 64). However, uncertainty about one's treatment and the potential of a bad experience certainly does not help. Because Canadian migrants tend to have better opinions of government employees and CIC than their American counterparts, they are less apt to view naturalization as a potentially unpleasant task and consequently more likely to file an application for citizenship.[25]

It is difficult to know whether normative stances—toward enforcement in the United States, toward integration in Canada—make adjudicators in the INS more likely to refuse potential citizens than Canadian officials. Comparison of standard questions used in American and Canadian citizenship tests suggests that the two require similar levels of knowledge.[26] An INS official might ask an applicant, "What are the colors of our flag?" "How many senators are there in Congress?" or "What are the 49th and 50th states of the Union?"[27] In Canada, a would-be citizen might be asked, "What is the capital of Canada?" "How many electoral districts are there in Canada?" or "What is the name of Canada's new territory in the north?"[28] In both countries immigrants who undergo an in-person exam are subject to the examiner's arbitrary choice of questions. In the last fifteen years, both the INS and CIC also administer a written exam.

Accurate statistics on refusal rates are difficult to compile and are not perfectly comparable. Figures from the INS *Statistical Yearbook* suggest that from the 1960s through the 1980s, only 2 percent of citizenship claims were denied. However, this does not mean that 98 percent of applicants successfully acquired citizenship. The number of denials is based on cases pressed to a final decision, while "a substantial but unknown percentage of those applying are neither denied nor granted citizenship; they simply drop out of the system" (North 1985: 37–38). North suggests that up to 25 percent are not formally denied but put on hold because of missing documents or because applicants are encouraged to try again later. In a similar manner, 3 percent of Canadian petitions are denied formally, but another 9 percent of applicants default after they fail to attend their citizenship interview (North 1985: 54). An additional and unknown percentage of would-be applicants in Canada withdraw applications on the advice of civil servants if an official feels that language skills need improvement or if the applicant needs to wait until a pardon is granted for a criminal conviction. In the 1990s INS denials rose sharply to about 15 percent, in part due to ineligible applications from individuals who had not yet met residence requirements but who filed since they were worried about legislation penalizing noncitizenship. Officials at Citizenship and Immigration Canada estimate that in the same period, about 10 percent of applications were denied.[29] It is probable that immigrants in Canada enjoy a slightly greater likelihood of a positive decision compared to those in the United States, but the difference would account for only a small portion of the cross-national gap in citizenship levels.

A focus on refusal rates ignores a larger issue: immigrants might be slightly more successful, on average, in acquiring Canadian citizenship than counterparts in the United States, but they are also much more likely to apply, in part because the government tries to demystify the process. All applicants in Canada are given a free booklet, *A Look at Canada*, upon submission of their naturalization application.[30] The booklet provides information about Canadian history, geography, and politics. Applicants are told that test questions will be drawn from the book. Publicly funded citizenship classes are available for those who want additional assistance, and many ESL classes go over some of the material in *A Look at Canada* as part of the instruction. In contrast, neither INS nor USCIS distributes free booklets detailing American history and politics, although both post the citizenship questions examiners may ask.[31] In Boston, ESL classes cover some citizenship material, as in Toronto, but there are far fewer courses available since, unlike in Canada, the federal government does not usually offer direct funding for newcomer language instruction.[32]

Perceptions of citizenship are also shaped by promotion activities. North calculated that in the mid-1980s, Canadian officials spent 6.8 hours on every citizenship file, compared to 3.3 hours in the United States. These figures might reflect greater efficiency in the United States, but "a significant part of the difference can be attributed to the amount of time and energy spent on [citizenship] promotion" (North 1985: 55). Staffing of naturalization services in the mid-1980s was virtually equivalent in the United States and Canada—397 adjudicators compared to 366, respectively—despite twice the number of naturalization petitions filed in the United States (North 1985: 55). Canadian officials could consequently spend more time with applicants. Since then, the two systems have moved a bit closer together: more money was injected into naturalization petitions in the United States in the 1990s, though mostly just to keep up with demand, while pressure in Canada during the 1990s for a more efficient and less costly bureaucracy led to the establishment of a centralized, and less personal, telephone call center approach.[33]

The hours worked on each application also exclude the activities of Canadian citizenship judges. Citizenship judges are individuals appointed by government to examine citizenship applicants, to preside over the formal citizenship ceremony, and to promote Canadian citizenship at special events and in community activities. In the mid-1980s, for example, a Portuguese-speaking citizenship judge went out to meet with about two hundred Portuguese farmworkers to describe the naturalization system (North 1985: 50). Citizenship judges are not regular court justices. In 2003 the group included a former public librarian, a former nurse, numerous teachers, retired politicians and civil servants, various businesspeople, and individuals with long histories in community service. Chosen for their contribution to Canadian society, the citizenship judges are frequently first- or second-generation immigrants, so they also serve as role models to would-be Canadians.[34]

Higher staffing levels in Canada generated a slightly faster turnaround of citizenship applications in the 1980s.[35] Both countries encountered processing problems in the 1990s, although they became more acute in the United States. The U.S. General Accounting Office found that while the INS took only four months to process a naturalization application in 1996, by 1997 the wait had exploded to thirty-one months (U.S. General Accounting Office 2001: 25). Wait time dropped in subsequent years, to two years in 1998, twelve months in 1999, and only about six months in 2000. Canadian officials faced similar problems. An internal CIC audit of the citizenship system in 1998 indicated that citizenship processing took on average ten to twelve months (Citizenship and Immigration Canada 1999b). Slight differences in processing times are not behind the North American naturalization gap, but they do contribute to immigrants' impression of government efficiency and their sense of immigrants' relative importance compared to other government priorities.

Indeed, the attitude and outreach on immigration and naturalization reflect more generally on *all* government institutions. Immigration officials are usually the first government representatives with whom newly arriving migrants interact. As such, they can symbolize the attitude of government writ large for newcomers. This has important repercussions on understandings of full citizenship. According to Soss's (1999) study of the U.S. welfare system, program clients perceive the agency with which they interact as a microcosm of the government, and they extrapolate from those experiences to form an understanding of their own role in the political system. Similarly, Aihwa Ong (2003) documents how Cambodians' experiences with refugee program officials, welfare agencies, and medical institutions transmit specific cultural norms of American citizenship. Negative experiences with immigration officials can undermine newcomers' confidence in their welcome by all governmental agencies and political actors, and it can set an example for nonimmigrants regarding their society's attitude toward immigrants.

NEWCOMER SETTLEMENT
AND MULTICULTURALISM POLICIES

Beyond the bureaucracies directly responsible for administering citizenship, other government agencies work to resettle and integrate newcomers. American efforts at incorporation largely focus on refugee resettlement; in Canada, programs are more extensive since nonrefugee populations also benefit from public support. Programs in both countries provide newcomers with material resources, individually or as a community, and they serve symbolic functions, signaling government's interest (or disinterest) in extending a helping hand.

Multiculturalism policies, a second set of policies with incorporation consequences for immigrants, also provide material and symbolic resources to newcomers. Overall, Canada's policy of official multiculturalism offers a more developed public rhetoric of *immigrant* integration and more direct funding to ethnic communities. The tenets of Canadian multiculturalism—promoting ethnic pride while facilitating incorporation into Canadian society—imply that acquiring Canadian citizenship does not require renunciation of former identities and loyalties and that political participation is not at odds with continued attachment to the homeland. In the United States, multiculturalism also involves pride in diversity, but rhetoric and programs primarily speak to the native born. American multiculturalism is usually defined in racial terms, but pan-ethnic racial identities, such as Asian American, often stand at odds with first-generation immigrants' self-perceptions. Diversity programs that work to eradicate ethno-racial discrimination or offer assistance in overcoming discrimination can help nonwhite immigrants, thereby easing integration. However, they are often not concerned with immigrants' unique settlement needs, especially those related to legal status and linguistic or cultural barriers.

Integrative Citizenship: Settlement Programs in Canada

Settlement programs—oriented to a newcomer's first years in Canada—aim to ease an individual's transition into the labor market and to promote integration into Canadian society, especially through language training.

Such programs can facilitate and encourage naturalization, even though that is not their primary purpose. For example, ESL classes (or, in the case of Quebec, French language classes) can make the language requirement for naturalization surmountable. Such classes can also increase interest in and understanding of citizenship. ESL teachers might provide instruction in Canadian social and political structures or even organize field trips, such as to the local city hall.

Prior to the 1950s, Canadian immigration officials focused on recruiting, processing, and screening would-be immigrants rather than on settlement. With the establishment of the Department of Citizenship and Immigration in 1950, newcomers were progressively offered a range of programs, including language and citizenship classes, job-placement services, and health and welfare assistance. By 1963 there were ninety-nine immigration officers across Canada wholly engaged in placement and settlement work and seventy-seven individuals working part time on newcomer integration (Hawkins 1988: 443, n. 8). Funding for settlement was limited initially but underwent rapid expansion during the Trudeau years (1968–79, 1980–84). The period also saw a philosophical shift: government would not only oversee immigration flows but would become an active player in the settlement process (Lanphier and Lukomskyj 1994). State intervention in this area paralleled a more general expansion of the Canadian welfare state as a national health care system was instituted and other social policies were expanded or created.

Following the split of immigration services from citizenship in 1966, the federal Department of Manpower and Immigration (later the Department of Employment and Immigration) catered to the immigrant heading for the labor market while the Citizenship Branch of the Department of the Secretary of State focused on social, political, and cultural integration.[36] A strong emphasis on the economic consequences of immigration and a belief that successful integration begins with reliable employment led government to direct most public money to programs aimed at working-age males, and it oriented government workers to define settlement in economic terms.[37] By the early 1970s, it was estimated that about half of all newly arriving immigrant workers visited one of 360 Canada Manpower Centres for job counseling and training (Hawkins 1988: 339). A survey of Vietnamese who arrived in Toronto between 1975 and 1978 found that 24 percent of respondents got their first job with the assistance of an employee with the Department of Manpower and Immigration and another 6 percent did so through a counselor at Welcome House, the provincial agency in charge of newcomer settlement (Vietnamese Association of Toronto 1979:

10). Similarly, a survey of Portuguese blue-collar workers in 1969 found that 19 percent found their first employment through immigration officials (Anderson 1974: 70).

Federal interest in settlement flows from Ottawa's primary responsibility for immigration policy. The Immigration Act of 1976 explicitly recognizes the importance of newcomer settlement for the "domestic and international interests of Canada," a sentiment reiterated and expanded in the new Immigration and Refugee Protection Act of 2001.[38] However, under the Canadian Constitution the main components of newcomer settlement—language training and education, and economic and social welfare—fall under provincial jurisdiction. Up to 2003, the federal government had entered into formal settlement arrangements with three provinces—Quebec, British Columbia, and Manitoba—but it had been unable to reach an agreement with Ontario, the biggest reception area of new immigration. A first-ever Canada-Ontario Immigration Agreement was finally signed on November 21, 2005.[39] Various provinces have set up their own independent agencies for immigrant settlement.

Ontario became active in settlement relatively early, gathering together programs previously dispersed in various ministries under a new provincial Citizenship Branch in 1961.[40] In its first year the provincial branch was small: it had a staff of five and a budget of $58,000 dedicated to translation services, information diffusion, English-language training, and citizenship instruction (Hawkins 1988: 209). Mirroring changing attitudes at the federal level, provincial intervention increased over the 1960s as the Ontario cabinet made newcomer settlement a priority. By 1970 the Citizenship Branch employed a staff of thirty-eight and oversaw a budget of more than $1 million dedicated to language training, citizenship, and reception and orientation services as well as a grants program for community organizations (Hawkins 1988: 209). According to Hawkins, expansion occurred after language training programs were judged a success, giving officials within the provincial Citizenship Branch more leverage against a disinterested Treasury Board, and after attitudes in the cabinet shifted from laissez-faire to prointerventionist. Increased political interest and bureaucratic clout led to further expansion, so that by the mid-1980s Ontario's Multiculturalism and Citizenship Branch had a staff of one hundred forty with expenditures of over $15 million (Hawkins 1988: 392).

In the 1990s fiscal retrenchment reduced federal and provincial funding for settlement programs. At the same time, however, programs expanded beyond the old orientation of helping immigrants, particularly the male breadwinner, with labor market placement. The shift in emphasis is evident in language policy. In 1990–91, 92 percent of the over $100 million directed by the federal government to language training was earmarked to employment-related programs, reaching an estimated 28 percent of newly arrived immigrants (Boyd, DeVries, and Simkin 1994). A new policy, started in 1992, split funding 20/80 percent between the Labour Market Language Training program and the more general Language Instruction for Newcomers to Canada (LINC) program. The aim was to serve 45 percent of adult newcomers.

The 1990s also ushered in a philosophical shift regarding the government's role in providing direct services. Service provision increasingly devolved to local community organizations or lower levels of government through grant-making and cost-sharing arrangements. Under CIC's Settlement Renewal Project, driven by the department's desire to formulate a ten-year strategic plan and by a federal government review of its activities, CIC decided to withdraw completely from direct administration and delivery of federal settlement programming by the end of the decade (Citizenship and Immigration Canada 1995). The province of Ontario also cut back much of its direct service provision, only replacing a portion of these programs with grants or contacts to local community organizations.

In the mid-1990s the program budget of the federal Settlement Branch of CIC stood at $166 million in the 1995–96 fiscal year, a slight decrease from the $175 million of the year before (Citizenship and Immigration Canada 1995). This amount has held steady in the intervening years, with $173 million allocated to settlement in 2003–04.[41] The major programmatic areas over the past ten years include LINC; the Host program, which matches Canadian resident volunteers with newly arriving immigrants to provide early settlement support; and the Immigrant Settlement and Adaptation Program (ISAP). ISAP funds community organizations to provide immigrants with direct service delivery in areas such as reception, orientation, translation, interpretation, referral to community resources, and paraprofessional counseling. In 2003–04, $100 million went to LINC, $2.8 to the Host program, $30 million to ISAP, and $47 million to the Resettlement Assistance Program, which provides financial assistance to certain newcomers (Canada. House of Commons 2003: 2).

Critics of the settlement program's stalled spending note that the proportion of CIC's budget devoted to settlement decreased from 46 percent of the total in 1997–98 to 37 percent of net planned spending in 2003–04 (Canada. House of Commons 2003: 6). Compared to the United States, however, the disbursement of public monies for newcomer integration is very generous. In 2000–01 the Canadian federal government gave out approximately $1,500 per new immigrant admitted that year.[42] In addition, provincial and municipal agencies might offer settlement programs, multiplying immigrants' potential access to services and contact with government. Although lack of coordination continues to plague newcomer settlement— often there is little consultation between federal and provincial officials beyond cost-sharing agreements—generally one level of government supplements or adds to services offered by another (Lanphier and Lukomskyj 1994).[43] As we will see in later chapters, the existence of services positively influences immigrants' understanding of their relationship to the state and their sense of citizenship, and the actual monies transferred to community-based organizations help establish and sustain institutions that can promote political incorporation.

The New Canadian Nationalism? Official Multiculturalism

The growth and expansion of immigrant settlement services was complemented and reinforced by the rise of official Canadian multiculturalism. Today settlement services address migrants' needs shortly after arrival in Canada; multiculturalism speaks to a broader audience, including newcomers, established groups, and the second generation and beyond. According to Hawkins, in many ways Canadian multiculturalism "is a new name for an old activity, namely the long-standing efforts of the federal Citizenship Branch to encourage harmonious community relations in Canadian cities, and to protect and assist ethnic groups" (1991: 218).

Like the kaleidoscope to which multiculturalism is sometimes compared, definitions of multiculturalism shift and change. Depending on the speaker or context, multiculturalism is a label to describe the objective presence of ethno-racial diversity in Canada, a public ideology of harmonious interethnic relations, or an official government policy with attendant programs (Fleras and Elliott 1992; Kallen 1982). Multiculturalism in Canada also provides a normative framework for government and residents that legitimizes multiple identities while promoting Canadian citizenship. I am primarily interested in multiculturalism as official policy and, due to its legitimization by government, its underlying promotion of a specific normative framework of identity and intergroup relations.[44] In this way, multiculturalism provides material and symbolic resources to immigrants that they can use to make claims and access political debates.[45]

In Canada, conflict over diversity has historically centered on ethnicity—understood in terms of language, religion, and culture—rather than race. Canada's climate was not amenable to a plantation economy built on slavery.[46] Instead, British conquest of New France in 1659 produced a country divided into two linguistic and cultural groups, French Catholics and British Protestants. To accommodate "two nations warring in the bosom of a single state," as Lord Durham characterized the situation in his 1838 report, the Constitution Act of 1867 outlined a political solution by establishing a federal state and guarantees for the languages and religions of both groups.[47] Formal structures helped to mediate conflict, but continued interethnic inequalities—what John Porter (1965) called the "vertical mosaic"—spawned threats of Quebec separation in the 1960s and 1970s at the same time that the United States dealt with racial conflict.[48]

Prime Minister Pierre Elliot Trudeau first introduced a policy of multiculturalism during a speech in the House of Commons in 1971 as part of the government's response to the recommendations of the Royal Commission on Bilingualism and Biculturalism. Established in 1963 to counter rising French Canadian nationalism, the commission's mandate was to report on the status of bilingualism and biculturalism in Canada and to offer recommendations to further the "equal partnership between the two founding races, taking into account the contribution made by other ethnic groups to the cultural enrichment of Canada." Non-English and non-French ethnic groups protested these terms which, they claimed, relegated them to the status of second-class citizens.

In 1969 the government addressed the issue of bilingualism with the passage of the Official Languages Act, legislating English and French as the official languages of the federal Canadian government. The government was silent, however, on the idea of biculturalism. Then in 1971, the prime minister announced the government's new policy of multiculturalism in the House of Commons. To applause from all the opposition parties, Trudeau argued that "biculturalism does not properly describe our society" (Canada 1971: 8581).[49] By decade's end, multiculturalism had become an issue that none of the three major federal parties could criticize (Abu-Laban 1994), a stunning change for a society that in 1963 still spoke of the country's "two founding races."

The new federal policy was unabashedly interventionist. With the caveat "resources permitting," Trudeau committed his government to providing support to ethnic organizations, eliminating cultural barriers to participation in Canadian society, promoting dialogue between all Canadian cultural groups, and assisting immigrants to learn one of Canada's two official languages (Canada 1971: 8546). The pursuit of these objectives would involve government because "We are free to be ourselves. But this cannot be left to chance. It must be fostered and pursued actively" (Canada 1971: 8547). Trudeau argued that adhesion to a cultural community was a matter of individual choice, but that for the members of minority groups, the ability to choose was threatened without government intervention.

Multicultural policy and ideology have always been intimately linked with promotion of Canadian citizenship.[50] The prime minister assigned primary responsibility for multiculturalism to the Citizenship Branch of the Department of the Secretary of State. Initially given funding of $5 million in 1972—an amount which would double the following year then decrease later in the decade—the newly established multiculturalism branch administered six programs: multicultural grants to community groups, a cultural development program, grants for writing ethnic histories, funds for Canadian ethnic studies, promotion and support for official language instruction, and joint programs with other federal agencies dealing with cultural issues.[51] Government funding of multiculturalism—separate from existing settlement services—financed local ethnic associations, promoted cultural activities, and even supported programs such as heritage language schools, where the children of immigrants could learn the language of their parents.[52]

In its first decade, multiculturalism responded mainly to European immigrants' desire for recognition and support. As late as 1981, census statistics showed that three-quarters of all immigrants in Canada were born in Europe or the United States.[53] The face of Canadian immigration was changing rapidly, however, as new immigration increasingly originated from Asia, the Caribbean, and the Middle East. In response, the tenor of government and public discourse shifted from celebrating ethnic diversity to acknowledging racial barriers to participation in Canadian society (Canada 1984).

Government activities remained integrationist. Over fiscal year 1987–88, the multiculturalism program distributed more than $20 million in grants, with almost $6.5 million directed at "Citizen and Community Participation" (Pal 1993: 200).[54] Official multiculturalism reached a political and bureaucratic apogee with the passage of the Multiculturalism Act and the creation of a new Department of Multiculturalism and Citizenship in 1988. By enshrining multiculturalism into law with the Multiculturalism Act, the federal government committed itself to recognizing and protecting cultural differences, ensuring equal employment opportunities in federal institutions, and establishing "policies, programs and practices that enhance the ability of individuals and communities of all origins to contribute to the continuing evolution of Canada" (Multiculturalism Act, 1988, 2[b]).[55] These broad terms give policy makers the freedom to interpret the act as expansively or narrowly as they wish.

Constitutional crises in the 1990s led some politicians and public commentators to proclaim that the focus on diversity was undermining Canadian unity. Not coincidentally, these critiques gained force as Canadians faced the real possibility of Quebec's independence with a referendum on separation in 1995. As in the 1960s, discontent about the place of French Canadians and Quebec in confederation significantly affected immigrants through the reimagining of Canadian citizenship and nationalism. Multiculturalism was demoted to being a branch of Canadian Heritage and policy objectives were revisited, so that promotion of citizenship was put front and center. The revamped multiculturalism program of 1995 states that one of its three fundamental goals is civic participation, which involves "developing Canada's diverse people into active citizens with the capacity and opportunity to participate in shaping the future of their communities and their country" (Canadian Heritage 2002: 7). Grants for the promotion of civic participation and citizenship are available to a variety of groups, including nonprofit organizations, community associations, educational institutions, businesses, and provincial or municipal governments. The other two fundamental goals are promoting social justice and identity, with the latter focused both on diverse backgrounds and attachment to Canada.

Funding cutbacks followed bureaucratic demotion. In the 1996–97 fiscal year, the government spent almost $60 million dollars on multiculturalism programs, but the following year the multiculturalism budget was cut in half, to just under $30 million. Most of the cuts occurred in administration and public programming. Grant money for community organizations was also scaled back, but more gradually, from $17 million in 1996–97 to $15.9 million in 1997–98. The overall downward trend continued, hitting a low point in 2001–02 when the federal government disbursed only $7.5 million in multiculturalism grants. More recently, grant funding has increased modestly, to stand at $11.2 million in 2003–04.[56]

Scholars and pundits spiritedly debate whether multiculturalism has mattered and what effect it has had on Canadian society. Trudeau apparently took little interest in the policy following his initial speech in the House of Commons, and government spending has heavily favored bilingualism over multiculturalism. Grants to ethnic organizations tend to be modest, often directed at national umbrella groups or disbursed for pilot projects.[57] Nonetheless, as I outline in later chapters, multiculturalism has had four important consequences on immigrant political incorporation: (1) it legitimates immigrants' sense of being attached to both Canadian society and their homeland; (2) it provides resources to community organizations that, directly or indirectly, promote citizenship and participation; (3) it orients ethnic community leaders toward a language of inclusion centered on citizenship and allows them to make claims on the state when immigrants are not included; and (4) it has changed the symbolic landscape of Canadian public discourse so that other political actors, such as political parties, must make some accommodation for ethno-racial minorities.

Newcomer Settlement in the United States: Refugees Only

In discussions of American "exceptionalism," commentators often contend that Americans have a pronounced distaste and suspicion of interventionist government policies. As evidence, we could point out that the INS has not offered settlement assistance to newcomers in the post–World War II period, assuming that those granted permanent residence through employment preferences have the skills necessary to integrate while those sponsored by family members can turn to kin for help.[58] Unlike in Canada, where public grants fund services delivered by community-based organizations, the INS did not have legal authority to act as a grant-making agency under the terms set by Congress. To have done so, the INS would have had to ask Congress for a legislative change granting authority to disburse funds to community groups or it would have had to funnel grants through other structures of the Department of Justice, such as the Office of Justice Policy. Given Americans' political culture of antistatism, we might not find it particularly surprising that the United States failed to develop settlement and multiculturalism policies such as those found in Canada.

The problem with such an account is that it ignores the fact that the United States *has* developed settlement policies for certain migrants and that it clearly does pursue diversity policies, even if the country does not have an explicit federal multiculturalism program such as in Canada. The tenor and breadth of these policies differ, however, because they evolved from different logics: foreign policy considerations in the case of settlement assistance and struggles over civil rights in the case of diversity policy. Thus, the noninterventionist position of the INS stands in stark contrast to that of the Department of Health and Human Services, within which is housed the Office of Refugee Resettlement (ORR). In accordance with the special status of refugees, ORR is mandated to give public monies to public and private organizations that provide social services to refugees. In addition, the State Department, through its Bureau of Population, Refugees, and Migration (formerly the Bureau of Refugee Programs), also provides funds for refugee resettlement. Such funding, as well as ideological support for allied aliens, supports integration programs, facilitates the development of refugee organizations, and promotes a norm of inclusion.

Before 1945 the United States and Canada made no formal distinction between immigrants and refugees. Even as Europe was engulfed in humanitarian crises, from the Turkish persecution of Armenians to the horrors of the Holocaust, American and Canadian governments refused to enact special refugee provisions (Abella and Troper 1983; Zucker and Zucker 1992). It was only following World War II that both countries cautiously opened their doors to the hundreds of thousands of displaced persons in camps across Europe.

In the United States, refugee policy from 1945 to 1980 consisted of a series of ad hoc and disparate presidential directives, special legislative acts, and grants of parole status by the U.S. attorney general. Under the Immigration and Nationality Act of 1952, also known as the McCarren-Walter Act, the attorney general could grant "parole" status to certain individuals or groups, allowing them to enter the United States outside regular immigration quotas. Grants of parole quickly became an integral part of America's cold war foreign policy, handed out almost exclusively to those fleeing communist regimes. The attorney general first used the parole provision on a mass scale to admit Hungarian refugees in 1956 and then, starting in 1959, to let in Cubans fleeing the Castro regime (Zucker and Zucker 1992). It would also be used in 1975 to admit Vietnamese, Cambodians, and Laotians fleeing war and upheaval in Southeast Asia.

After many of the Cuban migrants settled in Miami, the city, county, and local voluntary agencies found themselves overwhelmed by settlement demands, from ensuring adequate accommodations and job training to providing education, health, and social services to the newcomers. Officials and politicians in southern Florida argued that since the federal government had allowed Cubans entry, federal dollars should pay for the cost of the influx. In response, Congress passed the Migration and Refugee Assistance Act of 1962, the first piece of federal legislation authorizing and financing a broad array of domestic assistance services to refugees in the United States.[59] The act, restricted to a single group and locality—Cubans in Miami—remained the sole program of domestic assistance to newcomers until 1975 (Holman 1996).

In 1975 war in Southeast Asia and the fall of Saigon precipitated the arrival of 130,000 new refugees and a new array of settlement policies and practices. Because the Indochinese refugee flow was largely unanticipated, the institutionalization of a bureaucracy and policy to handle refugees began as a piecemeal process. In April 1975 President Ford used $98 million in U.S. Agency for International Development money, initially targeted for postwar reconstruction in Indochina, to pay the Defense Department to transport and house the first wave of Vietnamese refugees (Hein 1993: 22). Ford then created the Interagency Task Force for Indochina Refugees (IATF) to operate four camps in the continental United States to house and resettle the new arrivals.

Oversight of settlement quickly moved from the domain of foreign policy to domestic social services. At the IATF's founding in 1975, an official from the State Department served as the director of the presidential task force, but direction of the IATF was soon transferred to Social and Rehabilitation Services, a branch of the Department of Health, Education, and Welfare (HEW) concerned with senior citizens, the handicapped, and Native Americans (Hein 1993). In 1977 it was again relocated, this time to the Office of Family Assistance in the Social Security Administration. In 1980 the new Office of Refugee Resettlement would be established in the Department of Health and Human Services.

Using the same authority and logic as had been used for Cuban refugees in 1962, Congress passed the Indochina Migration and Refugee Assistance Act in 1975. It established the Indochinese Refugee Assistance Program, or IRAP. IRAP gave states federal funds to provide medical assistance and financial support to needy refugees, and it paid for integration programs such as ESL and employment training.[60] The act also made refugees from Vietnam and Cambodia eligible for Supplemental Security Income, Medicaid, and welfare benefits from Aid to Families with Dependent Children under criteria more generous than those accorded to American citizens: refugees had to meet economic eligibility criteria, but they were exempted from family composition requirements.[61] The 1976 Indochinese Refugee Children Assistance Act reimbursed states for education and special language instruction costs. Unlike the Cuban Refugee Program, IRAP was national in focus. Reauthorized in 1977, the act continued the flow of federal monies to the states via compensation programs, it expanded some forms of assistance, and it made the refugees permanent residents.

As larger sums of federal monies were released and a new wave of Indochinese refugees began to arrive in 1979, the lack of a clear policy became apparent. In response to this and Congress's growing anger at White House circumvention of congressional power through the use of parole provisions, Congress passed the Refugee Act of 1980. The act sought to define who qualified for refugee status and it codified the settlement obligations of the federal government.[62] A special program separate from public welfare, Refugee Cash Assistance, made the federal government responsible for supporting refugees, thereby avoiding interstate differences in the provision of social benefits.[63] Other programs defrayed states' expenses for services such as provision of medical assistance and gave funds for community integration programs.

In addition to defining federal responsibilities, the act made clear that states needed to assume a significant role in the development, implementation, and administration of settlement programs. ORR established a disbursement policy that required state governments wanting access to federal funds to submit a refugee resettlement plan, designate a state agency to administer the plan, and appoint a state refugee coordinator. The existence of federal legislation and the enticement of federal funds were critical. In Massachusetts, "Between 1978–82, Massachusetts, under Governor Edward King, had no refugee policy or, more accurately, a policy of benign neglect. Refugees admitted to the state were the responsibility of VOLAGs [voluntary agencies] and their sponsors. The state served only as a conduit for federal refugee cash and medical assistance grants" (Pho 1991: 8). Over the course of the 1980s, amid political jockeying by pro- and anti-immigrant politicians and advocates, Massachusetts established the Office for Refugees and Immigrants, created the Governor's Refugee Advisory Council, continued its partnerships with established voluntary organizations, and promoted the development of ethno-specific refugee associations.[64] Federal action thus spurred the establishment of refugee services at lower levels of government.

As in Canada, government intervention also helped to develop an infrastructure of ethnic community organizations. Between 1945 and the 1962 Migration and Refugee Assistance Act, the U.S. government left settlement activities almost exclusively to private voluntary agencies. The arrival of Southeast Asian refugees in 1975 heralded the development of much more complex and mutually dependent public-private partnerships. Nearly 115,000 of the over 129,000 Vietnamese in the first refugee wave of 1975–76 were settled in the United States through one of nine established American voluntary agencies (VOLAGs).[65] The State Department provided these voluntary agencies with $500 for each refugee they helped to settle.[66] As policy evolved to encourage language instruction, employment training, job placement, and other such services, ORR and the states regularly turned to local nonprofit organizations to administer and run resettlement programs, financing activities through public-private contracts and grants.

Although the mainstream American voluntary agencies had prior experience with resettlement and many ordinary Americans and local churches worked hard to welcome the newcomers, it quickly became clear that the refugees needed local agencies that could provide linguistically and culturally sensitive support services.[67] The government therefore began promoting the development of coethnic Mutual Assistance Associations (MAAs). At first MAAs functioned as advisory bodies, but by 1976 the IATF established an Indochinese Mutual Assistance Division to help MAAs evolve into grant-receiving service providers. In its 1977 annual report to Congress, the newly established Refugee Task Force in the Department of Health, Education, and Welfare claimed that government officials were providing technical assistance to 138 Indochinese MAAs; in 1978 the number rose to 178. According to Bui (1980), 500 Southeast Asian MAAs were created across the United States between 1975 and 1980; of these, 340 associations catered to Vietnamese refugees.

When first established in 1976, the Indochinese Mutual Assistance Division offered only liaison services and technical assistance. In its 1976 report to Congress, the Refugee Task Force claimed that provision of direct financial assistance to MAAs would be "premature." Four years later, however, ORR began a formal policy of funding MAAs using competitive grants under the new MAA Incentive Grant Initiative. The grants, totaling $1.2 million in 1980 with a maximum allocation of $50,000 to any one group, were justified to Congress based on "the great importance and the historic appropriateness of refugees helping their newly arrived fellow countrymen" as well as the existence of unmet needs in various refugee communities (U.S. Office of Refugee Resettlement 1981: 13).[68] Organizations received funding for refugee orientation, information referral, vocational training, ESL instruction, and translation and interpretation services.

Hoping to encourage state and local support for MAAs, ORR also launched a program of incentive grants in 1982 that provided an extra $25,000 to $100,000 to states that allocated a portion of their refugee social service budgets to MAAs rather than traditional social service providers. These allocations were in addition to direct grants awarded to MAAs by the federal office. In its first year, ORR disbursed $791,462 to twelve states. The following year, incentive grants totaling $917,478 were given to fourteen states, including a first-time grant of $75,000 to Massachusetts. The federal Office of Refugee Resettlement had clearly moved to an interventionist stance in community building, arguing in its annual report, "Successful refugee resettlement . . . cannot be fully realized without the development and encouragement of effective refugee leadership and organization" (U.S. Office of Refugee Resettlement 1985: 114). Between 1982 and 1994, ORR allocated almost $30.5 million to state governments to promote the growth and participation of refugee associations in the resettlement process; of this amount, the state of Massachusetts received about $1.2 million.[69]

In place since 1980, federal settlement assistance to refugees provides hundreds of millions of dollars each year to states, individual refugees, and various nonprofit organizations. Since the mid-1980s, ORR's total annual allocations have fluctuated between about $350 million and $450 million.

The bulk of these funds go to social welfare costs such as Refugee Cash Assistance and medical expenses, but in any year ORR provides VOLAGs and local MAAs with tens of millions of dollars to help integrate refugee newcomers. For example, in 2000 and 2001, ORR disbursed $54 million and $61.5 million, respectively, to nonprofit groups under the Voluntary Agency Matching Grants program.

Three important consequences flow from U.S. refugee resettlement policy. First, the American federal government set in motion the development of a special refugee bureaucracy, not only within the federal government but also at the state level, creating multiple levels of government responsible for refugee resettlement. Second, it promoted the creation of a grassroots infrastructure through MAAs and other organizations receiving grants or contracts for refugee resettlement. Although the federal government determines eligibility for refugee programs, many of the actual settlement services are localized through cash transfers to lower levels of government and grants to third parties. Finally, unlike in Canada, services are exclusively for refugees and not available to ordinary immigrants. Not only does this provide differential resources to different communities, unequal government treatment has the potential to create distinctions, in the minds of newcomers and native-born Americans, over the relative standing and legitimacy of different immigrant groups.[70]

Canada also administers a refugee policy in addition to immigrant settlement and multiculturalism programs, and in some respects the evolution of Canadian refugee law parallels dynamics in the United States (Zolberg 1992). Canadian refugee policy became formalized four years earlier than in the United States with the passage of the 1976 Immigration Act.[71] The 1976 act recognized convention refugees, as defined by the United Nations Convention Relating to the Status of Refugees, and humanitarian refugees, a designation given by the cabinet to groups of displaced and persecuted persons who do not necessarily meet the stricter convention definition.[72] In January 1979 the cabinet used its power to designate a special Indochinese class of humanitarian refugees.

As in the United States, refugee resettlement involves private-public partnerships. The 1976 Immigration Act outlined sponsorship regulations under which a group of five or more Canadian citizens or an incorporated body such as a voluntary agency could sponsor a refugee and dependents by providing lodging, maintenance, and resettlement assistance for one year. In the case of Indochinese refugees, the federal government agreed to admit fifty thousand Indochinese over 1979–81 following strong public pressure to help the "boat people." Half would come under private sponsorship provisions, the other half under government support. When offers for private sponsorship surpassed expectation, totaling forty thousand, the government agreed to increase the two-year quota to sixty thousand, with the remaining twenty thousand supported by the government.

Government sponsorship was handled through Employment and Immigration Canada by a special refugee task force created for the purpose. Language training was available to those destined for the job market, and refugees were eligible for up to one year of government income support. While some of the resettlement services were offered directly by government, others, such as language training, were contracted out to local organizations.[73] Today, the Resettlement Assistance Program offers very similar support to convention and humanitarian refugees for the first year in Canada, while the Interim Federal Health Program provides health insurance coverage until individuals are eligible for provincial health care plans. In many respects, these programs parallel efforts in the United States.

However, while the American approach to refugees often envisages these individuals as needing temporary asylum and then repatriation, Canada has largely viewed refugees as permanent immigrants with special needs. Thus, once accepted as refugees, individuals can quickly gain permanent residence and access general settlement programs.[74] This facilitates a citizenship discourse for displaced persons who become permanent residents. Further, although Canadian policy has been sensitive to foreign policy concerns, it has been less dominated by them—and by a concern with communism— than United States policy.[75] Lacking America's status as a great power, Canada began to forge an international identity in the 1960s and 1970s as a country committed to humanitarianism and multilateralism through structures such as the United Nations. The nation-building dynamics that inform the evolution of Canadian multiculturalism also play a role in the evolution of contemporary Canadian refugee policy.

Race-Based Multiculturalism and Poverty Programs in the United States

In the next chapter I show that Americans are much like Canadians in their acceptance of social and cultural multiculturalism. Whatever the past reality of the American "melting pot," most of the immigrants with whom I spoke feel that they can continue cultural and religious practices from their homeland and still be accepted as Americans. In this way, the ideology of the Canadian multicultural mosaic differs little from the American metaphor of the salad bowl. In both countries immigrants may retain distinctive ways while also contributing to a new whole.

In contrast, *political* multiculturalism in the United States differs in important and consequential ways from Canadian government policy. Although there is no single "official" U.S. multiculturalism, contemporary America embraces a version of political multiculturalism that centers on racial categories. Socially, immigrants and their descendants can talk about being Vietnamese American or Portuguese American, but in the political and policy arenas individuals from these communities are understood as Asian or white. As Judith Shklar (1991) has noted, one cannot understand U.S. citizenship without taking into account the legacy of slavery and the concomitant sense of hierarchy and standing in American society that is predicated on race.[76] Much of this legacy centers on the black-white color line, a racial divide used into the 1960s to ensure government-supported second-class citizenship for African Americans. The black-white color line fundamentally shapes immigrant incorporation dynamics.[77]

It is important to remember that today's government-approved categorization of ethno-racial groups—white, black, Asian, Native American, native Hawaiian/Pacific Islander, and Hispanic/Latino—is a recent construct rooted in the African American civil rights movement of the 1950s and '60s.[78] Black Americans' mobilization produced a fundamental shift as federal and state laws moved from the exclusion of nonwhites to practices of inclusion based on minority status. Important milestones include the Civil Rights Act of 1964, the Voting Rights Act of 1965, the Fair Housing Act of 1968, the Equal Credit Opportunity Act of 1974, and the Home Mortgage Disclosure Act of 1975 as well as the development of equal opportunity measures and affirmative action programs.

When the Voting Rights Act, passed by Congress in 1965 to assure African Americans' access to the ballot box, was renewed in 1970 and again in 1975, the second renewal extended its guarantees to linguistic minorities. Similar extensions occurred for other laws and programs. The extension of minority status occurred in an ad hoc process, based on past administrative practices, the need to count groups for civil rights legislation, and incremental program expansion by federal bureaucrats (Skrentny 2002; Graham 2002). The expanding set of minority legislation then became a part of the interests and discourse of new social movements dedicated to native rights, Chicano rights, and Asian American rights. These groups were inspired by the black civil rights movement and motivated by their own historic mistreatment and grievances. Discourses of redress, framed in the language of civil rights, overshadowed the reality that new immigration laws were allowing in tens of thousands of nonwhite newcomers. These people had not suffered discrimination in the United States like native-born minorities, but

they faced unique barriers to participation in American society based on foreign birth. Race played a role in these barriers, but only in part.

The dynamics of this process of race-based multiculturalism can be seen
in the evolution of minority group classification. Government agencies
quickly realized that they needed clear and consistent definitions for minority groups. In 1974 the Federal Interagency Committee on Education created
the Ad Hoc Committee on Racial and Ethnic Definitions to develop such
definitions. Its report, released the following year, would serve as a basis
for the eventual administrative-wide statistical standards, known as Directive 15, imposed in 1978 by the U.S. Office of Management and Budget
(Edmonston, Goldstein, and Tamayo Lott 1996: 7). Between 1975 and 1978,
groups jockeyed to be included in or excluded from the minority designation. Congress passed Public Law 94–311 in 1976, requiring various federal
departments to collect economic and social statistics on the status of
Hispanics. In defining the Hispanic category, government officials decided to
include those from Spain—people who speak Spanish but normally would
be considered akin to other white European ethnic groups—and to include
people with origins in Spanish-speaking countries who no longer speak
Spanish, such as third-generation Mexican Americans. Congress *excluded*
individuals who speak Portuguese—such as those from Brazil, Cape Verde,
and Portugal—despite strong cultural and socioeconomic similarities to the
Hispanic population.[79] Persons with origins in the Indian subcontinent were
reclassified from the white category to the Asian/Pacific Islander category
(Edmonston, Goldstein, and Tamayo Lott 1996: 7).

These political, administrative, and bureaucratic decisions about minority status show the social construction of ethno-racial categories. More
important for immigrants, by classifying minorities into racial categories
and considering this to be the central way of understanding inclusion and
incorporation, the United States failed to develop specific policies around
immigrant integration outside race-based multiculturalism. Consider the
Voting Rights Act. "Linguistic minorities" are guaranteed access to ballots,
instructions, and voter information pamphlets written in their own language as well as to multilingual poll workers if a political jurisdiction contains ten thousand people or 5 percent of the population who speak a language other than English and report limited English competency as
measured by the census.[80] This provision should provide a resource for any
large immigrant community speaking the same language. However, the act
limits its coverage to "persons who are American Indian, Asian American,
Alaskan Natives, or of Spanish heritage."[81] In Massachusetts, where the
Portuguese constitute the largest foreign-born group in the state and where

we also find significant Brazilian populations, the cities of Lawrence, Holyoke, Springfield, Boston, and Chelsea had to provide Spanish-language services to electors during the 1990s, but Portuguese speakers received no special assistance.[82]

U.S. governments have occasionally used preexisting funding and bureaucratic structures, aimed at native-born minority populations, to deal with immigrant integration problems. For example, ORR initiated joint projects under the Small Business Administration's 7(j) program, aimed at "socially and economically disadvantaged small businesses in order to overcome historic flaws in the free enterprise system," to help refugee newcomers, and it was able to secure slots in Job Corps for refugees (Hein 1993: 67). Refugees and immigrants become recast as racial minorities within government programs.

Federal, state, and municipal social service and community development programs can also provide resources to immigrant communities through regular grants and contracts.[83] For example, the most significant Portuguese organization in the greater Boston area, the Massachusetts Association of Portuguese Speakers (MAPS), got its start with monies disbursed under Lyndon Johnson's Great Society and War against Poverty campaigns. More recently, younger Vietnamese Americans in Boston established Viet-AID, the only Vietnamese community development corporation in the country, in part through the use of government urban development monies, funds that also find their origins in the Great Society wave of government intervention. Lacking an established immigrant settlement or integration policy, newcomer communities in the United States have tapped alternative resources to help build an organizational infrastructure and to provide certain services to their members. Given, however, that the American welfare state is less developed than the Canadian one, there are relatively fewer opportunities for public-private partnerships.

These programs also do not serve exactly the same function as settlement and multiculturalism policies in Canada. Two important caveats are in order. First, these programs were not created with immigrants in mind. Naturalization, for example, is rarely a priority since it is assumed funds will be going to Americans. Second, in many cases the fight against poverty has become synonymous with helping disadvantaged racial minorities.[84] Newcomers are consequently viewed as racial minorities or urban poor, not as individuals who must adjust to a new social, economic, and political environment.

More detailed analysis of the roots of contemporary Canadian and American settlement and diversity policies lies outside the scope of this book. Here the focus is on the consequences of such policies. We can nonetheless high-light certain dynamics privileging greater intervention in Canada. First, con-temporary Canadian governments have more strongly identified immigra-tion as an important foundation for state building. Declining birthrates, fears over the ability to pay public benefits to an aging population, and a large landmass create the perception among policy makers that immigration is important to Canada's future. In a way, this favorable bias toward immi-gration recalls American thinking in the nineteenth century. In contempo-rary times, however, U.S. policy makers stand divided over the wisdom of large-scale immigration. A large population, steadier birthrate, and a strong link in the public mind between immigrants and illegal migration dampens enthusiasm for the type of mass migration the United States witnessed in the early twentieth century. It is probably not surprising that a country with a greater interest in immigration will welcome newcomers more than one that is ambivalent.

Second, Canadian governments, especially the federal government, seek to encourage unity and pride in Canadian citizenship as an antidote to Quebec nationalism. Immigration consequently feeds into nation building. Official multiculturalism arose, in part, due to the lobbying efforts of non-British and non-French groups, but a strong argument can be made that politicians' attraction to multiculturalism also lies in its ability to defuse claims of Quebec's special character. By celebrating all ethnic and cultural backgrounds, French Canadians become one among many. Since Canada's central ethno-racial conflict has historically been defined in ethnic terms, that is, around Quebecers' unique culture and language, it is relatively easy to celebrate other cultures and languages. Multiculturalism—which Trudeau largely ignored after he introduced it—was embraced by immi-grants as a meaningful new way of conceiving Canada and adopted by many native-born Canadians who wished to move away from an identity as British subjects. Once embraced, future governments found it difficult to ignore.

In the United States, the central ethno-racial issue has been defined as black-white relations: the forced migration of African slaves and the subse-quent treatment of their descendants. Given that those who arrive in the United States after 1965 tend to be nonwhite, it is not surprising that the language of race infuses discussions of immigration. However, voluntary immigration and integration are fundamentally different from the chal-lenges that stem from the legacy of slavery and second-class citizenship of African Americans. Rather than placing it into a civil rights framework, immigrant incorporation could be cast as an extension of America's immigrant past. Why do activists in the United States adopt the language of race instead of hyphenated Americanism?

A large part of the answer appears to lie in a final factor affecting newcomer settlement policy: the relative development of a country's welfare state. Since the 1960s, the provision of public benefits in the United States is more restricted than in Canada. Limited benefits, especially those that are means tested rather than universal, give rise to the perception that more for one person—such as an immigrant—entails less for others. The black civil rights movement—and the parallel movements spawned around native rights, Chicano rights, and Asian American rights—revealed fundamental problems with the myth of American social unity. These upheavals forced government response. Since the primary cleavage centered on race, remedial policies such as the Voting Rights Act, antidiscrimination measures, and affirmative action programs attempted to redress problems using categories of race. In many cases, these remedies were imposed—on southern states, government contractors, public and private institutions—using the federal government's legal and coercive apparatus. Immigrants can take advantage of these policies and programs, but when they do, the helping hand of the U.S. government is extended on the basis of race, not citizenship or membership in a common enterprise. These dynamics can be seen in the ways Portuguese and Vietnamese migrants talk about citizenship and belonging, the subject of the following chapter.

4. The Meaning of Citizenship

I don't see America as a melting pot. No. And that racism and
discrimination will be there until the end of time. . . . We can
only go to a certain level. If we become too strong, we [will]
be eliminated. Look at Martin Luther King. Look at Chavez.

MOC VAN, *Vietnamese American, Boston*

The melting pot is, yes, good . . . for some people with a certain
degree of integration. But for the rest—you are just garbage.
Here [in Canada] we try to provide an opportunity for everybody.
It doesn't matter whether you have a language ability or you do
not have a language ability. You, as a person, you have the right
to live, you have the right to access, to service, to government.

HAI, *Vietnamese Canadian, Toronto*

Moc Van, who lives in Boston, and Hai, who lives in Toronto, both dismiss
the melting pot metaphor as an unrealistic description and inappropriate
prescription for managing diversity in the United States and Canada. The
tone of their comments, however, differs. Moc Van, reflecting the dominant
multicultural discourse in the United States, views the problem of intergroup relations through the lens of race. The Vietnamese experience—one
largely of refugee flows since 1975—is compared to struggles by African
Americans and Latino farm workers. Hai, reflecting Canada's version of
multiculturalism, describes barriers based on cultural markers such as language, an obstacle of particular concern to foreign arrivals. Moc Van's
assessment of the future, including his assessment of American society and
government's ability to resolve problems of diversity, is bleak. He and people like him are kept down. Hai sounds more optimistic. He sees opportunity in Canada, and government figures as part of the solution. Citizenship
holds out greater possibilities for Hai than for Moc Van.

Moc Van's tone is more bellicose than many Vietnamese Americans, but
he clearly expresses a widespread sense of American citizenship infused
with racialized understandings of group relations and limited trust in government's ability to solve problems. Hai reflects many Vietnamese Canadians' sense of their own ethnic distinctiveness and most immigrants' belief
that although imperfect, Canadian governments care about newcomers.

These understandings of citizenship derive in part from the bureaucratic practices, policies, and programs examined in the previous chapter. Policy and practice carry symbolic repercussions. They shape the meaning of citizenship for immigrants and their fellow citizens.[1]

Before migrating, most Portuguese and Vietnamese had limited experience with the breadth of ethno-racial diversity found in North America. Vietnamese from cities such as Saigon might have had some contact with the Chinese minority there or have seen American soldiers; those in Portugal might remember the government's attempts to incorporate its African colonies within a common Lusophone space. By and large, however, these people arrive from relatively homogenous societies. As immigrants in North America, they must develop an understanding of their place in a new society and an account of how "Canadians" or "Americans" are produced from so much diversity.

This chapter shows how national beliefs about diversity and the appropriateness of political intervention structure immigrants' conception of their interests and their identities. There are two elements to the symbolic meaning of citizenship: public versus private recognition of diversity, including the categories used to describe ethno-racial diversity; and the extent to which government intervenes to legitimize and help migrant newcomers. Public ideologies act as cognitive maps or moral schemas, signaling the relative standing of particular groups or individuals.[2] Immigrants look for signs of government's openness to outsiders like themselves. Government policies, especially those directed at newcomers, become symbols of how much the state cares about its citizens. Perceptions of government concern encourage political involvement and interest. Much in the way that social movement scholars talk about framing strategies, public discourses, embedded in multicultural policies and settlement programs, also provide symbolic resources that immigrant communities can use to make claims on government or fellow citizens.[3]

DEALING WITH DIVERSITY: THE MOSAIC AND THE MELTING POT

Canadians like to contrast their own perceived multicultural "mosaic" to the American "melting pot." These contrasting images imply that in Canada, immigrants and their descendants can retain their unique ethnic heritage and simultaneously contribute to the Canadian whole, like a multitude of distinct tiles that create a mosaic. Immigrants in the United States may contribute some customs to an evolving "American" way, but they must largely abandon former identities and traditions. According to Canadians, the United States demands one-way assimilation into a patriotic, single national identity while Canada welcomes diversity within its nationalist vision.

Many Canadians celebrate multiculturalism as superior, marking a distinctly "Canadian" approach to managing ethno-racial diversity. Even immigrants absorb this conventional Canadian wisdom. Cong, a Vietnamese Canadian businessman, explained, "when you go to the U.S., you forget about your background. But here, we still maintain some." Canadian Heritage, the department responsible for the federal multiculturalism program, proudly noted in its 1999–2000 annual report that multiculturalism comes second only to health care as a policy that Canadians name to distinguish their country from the United States (Multiculturalism Program 2001: 3).[4] Overwhelming majorities, between three-quarters to four-fifths of Canadians, believe that multiculturalism is a source of national pride and a cornerstone of Canadian culture (Jedwab 2005).

Despite their popularity, the mosaic and melting pot metaphors obscure multicultural realities in the two countries more than they illuminate them. Cultural and social pluralism are largely accepted on both sides of the Canada-U.S. border. Immigrants in both countries believe that fellow residents accept diversity. Most newcomers welcome this recognition. Indeed, many list tolerance for diversity, in Canada or in the United States, as one of the great things about their new home.

The political variants of multiculturalism differ, however. The first consequential difference lies in the official categorization of diversity. The Canadian version of public multiculturalism tends to legitimize small ethnic groups, usually defined by country of origin (e.g., Portuguese Canadian, Vietnamese Canadian). In the United States, these groups are categorized into broader ethno-racial classifications (e.g., white, Asian American, Latino/Hispanic).[5] The U.S. government adopts no formal policy on immigrant diversity, but a patchwork of civil rights legislation and minority policies provide immigrant groups with a strong incentive to redefine themselves in racial terms.[6] In Canada, multiculturalism's origins in ethnic, cultural, and linguistic categorizations persist to the present. While Canadian multiculturalism programming since the 1980s increasingly focuses on race-based barriers to inclusion, race is conceived differently: government officials speak, somewhat awkwardly, of *visible minorities*, putting all nonwhite residents in one group but refusing to use *white* and *nonwhite* labels.

Canadian multiculturalism makes it somewhat harder to address racial barriers to integration, but for first-generation immigrants, the symbolism of a multicultural mosaic is more attractive and fits well with how most immigrants, in Canada and the United States, understand their group's specificity. Regardless of whether a migrant comes for political, economic, or family reasons, many of the first generation feel a tug between the land they left and the one in which they reside. Language, culture, and memories of home lead most to embrace multiple identities. Because citizenship in North America provides not just legal status and political rights but also a national identity, most immigrants appreciate recognition of their multiple ties: they are American *and* Vietnamese, Canadian *and* Portuguese. One Vietnamese senior in Toronto explained approvingly, "here the people from the minority groups can keep their own traditions, respect cultures like ours, like we can have the Gio To Hung Vuong [First King, Hai ba Trung ceremony] every year and organize that. The Muslim people can celebrate their religion." In making distinctions between themselves and others, many immigrants point to language and cultural traditions, an understanding of diversity that is primarily "ethnic." One is Vietnamese, not simply Asian; one is Portuguese, not just part of the white mainstream.

Ethnic rather than race-based multiculturalism is also perceived as providing a better starting point for inclusive citizenship and intergroup dialogue than the more prevalent zero-sum framework of race relations in the United States. As Joppke suggests, "Race is different. Its content is not a positive heritage (however modified) transplanted into the new society, but the negative experience of oppression at the hands of the receiving society. Its direction is not integration into a (white) majority . . . but restitution for harm and public existence as a protected, separate group" (1999: 143). Canadian multiculturalism appears to foster political integration more than the American variant.[7]

The Canadian Melting Pot?

Canadians underestimate contemporary Americans' tolerance for cultural diversity and overestimate their own support for substantive multiculturalism. In some ways the integrationist thrust of government-sponsored multiculturalism means that Canadians embrace more of a "melting pot" approach to ethno-racial diversity than Americans. Canadian multicultural policy legitimizes and promotes symbolic ethnicity while also pushing for immigrants' incorporation into the social, economic, and political fabric of Canadian society. This project has more similarities with old-fashion assimilation than many Canadians might be ready to admit.

Multiculturalism is different from assimilation in that immigrants in Canada are not asked to give up prior identities or cultural practices. Indeed, cultural heritages are given symbolic legitimacy and some public support under official multiculturalism. Two of the policy's original four goals—supporting ethnic organizations and promoting intercultural dialogue—provide resources for cultural retention and public education efforts. Most immigrants and community leaders endorse these policy goals. One Portuguese Canadian woman explained, "What [multiculturalism] means to me is different nations of people, all types of people gathered. And we do have something here in Toronto in the summertime—it's organized by the Portuguese program. And then you have the Spanish, Chinese, Polish. They do all this in the park and they have all kinds of people going in there and you meet a lot of people from different nations and different countries. And they tell what they do in that country, what we do differently." Recognition of difference becomes part of a campaign to foster interethnic tolerance and understanding.

Multiculturalism policy does not, however, provide ethnic minorities with the structural and institutional resources necessary to sustain autonomous communities, a "stricter" version of multiculturalism that would permit more durable group-based pluralism (Kallen 1982; Li 1999). Children of immigrants can take "heritage language" classes to learn their parents' language—a program initially funded by the federal government and now supported by local governments and school boards—but such classes usually take place on weekends or after school; they are not integrated into the public curriculum. Governments largely expect immigrant children to attend Canadian public schools rather than separate "ethnic" schools.[8]

Indeed, integration features prominently in Canadian multiculturalism. The other two policy goals outlined in the 1971 pronouncement on multiculturalism direct government to eliminate barriers to participation and offer language assistance to newcomers. Subsequent evolution of the program has reinforced the integrationist thrust, first by shifting focus to barriers impeding participation by racial minorities and, since the mid-1990s, by increasingly promoting the language of Canadian citizenship. In 2005 Canadian minister of state for multiculturalism Raymond Chan challenged the idea that the simultaneous promotion of integration and diversity is paradoxical by appealing to common citizenship: "Ideally, we want to get to the point I think where multiculturalism is associated with our shared interests, as Canadians, in institutional inclusion and equality of opportunity. The idea is that we need to be able to respect diversity and at the same time recognize one another as equal citizens" (2005: 3).

In this context ethnicity becomes primarily symbolic since its content is largely made up of affective identities, private practices, and a voluntary choice of which markers of ethnicity will be retained or displayed. Originally applied to third-generation and later descendants of European immigrants in the United States, the concept of symbolic ethnicity can be extended to non-European immigrants in Canada.[9] Under Canadian multiculturalism, newcomers and their children are free to celebrate their ethnic foods, maintain separate languages in the home, practice their religion, and establish ethnic-specific community organizations. These activities are legitimated by official government discourse. They are also largely relegated to the private sphere, albeit supported with some public funding.

Immigrants have largely internalized this understanding of multiculturalism as symbolic ethnicity within common Canadian citizenship. Asked about multiculturalism, one Vietnamese Canadian responded, "It is good that people can promote and demonstrate their cultures. I saw the Caribbean festival [in Toronto] and it is very interesting." Discussing her support of multiculturalism, a Portuguese Canadian woman explained: "I think we're all better for it. It opens up other people to see the diversity of other people, and the culture. And I think that these people bring quite a bit with them, customs, foods. [A] big attraction is foods. People go for Thai food, or 'Where do you want to eat tonight? Chinese? Or do you want to eat Italian?' And that opens up your horizons; it opens up your mind to other cultures, and you don't become so . . . narrow-minded." In these accounts, public celebration of pluralism and diversity denotes cultural tastes such as food and dance.

Indeed, Canadians, native born and foreign born, express ambivalence about the degree to which newcomers' should continue to hold and act on values or traditions found in their homeland. A 1991 survey commissioned by the Department of Multiculturalism and Citizenship found that 76 percent of respondents supported recognition of cultural and racial diversity as a fundamental characteristic of Canadian society, but at the same time, 46 percent agreed that "People who come to Canada should change their behavior to be more like us," a level of opinion relatively constant since 1974 (Li 1999: 162; Reitz and Breton 1994: 36).

The most frequent drawback to multiculturalism mentioned by my Toronto respondents was a concern over immigrants' failure to integrate into mainstream society. Tom, a Vietnamese Canadian who has lived in Canada about a dozen years, feels that multiculturalism mainly benefits those unable to adapt. According to him, "multiculturalism doesn't make much of a difference. It is good for some people, those who don't want to integrate. There are some small funds. You see, there are some people who were important, had high status, back [in Vietnam]. They come here and they have nothing; they are not important. So, these people get some money and they can have an office." Similarly, Mario, born in mainland Portugal, calls the policy "a coin with two faces." On one hand, Portuguese seniors benefit from having services in Portuguese, going to their clubs, or being able to get their news in Portuguese since, according to Mario, their age prevents them from integrating. However, for others: "Once they are supported, they don't have the incentive to break and say, 'I am going out there.' And live and learn more with others. So they feel very comfortable, they are subsidized in many areas, and they use this for their own benefits instead of using them to develop their skills, their culture. Instead of getting involved with the Canadian society, the Canadian culture. They isolate themselves. . . . It becomes, I'd say, a little bit selfish." Many immigrants support a certain assimilatory trajectory as they become "hyphenated" Canadians.

Multicultural ambivalence—respecting diversity but within limits— arose in a number of interviews. Tilla, a Portuguese Canadian in her late fifties, explained that she liked multiculturalism, "Because it's rich. . . . We have a chance, like perhaps I never have this chance in Portugal, to communicate with lots of people all over the world." Yet she also worried:

> You have a chance to come in here, like everybody has, you should involve yourself in this country. Politics, language, and the really Canadian style. Like, I'm going to give you two examples. You come from Iran, you cover yourself. I come from Portugal, perhaps I like to wear something [of] my customs to work. I not agree with that. I am Portuguese. I wear this in Portugal. I wear this at my house. But as soon as I go to work, I should behave like I—how can I explain? I have to dress like the majority. I have to be involved [in] what it is in this country.

Thuy, who arrived in Canada from Vietnam in the late 1970s, shares such concerns. She also calls Canadian multiculturalism "rich," but she says, "I also think sometimes, because of different backgrounds, and sometimes some nationalities, some nations, bring their own preconceived values into Canada. . . . And some of their ideas, they want to proselytize the government to change from what already exists. I'm not sure whether that's healthy. So yeah, I feel that is a danger of multicultural country." These women suggest that multiculturalism works best with some assimilation into dominant Canadian norms.

The ability to integrate is not just a function of newcomers' practices but also outsiders' perceptions. Choosing mainstream practices does not guarantee acceptance. Because phenotype makes non-European immigrants more obviously different from white Canadians, they can experience prejudice at the hands of others. Multiculturalism, in celebrating symbolic ethnicity, promotes acceptance of difference and a certain level of intergroup tolerance, but it deals poorly with race-based barriers to equal participation.[10] Thus Mai, a Vietnamese senior, expressed doubts about the policy of multiculturalism, "I think it's okay. I respect everybody, but I'm not sure they do." The landlord of her seniors' residence had organized a multicultural party where all the residents were asked to share food and drinks from their homeland, "But then they [non-Asians] don't share theirs with us. So we learned our lesson, we don't share drinks with them anymore. Not the Asian people, they share, but people from other countries [don't]."

Almost every immigrant or refugee I interviewed in Toronto failed to associate multiculturalism with a concerted policy of antiracism, despite governments' efforts to recast the program as one targeting racial inequality. Multiculturalism preaches tolerance, so being Canadian includes acceptance of fellow citizens regardless of phenotype, but the policy and program of multiculturalism continues to be viewed as largely about culture and language.[11] This implies a certain failure of "new" Canadian multiculturalism.

Canadians, including those born in Portugal and Vietnam, assume that certain groups integrate more easily into the "Canadian way" than others. Interestingly, although race was regularly brought up as a barrier, doubts about integration centered most on religion, especially the ability of Muslims to become Canadian. These opinions, expressed before the terrorist attacks of September 11, 2001, and the wars in Afghanistan and Iraq, are probably even more salient today. Vietnamese Canadians, despite being phenotypically different, perceive that their values are within the realm of mainstream Canada since they are Catholic, Buddhist, or another "acceptable" religion. Antidiscrimination policies in Canada and the United States have a strong focus on race, given historic injustices and contemporary prejudice based on phenotype. Future efforts need to also take seriously prejudice and discrimination based on religion.

The American Mosaic and Race-Based Multiculturalism

If Canadian residents, including immigrants, exaggerate their support for substantive multiculturalism, they also misunderstand Americans' attitudes toward cultural diversity. The available empirical data challenge the notion that Canadians' support for multiculturalism eclipses that of Americans. A 1989 cross-national survey found that 47 percent of Americans favored cultural retention, but only 34 percent of Canadians felt the same way, a difference that persists across almost all demographic subgroups (Reitz and Breton 1994: 27–32).[12] Many immigrants to the United States share with Canadian newcomers a sense that mainstream society accepts their cultural background and that it is possible to be American and ethnic at the same time. Assimilation might have been the mantra of the Americanization movement of the early twentieth century, but at the dawn of the twenty-first century the United States embraces its own form of multiculturalism, born out of the African American civil rights movement, extended by activists from the Latino, Asian American, and Native American communities, and supported to a degree by ethnic "revival" among European Americans. In the words of one celebrated proponent of America's assimilatory impulse, "We are all multiculturalists now" (Glazer 1997).

The effects of these changes can be seen in my interviews. A few older Portuguese Americans recount harrowing experiences with forced assimilation, but none of the Vietnamese newcomers share such stories.[13]

The Portuguese who have lived in the United States the longest often remember pressures to conform to American ways. Joe, who arrived in the United States as an adolescent during World War II, quickly dropped out of school, in part because he was given a "hard time" as a foreigner. Five years later he became a U.S. citizen, in his words, "Because I became Americanized, one of the boys." Ilda, who also migrated to the United States as an adolescent, remembers similar problems in the early 1960s. She attended summer school to learn English, but despite a "wonderful teacher," she entered eighth grade with limited comprehension. Her new teacher made no accommodation and instead criticized her work. He found her method for doing long division, a technique different from what he taught the class, a particular annoyance. This seemingly minor difference had major repercussions: "I was doing division the Portuguese way, not the American way, and he caught me. He started yelling at me, in front of the whole class, saying I had to do division 'the American way.' He made me come up to the blackboard and do it again, and—[Ilda breaks off, crying.] I had to stay after class, and after that, I went home crying. I told my parents I wouldn't go back. They weren't happy, but they didn't make me, and I never went back." The incident so marked the young woman that five years later, when she worked up the courage to take the test for a high school equivalency diploma, she was unable to finish when confronted by a question requiring long division and fled the exam room. Ilda never returned to school and never achieved her dream of becoming a nurse.[14]

The Vietnamese Americans I interviewed—all of whom arrived since 1975—expressed very different perceptions of immigrants' need to assimilate. When asked specifically about the idea of a melting pot, a few Vietnamese in Boston had never heard of the term. Among respondents who expressed vague familiarity with the phrase, a number voiced confusion between the theory and what they saw around them. For ordinary Vietnamese, the social reality of their neighborhoods, workplaces, and schools makes a homogeneous melting pot unthinkable. This seemed the case for Thien, who had lived in the United States for about ten years:

I: *Have you heard of the words "the melting pot"?*
T: Yes, I heard that many people from many countries are living in the U.S. I didn't know what it meant. I heard it a long time ago from many people so I don't remember when I heard it.

I: *What do the words mean to you?*
T: I don't know what to think. I see that there are many different cultures living in the U.S. There are Chinese people, Spanish, whites, and blacks.

Given the disjunction between the idea of the melting pot and what they experience, some Vietnamese agreed with the melting pot metaphor as a description of American society but then reinterpret the phrase until it resembles the idea of a multicultural mosaic. According to Yen, "I think there's a part melting pot. Everybody comes here; they become a member of the society. They then enrich the society with their own culture. I think that is the melting pot. They may become one, and also they have their own distinguished culture." The resulting "multicultural melting pot" strongly resembles the vision offered by immigrants in Canada.

Others rejected the idea of a melting pot outright, explicitly preferring multiculturalism or an alternative metaphor. This was the case for Lap:

I: *Sometimes people say that the U.S. is a melting pot. What do you think about that?*
L: I don't think it melts at all. It's more like a salad bowl.

I: *Why do you say that?*
L: I think, like the Chinese, they still have—even if they live here [many years]—they still keep their culture. . . . And the same thing, with the Portuguese people. . . . They still have their own group, and they live together.

Likewise, Buu explained, "When I first came to America, I think so [that the United States is a melting pot]. But later, I changed my mind. [The] U.S. is not a melting pot. . . . Each community should be separate, should keep their identity. . . . They have their own traditions, different way of thinking."

Buu did not offer an alternative description of American society, but among those who had heard of the term *multiculturalism*, almost all preferred it. I asked Luan what it is like for an immigrant to live in the United States. She responded:

> I will share with you my dream. My dream is to marry someone and have kids and teach my kids to learn my own language first. And having them learning English because they [are] born here. Now why I'm saying that? Because to me, America is the picture of multiculture, multi-languages. . . . As long as we have many different cultures, many different languages, we make the country richer. Not like my country. We only speak one language. . . . Here we have more chance that a lot of people will speak different languages and [have a] different perspective.

The picture Luan paints is similar to how Thuy describes multiculturalism in Canada, "people of different nationalities who come to Canada to have their lives and try to get along. English is the vehicle for us to communicate among one another. But we keep our own heritage. So that diversity [is] in our society." From the perspective of these Vietnamese migrants, Americans and Canadians tolerate cultural diversity in a similar way.

Sometimes perceptions of America's tolerance for diversity are used to make a case for legal citizenship. Joe, the Portuguese American who came to the United States during World War II, naturalized because he became "Americanized." In contrast, Vietnamese American Moc Van tells newcomers: "I explain to my countrymen, I say, 'If you apply for U.S. citizenship, you are not a traitor. Why? Because the U.S. is a nation of nations. There are Italians here, there are Dutch, Irish, you name it. And everybody belongs some place else.' It's like everybody has a dual citizenship." Similarly, Tong, a former political detainee in Vietnam who is currently in the process of acquiring U.S. citizenship, believes he is expanding his identity by naturalizing, rather than being asked to give something up: "I want to be an American citizen, but I would like to retain my culture. The United States is like the world. There are so many different people here and the people can retain their Vietnamese culture or their Puerto Rican culture. So that we can maintain our culture but are still American."[15] In this way, the everyday availability of "hyphenated" Americanism provides an opening to participatory citizenship.

At the same time, *public* discussions of multiculturalism in the United States subordinate cultural and linguistic differences in favor of pan-racial categories that stand at odds with immigrants' self-understanding. When I asked Vietnamese in both countries about their affinity with other Asian groups, such as the Chinese, many stressed a lack of any "natural" link. As one person explained, "back in 1979 the Chinese tried to 'teach' [the] Vietnamese a lesson, you know? And, it's funny enough, in lots of Chinese people's mind, in their brain, Vietnam is just a piece of land of China." Most Vietnamese beg to differ, adamantly. In accordance with emerging survey research on Asian Americans' identity, I found that few ordinary Vietnamese considered *Asian American* an important or appealing way to understand their membership in American society. Vietnamese immigrants feel a slight affinity to certain East Asian groups through a shared high regard for education or for children's respect of elders, but definitions of community are overwhelmingly about being Vietnamese.[16] Many ordinary Vietnamese find pan-racial categories alienating rather than a basis for common American citizenship.

In contrast to first-generation Vietnamese Americans, some younger community activists embrace race-based multiculturalism as a salient political tool and as a way of understanding American society. Community leaders quickly find that culturally defined hyphenated Americanism carries limited political salience, given the lack of a specific discourse to deal with immigrant-generated diversity.[17] Unlike ordinary Vietnamese, activists were less likely to reinterpret the metaphor of the melting pot to mean cultural diversity and interethnic tolerance. Instead, various advocates considered the melting pot a racist ideology. Moc Van told me emphatically, "I don't see America as a melting pot. No. And that racism and discrimination will be there until the end of time. . . . We can only go to a certain level. If we become too strong, we [will] be eliminated. Look at Martin Luther King. Look at Chavez. . . . The Congress is very racist because during the '90's the color of immigration has changed completely." While Moc Van describes America as a place of "dual citizenship" when it comes to identity, culture, and legal standing, he associates political citizenship primarily with the Caucasian native born.

Another Vietnamese American, a young woman who moved to the United States when she was nine, offered a similar analysis, one that led her to reject the rhetoric of symbolic ethnicity and intercultural tolerance: "You know, it doesn't matter if the majority of this country are people of color . . . because the critical issue is who's in power. . . . It doesn't matter if people say, 'Well the diversity is here. The cultural background is rich.' You know that rhetoric? But if you don't have [a] system that changes to be equal to all residents, white people and people of color, then that's institutional racism."

Almost all Vietnamese Americans who hold a strong racialized understanding of American diversity began to develop such an outlook while attending a U.S. institution of higher education, either as a young adult or as a midcareer student. For example, Khoi found that his views of ethno-racial relations changed during a one-year program he attended as a mature adult at a local university: "they discuss concepts here and there, and the whole civil rights movement, and how everybody else fit in with everybody else." Khoi and other activists recognize the substantial debt owed to African Americans in paving the way for race-based legislation and policies and in raising public acknowledgment of racial barriers, efforts that benefit Vietnamese newcomers today. According to Khoi, mutual recognition of minority status leads to good relations with blacks: "In Boston, we've had a very positive experience with African Americans." The logic of race-based multiculturalism means that Vietnamese American leaders can identify "natural" coalition partners based on minority status.

At the same time, Vietnamese American activists are aware of the limits of race discourses for addressing distinctly immigrant issues, such as concerns about English-language training and settlement assistance. Reflecting on her first year in college, Becky, a Vietnamese refugee who arrived in the United States as a young child, remembers that as one of the few Vietnamese on her campus, she received a warm welcome from "international" students—a designation that was supposed to apply to temporary, foreign students, not permanent residents such as she.[18] With time, she began to pay attention to Asian American issues and found that those most politically active were American-born natives of Chinese, Korean, and Japanese origin. The lack of participation by the foreign born was, according to her, a problem: "I was also looking at the Asian American agenda, which at that point—and I still see—as this glass ceiling. . . . Not really representing the issues that I was concerned about. . . . Like the Asian American agenda hasn't expanded to figure out how to deal with refugees." However, with no alternative discourse, plus the advantage of forming political coalitions with other Asian groups or people of color, community leaders adopt and employ race-based multiculturalism.

As a consequence, immigration issues often become recast as race-based civil rights issues. For example, one public employee in Boston, who works on behalf of immigrants, links the distinct treatment given to noncitizens with racism: "A green card, like, they would call it an alien card. They would label you as an alien, because you are not white. You are considered as an alien. And people still use that term, like an alien card. And if you walk into INS, you know, people come out and ask you for an alien card. And then, I remember, when I went to the customs department, they said, 'Aliens over this side, and U.S. passports over this side.' That's how blunt they are— that's racism! And people just follow that line." U.S. immigration policy has certainly incorporated many racist elements, but the categorizations that this individual mentions are legal designations affecting all immigrants, regardless of race. The link she makes between the two is, however, common.[19] While most Americans celebrate, at least symbolically, the country's immigrant past, there is no parallel image of a positive, common immigrant future.

The link between immigration and race can hurt certain groups. Portuguese Americans find it difficult to make group-based political claims in the American system. They are not third- or fourth-generation "ethnics" like the Italians and Irish since they face linguistic, cultural, and socioeconomic barriers similar to Vietnamese refugees. Yet they are not quite immigrants in the eyes of many activists, because immigrants are conceived of as nonwhite. The Portuguese, today considered white, are viewed as privileged. They are consequently sometimes excluded from efforts in support of immigrant rights or justice for low-income individuals.

Ironically, although the Portuguese are a European group, their status as white in American racial classifications was not a foregone conclusion. In Hawaii, the lower-class status of the Portuguese made them historically part of the local nonwhite population rather than members of the European-origin "Haole" community, a distinction reflected in Hawaiian census reports from 1853 to 1930.[20] In Massachusetts, the presence of darker-skinned Cape Verdeans led some Americans to consider all Portuguese black, an experience recalled by some of my older respondents. The desire to escape such classification prompted some Azorean and mainland Portuguese organizations to exclude Cape Verdeans in the early part of the century, despite the insistence of the Portuguese government that all individuals in Portuguese-controlled lands, including Cape Verde, were Portuguese (Pap 1981).

Internal debates over minority status grew heated in the 1960s and 1970s as government bureaucracies established evolving definitions of Hispanics as a minority deserving special protection and assistance. Under Section 720 (9) (a) of the Ethnic Heritage Program, Portuguese were classified as a minority with African Americans and Latinos (Rogers 1974: 53). There were indications that Congress would extend this logic to other federal programs, and the Census Bureau appeared set to tabulate Portuguese as part of the Hispanic/Latino ethnic category. The Portuguese would thus join Spaniards as European and a minority.

There were good reasons for the Portuguese to be included in the Hispanic/Latino ethnic category. The majority of participants at a 1973 conference on Portuguese Americans agreed that minority designation made sense culturally, geographically, and socially.[21] Perhaps most important, many poor Portuguese would presumably get a boost from access to special programs directed at minority business owners, preferential hiring in the public sector, and assistance in pursuing higher education. One researcher who surveyed the Portuguese populations of Cambridge and Somerville in the 1970s summed up the general attitude when he argued: "Whatever the national political logic of this position, it [the Hispanic category] is conceptual nonsense in terms of defining minorities as far as this local area is concerned. If speaking a different language, sharing a foreign cultural background, or being an immigrant population is sufficient reason to be considered a minority in the case of non-Black Hispanics, then the Portuguese are definitely a minority." (Ito-Alder 1980 [1972, 1978]: 25).

However, Francis Rogers, a Portuguese American professor of Portuguese studies at Harvard University, opposed the designation, arguing for the distinctiveness of Portuguese culture vis-à-vis that of Hispanics. Others were apparently also worried about being grouped with racial minorities. A letter by two Massachusetts Portuguese Americans read into the *Congressional Record* in 1975 objected to the planned inclusion of Portuguese as minorities in an education bill, arguing, "The one million Americans of Portuguese descent unequivocally and respectfully state to the Congress of the United States that we can, and will continue to, compete freely with all our fellow Americans, on individual merit in all fields of endeavor, and that we neither seek, nor need, any advantage, whether by law or executive fiat, over our fellow Americans. . . . We believe the Congress of the United States has seriously erred by the inclusion of the 'Portuguese' as part of the minority in PL92–318."[22] Some community members point to this as the key event, combined with Rogers's status as a professor at Harvard, that prompted Congress to exclude the Portuguese from the minority category.

Thirty years later, questions over Portuguese Americans' minority status continue. A 1999–2000 survey of Portuguese Americans in southeastern Massachusetts found respondents equally divided regarding the perceived benefits of applying to the federal government for official minority status (Barrow 2002: 29). First-generation Portuguese immigrants continue to see limited affinities with Mexican or other Spanish-speaking immigrants. Younger Portuguese American activists, especially if they are born and raised in the United States, instead claim significant cultural overlap with Hispanic communities. There also exists a certain jealousy, rarely stated, that Hispanic immigrants in Massachusetts receive public benefits directed at minorities, but that the Portuguese, possessing very similar backgrounds and facing similar barriers, cannot access these programs.[23] These American-born advocates hold fewer reservations about being labeled as a minority, and they anticipate significant benefits for a community that has remained largely working class. They thus try to promote an expanded, race-based political multiculturalism that the immigrant generation largely rejects.

THE IMPORTANCE OF GOVERNMENT RECOGNITION

Beyond the definition and recognition of ethno-racial groups lies the important issue of *who* recognizes. The second consequential difference in Canadian and American visions of multiculturalism centers on the role of government. Popular attitudes toward diversity in Canada and the United States might be similar, but the fact that in Canada *government* officially recognizes, celebrates, and financially supports diversity—in however a limited manner—favorably influences immigrants' understanding of citizenship and their place in society.

The Canadian state's official endorsement of multiculturalism gives immigrants normative standing in the political system. Government programs for immigrants or refugees provide newcomers with a stronger sense of linkage to the state. Absent such programs, citizenship becomes a passport or legal status with accompanying rights, but it does not carry a sense of engagement in policy issues or electoral contests.[24] This is not to say that new Americans do not recognize and value the right to vote. Many do, especially when compared to the lack of such rights in the countries they left. Nonetheless, I found a subtle, persistent difference in the way immigrants in Toronto spoke of citizenship as compared to those in Boston. Those in Canada valued governmental protections and felt, despite problems, that they could count on the state, fostering a sense of obligation to participate and give back. In Boston, American citizenship evokes rights and economic opportunities but entails a more modest sense of engagement. Because Americans' support for cultural diversity is social and relegated to the private sphere, immigrants see less of a natural link with participatory citizenship.

Public Intervention, Standing, and Political Claims

Various scholars have argued, correctly I believe, that one of the most significant consequences of Canadian multiculturalism is the reordering of symbolic ethnic hierarchies (Breton 1986; Abu-Laban and Stasiulis 1992). Canada's political history largely unfolds as a story of French and English accommodation, with little mention of other groups. Multiculturalism makes room for others. As Portuguese immigrant Maria Clara says, "It shows that everybody can get along together. It's not discrimination against anybody. We all feel that in some way we are important to each other, that this person is not better than a Portuguese person, not better than the next person. To me it's *very* important." It is critical that government offers such recognition and intervenes. Hiep, a Vietnamese Canadian senior, explains the importance of Canadian multiculturalism in the following way: "To my understanding, Canada is a country with a true meaning of multiculturalism. It is very good and suitable to this country. Why? The Canadian government listens to the voice of the people's will, the requests, and helps to respond. They not only respect the cultures of the different community backgrounds, but they always try to develop the culture and the tradition of that community more." Appreciation of government support goes beyond multiculturalism and settlement assistance to include social services such as universal health insurance, pensions, and other programs. Immigrants' sense of equality and dignity are enhanced by the fact that such social programs are open to foreign-born permanent residents as much as to native-born citizens. Rather than removing incentives for naturalization, universal access to public programs enhances newcomers' sense of citizenship.

In the United States, race is an imperfect discourse in dealing with immigrant integration, in part because the limited nature of government assistance generates rivalries and competition. Certain government programs are restricted to specific minorities or, when they are open to all individuals under a certain poverty threshold, programs often carry an implicit connotation of being race based.[25] Some African American activists consider these programs the outgrowth of their community's militancy, and they express subtle proprietary rights over program benefits, a feeling reinforced by their own long history in the United States compared to newcomers' recent arrival. Remembering an incident where the presence of a nonblack worker generated antagonism in one agency, a Vietnamese American advocate explains, "Because all black people, they think that Healthy Start is for the blacks. But it was a federal grant. [Under a] federal grant you have to hire all races, to work with ALL races to reduce infant mortality." Tensions arise when policies perceived by some to compensate for past injustices are redirected to newcomer settlement and social services. Some immigrant community leaders, like Moc Van, even wonder whether the government harbors more sinister motives: "I think that the government invented some programs to divide us, to conquer. For example, Section 8 housing. Welfare. That kind of thing. Different. In your eyes the government is so good, they help us. I don't think so. Because there are too many people chasing too few goods. We are so busy fighting each other we cannot become politically strong." A perception of scarce resources generates antagonistic relations, where a gain for one is a loss for another. Such feelings provide a meager basis for inclusive and participatory citizenship.[26]

For community leaders in Canada, ethnic multiculturalism combined with the largely universal nature of Canadian settlement and social programs create two contradictory impulses: a sense of integration and welcome but also a fear of political isolation through ethnic "ghettoization."[27] As in Boston, some advocates worry about the use of public programs to marginalize minority communities. The tenor of such critiques is different, however. One Portuguese Canadian explained, "I think official multiculturalism . . . is used to pander down, to buy votes, and to kind of ghettoize a little bit. This whole ethnic thing also bothers me. . . . Because I think that's another way in which the immigrant communities are kind of marginalized and ghettoized." Noteworthy in this assessment is the respondent's belief that politicians seek to "buy votes" through such programs, whereas Moc Van concludes, "By chasing those things [government programs], black people hate Vietnamese. Vietnamese hate Cambodian. Vice versa. How come you get and I don't get it? And [so] they don't have time to get politically involved." In the first case, all individuals are implicitly provided with certain universal services, on top of which politicians might disburse ethnic "extras." In the second, there are no extras; competition centers on basic, limited, particularistic services.[28]

Since the negative valence of race is less apparent in Canadian multiculturalism—everyone is an "ethnic"—community leaders in Toronto use multiculturalism to encourage political integration as an antidote to ghettoization. When organizations receive money and legitimacy from government departments or programs with *multiculturalism* or *citizenship* in their titles, community advocates make an implicit link between government, inclusion, and participation. From the point of view of leaders such as Celia, the state welcomes newcomers, and while it clearly could do more, a certain loyalty emerges:

> I know that a lot of people resent the multiculturalism policy; they feel that it ghettoizes us, and puts us into separate little communities, and it prevents us from fully integrating, and so on. There is a bit of truth to that. . . . Having said that, however, on another level we have fought and we have gained, and other organizations have fought for services, social services, health care services. . . . A system that has had a lot of faults— that's why we're still lobbying and advocating for a lot of things—but a system that gives us, from what we hear from other jurisdictions and other countries, [a system] that I think has been incredibly good to newcomers in terms of trying to address a lot of the different needs.

Such sentiments encourage community leaders to mobilize in favor of citizenship and political participation.

Multiculturalism and settlement policies also provide a public discourse that community leaders can use to talk about problems and make political claims. Hai, who serves on the board of a Vietnamese Canadian organization, appreciates government-sponsored multiculturalism because it provides a language of rights and claims making:

> The melting pot is, yes, good . . . for some people with a certain degree of integration. But for the rest—you are just garbage. Here we try to provide an opportunity for everybody. It doesn't matter whether you have a language ability or you do not have a language ability. You, as a person, you have the right to live, you have the right to access to service, to government, you have the right to access to education. You shouldn't be discriminated [against] because your English is so poor, as long as you prove that you have intelligence and you can do it.

Another activist explained:

> [This organization] does not believe that the Multiculturalism Act has done very much in terms of eradicating racism in Canada. Personally I think that it has given our political people an excuse to not pay real attention to some of the issues. That on the international scale, they are able to hold up the Multiculturalism Act as if that somehow makes Canada less racist than it really is. On the other hand, I think what the act does do is to recognize the plurality of cultures within Canada. And so as a discourse, at least it keeps the conversation going. As you probably heard, people take different positions on it, but at least the conversation is on the table and it's an end to talking about issues of race and racism in Canada.

Newcomers in Canada see multiculturalism as a means to enter into dialogue with government and other Canadians.

Rights, Protections, Legal Citizenship, and Full Participation

Government can also offer protection when fellow citizens threaten immigrants, an issue raised by respondents in both Toronto and Boston. Van, who was born in Vietnam, is in his thirties and has spent more than half his life in Canada. He graduated from a Canadian school and feels relatively comfortable in his adopted country. Yet he values policies such as multiculturalism because they direct government to intercede on immigrants' behalf against native-born Canadians: "What it means for me is I have the right to be who I am and practice whatever religion I believe, my cultural background, you know. I should be able to display myself in this country without being afraid of being harassed or anything. . . . And those who criticize that, those people are the ones born here, grew up here."

Similarly, immigrants in Boston appreciate the guarantees offered by the

American Constitution and legal system. When I asked Thien whether he thought it a good thing that the United States welcomes so many people from different cultures, he responded, "There are some good people and there are some bad people in every country. The good thing about the U.S. is it has a very strong and effective law system. It can handle and watch everyone in the U.S. It is a great thing, because the U.S. can monitor all these people." However, while the legal system offers protections, Thien does not see a strong relationship between his life and government. Thien continues:

> Life in the U.S. is flexible. If you go to work you will have money. You have all the necessities that you need. But if you don't work then you won't have any money. So if you want to be a bum, then be a bum in Vietnam and don't come here. I don't have much more to say because my whole life surrounds only these things. If I work hard then I can buy a car and a house. I also have the freedom to travel. But if I commit a crime then I will go to jail.

For Thien, citizenship provides guaranteed residence, access to economic opportunity, and a passport for travel.[29] It also entails the responsibility of obeying American laws. Citizenship does not, however, include a strong participatory element. Thien does not vote—"I have no time, and because I just came to the U.S. I don't know who is good or who is bad"—nor does he engage in other political activities. As Gilbertson and Singer (2003) find, citizenship becomes largely a defensive or protective measure.

At the end of my interviews I would ask respondents to list three things they liked most about their adopted country and three things they disliked or would want to change. Whether in Boston or Toronto, the list of positive characteristics frequently included freedom, especially by Vietnamese refugees, and access to economic opportunity, although respondents often added the caveat that work in North America consumes one, leaving little time for family or relaxation. Vietnamese Americans were more likely to name education and access to Boston's colleges and universities as a benefit. In Toronto, Portuguese and Vietnamese Canadians consistently listed cultural tolerance and various forms of government intervention as something they valued, even though they might also complain about the taxes that fund those programs. A Portuguese immigrant who had lived twenty years in the United States and thirteen years in Canada offered an excellent summary of the trade-offs I consistently heard through my interviews:

I: *What are the best three things about Canada?*
R: The best three things? Well, like I said, the welcoming, the open-mindedness. The friendliness, that would be one. And the respect

for who you are, what you are, especially about ethnicity and for immigrants. [Pause.] And a third thing? Well, like I said, the sense that the government cares, especially Medicare.

I: *What about the United States? What are the best things about the United States?*

R: Well, it's the best country in the world . . . economically, it is so strong, the dollar is strong. Life is cheaper here. Another thing. . . . People are very patriotic here. That brings a certain unity with it, maybe a certain conformity, depending on the word you use. Hmmm . . . It's a land of opportunity. *Both* provide great opportunity. It doesn't matter what your background is, it doesn't matter who you are, you have the opportunity to make something, do something.[30]

Currently living in Boston, the speaker holds both Canadian and American citizenship and he considers himself "a North American citizen." The United States is economically "the best country in the world," and family will keep him in Massachusetts a few more years. However, at the end of the interview he told me that he dreams of going back to Toronto, "It's just the place that I feel [at] home." It is an emotion that stems in large part from his sense of welcome, "the way the government runs things—I guess the great support, the multiculture stuff, the social assistance. We pay a lot of tax[es], that's true. But the great concern of government, the help for the citizens themselves." Citizenship consequently becomes something more than legal status.

Contrary to conventional Canadian wisdom, the United States can no longer be considered home to a melting pot ideology. As we have seen, ordinary immigrants today perceive widespread social acceptance of their multiple identities. The possibility of "hyphenated" Americanism provides an opening to citizenship and participation. However, the lack of a specific discourse to deal with *immigrant*-generated diversity means that activists couch political claims in the language of race.

For a group such as the Portuguese, race-based multiculturalism has meant political invisibility: they have difficulty making claims in the public space since government and ordinary Americans do not see them as requiring assistance. They blend into a "white ethnic" mass that places them on equal footing with fourth-generation Irish and Italians, despite the fact that they experience problems similar to other first-generation immigrants, problems compounded by limited education and language skills. In the Vietnamese case, a minority label provides resources and, in some cases, access to political structures but at the cost of having to negotiate the enduring American race dilemma, so long defined in terms of black and white. Race-based multiculturalism is a salient political tool, but it is one that resonates poorly with ordinary community members who find it difficult to rally around a construct of *Asian* or *people of color.*

Canadian governments also address issues of racial discrimination and institutional barriers through the catch-all designation of *visible minorities,* but it is rare to talk about *Asian Canadians.* Canadian multiculturalism is primarily ethnic; groups are recognized based on national origin or, more rarely, by subnational ethnicity if the group is relatively large and cohesive. People are of Vietnamese, Chinese, Indian, or some other Asian origin. A major advantage of such public rhetoric is that it accords well with most immigrants' self-perceptions; most first-generation Vietnamese, for example, feel distinct from other Asian groups. A major disadvantage is that despite government efforts to the contrary, the predominantly ethnic understanding of multiculturalism makes the policy less effective in addressing race-based problems.

Canadians have engaged in substantial debate as to whether public multiculturalism matters and what effect it has had on Canadian society. The original government policy sought to integrate ethnic minorities while also recognizing their unique cultural heritages. Critics assert that, at best, the policy does little—"'multi-culturalism' turns out to be a choice of pizza, wonton soup and kosher 'style' pastrami sandwiches" (Brotz 1981: 44)—or, at worst, it hurts interethnic relations by acting "as an institutional system for the marginalization of the individual" and creating "the hyphenated Canadian with divided loyalties" (Bissoondath 1993: 78, 383; Li 1999). Such charges echo some Americans' worries that multiculturalism leads to the "disuniting" of the United States (Schlesinger 1998).

Here I offer a different view. Despite its problems, multiculturalism's "mere" symbolism promotes incorporation; the policy's effects, rather than being divisive, promote integration, at least within the political system. The new Canadians with whom I spoke tend to view multiculturalism as a celebration of symbolic ethnicity, and some worry about ghettoization. Nevertheless, almost all feel that multiculturalism is consequential in its recognition of diversity and its ability to allow immigrant voices into the public sphere. In this way multiculturalism, and government intervention around newcomer settlement more generally, promotes immigrants' sense of full citizenship in the polity, encouraging naturalization and participation. The upshot is that the ideology of multiculturalism in Canada, commonly understood as public recognition of one's cultural background and support for interethnic tolerance, carries a stronger assimilatory impulse than laissez-faire integration and de facto race-based multiculturalism in the United States. And, as we will see in the following chapter, interventionist policies not only shape understandings of political citizenship but also provide the material resources needed to actually undertake various forms of political incorporation.

5. Community Organizations and Political Mobilization

> Well, of course there is this perception out there that government in the past has wasted all this money subsidizing organizations that end up lobbying government, and how incestuous can that be? But in reality, that is not true. Government has never really subsidized organizations to do advocacy or lobbying. We are subsidized to do settlement and integration programming and community development work in our communities . . . [but] we also have to take action on behalf of our communities around issues.
>
> PORTUGUESE CANADIAN STAFF MEMBER,
> *Portuguese Interagency Network, Toronto*

How do we link the national policies that structure political incorporation with newcomers' personal and localized experiences of naturalization and political participation? We have already seen in chapter 2 that community organizations offer assistance and actively nudge immigrants and refugees toward political integration. From the newcomer's perspective, this is largely an individual story of learning about citizenship, figuring out how to acquire it, and then taking steps to use new political rights. It is not obvious that these personal decisions and actions link up to national government policies or ideologies of multiculturalism, especially for those who report never having heard about such policies or ideologies.

To show how policy environments shape immigrants' experiences, this chapter traces the effect of integration and multiculturalism policies on the founding, survival, and activities of community organizations. Governments can promote immigrant organizing through the provision of vital resources. This usually takes the form of grants and contracts, but it also occurs by providing technical assistance, developing a friendly regulatory environment, establishing norms of inclusion, and opening "access points" to public officials. In environments with such support, newcomers establish a greater number and diversity of community organizations. Although public dollars come with trade-offs, organizations receiving government assistance often help facilitate public engagement.

A COMMUNITY'S CAPACITY TO ORGANIZE
AND THE ROLE OF GOVERNMENT

Despite their role in political incorporation, advocacy, and service delivery, immigrant and refugee organizations have received little attention from migration scholars. Instead, researchers focus on social capital, a resource based on interpersonal ties that can be cemented by common culture, ethnicity, religion, geography, or immigrant experience (Zhou and Bankston 1998; Portes 1995). In part, the lack of interest in organizations reflects the priorities of many newly arrived migrants. Faced with the challenges of finding employment, learning a new language, and adjusting to a foreign environment, establishing organizations sits low on a list of adaptation concerns.[1]

Yet organizations provide benefits beyond social capital, especially in politics.[2] They concentrate community resources, they bring people together on a regular basis, and because they offer a measure of permanence, they facilitate sustained collective action over time. The greater the prevalence of ethnic organizations, the more "institutionally complete" the immigrant community (Breton 1964).[3] Immigrants' political incorporation rests in part on the community's capacity to organize, that is, on the available stock of organizations serving new and established migrants.

Predictions about State Intervention

Can government help establish and sustain community organizations? Some argue that state involvement crowds out civic participation.[4] When government steps in, it grows like a weed, choking off grassroots organizing, undermining citizen participation, and fostering an unhealthy dependence on state initiative. According to Joyce and Schambra (1996), immigrant groups face a particular threat, since government bureaucratic expansion attacks ethnic ties, weakening ethnic communities.

A model of structured mobilization suggests the opposite: government support should increase local organizational capacity by providing legitimacy, material resources, and technical assistance. In this view, government sows seeds that help immigrants grow and nurture their own communal groups. According to Grønbjerg (1993), government is especially likely to cooperate with nonprofit organizations in instances where service provision is needed but business activity is limited. Such is the case for newcomer settlement in Canada and refugee settlement in the United States. When state intervention is accompanied by policies of multiculturalism, ethnic or racial ties are reinforced, perhaps even reified, not undermined.

The Portuguese and Vietnamese communities in Toronto and Boston provide a way to adjudicate between these two accounts. If we believe the model of structured mobilization, migrants will organize more in contexts where they receive more public support. All things being equal, we would expect a greater number and diversity of organizations from the Portuguese community in Toronto than the one in Boston, due to more extensive Canadian funding of newcomer communities. Conversely, we would expect the number and diversity of organizations in the Vietnamese communities to be comparable in Toronto and Boston, given the U.S. government's commitment to refugees. The Boston Portuguese community should have fewer organizations than the Boston Vietnamese community because of the American laissez-faire attitude toward economic and family-sponsored migrants. The crowding-out argument suggests the opposite: more public programs should engender fewer community organizations.

We can also consider a third hypothesis, namely that the dispute over state intervention is much ado about nothing. Government support might be irrelevant to community organizing. If so, we should find no relationship between policy and the number of immigrant organizations. Instead, organizational capacity should vary with other factors, most obviously the size of the group. Communities with a larger population should have more organizations since there are more people to establish and sustain them.[5] Of the communities considered here, population sizes are similar within ethnic groups and roughly proportional across them. Comparing metro Boston (population 3,398,000) and the city of Toronto (population 2,364,000), we find about 87,200 and 78,500 individuals of Portuguese ethnicity, respectively.[6] Metro Boston is home to just under 22,000 individuals of Vietnamese origin and Toronto to just over 25,000. Thus across the two cities, the ratio of Portuguese and Vietnamese is roughly one to one. In Boston the ratio of Portuguese to Vietnamese is four to one, while in Toronto the proportion is three to one. If government intervention has no effect on organizational capacity, the number of organizations should approximate the population ratios.

Evidence for Structured Mobilization

Using community directories, resource lists, and interviews, we can count all organizations located in the heart of the Portuguese and Vietnamese communities of metropolitan Boston and Toronto.[7] Reliance on a simple organizational tally has limitations, since it does not reflect the relative strength—in resources or membership—of the community organizations. Nevertheless, counts can be an important indicator of social and political mobilization (Kaufman 1999; Minkoff 1994).

TABLE 7. ORGANIZATIONAL CAPACITY OF THE PORTUGUESE AND
VIETNAMESE COMMUNITIES IN BOSTON AND TORONTO, 2000

Organization Type	Portuguese		Vietnamese	
	Boston	Toronto	Boston	Toronto
Advocacy	—	7	3	3
Political	—	2	5	4
Social clubs	8	37	—	—
Professional	1	4	1	2
Social service	4	16	12	19
Media	2	28	4	6
Catholic churches	1	4	3	1
Temples	—	—	4	5
Total	16	98	32	40
Total excluding clubs and temples	8	61	28	35

SOURCE: Author's compilation.

Table 7 shows that the number of ethnic organizations in the two cities
supports the predictions of structured mobilization: the Portuguese in
Toronto have many more organizations in a broader array of categories
than those in Boston; the Vietnamese in Boston have a greater density and
diversity of organizations than the Portuguese in the same city; and the two
Vietnamese communities are quite similar in organizational capacity.

Table 7 also breaks down the total number of organizations in each community into seven categories: advocacy, political, social, professional, social
service, media, and religious.[8] This helps us examine how policies might
have differential effects depending on the type of organization. The advocacy category counts nonpartisan groups organized along ethno-specific
lines that speak out on a specific set of issues. Political groups focus on an
explicit political aim, be it home country politics or political participation in
the host country.[9] Social organizations include fraternal associations and
Portuguese social clubs. Professional associations are ethno-specific groups
organized around particular occupations, including business ownership. The
social service category includes all groups that offer settlement support or
other services that help immigrants adjust to life in the host country. These
groups can be multiethnic, serving a wide array of clients, but they must
have at least one staff person dedicated to the Portuguese or Vietnamese
community and substantial outreach to immigrants. The media category

includes local organizations providing print, radio, or television programming in Portuguese or Vietnamese. It excludes imported media, such as the Portuguese international television station, available via satellite in both countries, and Vietnamese newspapers published in California that circulate in Boston and Toronto. Finally, religious organizations include the number of Catholic churches offering mass in the language of the immigrant group and, for the Vietnamese community, Buddhist temples.[10]

Organizational Capacity among Portuguese in Toronto and Boston Overall, there are many more organizations serving the Portuguese in Toronto than in Boston. We find no one to one ratio as we might expect given the number of ethnic Portuguese in the metro Boston and Toronto areas. These results support the contention that government assistance, through policies like multiculturalism and newcomer settlement, promotes immigrant organizing more in Canada than in the United States.

The picture becomes more nuanced when we consider various categories of organizations, as the effect appears to vary across organizational type. Critically, government policies might provide the most fertile ground to the groups most central to political incorporation, advocacy, political, and media organizations. In Toronto, we find seven groups directly engaged in advocacy, from gay and lesbian issues to an association of seniors that speaks out on elder abuse, and two groups with explicitly political purposes. These organizations are not equally active, but they have much more political potential than the ones in Boston. In Boston, we find no Portuguese group primarily dedicated to advocacy or political goals.

The greater number of advocacy and political organizations in Toronto can be linked back to public support. Many of these groups have limited resources, but small grants, often from government, keep them going, helping to pay for newsletters or to organize periodic events. For example, funding from the provincial and federal governments helped establish the Portuguese Interagency Network (PIN). PIN has prepared needs assessments of the community to better lobby government for services, has appeared before municipal and provincial legislative committees to speak on behalf of the Portuguese, and spearheaded the organizing effort behind the founding of the Portuguese Canadian National Congress, a national advocacy organization. Others have documented how the Canadian government appears to fund its own critics at the national level through programs like multiculturalism (Biles 1997; Pal 1993). These results suggest that the effect of government intervention spills over to local communities as well.

The relatively greater number of Toronto media organizations is more surprising. The ethnic media tend to be organized as private for-profit businesses. In contrast, all of the other groups enumerated in table 7 are voluntary or nonprofit organizations. The latter should be most affected by external assistance since many are resource poor and could benefit from funding and technical help. It is thus noteworthy that the media category shows one of the biggest imbalances in organizational ratios. Whereas there are twenty-eight different newspapers, radio stations, or TV programs for Portuguese Canadians in Toronto, there are only two in Boston. The difference is consequential, since ethnic media are important conduits of information about the community and mainstream society and they can encourage civic or political mobilization. The Toronto ethnic media has been a particularly fertile ground for forming and promoting community leaders, including politicians. One former Portuguese Canadian member of municipal government had a regular radio show before being elected, a former school trustee works as a newspaper journalist, and at least two elected school board members have worked on Portuguese-language television.

Part of the imbalance in media offerings stems from the two cities' relative importance as foci for the larger provincial or state Portuguese community. In Ontario, Toronto is a center for Portuguese activities, but larger and older Portuguese communities in New Bedford and Fall River, towns in southeast Massachusetts, produce newspapers and some radio programming that are consumed in Boston.

Yet government support for immigrant communities also plays a role. The federal Canadian Radio and Telecommunications Council provides greater regulatory support for multicultural radio and television programming. Toronto boasts two TV stations dedicated to the city's linguistic minorities, and various radio stations offer multicultural programming, including music, call-in shows, and news commentary. The Portuguese usually have a few hours per day or per week on these multiethnic channels. In contrast, without a clear national policy in favor of multicultural broadcasting, ethnic communities in the Boston area are dependent on local authorities. City governments require cable companies to provide community television channels in return for distribution contracts. A few Portuguese Americans have used these local channels to produce a weekly call-in show and to broadcast community events, but access is not guaranteed and community members complain that distribution of the shows is excessively localized given complicated cable agreements.

The cross-national differences are less stark among religious bodies, professional associations, social clubs, and social service providers. In Toronto we find about four of these organizations for every one in Boston, a ratio that mirrors the Portuguese population in each area's historic site of first settlement.[11] In these cases we find no support for the crowding-out argument, limited support for a model of structured mobilization, but some evidence of a population effect. Ethno-specific Catholic churches are among those organizations most dependent on a local population because of the parish system and least likely to be influenced by government support, although in Toronto some Portuguese churches have received government funds for settlement. The same is true for social clubs and professional associations, groups that largely rely on a membership base for resources and support. It is thus not surprising that the number of these groups is more a function of the size of the local population than external funding.

The relatively modest four to one ratio for social service organizations is more surprising given the stronger Canadian support for immigrant settlement. The relatively large Canadian welfare state might play a role here, making government less reliant on ethnic associations for service delivery. In contrast, given a much more limited American welfare state, governments in the United States tend to contract with nonprofit organizations for service provision.[12]

Organizational Capacity among the Vietnamese in Toronto and Boston
The organizational landscape changes dramatically when we compare the Vietnamese in Toronto and Boston. Given roughly equal populations and similar government support, we would expect few differences in organizational capacity. Indeed, the total number of organizations is roughly similar, thirty-two in Boston and forty in Toronto. There is also much greater parity across organizational types. The number of advocacy associations, political organizations, professional groups, and temples is almost identical. In Boston, we find three Catholic churches offering regular mass in Vietnamese compared to only one in Toronto, but the difference most likely stems from the higher proportion of Catholics among Vietnamese in the United States, not the presence or absence of government support.[13]

The difference in media organizations is much less remarkable for the Vietnamese than it is for the Portuguese. Both Vietnamese communities have developed local ethnic media, although both also rely on newspapers produced in Southern California, home to the largest concentration of Vietnamese in North America. The effect of multicultural programming is still somewhat in evidence in Toronto. Vietnamese Canadians boast regular television programming on the multicultural channels, although community members complain that the larger, more established ethnic groups have monopolized the best times.

The only other discrepancy appears in the slightly larger number of social service and settlement organizations in Toronto, nineteen, compared to twelve in Boston. The difference is driven mostly by a greater number of multiethnic agencies in Toronto. A number of settlement and neighborhood groups, established decades earlier, have recently added Vietnamese staff and programs to serve the growing Vietnamese population in downtown Toronto. In Boston, experienced refugee resettlement agencies such as the International Institute of Boston, Catholic Charities, and Jewish Vocational Service undertook a similar expansion, and some preexisting Chinese organizations transformed themselves into broader Asian American agencies. On the whole, however, fewer established organizations in Boston have made moves to include Vietnamese. Vietnamese Canadians integrate into a general newcomer infrastructure, while Vietnamese Americans are channelled into an organizational universe of refugee resettlement or Asian-specific minority services.

Organizational Capacity in Boston: The Portuguese and Vietnamese Compared   In the absence of government intervention, we would expect the Portuguese population in Boston to support many more organizations than the Vietnamese. Portuguese migration has a much longer history and it has been fed by larger waves of immigrants. The community has had more time to establish a strong organizational infrastructure and it can call on significant resources, both material and human, from first- and second-generation individuals. Based on population, we would expect up to four times as many organizations in the Portuguese community as compared to the Vietnamese.[14]

After discounting Vietnamese temples and Portuguese social clubs—which have no equivalent in the other community—we find instead three and half times more Vietnamese organizations than Portuguese ones, twenty-eight to eight, respectively. The imbalance appears in almost every organization category: advocacy, politics, media, social services, and even in the number of Catholic churches providing mass in the migrants' language.

The difference could stem from the more recent nature of Vietnamese migration. Many Vietnamese moved to Boston after 1985, and they likely have a greater need for settlement and social services than a more established group like the Portuguese. However, relative newness does not explain the difference in media offerings, political groups, or Catholic churches. Rather, the normative support accorded to refugees acts in a way similar to multiculturalism in Canada, altering the perception of mainstream actors such as the Boston Archdiocese toward accommodation of newcomers.[15] Refugee settlement monies provide seed funds that produce spillover effects for further organizing (see also Hein 1997). Thus, the Vietnamese Seniors of Metropolitan Boston, an advocacy group, grew out of informal meetings held at the Vietnamese American Civic Association (VACA), one of the mutual assistance associations (MAAs) established with help from the federal government (With 1996). Vietnamese Americans have benefited from such support while Portuguese Americans have not.

Government policies promote organizational formation and persistence through favorable regulatory environments, technical assistance from public officials, allocation of physical space for group meetings, and probably most important, public funding. While many immigrant organizations do not receive public monies—professional groups, for example, are largely financed through members' fees and private fund-raising—the largest and most powerful generally do. These are the ones most likely to engage in political mobilization and advocacy.

Indeed, the financial records of key organizations in the Portuguese and Vietnamese communities reveal that government grants and contracts finance two-thirds to over four-fifths of annual budgets. The Massachusetts Alliance of Portuguese Speakers (MAPS), a social service and advocacy agency, owes 79 percent of its budget to government monies.[16] PIN in Toronto is even more dependent, receiving 86 percent of its income from government grants and contracts. Government funding accounts for about two-thirds of revenues for St. Christopher House (a multiethnic community center in west downtown Toronto serving, among others, Vietnamese and Portuguese residents), the Vietnamese Association of Toronto (VAT), and VACA (both mutual assistance associations engaged in advocacy and service provision). The remainder of these organizations' revenues come from the United Way, grants from foundations and businesses, program fees, fund-raising efforts, membership fees, and investment income. The relative importance of public versus private funding sources is very similar to what Cordero-Guzmán (2005) found for immigrant community-based organizations in New York City, and these findings support Hein's contention (1997) that "welfare state channeling," in the form of government grants and contracts, explains the prevalence of Indochinese MAAs better than general resource mobilization accounts or explanations centered on ethnic competition.

Immigrant and refugee groups are not alone in their reliance on government. Salamon (1999: 114–16, 141) estimates that governments in the United States provide, on average, 37 percent of revenues for all nonprofits offering social services and a surprising 51 percent for civic and advocacy organizations that file tax forms.[17] In Canada, governments provide a similar 47 percent of all revenues for civic and advocacy organizations and a much more significant 66 percent of income for social service organizations (Hall et al. 2005: 17). In a comparative study of the nonprofit sector in various countries worldwide, researchers estimate that the governments of "Anglo-Saxon" countries—the United States, United Kingdom, and Australia—disburse the equivalent of 2.5 percent of GDP to nonprofit organizations. Canada is usually grouped among the Anglo-Saxon countries in this sort of global analysis, but in this case Canada falls just outside the model. Canadian governments instead devote 4.4 percent of GDP to funding nonprofit organizations, a level on par with countries such as France, Germany, and the Netherlands (Hall et al. 2005: 19). Nonprofit organizations in the United States and Canada thus share a reliance on government, but since the overall level of public support is greater in Canada, more organizations and more communities, including newcomer communities, benefit.

THE CONSEQUENCES OF STATE SUPPORT
FOR IMMIGRANT ORGANIZING

We must not be blind to potential trade-offs accompanying government support. The crowding-out argument contends, mistakenly, that one of the pathologies of state intervention is the stifling of civic organizing. A second potential pathology is the risk of co-optation and depoliticization. Government policies may well breed more organizations, but do these groups promote political engagement?

Government intervention could compromise nonprofit and civic organizations' ability to act as effective political agents. State support is not merely an act of benevolence: government agencies and officials often need community organizations to deliver services that the state cannot or will not provide, and they use community-based organizations to convey and gather information needed for the effective functioning of the government (Salamon 1995; Simmons and Keohane 1992; Smith and Lipsky 1993). Scholars and community activists warn that government financing of private civic groups can undermine such groups' autonomy and deflect their activities through the explicit or subtle co-optation of organizational goals (Indra 1987; Joyce and Schambra 1996; Smith and Lipsky 1993). For example, grants from the Canadian multiculturalism program might promote government agendas rather than serve the interest of ethno-racial minorities (Fleras and Elliott 1992; Pal 1993). Chasing government grants can encourage organizations to adopt issues and programs of peripheral interest to the community while more pressing needs are ignored, a phenomenon called "mission drift" by those in the field (Jenkins 1987; Smith and Lipsky 1993; Hall 2003). More generally, government contracting risks diminishing organizations' real or perceived ability to advocate on their community's behalf: if financial stability rests on public funds, organizations might be reluctant to bite the hand that feeds them (Salamon 1995; Chaves, Stephens, and Galaskiewicz 2004).

Such dire predictions can be countered by arguments *for* politicization. Government subsidies for community services can produce spillover effects into advocacy and mobilization (Chaves, Stephens, and Galaskiewicz 2004). Community organizations often build up a constituency that can counteract, through public outcry, voting, and demonstrations, policy choices perceived as detrimental to the community (Kramer and Grossman 1987; Marwell 2004; Nowland-Foreman 1998; Smith 1999). Finally, dependence is a two-way street: when governments rely on community organizations to collect information and provide services, powerful community groups can channel government behavior by controlling the information conveyed and activities pursued.

The quandary of government co-optation entails three separate questions. (1) Does reception of government assistance affect the *level* of political activity, that is, increase or decrease it? (2) Does reception of government assistance affect the *type* of advocacy and mobilization, channeling activism to institutionalized politics or to contentious action? (3) Does reception of government assistance affect the *direction* of political action, favoring the government's agenda rather than the community's agenda?

My data cannot provide a quantitative assessment of this question, but they do permit an evaluation of how those involved perceive these trade-offs and of the programmatic and advocacy choices taken by community organizations. In line with optimists' viewpoint, government support promotes involvement in mainstream political institutions: the overall level and interest in politics appear to increase, as does the ability to be involved. Government policies provide material resources, they open access points to political actors and public employees, and they increase opportunities for political learning from other organizations or from civil servants. Much of this learning and building of networks direct immigrants to "regular" channels of political influence, so government support does appear to prejudice contentious behavior. Public funding channels programmatic choices and, to a lesser degree, political advocacy, but not at the expense of eliminating activism. In sum, government intervention promotes normal, institutionalized political activity, helping to explain greater immigrant political incorporation in Canada.

Levels of Participation: Building Political Capacity and Interest

State support is translated into greater organizational political engagement through a variety of mechanisms. The process of applying and receiving government grants necessarily places an organization in contact with government, opening channels of communication that immigrant groups can use to convey policy preferences, build networks, and engage in political learning. The funding relationship can be purely administrative: a grants officer at a community-based organization files a proposal and periodic reports; a government official cuts a check. But sometimes funding relationships evolve into discussions over policy. For example, the Ontario Council of Agencies Serving Immigrants (OCASI) holds regular meetings with government departments that fund immigrant organizations:

> We meet two or three times a year where we look at program needs from the [nonprofit] sector's perspective. And program plans from the government perspective. And we thrash it out. I must say that I think both levels of government [federal and provincial] have been good. . . . We invite them to participate at our events. For example, every year at our professional development conference, we have a panel with all of the funders of the community-based sector. . . . And it's an opportunity for the sector to hear from government and for government to hear from the sector. And we find that that probably works. And then we also don't shy away from sending off nasty letters!

The bureaucracy accompanying public monies can penalize new groups with less expertise in grant writing. As one Vietnamese Canadian explained:

> It was really hard to get the funding. . . . We, as a brand-new group—and we didn't have a connection to the government, so we didn't have an expert to write [a] proposal—we find it hard. We put in a lot of applications, and you know what their comment is? "Well, your application was good, but it was not meeting our criteria. So sorry, we cannot fund you anything." That happened all the time! I was shouting, "You guys from the state know that we are new, we don't know about criteria, so if you want us to write exactly what you propose, you have to tell us what it is!"

To overcome these obstacles, organizations engage in a process of learning from past mistakes and develop contacts with knowledgeable individuals, including community outsiders who work in government or for other organizations. Such learning is facilitated by the existence of policies of refugee resettlement or multiculturalism that encourage information sharing between immigrant and established groups.

In this way Viet-AID built networks to political actors inside and outside of government while trying to acquire public monies. One organizer remembers:

> The federal government is the most political one. We got a huge grant from the federal government and in order to do that, we need to get the support of our senators, because the senators are the ones who decide how much funding [will] go to that agency. So what we did was, as soon as we sent in a proposal, we got a letter of support from our senator. When they review our proposal, we get our senator to give them a call. . . . We are lucky in Massachusetts. We have a senator who really cares about immigrants and refugee issues. . . . And you go in and you do the right dance and you sing the right song.
>
> And also, when you don't have enough political power, you have to get someone else to introduce you. And that's what we did. . . . When we approached [Senator Edward] Kennedy we went through a Jewish organization. . . . We talked to the leader of that nonprofit, who knows Kennedy very well. And that person talked to Kennedy's staff. . . . I called [the staff person] up and I said, "Hi. This person called your office and your office asked me to give you a call." So that's how it works. Otherwise, if I called first, it would be "Hah—who the hell are you?"

The lessons learned in securing funding prove useful later when the community mobilizes around other issues.

Receiving public funds also makes it more likely that a group will join an umbrella organization devoted to immigrant and refugee issues. Such umbrella organizations, like the Massachusetts Immigrant and Refugee Advocacy coalition (MIRA) and OCASI, provide technical information about administering and applying for government and foundation grants, track legislative changes that are of concern to their members, and call upon member organizations to mobilize around relevant legislative debates, as in the case of cuts to the Massachusetts Citizenship Assistance Program, changes to U.S. welfare policy, or health care reform in Ontario.[18] Umbrella organizations draw local community groups into larger debates around domestic politics.

The public employees who manage and administer government programs can also promote immigrant political engagement. In some cases, a desire to validate their jobs pushes public employees to mobilize ethnic communities to support the programs they run. Many, however, are genuinely interested in making government less opaque to newcomers. Staff might be members of the communities that receive government support, and they sometimes have prior experience in community-based organizations. In the city of Boston's Office of New Bostonians, a municipal office that promotes immigrant involvement in city affairs, the founding director had been head of the nonprofit Asian Task Force against Domestic Violence, and a resource development officer previously worked for the advocacy group Asian Pacific Youth Coalition. Similarly, various employees in the city of Toronto's Task Force on Access and Equity have been active within community-based organizations, either as staff or volunteers. Such experiences orient civil servants to include ethno-racial communities in the business of government.[19]

Some public officials and bureaucrats want to empower minority communities; others espouse more modest goals of public service. In either case, they can facilitate political incorporation. Boston's Office of New Bostonians, after meetings with community leaders, service providers, and activists, established a four-point mission, including the goal of increasing civic participation among immigrants and refugees. As part of this mission, employees in the Office of New Bostonians coordinated a voter registration and turnout effort, Boston Votes 2000, that involved approximately two hundred fifty civic associations, social service providers, and other community-based organizations as well as various city departments. One staff member estimates that five thousand people were registered through the Boston Votes campaign. The project culminated with New Bostonians' Community Day. Immigrants were invited to City Hall to meet elected officials and the mayor, and they were given tours of the city departments to familiarize themselves with the available services.

Public employees can also provide targeted help to specific groups. Grassroots organizing and government support transformed an informal group of university students and recent graduates, the Fraternal Association of Overseas Vietnamese, founded in 1972, into the Vietnamese Association of Toronto (VAT), the largest Vietnamese social service and settlement agency in Toronto. The group, initially established to organize a Tet celebration for the Lunar New Year and let members socialize with the few other Vietnamese in Toronto, became involved in resettlement after the communist take over of Saigon in 1975. The group coordinated a network of volunteers to greet displaced compatriots at the airport, act as interpreters, and provide resettlement assistance. In response to encouragement from the secretary of state for multiculturalism, the president of the association applied for and received a one-time grant of $3,000 to help defray the organization's expenses (Wilson 1997).

A few years later, with the influx of new refugees during the boat people crisis, government representatives, churches, and voluntary agencies began to contact the Fraternal Association's members for advice and help with resettlement efforts. In 1978 the group changed its name to the Vietnamese Association of Toronto and registered the following year as a charitable (nonprofit) organization. It conducted a needs assessment of the Toronto Vietnamese population with a grant from the provincial Ministry of Culture and Recreation (Vietnamese Association of Toronto 1979). With encouragement from Immigration Canada, the association received federal funding for resettlement services. The provincial government gave the association free space in a provincial government building as part of a partnership with an interfaith council for refugee resettlement. In 1985 a provincial Community Facilities Improvement Program Grant facilitated the purchase of a small, two-story building with two meeting rooms and several offices to serve as a permanent home for the association. VAT's revenues, $120,000 in 1984, reached almost $920,000 in 1997. Today it organizes social and cultural events, oversees ESL programs, runs citizenship classes, offers job placement and counseling, and regularly speaks out in public on behalf of Vietnamese Canadians in Toronto.

A major advantage of government money is that it often comes in larger amounts and over a longer period of time than alternative funding sources, thereby helping to provide organizational stability and to expand an organization's agenda and activities. The cost is increased administration. In the words of one Vietnamese American executive director:

> [Foundations] don't come with a lot of requirements. Usually they give you a grant for the whole year; they just give you a check and they expect you to give them a report by the year end. Government? Whoa! First you have to submit a bill every month and you get reimbursed. And you have to do a report every quarter. And all kinds of stuff. A lot of requirements.
>
> But for foundations, it's a one-year thing, so you have to reapply every year. So that's the negative. For government, in many cases it could be a two year or a five year, so if you get selected, then it's longer term.

All grant-based funding demands some formalization of operations, but receiving public monies appears to exacerbate this tendency. Government prioritizes accountability and fiscal integrity when disbursing public funds, forcing community organizations to assign individuals to administering, overseeing, and reporting on such monies (Smith and Lipsky 1993). Such professionalization runs the risk of bifurcating political involvement: paid professionals engage in sustained, full-time activity while ordinary individuals do little (Skocpol 1999, 2003).

Yet eschewing government monies does not necessarily eliminate problems of professionalization, and it can exacerbate the divide between organizational elites and average community members. Political or advocacy groups that avoid public monies are often supported by elites who possess significant personal resources and technical expertise. Given these assets, such organizations can be even more professional than groups that rely on government support, and because they are less reliant on broad-based community support, they do not necessarily encourage mass participation (Bloemraad 2002).

In contrast, public funding can encourage democratic processes within organizations, with spillover effects into mainstream politics. To secure public funding, leaders must satisfy government officials that there is community support and participation in their proposed initiative. As one Vietnamese American put it, "it's all political when you go to government. . . . You have to have a lot of community support. You have to get everyone on board." Regulations accompanying government monies often require grant recipients to hold annual meetings or regular public consultations, thereby preventing the dominance of one charismatic leader or movement entrepreneur (Staggenborg 1988). It can also promote bridges between first-generation immigrants and more "North Americanized" 1.5- and second-generation members of the community.

Such was the case for Viet-AID, the first and apparently only community development corporation (CDC) in the United States established by Vietnamese Americans. Dreamed up by a tight-knit group of friends who had migrated to the United States as adolescents, Viet-AID's success relied on a partnership across generational lines and with mainstream actors. The young founders brought professional skills and organizational savvy to the project. The executive director had worked as a lawyer for Greater Boston Legal Services and had learned about the CDC model through relationships with American-born lawyers and activists. The future president of the board, who worked for a time as executive director for another community-based organization, had developed relationships to other nonprofit workers at the local, regional, and national levels. These relationships taught him more about CDCs and funding options. Given their experience, the group successfully pitched a proposal to private foundations for a small seed grant. There was, however, substantial suspicion from some older members of the Vietnamese American community over the group's goals—which were focused on the United States rather than anticommunism in Vietnam—and the perceived threat to established leadership.[20]

As the fledgling organization gained steam and showed results, various levels of government signaled an interest in providing funding, but they

demanded coalition building. Organizers had to convince government officials that they enjoyed the support of all Vietnamese Americans and that
they could legitimately represent their interests. The group consequently
cultivated good relations with older and more conservative Vietnamese by
holding regular community meetings and asking a prominent elder to chair
the steering committee of the new community center. Within four years,
public monies supported approximately half of the agency's activities, and in
the ensuing years government provided half to two-thirds of Viet-AID's
budget. Founded in 1994 as a small one-person operation with a total budget of $37,500, by 2000 Viet-AID had revenues of $916,064 and a staff of
ten. Its community center project, completed in November 2002, is considered an important symbol of the community's empowerment. According to
Executive Director Long Nguyen, "This center says to everyone that the
Vietnamese community is here. The center signifies our existence in terms
of political power" (*Boston Globe*, July 18, 1999). While many might
assume that prior political power led to government support of the community center, it was actually the process of securing funding and constructing
the building that taught the Vietnamese community political skills,
increased its public visibility, and augmented its ability to exercise its political voice.

Autonomy and Co-optation: Normalizing Public Intervention

Through funding relationships, networking, and teaching political skills,
settlement and multiculturalism policies increase political interest and participation among ethnic organizations and, in turn, among ordinary immigrants. Newcomer policies also privilege normal rather than contentious
politics. The Office of New Bostonians promotes voter registration and electoral participation, not street demonstrations. Citizenship classes at VAT
and MAPS teach pride in national political institutions. These classes raise
issues of historic political exclusions based on gender and race, but the overall message is one of working within the system. A good citizen pays attention to current events, votes, writes letters to local politicians, and is proud
to be an American or Canadian.

Organizations are also encouraged to work within the system. The very
existence of newcomer policies leads political actors to consult with immigrant communities on program implementation or future directions. Canadian ministries occasionally convene roundtables with private sector "stakeholders" when they formulate policy. Such meetings allow direct access to
political decision makers and can serve as a point of access for future issues,
even when a group fails to influence current policy (Simmons and Keohane

1992). An executive director of one Toronto nonprofit organization met senior Treasury officials during a government-sponsored roundtable. Using this contact, he later scheduled a meeting between community-based organizations and Treasury officials to discuss funding for immigrant settlement. Canada's wider array of newcomer policies and the greater role played by the civil service in Canada's parliamentary tradition facilitate this route of political access more in Toronto than Boston.[21]

Some question the wisdom of incorporation into existing institutional politics, especially when the current system might disadvantage political outsiders. According to Katznelson (1981), normal American politics assumes a separation between the politics of the workplace and the politics of community, the latter often centered on ties of ethnicity and race. The division diffuses credible challenges to the political status quo. Piven and Cloward (1977) warn that organizing for political ends has little use, since those with more power inevitably organize more successfully. Because a few powerful groups or individuals control decision making, political outsiders must engage in threats of disruption and mass protest to have an impact.[22] According to this view, government support of immigrant organizations undermines political effectiveness by channeling groups away from contentious politics.

Yet most immigrants prefer insider access, participation through the electoral system and normal advocacy work to disruptive politics. They will engage in contentious behavior when necessary, but the great majority favors less aggressive tactics. Importantly, most do not perceive incorporation into normal politics as "co-optation." Rather, a voter registration drive organized by city hall signals mainstream society's acceptance of newcomers' legitimate place in Canadian or American politics.

Organizational leaders also do not consider themselves to be substantially constrained by public funding. A former staff member of a Toronto-based Portuguese Canadian organization explained:

> Well, of course there is this perception out there that government in the past has wasted all this money subsidizing organizations that end up lobbying government, and how incestuous can that be? But in reality, that is not true. Government has never really subsidized organizations to do advocacy or lobbying. We are subsidized to do settlement and integration programming and community development work in our communities. But what it means though, too, is that government here in Canada, at least thus far, has been rather accepting and open of the fact that we also have to take action on behalf of our communities around issues. So there has been a certain acceptance and understanding that this is part of our role.

When access does not result in desired outcomes, community organizations will employ different tactics, as described by one staff member: "The picture that I think that I would like to portray is that it has been a long road. It has been very hard; we've had to work very hard and lobby very hard to ensure that services are there. . . . We have had to be in their faces many times. We've had to write letters, we've had to make noise, in terms of insuring that there is accessibility." Despite their dependence on public largesse, newcomer organizations do not fear criticizing government.

For example, St. Christopher House of Toronto is a regular critic despite its dependence on public funding. "St. Chris," as it is affectionately known, serves both the Portuguese and Vietnamese communities in west downtown Toronto. Established in 1912 by the Presbyterian Church of Canada, St. Chris began with a clear mandate to Canadianize and Christianize. Within a decade of its founding, tensions arose between the board, interested in promoting the "influence and the fellowship of the Christian Church," and settlement workers, primarily concerned with social improvement and good citizenship (O'Connor 1986: 33). In 1963 St. Chris incorporated as a nonsectarian multiservice community organization, and today its mission is "the enabling of less-advantaged individuals, families and groups . . . to gain greater control of their lives and within their community." The organization focuses on service provision, leadership development, community relations, and "advocat[ing] for changes in social systems that will ensure dignity, quality of life, and equal opportunity for all" (St. Christopher House 2000: 1).

Following incorporation, St. Christopher House became increasingly dependent on public monies from all levels of government. In 1964, 22 percent of the organization's revenues came from the city of Toronto.[23] Ten years later, government contributions increased to 34 percent of the total, in 1984 they stood at 42 percent, and by 1994 the proportion had swelled to 65 percent, a percentage that remained stable into 2000.

The increased reliance on government money, including settlement and multiculturalism grants, has not muzzled the organization. In the 1960s staff participated in the social change movement. A particularly activist period in the mid-1970s resulted in Cleaners' Action, a program to help mostly Portuguese cleaners in downtown office buildings learn about their rights under labor codes and organize for better work conditions.[24] Today, the volunteer board regularly speaks out for the disadvantaged, and paid staff advocate at the municipal level for affordable housing, seniors' services, and help for the homeless, while at the provincial level they have been vocal opponents of welfare cuts. In many ways, St. Christopher House embodies the ideal of a "third space" of civil society: autonomous from government and the market, engaged in advocacy and problem identification, valorizing action for public purposes, and promoting the development of local social capital (Van Til 2000; Salamon 1999: 16–17). Yet much of its work over the last thirty years would have been impossible without government partnership.

Agenda Setting: Programmatic Channeling and Creative "Program Slippage"

Even with a shift to institutionalized tactics and away from disruptive direct action, organizations of political "outsiders" can exert real influence (Staggenborg 1988). Normalization of political tactics is not necessarily a problem if an organization can keep "outsider" goals. A third strand of concern about state co-optation worries that government priorities and programmatic guidelines will dictate the activities and agenda of organizations that receive public funds. Community leaders beholden on public monies, for their jobs or for their organization's survival, might be less likely to demand dramatic changes in the way immigrants are treated. Chung (2002) found that a radical Korean American advocacy organization in Los Angeles, which largely failed to attract government funding, suffered from a reduced financial base but perceived greater liberty to pursue controversial political agendas.

Among Portuguese and Vietnamese social service and advocacy groups, government policy has a noticeable effect on *programmatic* decisions but less of an impact on *political* activity. The desire to expand services and to increase the size and financial resources of an organization leads community groups to chase government dollars, even if the priorities of a certain contract or grant do not necessarily overlap with the most critical needs of the community. At the same time, major political issues can mobilize an immigrant community regardless of government grants, and organizations regularly formulate advocacy goals independent of public funding.

Finding direct evidence of government agenda setting is not easy. Community activists and nonprofit staff show substantial creativity in arguing for a particular, and critical, community need that also happens to match a current government program. Nonetheless, almost all directors of community-based organizations acknowledge that programmatic channeling occurs. Its impact can be seen best in the absence of certain programs. Naturalization among Portuguese in Massachusetts is relatively low, but MAPS did not employ a full-time citizenship counselor until state funding for the Citizenship Assistance Program became available in the late 1990s. The need for citizenship assistance clearly existed earlier, but MAPS concentrated on health and social services, two areas for which there are substantial public contracts.

In a similar manner, school dropout is a significant problem among Portuguese youth (Nunes 1998), but few Portuguese social service agencies in Boston or Toronto have developed youth education programs.[25] In the Boston area, the lack of mobilization stems in part from a general policy framework that understands stratified educational outcomes as primarily an issue of race rather than socioeconomic status.[26] In Toronto there has been more advocacy—a group of activists with an interest in education, including a former member of the school board and an employee of the public school system, have spoken out and formed parent groups—but the Portuguese community lacks significant programming to combat school dropout and "streaming" that directs students to technical high schools rather than regular institutions. Instead, resources are directed at seniors, family violence prevention, health care, and immigrant settlement. These issues are also important, but the presence of these programs reflects funding availability more than a sustained dialogue about their relative merits compared to other needs.[27]

This tendency toward programmatic channeling worsens under government contracting as compared to government or foundation grant programs. Under contracting, government pays an organization to undertake a very specific task. In the words of one staff member, "the money that comes from the state, it's all for a different program, and you can only spend that money providing that specific service. Sometimes the community has other needs, but, you know, we can't provide those services because that's not what the funding is for." Evaluating the "contracting regime" in the United States, Smith and Lipsky claim that "control over government purse strings allows public officials to dominate the policy debate . . . to determine where the greatest need exists . . . [and] to decide which service philosophies are most appropriate" (1993: 15). In contrast, grants give an organization greater liberty in the use of funds. Organizations receive money for projects that they propose rather than a service that the state wants to outsource. Through the 1980s and into the early 1990s, Canadian governments were more apt to distribute grants while American governments were more likely to administer contracts. This provided more room for advocacy and political integration projects, helping to explain greater immigrant political activism in Canada. However, in the late 1990s Canadian governments cut back on grant making and, as was the case in the United States, increasingly restricted disbursements to project costs rather than general operating expenses (Hall et al. 2003).[28]

The power of government agenda setting is mitigated in two ways. First, many organizations engage in creative "program slippage": they construct liberal definitions of project guidelines to address problems that do not receive financial support. Second, groups exert some say over program guidelines and priorities through advocacy work. Such influence is difficult since government decision making is embedded in larger political debates and complex bureaucratic processes and tends to be reactive rather than proactive, but community organizations can sway political agendas.

Bending the Rules: Program Slippage　Staff who engage in program slippage allocate small amounts of monies from various grants to run community development programs that are not otherwise funded, or they use liberal understandings of program goals to pursue empowerment and advocacy work. The use of public funds for HIV/AIDS education illuminates this strategy particularly well.[29] The Women's Health Leadership Initiative, part of the Massachusetts Asian AIDS Prevention Project, formally aims to educate Vietnamese women about HIV/AIDS and prevent its spread in the community. The actual program is much more ambitious.

The coordinator of the Women's Initiative trains Vietnamese immigrant women to become paid peer counselors. These women are frequently receiving social assistance, so the project also functions as a de facto employment program. The peer counselors hold a series of "home parties" to which they invite friends and acquaintances. During the gathering, counselors steer the conversation to educational efforts. Topics include HIV/AIDS but also general discussions of sex, contraceptive methods, pregnancy, sexually transmitted diseases, general communication techniques in the home and workplace, and information on how to access social and health services. Staff members justify the greatly expanded agenda by reasoning:

> There's a need to attack the social change that Asian women would
> have to undergo to reach their potential, their full potential as a member
> of this society. . . . We end up doing a lot of things beside HIV/AIDS
> awareness. . . . They need to understand the health care system. They
> need the language. And they need to get out of the box. They've been
> in the box so long. What do I mean by getting themselves out of the
> box? The women tend to stay at home and take care of their family.
> Think of their family always, all the time, before they think of them-
> selves. . . . We tell them that if you not healthy, how [are] you going
> to maintain your family?

Other organizations engage in similarly creative redefinitions of program objectives. The ability of St. Christopher House to pursue its agenda of social change, despite the constraints of government funding, is due in large part to the use of "program slippage" techniques.

"Educating" for Change If government policy channels community groups' activities, ethnic organizations can also try to shape those policies. They must tread carefully, however, and the line they walk seems narrower in the United States than in Canada. In the United States, organizations that wish to set up as nonprofit groups—bodies that do not have to pay taxes— must file for this status with the Internal Revenue Service. Those who file under the tax code's 501(c)3 provisions can provide private donors with tax benefits for their charitable contribution. In return, the tax code requires that no "substantial" portion of a group's activities go to political lobbying.[30] The law also prohibits nonprofits from directly supporting a specific political candidate, party, or political action committee. As a result, community organizations claim to "advocate" on behalf of their community through educational activities: they educate their members, the mainstream community, and policy makers about issues of concern.[31] As one advocate describes it, "We don't consider ourselves lobbying; we just consider ourselves educating our public officials about the issues of the community. Making them responsive to the community, that's all. . . . Lobbyists can give people, you know, free rides, different things, and bonuses, and bring them on vacation. . . . That's not what [we] do." Board members and administrators often fear that overt political activity can hurt an organization's legal standing or damage funding opportunities if it is perceived as partisan.

At the same time, terms such as *advocate* and *educate* offer substantial interpretative leeway, providing an opening for political activity and mobilization. An employee of a community-based organization in Massachusetts pointed out gray areas: "Officially, we can't lobby, we can't pay people. We cannot lobby. But, we lobby on a daily basis. We advocate on behalf of our clients daily, when we deal with other services—with other organizations, governments. . . . So indirectly, we're lobbying, on behalf of our clients. But we also advocate with our government. We call [it] advocacy. We go out many times into the state and meet with our public officials, our legislators, and talk to them about our needs. You know, they need to know the needs of the community."

The line between lobbying and advocacy becomes particularly thin when budget decisions are made about public funds or when legislation directly affecting immigrants and refugees is debated. It is often at this point that organizations try to mobilize individuals directly into the political process, asking them to appear before legislative committees, to call their local politicians, or to write letters in support of a particular policy or program. As one staff member at a Vietnamese American agency put it, "the agency, its status does not allow us to do any political thing. We cannot lobby for our client to vote for that candidate or the other candidate. . . . But we do, within the limit of the law, we do advocate people to register to vote. When you become [a] citizen, you have to vote. Your vote will bring benefit back for the community."

In Canada, many fewer groups benefit from charitable status. While Canadian regulations appear to mirror those in the United States—intending charitable status to be reserved for organizations working for the relief of poverty, the advancement of education or religion, and "other purposes beneficial to the community"—they have been applied restrictively, excluding many ethno-cultural groups because they are perceived as too narrow in their public purpose (Hall et al. 2005: 29). Unlike in the United States, many ethnic groups cannot offer tax benefits to donors.

While various executive directors bemoan their reduced ability to attract private gifts, they might gain by having slightly more leeway for political activism. Members of Canadian community organizations feel political constraints similar to American counterparts.[32] An executive director of a Toronto nonprofit explained, "What agencies have tried to do is to advocate on issues but never ever align themselves with a political party. . . . On issues, yeah, agencies have spoken up. Will and always will. We'll come up with the research, will try link up with other groups. You know, sometimes there are coalition groups and we'll try to join. But it's a fine line you walk." Yet community advocates in Toronto appeared more willing to use their organizations for political ends than activists in Boston.

Indeed, Canadian government officials appear proud to tell international counterparts that they have no philosophical problem funding their critics. Asked whether the multiculturalism program gets attacked for giving taxpayer money to private groups who then pressure government, one senior civil servant claimed that this was "a nonissue": "We don't see it as a problem. The ultimate goal is to have equality in participation. Since that is not the case now, we have to take steps to achieve that goal. . . . We still get calls from some people who say we shouldn't be giving money to these groups because it hurts Canadians and these groups become too powerful. But, history shows they are underrepresented and far from having too much power." Given the ideology of multiculturalism as a policy of inclusion, officials and community activists share a certain agreement that groups can challenge government even if they receive public funds.[33]

We can see openness to political engagement in the activities of OCASI, the Ontario umbrella organization for immigrant-serving agencies. In the late 1990s it received 80–90 percent of its funding from all three levels of Canadian government: Citizenship and Immigration Canada (CIC), the provincial newcomer settlement program, and the City of Toronto Access and Equity unit. In turn, OCASI spent about 60 percent of its time and energy on policy development and promotion, 30 percent on public education campaigns, and 10 percent on support to member organizations.[34] Its political activities run from high-level face-to-face meetings with government ministers and senior civil servants to letter-writing campaigns in favor of particular pieces of legislation. Staff at OCASI feel that they generally have the freedom to advocate as they wish, despite their reliance on public funds.

American activists and employees of nonprofit organizations perceive less latitude. They fear being branded as partisan by elected officials who could subsequently cut them off from public funds.[35] The rationale for banning the use of public funds for political purposes lies in the pluralist tradition: the state should stay neutral to alternative political orientations. The lack of a diversity policy toward newcomers reinforces the idea that they should play the political game like everyone else. However, when groups such as immigrants and refugees have few alternative resources to public funding, government can affect the agendas of community-based organizations' in a repressive manner: legal and political fears cause organizations to avoid certain issues or to abstain from certain activities.

Such silencing is a danger, though it is far from complete. American organizations do have an alternative resource, private foundations, which are much less prevalent in Canada. Nonprofit groups in the United States cannot escape tax law, but they can avoid charges of misusing public funds by relying on private donations, especially from philanthropic foundations.[36] Foundations frequently provide start-up funds for new or controversial projects.[37] As a member of Viet-AID explained, "usually [foundations] are willing to try new things. They want to promote innovation, so when you have a new idea, usually you go to a foundation first to test out that idea. And then when it's proven successful, then you can go to the government." Massachusetts's equivalent to OCASI, MIRA, is significantly less dependent on government monies than the Ontario organization, and it engages in political and public education efforts similar to OCASI's. In 1997 only 16 percent of total revenues came through public grants or contracts.[38]

Does it make a difference if American and Canadian advocacy organizations such as MIRA and OCASI rely on public funds to different degrees? Both groups are politically active, and both pursue similar agendas. Because of its dependence on government funding, OCASI has fewer options when public funding ends, but commitments tend to be long term and relatively stable except in periods of substantial government cutbacks. MIRA enjoys more freedom from government thanks to private donations, but private monies are less stable and require more sustained fund-raising. Perceived anti-immigrant legislation passed in 1996 helped fuel donations to MIRA, resulting in an annual budget for 1997 of over $800,000. By 2000, however, revenues fell to $483,000, a decrease of 40 percent.

Beyond income, government grants also build a relationship with those employed in government agencies and departments. The result is that government funding can open access points for advocacy and mobilization, although it also routinizes political activity. As Smith and Lipsky (1993) note, despite the drawbacks of government contracting, such arrangements help foster organizational capacity in cases where it is limited or does not exist, a situation characteristic of many newcomer communities.

Breton suggests that the effect of institutional completeness is at least partly political: a more organized immigrant community increases ethnic sentiment and solidarity, arouses greater intracommunity debate and interest, and spurs leaders of organizations to maintain or enlarge the clientele of the group (1964: 199–200, 1991). All things being equal, communities with greater organizational capacity will be more politically active and better able to encourage individual immigrants to become politically involved.[39] Evidence from the Portuguese and Vietnamese communities in Toronto and Boston suggests that government intervention facilitates the creation and persistence of community organizations. State support is not a necessary condition for the establishment of community organizations, but the presence of settlement and multicultural policies is associated with a greater degree of organizing. Furthermore, the most prominent ethnic organizations in each community rely heavily on public funds.

According to much of the neo-Tocquevillian thinking on civic participation, such a symbiotic relationship between government and civic groups should not occur. State intervention should crowd out associationalism. Joyce and Schambra claim that the zenith of this process occurred under Lyndon Johnson's Great Society project: "The Great Society probably came as close as any other effort in the twentieth century to capturing progressivism's ideal: public policy securely in the hands of an elite cadre of professionals, dispensing programs through vast, gleaming, rational bureaucracies" (1996: 20). Statism stands in contrast with ordinary people's "yearning for the intimate, face-to-face, participatory community to be found in small groups, family, neighborhood, church, and ethnic and voluntary associations" (Joyce and Schambra 1996: 20).

Ironically, and in stark contradiction to this view, the group that has benefited the least from government largesse—the Portuguese in Boston—owes the existence of the community's central service provider and advocate, MAPS, to the very Great Society initiatives that Joyce and Schambra criticize. The Portuguese, with no established settlement programs on which to draw, benefited from government urban renewal and community development programs administered through the Model Cities program of the late 1960s and early 1970s (Dreyer 1978; Ito-Alder 1980 [1972, 1978]). It is perhaps no coincidence that as such programs faded away or were redirected, the Portuguese community largely failed to develop new organizations.

We need to weigh the costs and benefits of government intervention, in particular the trade-off between the increase in resources and political access that comes with government intervention versus the concomitant pressure to conform to governmental agendas. Reliance on government policies channels programmatic decisions and normalizes political behavior. Yet it does not appear to determine political activities and, in fact, seems to increase overall political interest and activism.

For those who wish to avoid government support, what are the options? Organizations can turn to private donations, rely on internal revenue generation, or depend completely on the voluntary energies of their members and supporters. Vietnamese organizations directed at homeland politics, Portuguese social clubs, and a host of private recreation groups do not use public funds. Such autonomy appears easier in the United States, where we find more private foundations, fewer government grants, and more generous rules regarding private charitable donations.

Independence from government is, however, rare among the most important advocacy groups, probably because an independent strategy comes with its own trade-offs. Vietnamese and Portuguese immigrants are generous with donations in the face of natural disasters or special fund-raising campaigns, but limited economic means make it difficult to sustain political or advocacy organizations purely on internal fund-raising. Organizations that eschew public support tend to be less permanent and more subject to periods of relative inactivity once the voluntary, financial, or ideological energies of the founders become exhausted. Among organizations that avoid government assistance, the most successful tend to be run by the most privileged members of the immigrant community, relying on the generosity of wealthy and prominent community members. These individuals can establish effective, professional organizations, but at a potential cost of creating a disconnect between organizational leaders and ordinary immigrants.

Importantly, organizations that receive government funding seem more likely to assist those who are less apt to become politically engaged: the poor, women, and those facing particular hurdles to political incorporation. As Berry (2003) argues, government support of nonprofit, voluntary organizations provides an important resource for underserved populations to develop a political voice. To the extent that government support helps organizations reach out to marginalized segments of the community, public intervention promotes a more diverse citizenry.

6. Learning to Lead and Winning Political Office

> If I had maybe found a job with [a large corporation], I might have gone into a different direction, if you know what I mean. But my occupation brought me to very close dealings with the community. . . . You live in a community, you have to be part of the community. And in whatever small way you can, you have to do something.
>
> AGOSTINHO, *Portuguese immigrant, Toronto*

> It must be destiny, because when [my friends] graduated, the economy—[there were] no jobs. So they all moved into the nonprofit sector. If the economy at that time was as hot as the economy two years ago, I don't think . . . It would have been a totally different story. . . . As soon as you work as an engineer, making money, then you totally think differently.
>
> THANH, *Vietnamese refugee, Boston*

Community leaders are central to much of the story of immigrant political incorporation told thus far. They promote naturalization, encourage political participation, and build and sustain community organizations.[1] Leaders also serve as bridges, linking the debates and concerns of the immigrant community to the politics of mainstream society.[2] Being able to speak with a more or less unified voice through the figure of a leader facilitates political claims making since "the state and polity's authorities cannot deal with abstractions, but have recourse to privileged actors or individuals, namely to ethnic leaders and elites" (Martiniello 1993: 241).[3]

This chapter focuses on two types of leaders, community advocates and elected representatives. Leadership can be defined in a variety of ways, but I concentrate on what Jenkins has termed *policy advocacy,* "any attempt to influence the decisions of any institutional elite on behalf of a collective interest" (1987: 297).[4] Successful leadership in this context means the ability to enter into dialogue with political actors, to articulate an immigrant community's interests to mainstream authorities, and to mobilize community members toward electoral or policy ends.[5]

When we examine the career trajectories of community leaders and the dynamics that brought them to prominence or to elected office, we find that government settlement and diversity policies often eased their path. Such policies provide formal and informal leadership opportunities through the organizations that they support and legitimize the idea of ethnic advocacy. Canadian settlement and multiculturalism policies—combined with stronger political parties, easier entry into the electoral system, and dynamics of ideological congruence—also account for the much higher percentage of foreign-born politicians in Canada than in the United States. The difference matters deeply, because most newcomers feel that having "one of our own" in politics provides better community representation, easier access into political circles, and important symbolic affirmation of the ethnic community.

ADVOCACY AND NEWCOMER SETTLEMENT

Most community advocates learn to lead. Many of the skills of leadership, such as feeling at ease with public speaking or having organizational acumen, can be learned and perfected through participation in voluntary organizations and formal work settings (Verba, Schlozman, and Brady 1995). In the previous chapter we saw that government settlement and diversity policies help establish and sustain community organizations. These same organizations act as important training grounds for would-be advocates. Indeed, the constellation of organizations, agencies, and programs—whether nonprofit, public, or for-profit—that caters to the adaptation needs of newcomers, what we can call the newcomer settlement industry, repeatedly figures in the personal narratives of many community leaders.[6] The traditional sources of ethnic leadership lie in religious authority, business success, and/or having held a position of importance in the home country.[7] In all three cases, leadership heavily favors wealthier or more educated men. Government policies, by helping to build organizational infrastructures and legitimizing settlement and diversity initiatives, can promote new, alternative routes to leadership. Where such policies are more prevalent, as in Canada more generally or in the United States' refugee resettlement programs specifically, we find greater opportunities for advocacy and a greater diversity in the types of people who become community advocates.

Settlement Jobs and Recruitment to Advocacy

Many advocates find themselves working in institutions of newcomer settlement, by desire, by chance, or because they lack other options. In some respects the newcomer settlement industry functions like any other industry, providing individuals with careers ladders, common purposes, and interorganizational networks.[8] In addition, however, participation in settlement and diversity initiatives teaches leadership skills, provides visibility within and outside the community, and fosters confidence in would-be advocates' ability to represent and mobilize community members. Settlement work also helps deepen an ideology of advocacy, particularly the belief that immigrants' participation and political claims are legitimate.

In this way, the newcomer settlement industry provided the professional training ground for Dan, the Canadian-born son of Portuguese immigrant parents. Dan had a prior interest in community service that found an outlet in various jobs related to the Portuguese. As he recalls:

> I remember going through high school and being encouraged to become an accountant, and being encouraged to become a lawyer. The guidance counselor had me pegged for one or the other . . . but I just couldn't stand it. You know what I mean? I always just wanted to go the social services route. I always just wanted to listen to people and to help people, as best I could. You know, the sappy reason why all of us social work types get into this type of work. . . . And I've always wanted to do that with the Portuguese community, because I've always [seen] the need here as being the greatest and it's my roots, and it's always been the community that I wanted to work with.

After completing his university degree, Dan found employment helping immigrants as a coordinator of interpretation services, a paralegal specializing in immigration matters, and a staff member in various ethnic nonprofit organizations. Today he runs one of those agencies.

Continuous employment in nonprofit and private settlement organizations allowed Dan to sustain and deepen his interest in helping the Portuguese. Dan, like many, has had occasional doubts, "At times I've wondered, in terms of my own career path, that perhaps I should have just strayed a little bit. I might be earning a little bit more money. . . . Perhaps achieving a little more respect." However, daily contact with immigrants reaffirms his belief that such work is important: "I've been fighting for so long. It's one thing to say that these people should learn English, but what if they don't? What are you going to do? Every service that we offer works toward giving empowerment, works toward that ultimate goal of being self-sufficient. But you've gotta start where people are, and you can't start anywhere else, or otherwise you're marginalizing. So, that was an argument that we'd been making for so, so long." Such feelings led him to advocacy and engagement with municipal and provincial decision makers.

Others follow a serendipitous path to community leadership. These people often begin working with the immigrant community because they need a job, not from a strong internal conviction. Celia was born in Portugal and came to Canada as a child. She went to a Canadian high school and completed a degree in the humanities at a local university. Searching for a job after graduation, she stumbled onto a government communications post that required language skills. By coincidence the position focused on immigrant outreach. This job then drew Celia along a path to leadership within the Portuguese community. She began to see the work that she did as important, and she gained confidence in her ability to help people and advocate on their behalf:

> I wasn't interacting with the Portuguese community all that much at that time. . . . It wasn't until I worked [for the government] that my interaction became more interaction of people calling and saying, "Do you know where we can get grants?" and "Do you know who I can call to get this information and that information?" Because, once a member of your own community is in a place where you're perceived to have some knowledge or some power, you automatically get those calls, and an invitation to go to events, and so on. Even though I wasn't filling a powerful position, by no stretch of the imagination. . . .
>
> And those were very positive experiences. . . . It also gave me an opportunity to make [government] a little more accessible to ethnic groups who hadn't before had the opportunity to step in there and to get a feel of how the government works and so on.

This initial positive experience led Celia to stay in immigrant advocacy: she later worked for a nonprofit community agency and more recently in another government department. Over the last fifteen years, she has been actively involved in many community projects and in bringing more Portuguese into politics by promoting citizenship, encouraging voting, speaking to candidates, and being actively involved in a Canadian political party.

"We Became 'Parentified'": Recruiting Leaders from the 1.5 Generation
Individuals from the "1.5 generation" such as Celia—immigrants born overseas but who migrate as children or adolescents—are particularly likely to be recruited into newcomer settlement. These people frequently possess needed bilingual and bicultural skills. Their leadership path often begins with informal settlement work as a child, continues as a summer job or internship with a local community organization during high school or college, and then crystallizes in a permanent position with a nonprofit social service provider, advocacy group, public agency, or private settlement business in adulthood.

Community activists and political leaders of the 1.5 generation repeatedly mention how they were forced by circumstance to assume the roles of interpreter, translator, advocate, spokesperson, and even defense lawyer for their parents, relatives, and family friends. For those who migrate with their parents, this role is thrust upon them immediately. Rosana, a Portuguese American in her late thirties, works for an immigrant advocacy organization. She remembers, "I immigrated at the age of eight. And I became everybody's caretaker. . . . I learned English quite rapidly, so I was doing for everybody, you know? I became an advocate at the age of nine." Others, especially Vietnamese adolescents, sometimes precede family members by a few years. After struggling with their own adaptation experiences, they serve as "social workers," in the words of one young man, to later arrivals. It feels natural to continue this work as an adult, provided that the opportunity to do so exists.

Adolescent settlement and advocacy "training" comes at a price. Many speak of these experiences with some bitterness, feeling that they lost a part of their childhood. Marco moved to the United States when he was fourteen. Today, he is a senior staff member at a local community-based organization, a job he loves. It lets him work with fellow Portuguese Americans and serve as a liaison to mainstream American institutions, where he is an advocate for the community. Marco attributes his current work in large part to his experiences helping his parents and family friends when he was young. But he also remembers the worry associated with this role:

> We became "parentified." We really became the parents of the family. Because we knew the language and slowly began to learn—because we were in school—the system, we were the ones who, every time the mail came into the house, we were the ones providing interpreting/ translation. We were going with my parents to the doctor's, going with them to City Hall for every issue that they had with the house, all that stuff. Social Security. If they were unemployed, they became laid off from the companies—and there were some times when people became laid off in the mid-eighties—we had to go with them to the unemployment office. I mean, you name it, we did it.
>
> I became the social worker, I became the father. . . . You know, I was taking care of my parents, I was taking them by the hand everywhere. . . . I remember having nightmares the night before I had to go with my parents, because I always used to think, "What if I don't say it right, if I don't understand it right? What if I don't communicate well? Are my parents going to lose their house?"

Others told similar stories of how, at the age of ten, they would have to call a utility company and convince an adult employee not to suspend services when bills were past due, or how they would accompany their mother to the doctor's office at the age of fourteen and be asked to translate sensitive questions about their parents' sexual relations or communicate worrying test results.

The predominance of 1.5-generation immigrants stands out in particular among the public and nonprofit agencies of the newcomer settlement industry and in advocacy organizations. In the late 1990s the executive director and deputy executive director of Massachusetts Alliance of Portuguese Speakers (MAPS) were both 1.5-generation immigrants. So, too, was a Portuguese American advocate working for the Massachusetts Immigrant and Refugee Advocacy Coalition (MIRA) and the only Portuguese-born politician in the Massachusetts State House. In Toronto, the sitting Portuguese-origin municipal councilor, who later became a member of Parliament, came to Canada at the age of nine. Other 1.5-generation community leaders include the priest heading the Portuguese Pastoral Council in the Toronto Archdiocese, a prominent union organizer, and a municipal public employee who helped found the Portuguese National Congress. Among the Vietnamese we find a similar pattern, although the dominance of the first generation remains pronounced, given more recent Vietnamese migration. The founder of Viet-AID, a community advocate working for the state of Massachusetts, and the president of the Vietnamese Women's League of Massachusetts all are 1.5-generation immigrants. In Toronto, the former president of the board of the Vietnamese Association of Toronto (VAT) came to Canada at the age of eleven, while a vocal activist for the rights of gay and lesbian Asians migrated at the age of nine. Government settlement and diversity policies help provide an outlet for these individuals, allowing them to translate their childhood experiences into community service and leadership.

Personal Pain, Public Gain? Blocked Mobility and Community Leadership
Those of the 1.5 generation have attended some school in the adopted country, and they undergo a relatively easy transition into community work given their past experiences and skills. For adult immigrants who finished their schooling and entered the workforce in their homeland, the path to advocacy often begins with blocked mobility in the adopted country. This pattern, also an "accidental" path to leadership, is especially prevalent in the Vietnamese community, but it also occurs among the Portuguese. Individuals who previously were doctors, teachers, and engineers find that their credentials are not recognized in Canada or the United States. Hai, a Vietnamese Canadian who today works as a youth social worker, remembers:

> I was [a] graduate from university with [a] mechanical engineering degree. I was looking for [engineering] work with the Canadian govern-

ment or with any agency that can offer me the job. I was not really speaking English, so I got six months of English training with Human Resources.[9] And then I apply for jobs, I make a lot of résumés. Each time I go in, people ask me this: "We know that it's silly, we know that you just arrived here six months ago, but we want to know if you have a Canadian experience?" I say, "You already know that I [just] come here, I just go through six months of training. I do not have a Canadian experience at all." Most of them say, "Well, our policy is that if you don't have a Canadian experience, we cannot accept you. We cannot interview you."

Rather than work in manual labor or low-skilled service jobs, individuals such as Hai turn to newcomer settlement as a sector in which they can leverage their education and bilingualism, in some cases quickly advancing to become an executive director of a nonprofit agency or a manager of a government agency dealing with settlement or diversity issues.

Success in these jobs is, however, bittersweet: the positions these people hold are "cleaner" and of slightly higher status than those of many of their compatriots, but wages usually fall below what they might have earned if they could have found employment in their original field.[10] The blocked mobility of these well-educated, highly motivated individuals creates a public gain for the community but some private pain for the immigrant.

Such was the case for Hai. He found a lower-paying job, and then, as the first wave of boat people landed in Canada, he volunteered with the resettlement effort:

And I thought, "Well, I remember that my ideology was to go back to build up the country, and now I cannot do that, so why don't I spend my time, extra time, to help the people who are newly arrived here? I'm lucky enough to learn already English, and at least [I] know some experience in Canadian society." So I call Canadian Immigration. I say, "I know that there's going to be a lot of Vietnamese refugees coming in. I speak English. Can I do any volunteer help?"

And they're very lucky, they are very happy at the time to have somebody to call. . . . So they got me every night to go out to the airport and then welcome the people and take them to the hotel, and explain to them and try to buy food to feed them. You know? Because most of . . . You know how the government administrators are doing, they just walk through their time, and they go home. They don't care whether people are hungry or not hungry: "Next day we do it for you." So I was working on behalf of many of the immigration officers to help those families after they arrive here, in the evening or weekend, no pay at all.

And finally, somebody from the Ontario government . . . they got to know my name. And they say, "I know that you've been, in the last few months, you've been working so hard volunteering for the community. We know that you have a lot of experience helping them and we are desperately in need of somebody to work for [us], to help welcome the people, to help orient them." So they invite me to [take a] a job as a [settlement] counselor.

This position not only offered a better salary than the job he held at the time, but it provided formal experience in community work that Hai could put on a résumé. It also allowed Hai to build a relationship with newly arriving Vietnamese, ties that he later drew on when protesting police profiling of young Vietnamese and in helping to establish a community youth center. Hai never went back to mechanical engineering; instead, he built a career in newcomer settlement.

Sometimes individuals create their own job opportunities as they advocate on behalf of their community. Such was the case for Quan Van. A doctor in Vietnam, Quan Van found that in Canada, his foreign medical degree was not recognized. Although he eventually passed a Canadian equivalency exam, he was unable to find an internship and instead had to work as a medical orderly, "This is the bottom of the medical system. In my country, I am a doctor. In Canada, I start at the bottom." The job as an orderly contributed to the household income, but Quan Van also sought more rewarding activities by volunteering with various Vietnamese community organizations and attending public meetings on health care. In part, he was motivated by a desire to give back to his community and a Christian belief in good works. Also important, however, was the satisfaction that came when non-Vietnamese Canadians treated him with respect, listening to his opinions on the needs of Vietnamese newcomers.

While learning the ins and outs of the Canadian medical system, Quan Van became convinced of what he perceived as the failure of mainstream Canadian medicine to deal with the pressing health concerns of Vietnamese newcomers, from mental health issues to tropical diseases. He sought out Vietnamese community leaders, held meetings with Vietnamese refugees, and mobilized the community behind the idea of a health center dedicated to newcomers. He also built bridges to non-Vietnamese Canadians. With the assistance of people in the city of Toronto's Public Health Department and colleagues from other ethno-cultural communities, he wrote a proposal for a multicultural health care center in downtown Toronto. The project eventually received funding from the provincial government after a sophisticated lobbying campaign. Quan Van became a director of the new center, but he never succeeded in becoming a licensed doctor in Canada. He would have preferred to practice medicine, but Quan Van is happy that he was able to put his medical knowledge to good use and delighted to have been a driving force behind much-needed services for his community. Some in the community quietly criticize his tendency to act as a self-appointed authority on the needs of Vietnamese Canadians, but all recognize that without his efforts, the community would be without a strong voice in the Canadian medical establishment and lack many vital services that he helped to establish. The presence of multiculturalism policies facilitated Quan Van's efforts by legitimizing the idea that newcomers sometimes require special linguistic, cultural, and medical services.

Developing an Advocacy Framework

The newcomer settlement industry not only channels individuals into advocacy and mobilization activities, it also develops what I term an *advocacy framework*. An advocacy framework is a general worldview that the ethnic community deserves to exist as a community (as opposed to being completely assimilated into mainstream society), deserves to receive attention from government, and deserves to influence the political system. While these are not radical propositions, many immigrants in North America arrive with the view that they can make no claims on the host society—they are outsiders who have been given the privilege of entry, and they can expect little more. In contrast, community activists feel that immigrants and refugees quickly become citizens equal to the native born, in theory if not in practice. Leaders frame this view in different ways. Those right of center downplay service provision, highlighting all individuals' inherent right to equality of opportunity. Those left of center emphasize social justice, making appeals to equality of outcome. All promote newcomers' right to political voice.

A larger settlement industry encourages more people to become community advocates, in part because the individual's employment or status is tied to the community. Those who are being paid to do newcomer settlement work have a strong incentive to show government and other potential funding sources that their services are needed. More subtly and probably more significant, working with compatriots provides would-be advocates with a better understanding of the barriers that ordinary immigrants face in making a home in the adopted country. This is especially important, since leaders invariably differ from those they try to represent and mobilize. Leaders tend to have more education, come from more privileged backgrounds, and be employed in higher-status occupations. Development of an advocacy framework helps bridge the often substantial socioeconomic gap between advocates and ordinary immigrants.[11]

For example, Agostinho, a professional with a university degree, initially wanted little to do with the Portuguese community when he migrated to Canada. He felt a wide gulf between his socioeconomic background and time in Africa compared to the majority of Portuguese, who possess limited education and hail from the Azores.[12] He sought work in his field but failed to find a position because of an economic downturn and employers' reluctance to accept his foreign credentials and work experience. Eventually he turned to newcomer settlement: "You know, I still have fifty-two letters of 'Don't call us, we'll call you.' I've kept those. And eventually I decided, given my knowledge of English and Portuguese, to consider doing something else. And I put my name down for a few translation agencies and also approached the Immigration Department to see if they were in need of interpreters. . . . And so that's how I started. I started doing some translations. And then I was teaching Portuguese also, at the Portuguese Heritage School programs with the [Catholic] school board." Although these part-time jobs were not in his area of expertise, they were white-collar occupations and paid the bills. The work in the Immigration Department put Agostinho on a public service career ladder that provided some stability. Eventually, unhappy with the low wages in the public and nonprofit sectors, Agostinho started his own business providing immigration consultation services.

Agostinho's work led him to become more involved in community advocacy. In his words, "Once you get involved, it is always the same people, you know? Who are you going to call to do something? 'Well, what about the guy who has done that for those people?' So it goes in circles." When I ask why he remains active in the community despite his initial reluctance, his response evokes elements of self-interest and public service: "[It's] the nature of my business. . . . If I had maybe found a job with [a large corporation], I might have gone into a different direction, if you know what I mean. But my occupation brought me to very close dealings with the community, you know. I mean, I can't ignore . . . You live in a community, you have to be part of the community. And in whatever small way you can, you have to do something." Without the employment opportunities available in newcomer settlement, Agostinho would have directed his professional energies elsewhere. Instead, he has been active in lobbying government on behalf of a local social service agency, has worked with municipal officials on business improvement initiatives and community-police relations, and serves on the board of various nonprofit organizations.

A former employee of the Vietnamese American Civic Association (VACA), Thanh, tells a similar story about the group of friends that served as the driving force behind VACA's early expansion. Thanh studied social sciences at college, but most of his friends took engineering, a field that required math skills over English ability and which promised financial stability after the hardships of refugee resettlement. However:

> It must be destiny, because when they graduated, the economy—[there were] no jobs. So they all moved into the nonprofit sector. If the economy at that time was as hot as the economy two years ago, I don't think . . . It would have been a totally different story. . . . As soon as you work as an engineer, making money, then you totally think differently. I have a few other friends who were very active in college, but as soon as they became engineers, it's just that you hang out with a different crowd and you talk about different things. They began to talk about big houses, stock options, you know? It's just different.

For Thanh and his friends, working with ordinary Vietnamese helped to build a sense of solidarity and understanding that spanned generations and class divisions. Reflecting back, "When we started working . . . we had a lot of problems because we couldn't get the support from the community, especially from the older generation. They were skeptical of us, they were suspicious of us, and they thought we were arrogant and all that. . . . And I guess over time . . . we became more appreciative of what they went through, the more we looked at it. We had more respect for them." This understanding, and the relationship building that went with it, helped the Vietnamese to successfully mobilize to build a Vietnamese community center in Boston.

Community leadership also requires building relationships between the immigrant community and the mainstream political system. Individuals wholly involved in the immigrant community or wholly centered on mainstream activities do a poorer job involving others in collective action than those who bridge two social worlds, unless they form part of a larger leadership team (Ganz 2000). The previous chapter outlined one way to facilitate bridging: through funding relationships and partnerships between community organizations and actors outside the immigrant community. Another way is through job rotation between nonprofit, community-based organizations and mainstream public agencies. Job rotation provides access and ties to political actors and mainstream networks that advocates can leverage for their community. The former executive director of MAPS used knowledge and contacts from his days as an employee in the state's social services bureaucracy to help the Portuguese organization generate new revenues. The executive director of the Portuguese Interagency Network (PIN) leveraged government contacts she built during her time in public service to speak out on behalf of the Portuguese Canadian community. The public-private networks of various community members, including former directors of the Massachusetts Office for Refugees and Immigrants, helped the Vietnamese community of Boston get the ear of politicians at various levels of government. Indeed, working with public settlement or diversity agencies in Boston helped a number of Vietnamese Americans gain entrée into the party system, as was the case for the municipal employee invited to a party convention by a coworker.[13] Government sensitivity to the needs of newcomers can increase employment opportunities in "mainstream" government departments if political actors prioritize the hiring of employees who have bilingual or bicultural competencies. More generally, when government policies target immigrants and/or ethno-racial minorities, the chances of building public-private networks increases.[14]

What happens when there are relatively fewer positions in newcomer settlement? Some people still selflessly devote time, money, and energy to organize community events, run associations, or speak up on behalf of the community. However, in communities such as the Portuguese or Vietnamese, where many individuals work two jobs or long hours, those who can afford to give time and resources tend to be traditional community leaders, such as prominent members of the business community. Businesspeople and professionals unconnected to newcomer settlement can run sophisticated, successful organizations, but they have greater trouble connecting with ordinary community members. This is a particular problem in the Portuguese community of Somerville and Cambridge. People there repeatedly mentioned an "elite" society of Portuguese Americans who arrange events or speak out for Portuguese immigrants without including individuals of more modest backgrounds.[15] Criticizing the distance between these individuals and other community members, one Portuguese American argued, "they cannot forget that the global community, the people themselves, are very important. . . . If you don't have a message, they don't care. Because they are too busy with their jobs. They are too busy trying to get their bills paid, too busy with their kids' problems."[16]

Working for the Community

Others have hinted at the role settlement and diversity work might play in changing patterns of leadership and political influence. Thompson (1979) documents how renewed immigration and development of the Canadian multiculturalism program shifted the traditional bases of power in the Toronto Chinese community from an old merchant elite to newly arriving entrepreneurs and to social workers and professionals staffing community-based organizations. The latter could offer Chinese laborers settlement services and sociocultural events not tied to a business patron. Similarly, Indra (1987) traces the rise of middlemen in Vietnamese, Laotian, and Cambodian communities to the Canadian government's efforts to settle newly arriving boat people in the late 1970s. Some spokespeople achieved prominence after federal immigration officials hired them as bilingual workers; others accessed multiculturalism grants to start organizations celebrating Vietnamese identity. In Queens, New York, Jones-Correa found that Latina immigrants benefit from employment in the social service bureaucracy because it "gives them both financial security and entrée into American political life" (Jones-Correa 1998a: 180). In all these cases, immigrants combine advocacy with a steady income, job security, or professional advancement.

Of course, immigrants do not need to work in settlement to be involved. The Toquevillian image of the United States suggests that active citizens should contribute to their community within the broader category of *citizen* rather than *employee*. Indeed, research on volunteerism among the general American and Canadian populations suggests that the hours worked by volunteers equal about 3.5 percent and 2.7 percent of the economically active population in the United States and Canada, respectively (Hall et al. 2005: 11). Among Portuguese and Vietnamese in Toronto and Boston, individuals who do not hold paid positions in newcomer settlement agencies provide hours of volunteer time to community endeavors. At a leadership level, however, these people are rare. Most ordinary migrants who do not work in newcomer settlement have little time to devote to community activism— many work two jobs or regular overtime—and they have little chance to learn the skills needed to be community leaders. The low-skilled service and factory work done by many Portuguese and Vietnamese does not lend itself to learning civic skills.[17]

Since the size and diversity of the newcomer settlement industry depends in large part on the support of government, communities that enjoy more government support offer a greater number and more diverse routes to community leadership. Significantly, while volunteerism in Canada is somewhat less than in the United States, the number of paid positions in the overall nonprofit sector is much larger in Canada, the equivalent of 8.4 percent of the economically active population compared to only 6.3 percent in the United States (Hall et al. 2005: 10). The more opportunities that exist in immigrant-related service provision, diversity initiatives, or advocacy work, the more chances individuals have to learn leadership skills and establish standing in both the community and mainstream society.

Some criticize the way outside intervention can promote the rise of cer tain individuals as immigrant "middlemen," or "ethnic brokers." Since such leaders, helped to prominence by outsiders, are not elected (formally or informally) by ordinary members of the community, their interests might be aligned with those of the state, not the community.[18] Similarly, ethnic brokers tend to be more privileged than ordinary community members, biasing the leaders' views of community needs or at least causing them to downplay problems to avoid giving the community a "bad name" (Indra 1987: 158–60). Such observations carry some truth in the Portuguese and Vietnamese communities in Toronto and Boston, but they exaggerate the negative consequences of public support. It is not clear that the absence of a newcomer settlement industry would appreciably change the class and education biases in leadership structures, and it might aggravate gender biases by narrowing opportunities for leadership.

RUNNING FOR POLITICAL OFFICE: EXPLAINING ELECTORAL SUCCESS

Immigrant communities are also home to a second group of leaders, those with their eyes on political representation. Some come from advocacy backgrounds.[19] Others have histories of community involvement but as business owners or individuals active in the ethnic press. Some have occupational backgrounds outside the immigrant community, but they seek the immigrant vote once they run for office.

Most stories of political participation begin by considering electoral politics—voting, campaigning, and party involvement—because electoral contests determine who sits in office and the broad direction of government. To an important extent, however, voting, campaigning, and running for office are an end point of political integration. I therefore finish my examination of immigrant political incorporation with a discussion of newcomers' electoral success. Significantly, immigrants' chances for success appear better in Canada than in the United States. Only 8 of the 435 representatives in the 106th U.S. Congress were foreign born, compared to 45 of 301 members sitting in the House of Commons during Canada's 37th Parliament.

If the incorporation dynamics associated with government settlement and multiculturalism policies also affect electoral success—defined here as winning office—we should expect patterns similar to those we found for community organizing.[20] Portuguese Americans should have lower levels of political representation than Portuguese Canadians, since they are given less state support, and outcomes should be similar for the two Vietnamese communities if all other political resources are equal. Indeed, would-be Vietnamese and Portuguese politicians in Toronto and Boston confront similar barriers in mobilizing their compatriots: low average levels of schooling, political histories that discourage involvement in politics, internal fissures dividing the community, and the relative unimportance of politics when compared to immediate economic and social demands following migration.[21] From the perspective of a traditional model of electoral behavior, only two important differences stand out: the Portuguese have, on average, lived in North America longer than the Vietnamese, and the Vietnamese in Boston boast a larger percentage of highly educated community members than the other three groups.

Our predictions largely hold true. Despite the considerable similarities between the Portuguese populations of metro Boston and Toronto, Portuguese Canadians witnessed a remarkable surge in electoral success in the 1980s and 1990s while Portuguese Americans in Cambridge/Somerville remained invisible.[22] In Toronto, dozens of Portuguese Canadians have run for office at all levels of government, seven have held positions on local school boards, two have become municipal councilors, two have held a seat as a member of Provincial Parliament, and in 2004 Toronto residents elected the first Portuguese-born member of federal Parliament.[23] Table 8 provides an overview of those elected. All but one are first- or 1.5-generation immigrants.[24] Portuguese Canadians' representation on Toronto municipal council, just under 2 percent of all seats throughout most of the 1990s, is about half the community's proportion in the city, estimated to be 4 percent in 1996.[25]

In contrast, no Portuguese American from Cambridge or Somerville won city, state, or national office in the 1980s and 1990s. Only one Portuguese American, born in the United States to Portuguese immigrant parents, has made a successful bid for elected office; she sits on the Somerville school board.[26] Given that Portuguese Americans accounted for almost 4.5 percent of the population in Cambridge and over 8 percent in Somerville, their lack of political representation is striking.[27]

There are no Vietnamese-origin politicians in Toronto or Boston. Indeed, "white ethnics" dominate the political power structures of both Toronto and Boston, although Toronto appears more open to newcomer politicians. As shown in table 9, in 1997 the municipal council of the newly amalgamated city of Toronto counted fifty-seven members, twenty-seven of whom were of British origin (47 percent), eleven Italian (19 percent), six Jewish (11 percent), four Chinese (7 percent), and three blacks of immigrant origin

TABLE 8. ELECTED REPRESENTATIVES OF PORTUGUESE ORIGIN, METRO BOSTON AND TORONTO, 1980–2005

Politician	Elected to	Represents	Tenure in Office	Party	Generation	Occupation
Boston						
Teresa Cardoso	Public school board	Somerville	1991–present	Democratic	2	Office manager
Toronto						
Carl DeFaria	Provincial legislature	Mississauga	1995–2004	Progressive Conservative	1	Lawyer
Marques Domingos	Separate school board	Downtown	1991–94	New Democratic	1	Legal consultant
Christine Ferreira	Public school board	Downtown	1997–2003	New Democratic	2	Public relations
Peter Fonesca	Provincial legislature	Mississauga	2004–present	Liberal	1.5	Management consultant
Tony Letra	Separate school board	Downtown	1982–84, 1994–97	Liberal	1	Social worker
Nellie Pedro	Public school board	Downtown	2000–03	Liberal	1	TV producer (ethnic)
Maria Rodrigues	Public school board	Downtown	2003–present	New Democratic	1.5	Public employee
Vasco Santos	French public school board	Downtown	1985–87	New Democratic	1	Journalist (ethnic)
Mario Silva	City council	Downtown	1994–2003	Liberal	1.5	Politician
	Federal House of Commons	Downtown	2004–present			
Martin Silva	Municipal council	Downtown	1988–97	New Democratic	1.5	Radio announcer (ethnic)
	Separate school trustee to public board	Downtown	1985–86			

SOURCES: Author's interviews and published electoral returns.

(5 percent); the remainder were of various European ancestries, including one Portuguese Canadian (Siemiatycki and Isin 1997: 92).[28] None were Vietnamese. In comparison, the 1996 census found that those of British origin only made up 18 percent of the city's population, Italians 7 percent, Jewish 4 percent, Chinese 9 percent, blacks 10 percent, Portuguese 3 percent, and Vietnamese 1 percent.[29] The British thus enjoy three and a half times as much political representation as their numbers warrant and Italians twice as much, while visible minorities—the Canadian term for nonwhite populations—account for 43 percent of the city's population but only hold 12 percent of council seats.

In Boston, representation by minorities is no better, and if we consider those of immigrant background, it is worse. Following the 1999 election, U.S.-born candidates of European origin held eleven of thirteen council seats (85 percent), although only 49 percent of the city's population is non-Hispanic white. Most strikingly, Irish Americans held nine seats (69 percent), more than five times their proportion, 13 percent, in the general population. African Americans won the remaining two seats (15 percent), in a city where a quarter of its residents are black. Both African Americans were born in the United States to American parents, whereas one out of four black residents in Boston is foreign born.[30] There was no representation from the Latino or Asian American communities on the city council, although these communities make up 14 percent and 8 percent of the city's population, respectively, according to the 2000 census.[31] No city councilor was an immigrant.

Given their relatively recent arrival, we should perhaps not be surprised that no Vietnamese has ever been elected to office in either city. More surprising, no Vietnamese from the Toronto or Boston communities has ever run for elected office.[32] If we look to involvement with local political parties, often a first step to electoral bids, we find that Vietnamese in Boston have made further inroads than those in Toronto. A small group of about half a dozen Vietnamese American leaders has attended state and national conventions of both the Democratic and Republican parties. In Toronto, one individual was active enough in party politics during this period to be voted a delegate to provincial and national leadership conventions.[33]

What explains the cross-national and intergroup differences? Internal community resources play a part. The larger pool of well-educated Vietnamese Americans facilitates political activism among Vietnamese elites in Boston. A larger share of the answer, however, lies in resource differences generated by government intervention. A richer organizational infrastructure among Portuguese Canadians in Toronto provides groundwork for

TABLE 9. ETHNO-RACIAL REPRESENTATION ON THE CITY
COUNCILS OF BOSTON AND TORONTO, 1997 AND 1999

Boston

	Council Seats (1999 Election)		Proportion of Population (2000 Census)[a]
Ethno-Racial Group	*Number*	*Percentage of Total*	*Percentage*
Irish	9	69.2	13.0
Black[b]	2	15.4	24.9
Italian	1	7.7	6.9
Jewish	1	7.7	n/a[c]
Latino	0	—	14.5
Chinese	0	—	3.3
Vietnamese	0	—	1.8
Total	13	100.0	

[a] Based on single or first reported ancestry or race.
[b] In Boston, 24.8 percent of blacks are foreign born; in Toronto, 63.4 percent are foreign born.
[c] Unlike the Canadian census, the U.S. census does not allow *Jewish* as an ancestry/ethnicity.

political mobilization, while a more vibrant settlement industry and ethnic media have provided training grounds to many who successfully ran for office. More generally, higher levels of naturalization in Canada increase immigrant candidates' pool of potential coethnic voters.

Other institutional differences also play a role. A stronger and more competitive party system, greater ideological diversity between parties, and more localized nomination procedures assist immigrants in Toronto more than those in Boston. Campaign finance regulations make launching a campaign more expensive in the United States than Canada. We also need to consider the *ideological congruence,* or fit, between community leaders' views and the prevailing political discourses of the adopted country and its political parties. Taken together, the institutional environment greeting migrants shapes overall patterns of political incorporation in predictable ways, augmenting or dampening private interests and abilities.

TABLE 9. (continued)

Toronto

Ethno-Racial Group	Council Seats (1997 Election)		Proportion of Population (1996 Census)[a]
	Number	Percentage of Total	Percentage
British origin[d]	27	47.4	17.7
Italian	11	19.3	6.9
Jewish	6	10.5	4.4
Chinese	4	7.0	9.0
Black[b]	3	5.3	9.6
Portuguese	1	1.8	3.3
Other European	5	8.8	22.6
Latino	0	—	2.5
Vietnamese	0	—	1.1
Total	57	100.1[e]	

[d] Includes Irish (2.0 percent).

[e] Total does not add to 100 due to rounding.

SOURCES: Boston: author's tabulations, U.S. Census Bureau 2002; Toronto: Siemiatycki and Isin 1997; Ornstein 2000.

Networks and Organizations

Successful politicians use networks and organizations to mobilize support. Relative to the native born, would-be immigrant politicians face a significant obstacle: a lack of long-standing roots in a riding or district. As one immigrant politician puts it, "Because I came at fourteen, I didn't have the school buddies, the friends from elementary school that would be your natural supporters." Another politically active immigrant in Toronto told me she was interested in running for office, but she was intimidated by the obstacles faced by immigrant women: "no matter how you look at it, you don't always have the same connections. . . . I may have worked with them . . . [but] I don't rub shoulders with these people . . . I'm not part of that circle. I never have been, you know. I take a step in, I say hello, and I step out again." The disadvantage of limited networks is amplified for the

Portuguese and Vietnamese since limited financial resources prevent entrée through campaign donations.

A robust infrastructure of community organizations can mitigate some of these newcomer liabilities. Since political requests come disproportionately from acquaintances in civic and social organizations rather than from neighbors or fellow workers (Verba, Schlozman, and Brady 1995: 144–49), members of communities with more organizations have an easier time breaking into politics. Greater governmental support for Portuguese organizations in Toronto consequently plays a role in explaining Portuguese Canadians' greater electoral success.

For example, one former politician, Martin Silva, traces his political involvement back to two groups that received Canadian government support. One, the Portuguese Community Movement, provided an introduction to Canadian politics. Run through the local YMCA, the Movement was established using a federal government local initiative project grant to provide basic translation and interpretation assistance to neighborhood residents. As part of the initiative, a few young Portuguese Canadians began to publish a small newspaper, mostly reporting on issues within the Portuguese community. The external funding was critical, because "without the grant—and it was a minimal grant, it was $20,000 or $25,000—without it, we couldn't have published the newspaper. There was no money in the Portuguese community." Producing the paper led the young adults to engage in regular discussions and debates about Portuguese and Canadian politics. A few friends from the newspaper, already involved in the New Democratic Party (NDP), asked Silva to volunteer for his first political campaign, beginning his exposure to electoral contests.

The second organization critical to Silva's political career was a local ethnic radio station where Silva, starting in 1982, produced a morning show in Portuguese.[34] The radio station provided Silva with substantial exposure and name recognition and strengthened his involvement in community affairs. In the early 1980s, Portuguese Canadians affiliated with various parties came together in a nonpartisan effort to get more Portuguese Canadians on the ballot and into office.[35] Most of these efforts failed, but they led some in the community to suggest that Silva, due to his prominence, should run for a seat on the school board to raise political awareness in the community. He did, and he won. Later in 1988 he made a successful bid for a seat on the metro Toronto council. Other Portuguese Canadian politicians have also benefited from exposure in the ethnic media, while the lack of a strong, local, Portuguese-language media in Somerville and Cambridge contributes to that community's political invisibility.

Among the Vietnamese, especially those in Boston, many younger activists developed political interests and networks at college. Vietnamese American students would become involved in an ethnic organization as they built new relationships with students outside the ethnic group. The "insider" ties provided an organizational base to mobilize fellow Vietnamese, while "outsider" ties helped ground political action in domestic politics. In this way, universities' and colleges' tolerance—and outright assistance— to multicultural groups provides a setting within which political learning and organizing takes place.

For example, a number of Vietnamese Americans trace their activism to early participation in college Vietnamese students' associations. Most were attracted to the associations for social reasons: a desire to meet others— preferably of the opposite sex—who speak the same language, have the same cultural background, and have been through the same migratory upheavals.[36] For some, participation also built self-confidence, "the first couple years [I was] doing cultural things, because that was about my own search for identity. And celebrating culture and not being ashamed of it." A number of associations became politicized through opposing human rights abuses in Vietnam and helping newly arrived refugees. The focus on Vietnam opened these young adults' eyes to political activism for the first time. As one man remembers, "when I first went to Boston and met other Vietnamese students from different student associations, and they talked about organizing demonstrations, organizing protests, and . . . all those human rights violations in Vietnam, that exposed me to homeland politics."

At the same time, students also became exposed to non-Vietnamese peers active in North American politics. One man recalled with a smile: "My first year, I lived in the dorm, and a friend of mine, when I talked to him, he'd talk about American politics and how Reaganomics affected society . . . . And I was forced to watch [the] *McNeil/Lehrer [News]Hour* every day at 6:00 because he watched it every day. . . . They always talked about all those national, political, and social issues." Political learning in one setting could be transferred to another, and soon some students saw overlaps in their domestic and homeland concerns, for example, around the dynamics of refugee resettlement. As a result, some students pushed their ethnic student organization to broaden their political attention to include American politics. Personal ties developed in these organizations also proved important years later. For example, a number of those who established Viet-AID first met through the Vietnamese Student Association of Massachusetts. Collective action around homeland concerns can consequently provide a springboard to civic and political participation in the host country.

The Structure of the Political System:
Parties, Electoral Rules, and Financing

We also need to consider the structure of the political system, that is, the role played by the party system, electoral finance regulations, and the rules governing elections. All three areas tend to favor immigrants' greater involvement in Canadian elections by lowering barriers to electoral candidacy.

Running and winning political office almost always requires affiliation with a political party and involvement in the party system. Historically, urban political machines in the United States were lauded, or derided, for bringing immigrants into the political process. Reevaluation of these machines suggests that they were important vehicles for political mobilization but that incorporation depended on local party competition and tended to include only certain immigrant groups, such as the Irish, while keeping others on the sidelines (Erie 1988). Today, the remnants of these machines probably impede immigrant political incorporation by keeping power in the hands of party old-timers (Jones-Correa 1998a).

In a like manner, the dominance of the Democratic Party in metropolitan Boston hinders incorporation. Among registered voters in the city of Boston, 53 percent are Democrat and 9 percent Republican; in Cambridge and Somerville the figures are 56 percent versus 8 percent, and 55 percent versus 7 percent, respectively (Metropolitan Area Planning Council 2002). In contrast, residents of Toronto have two or three viable party choices, the Liberal Party or NDP in the urban core and the Liberal or Conservative Parties in the suburbs. Party competition increases interest in politics and spurs parties to reach out to new voters. Having a greater number of parties also increases the number of people who can run for office by providing more options for winning a party's nomination and a spot on the ballot. Of the ten Portuguese Canadians elected to office in metro Toronto, three different parties are represented. Relative to Boston, Toronto's more competitive party system provides an easier path to political candidacy.

The costs of securing a party endorsement are also lower in Toronto. The process of becoming a candidate for federal or provincial office requires fewer bodies or dollars than in Massachusetts. Would-be Canadian politicians need to get the nod from their party through a local riding association. Generally speaking, a riding association holds a binding election involving all party members in good standing, that is, those who have paid the membership dues.[37] These elections are not run through the formal electoral system but are instead organized by the parties who ask that all members come together in a specific location on a specific date to choose one person to stand for office.[38] Nominations are thus localized and intimate, rarely involving more than a few thousand, or even a few hundred, individuals. Importantly, would-be candidates can bring in new party members from their ethnic community to shore up their support. This practice of signing up "instant" party members generated intense criticism in the 1980s and 1990s, mostly because immigrant politicians were able to perfect a long-standing technique. By doing so, they challenged the dominance of older party elites (Stasiulis and Abu-Laban 1991). Independent of one's opinion on the appropriateness of "instant" members, being able to win a nomination battle by swinging a hundred votes lowers the threshold for immigrants' political participation.[39] Once nominated, the chosen candidate can then appeal to party loyalty to extend his or her support beyond the ethnic community.

In Boston, the primary system requires would-be candidates to run a campaign among all registered party members in a district, a process more akin to a general election. Given the bigger voting pool, generating support becomes a greater burden for immigrant politicians and involves more substantial fund-raising efforts. Since candidates largely have to raise their own money, each would-be politician must build his or her own personal electoral machine. The party is relatively less important, since, in the words of one former Portuguese American political candidate, "it doesn't support us as it should." For those who prevail in the Democratic primary, the subsequent general election requires less effort, since most Democratic candidates easily win their seat in the Boston metropolitan area.

The upshot of these differences is that many more immigrants in Toronto run for a party nomination than in metropolitan Boston. The cost of doing so, in both time and money, is significantly less than running in a primary. It is also relatively easier to become a candidate for the general election, given the greater number of competitive parties and easier nomination process. Conversely, the actual chances of winning the election in Toronto are probably less than for a Democratic nominee in Boston, given greater party competition.[40] Thus, an individual would-be politician in Boston or Toronto likely faces a similar overall probability of being elected, but with a larger total pool of immigrant candidates, the chance that *an* immigrant wins is greater in Toronto.

Political party differences should matter less in elections for school board and municipal council seats since most are nonpartisan and entail relatively low costs.[41] Party politics still play a role, however, since many candidates who stand for local election are affiliated with a political party. Background party support is a boon to Portuguese Canadians' political success. Often a party comes to some agreement as to who will run for a council or school board seat, and candidates can call on the volunteer efforts of party affiliates in addition to their own political networks. Candidates can implicitly or explicitly highlight their party affiliation. Mario Silva, a former Toronto city councilor, did not put "Liberal" on his campaign posters during municipal elections, but he did use red signs, the color of the Liberal Party of Canada. In 1997 Joe Pantalone, an Italian Canadian, and two Portuguese Canadians, Martin Silva and Christine Ferreira, joined forces to run a coordinated campaign under the NDP banner. Pantalone is a veteran city councilor with substantial support. By running with the two Portuguese Canadian candidates, the three candidates shared advertising costs and used the name power of Pantalone to help the newcomers gain office. This probably helped Ferreira get elected to the Toronto school board. In the words of one candidate, "The machine is crucial. . . . All of these people failed before because they just went with an ethnic machine and not with a party machine. Being nominated to be a candidate for a party gives you the credibility for people to come and work for you." This assertion finds confirmation in Cornwell's (1980) comparison of municipal elections in Providence, Rhode Island, and Fall River, Massachusetts. Cornwell found that Portuguese Americans consistently had a better chance of winning office when local elections were competitive and partisan.[42]

Since most political actors in Boston, Cambridge, and Somerville are Democrats, there is little explicit party competition of the sort found in Toronto. Instead, people hook up with different local power brokers, some of whom might be active within the Democratic Party. Teresa Cardoso, the Portuguese American school board representative in Somerville, put together a campaign team consisting of friends from the Parent Teacher Association, of which she had been president; her brother, who at that time was executive director of MAPS; a neighbor who was a former Somerville alderman; and friends from the ward and City Democratic Committee.

If limited partisanship hurts Portuguese Americans, would-be politicians living in Cambridge are further hindered, in the opinion of many community leaders, by that city's electoral system. The city uses a proportional representation system to elect nine city councilors and six School Committee members for two-year terms.[43] Adopted in 1939 as a way to install a powerful city manager and "guarantee majority rule and at the same time give minority groups representation in proportion to their actual strength," the system has weathered numerous referenda attempts to replace it.[44] Under the system, candidates run citywide, not in wards, and voters indicate all the candidates that they favor, in order of preference. Through a complex quota system, winners are declared after they pass a certain threshold of required votes based on voter preferences.

According to many Portuguese Americans, the system's complex nature dissuades ordinary immigrants from even entering the polling station. The costs of running citywide also pose problems. Expressing a common opinion, one community leader pronounced: "It's just baloney. Cambridge proclaims itself as the most democratic place in the United States. 'The People's Republic of Cambridge.' But proportional representation [PR] hurts the Portuguese. Within Cambridge, their numbers are relatively high, but politically speaking, they have no presence. Proportional representation absolutely does not help. They [people in Cambridge] feel so good; they feel that they are so understanding of difference. Baloney. PR is discriminatory; it's racist. It actually stops individuals from getting elected because of who they are. If they had precincts and wards, East Cambridge would be able to elect a Portuguese politician." Since holding local office frequently precedes a run for state or federal office, lack of voice in municipal politics carries ramifications throughout the political system.

Finally, more restrictive campaign finance regulations make personal wealth less important in Canadian elections than U.S. ones, usually an advantage for immigrant politicians. Funding considerations have an impact at all levels of office holding, even at the municipal level. Candidates for municipal council in Toronto face a spending limit calculated by taking a base figure and adding a variable amount tied to the number of voters in a ward. One Portuguese Canadian who has volunteered with numerous municipal campaigns estimates that most cost between $30,000 and $40,000.[45] In Massachusetts, there are limits on the amount that any one donor—individual, business, or committee—can give, but no overall spending limit.[46] During the 2001 election campaign for Cambridge City Council, at least six of the nineteen candidates spent more than $40,000.[47] The financial bar is consequently higher in Massachusetts.

Such differences fuel socioeconomic inequalities in leadership, potentially leading to greater class divisions among representatives and ordinary immigrants in the United States than in Canada. When I asked a Portuguese immigrant in Toronto how difficult it had been to raise money for a failed election bid, the question was dismissed with a shrug, "I didn't really raise funds. . . . If you intend to run, you have to let it be known; you have to start right away. If you establish your networks right away, it's okay." A Portuguese American in Massachusetts had a very different view, "It's very difficult to raise money. You have to start with your own natural constituency. But it's easier to organize a function to collect money for the parish—even one in the Azores—than to support a politician." Of those elected in Toronto, only two, Carl DeFaria and Nellie Pedro, appear to possess personal resources substantially greater than the community average.[48] In contrast, both municipal councilors, one of whom later became a member of federal Parliament, come from modest backgrounds. Their parents worked in construction, in cleaning, and on factory assembly lines.[49]

Ideological Congruence: Anticommunism, Social Justice, Ethnicity, and Race

Foreign-born candidates' political success depends on personal and organizational resources as well as the institutional structure of the political system, such as competitive parties and low barriers to participation. Formal institutional differences—what social movement scholars might call the political opportunity structure—should benefit Vietnamese Canadians as much as Portuguese Canadians. Indeed, among ordinary Vietnamese refugees, participation appears slightly higher in Toronto. However, Vietnamese community leaders in Boston have become more involved in domestic politics than those in Toronto. In part, greater elite penetration into Boston politics stems from the greater proportion of educated refugees in that city; the more educated tend to be more politically active. In addition, Vietnamese Americans benefit from greater ideological congruence, or matching, between their beliefs and American political discourse.

According to Seymour Martin Lipset, differences in American and Canadian political culture are reinforced by immigration. Each country's unique political ideology attracts likeminded immigrants, and these newcomers bolster existing ideological tendencies. Thus, in the nineteenth century, radical democrats migrated to republican America while conservative immigrants chose monarchical Canada (Lipset 1990: 183).

Whatever its historical accuracy, this prediction does not ring true in the post–World War II era.[50] Lipset is correct that the perceived ideological tenor of American and Canadian societies, in part institutionalized in bureaucratic practice, can act as a sorting mechanism. However, such sorting sends those with an orientation toward social justice to Canada and directs individuals opposed to the political Left to the United States. The most fervently anticommunist Vietnamese moved to the United States and found greater purchase in the American political system for their views. Anticommunism does not fit as naturally into the Canadian party system. In contrast, Portuguese Canadian leaders with social democratic leanings have found a welcoming home in the New Democratic Party and union movement. The extent of ideological congruence acts as a mechanism that further shapes trajectories of political incorporation.

Anticommunism and Vietnamese Refugees   Much of the argument so far has focused on how the host society, through policy and institutional arrangements, affects immigrant political incorporation once newcomers arrive in North America. This focus rests on the assumption that flows of Portuguese and Vietnamese have been largely similar. Among political leaders, however, we find some evidence for ideological sorting preceding arrival in North America.

Vietnamese refugees exercised little choice regarding their country of destination, although those who came as boat people were able to list their top three preferences for resettlement while they waited in refugee camps. Ultimately, policy and the individual decisions of Canadian and American immigration officers determined refugees' final destinations. These policies and decisions were not value neutral. The United States favored those who suffered severe reprisals from the communist government—usually those who had held positions of authority in the South Vietnamese government or military—or their families. Not surprisingly, the ideologies of people selected for resettlement in the United States tend to be ardently anticommunist.[51] The United States also received the bulk of those fleeing in 1975, a group that included many with ties to the South Vietnamese regime or to American government and business. In comparison, Canada received few 1975 refugees, and Canadian policy during the boat people crisis did not require proof of significant political persecution. Few, if any, of the refugees resettled in Canada are procommunist, but a greater proportion probably fled Vietnam for economic reasons.

In both Toronto and Boston, most refugees speak passionately against the communist Vietnamese government. Many tell painful stories of repression, persecution, and deprivation. However, anticommunism carries greater salience in Boston. Reflecting back to the 1980s, one Boston community leader remembers:

> There were a lot of organizations. There were political organizations. At that time, I think fighting for freedom in Vietnam was still very popular. So you had all those organizations, and their mission was to liberate Vietnam in the future, and there were so many of them in the Vietnamese community at that time. . . . [These groups] all have the same ideology. Maybe different strategies, different personalities. But they all want to liberate Vietnam from the communist government. And they

all believe in violence: "Organize an army and overthrow the Vietnamese government!"

God! I think that was the reason why I was not accepted to Harvard. [Laughs.] . . . I remember when I was interviewed by a Harvard guy and he asked me, "Okay, so what do you want to do in the future?" I said, "I want to liberate Vietnam from the communist government." And he asked me, "So how would you do it?" And I said, "I'd organize an army!" He must have looked at me and thought, "This guy is crazy!"

The speaker's views have since moderated, in line with others. In February 1994 President Clinton lifted the U.S. trade embargo on Vietnam, and an increasing number of Vietnamese visit family and friends in the homeland, making Vietnamese migration more similar to that of other immigrants. Nevertheless, anticommunism continues to affect political orientations and behavior.

Among those who vote in American elections—generally individuals with more education, greater income, and longer residence in the United States (Lien 2001)—loyalties tend to lie with the Republican Party because it is perceived as more strongly anticommunist. A 1994 *Los Angeles Times* survey found that 61 percent of Vietnamese are Republicans, 24 percent are Democrats, and 13 percent are Independents or report no party affiliation (Lien 2001).[52] Rose, a community activist in Boston, considers herself an atypical Republican due to her support for some Democratic social causes, but "the reason why I don't [want] to be a Democrat is because I believe in fiscal conservativism. And, also, I identify the word 'Republic' of Vietnam, you know what I mean? To [be] Republican [taking] a strong stand against communists. That's what I like about being Republican." The Vietnamese thus resemble Cuban émigrés, with opposition to communism directing political loyalties.

At the same time, the socioeconomic status of many Vietnamese—especially those working low-skilled service or manual labor jobs—puts their interests in line with the platform of the Democratic Party, a link reinforced by Republicans' perceived hostility to racial minorities. Younger and socially active Vietnamese are more likely to support the Democrats, although they often register as Independents. Almost all feel torn. One Vietnamese American, who usually votes Democrat, explained his reasoning as an order of priorities:

Not that I'm not anticommunist. No. I'm very anticommunist, but *how* you [are] anti, and [how you] express your thought or your action is very different. Because [on the] one hand I'm not procommunist. I do anticommunist. On the other hand there are many issues that we need to empower ourselves, exercise our right, right in this country. . . . There's got to be a process there. You cannot skip the first step and then jump to the second step. You cannot be hungry or not have a good job and then [be] anticommunist. You should have a good job and then [be] anticommunist. That's my way of belief, and that's the reason why we have to go with issues.

Another woman, who works in health education, describes the opposing pulls of family and work: "Here [at work] we really looking for support [from the] Democracy Party. But my family believes [in] the Republic [Party]. . . . It's very challenging. Vote for one party, but my work for another party." These younger Vietnamese stand poised between the two major parties.

Realizing that Vietnamese loyalties are up for grabs, the parties court community leaders. Among the thirteen Vietnamese American community leaders I interviewed, seven had worked on a political campaign, and three of the seven had attended a state or national party convention. Outreach to these elites is reinforced by subtle tokenism—having a Vietnamese American participate in a regional or national convention shows a party's openness to minorities. All three of those who attended party conventions did so after a non-Vietnamese party activist invited them, and all believe that the invitation stemmed in part from their status as a racial minority.[53]

Elite mobilization has not trickled down to the majority of the community. Neither party has undertaken a systematic effort to register or win over ordinary Vietnamese. Results from the 2001 Pilot Study of the National Asian American Political Survey indicate that Vietnamese were the most likely of the six Asian American groups surveyed not to vote because they did not register after gaining citizenship (Lien et al. 2001).[54] They were also the least likely to report having been contacted by a political party in the past four years, with only 15 percent of Vietnamese respondents reporting such contact, compared to 41 percent of the sample as a whole. Numerous Vietnamese Americans in Boston told me that they had never voted, despite acquisition of U.S. citizenship.[55]

In Canada, anticommunism provides fewer political returns. There is a decided American cadence to activism around homeland politics. One Vietnamese Canadian who regularly protests human rights abuses in Vietnam attributes her initial interest to a Vietnamese American speaker who visited her Canadian university campus:

One time, just by luck, I went by the auditorium and I saw a group of Vietnamese in there. They were having a political conference. And they had a guest speaker from the States, from Chicago. . . . I just stood at the door because I wasn't invited and I don't know who those people were. And I just saw this Vietnamese person standing up there and he was confidently answering all of these questions. . . .

Afterwards I just hang around and I got to talk to him. And I think he was the vice chairman of the group that I just mentioned. . . . He said, "Now that we're so lucky in Canada, we have all the freedom that we enjoy, and . . . we live in a democratic society, [but] unfortunately every second, every minute somebody in Vietnam is killed because he or she dares to speak differently or raises her voice or his voice." And he told me stories of thousands of people who have been put away in re-education camps. He himself was one, and he's seen torture, different ways of taking away your human dignity from you. And so that really made me think.

Following this experience, she persuaded peers in the Vietnamese Students' Association to mobilize around human rights and later became involved in a number of groups, some based in the United States.

Other American influences are subtler, a product of American articles in local ethnic papers and conversations with friends in the United States. Vietnamese Canadian veterans, for example, talk about Canadian parties using the names of American parties, the "Democracy" Party and "Republic" Party.

Because anticommunism carries less salience in Canada, opposition to the communist regime is expressed using the language of human rights.[56] Since all Canadian parties oppose human rights abuses, it is not clear whether one party would be more sympathetic to homeland concerns than another. To the extent that there is a partisan tendency among Vietnamese in Toronto, many lean toward the Liberal Party and the political center, primarily because other parties appear too extreme.[57] As one man explained:

We were victims of the Left, back in Vietnam, and even if the Left back there is different from the Left here, we still don't like the Left. So that is not an option. Even if rationally, logically . . . we should be very close to the NDP. We are at their level, closer to them economically, financially. We have that in common. But we were victims of the Left, so we don't want to get close to them.

And, then, the Right party, they are too far away from us. They are too rich, too protective. Maybe, in some cases, they are too far away from us because they don't like us, don't like visible minorities. Of course, they don't say that, but that is the sense that we have. So, you are left with the middle, the Liberals.

All the Vietnamese Canadian leaders I interviewed vote regularly, but none has become involved with a Canadian political party, in part due to the lack of ideological fit.[58] The only individual I interviewed who had attended a party convention—someone who does not consider himself and is not considered by others as a community leader—became active through non-Vietnamese friends and a local riding association. Today he participates in a Chinese Canadian Liberal caucus because a Vietnamese group does not exist.

Ethnic categorizations in Canada also make political parties less likely to seek out Vietnamese community leaders. Canadian discourse either classifies immigrant groups by ethnicity (e.g., Vietnamese, Chinese) or, in the case of nonwhites, lumps them together as visible minorities. Given the dozens of ethnic groups in Toronto, the presence or absence of Vietnamese leaders generates no particular concern, especially in the Liberal Party, which already has attracted significant support among visible minorities.[59]

Many ordinary Vietnamese Canadians harbor political antipathies similar to their compatriots in Boston, although a lack of survey data makes statistical generalizations impossible. It seems, however, that slightly more Vietnamese in Toronto report voting in Canadian elections. Many said they did so out of a feeling of obligation or pride for their Canadian citizenship. Doan, a senior living in subsidized housing, expressed this view with particular vigor, exclaiming, "I never missed any election! . . . It's not right to use the excuse that we are too busy. You have to make time to go to vote. . . . Being a citizen in a country, I must and am responsible to go to vote. It's that simple!" The sense of obligation overrides lingering fears about not understanding party platforms or not possessing sufficient information about the candidates. Those I interviewed also indicated slightly more contact with political parties than compatriots in Boston. Ideological congruence and greater interest by political parties encourage elite Vietnamese Americans to participate in the party system, while attitudes about citizenship and party outreach appear to diffuse class differences in voting among Vietnamese Canadians.

Social Justice and the Migration of Portuguese Dissidents   We also find dynamics of ideological congruence among a small minority of Portuguese elites who actively chose Canada for political reasons. They stand out because, without the barrier of immigration laws, the vast majority of Portuguese would have moved to the United States. At the height of postwar Portuguese migration, the United States was widely seen as *the* land of economic opportunity.[60] Stories from friends and relatives already in the United States bred familiarity; the American military presence in the Azores provided points of contact; and, quite simply, the United States exuded an aura of adventure, especially for young people. Canadian immigration officials who went to Portugal in the 1950s found that "people in the Azores did not 'emigrate' but rather 'went to America'" (Oliveira 2000: 86). For most immigrants, Canada was, at best, a second-place option. Almost all the Portuguese community leaders in Cambridge and Somerville cited economic opportunity as the driving motivation behind their (or their family's) move to North America.

This dominant narrative has an important variant in Toronto. While many echo the economic reasoning heard in Boston, a few community leaders explicitly call themselves political migrants, although none entered the country as a refugee.[61] Most of these "refugees" migrated from the Portuguese mainland and were involved with the Communist Party and its efforts to overthrow the dictatorship.[62] Some of these individuals embraced the Communist Party and its ideology. Others, a larger proportion, were less enamored, but they participated in networks or events organized by communists because there was no other viable opposition to the dictatorship. Many avoided the United States because of Americans' perceived anticommunism. Valadao, who was blacklisted by the Portuguese secret police for participating in opposition groups, found his chances for professional advancement blocked. He moved to Canada after careful research, including reading Canadian newspapers and learning more about the politics of Prime Minister Pierre Trudeau. Jose Manuel, who also had a dossier with the political police, came to Canada on the advice of a friend and because, as he puts it, "I don't fit in with the American mentality." Canada does not necessarily have a history of embracing Left-leaning immigrants (Whitaker 1987), but those involved in opposition to the Salazar/Caetano regime nevertheless saw Canada as the more welcoming country.[63]

These people brought a leftist mindset to Canada that found a home in the social democratic New Democratic Party. Originally "somewhere between" the centrist Liberals and left-wing NDP, Valadao threw his lot in with the NDP in the mid-1970s and has been an active party member ever since. Jose Manuel found a political home in the left-wing Portuguese Canadian Democratic Association and, through friends at the association and other activities, he became heavily involved with the NDP. Leftist orientations, often expressed in the language of social justice, were also reinforced through participation in the union movement or in newcomer settlement.

The Portuguese Canadian Democratic Association, established in 1959 "to form a front against the Fascist regime in Portugal" (Marques and Medeiros 1984: 156), offered friendship and solidarity to a number of left-wing migrants like Jose Manuel. The group brought together a small but energetic corps of two to four dozen activists.[64] Most hailed from the mainland but ranged in occupation from professionals to dock workers. They spoke, wrote, and demonstrated in favor of regime change in Portugal and the end of the colonial wars. Some in Toronto claim that the Portuguese International Police for the Defense of the State, a political police force, tried to infiltrate the Democratic Association (Anderson and Higgs 1976). Others recount harassment by fellow Portuguese Canadians, especially those opposed to communism and afraid that the radical Left would take over Portugal following the Revolution of the Carnations in April 1974.[65] In general, however, Canada proved an open environment to the group's political activities, which included bringing members of the Portuguese Communist Central Committee to Toronto to speak. In the words of one former participant, if Portuguese Americans were to organize such an event, "you will get the CIA, or the FBI, after you in a second."[66]

Indeed, no one with whom I spoke in Massachusetts can remember any antifascist club in the Boston area. There are some reports that in the early postwar period a few individuals wrote to Portuguese-language newspapers to advocate for a republican government along American lines, but any incipient attempts to organize a concerted opposition quickly fizzled into neutrality or apathy (Pap 1981; Rogers 1974).

The individuals who chose Canada for political reasons influenced a larger group of future community advocates. Some current community leaders trace their political beliefs and activism back to people like Valadao and Jose Manuel. Nelson came to Canada as a fifteen year old in 1968 to avoid being drafted into the Portuguese army. He began attending a Canadian high school and participating in the Portuguese youth group at his local church. He vividly remembers what he terms his first political awakening. Nelson innocently asked an older man why the local scout group could not be more like the Portuguese groups at home:

> [The Portuguese group] was a cross-breed of the scouts. They did a lot
> of camping, and knot-tying, and singing the praises of government. I
> only realized they were a fascist organization when I arrived in Canada,
> because one of the guys once had a scouts group, and I suggested, "Why
> not a *Mocidade Portuguesa* chapter?" And he was one of the ones that
> had been politically involved in Portugal with the Communist Party.
> He told me, "My God, can't you see that's a fascist organization, the
> way they salute with their fists clenched, and their arms outstretched?"
> And the "S" on the buckles was like a square "S," for Salazar, for a
> semi-swastika.
>   And it was only at the age of fifteen did I come to realize—and I
> had to come to Canada to realize that—that I had lived my first fifteen
> years of my life in a fascist government. I had never come to that con-
> clusion on my own.

As Nelson began to reevaluate his beliefs, he became more interested in Canadian politics. Initially the ideology of the NDP attracted him as an antidote to fascism, then later as a party opposed to any system of privilege. When close friends became active in electoral politics, he was drawn in.

These political activists do not represent the political ideology of the majority of Portuguese Canadians. In Toronto, most Portuguese immigrants support the Liberals, Canada's centrist political party. Loyalty to the Liberals is often tied to a person, former prime minister Pierre Elliot Trudeau, not a platform. For those worried about voting for the "wrong" side, the Liberals offer the Goldilocks advantage: not too far to the Right nor too far to the Left. Nonetheless, the left-wing minority has exercised a disproportionate influence on the tenor and success of Portuguese Canadians in the electoral system. Five of the ten Portuguese Canadians elected to office are affiliated with the NDP. These individuals serve as a role model to some or as a challenge to others who disagree with their political views. In either case, their presence spurs Portuguese Canadians to become politically active.

Similar dynamics are largely absent in Boston. In Massachusetts, ordinary Portuguese immigrants and community leaders tend to support the Democratic Party. Given their immigrant background, socioeconomic status, and the Democrats' political dominance in the Commonwealth, their choice is not surprising. Yet Democratic support is not usually animated by a strong ideological allegiance or commitment to social justice. Rather, many Portuguese see themselves as Kennedy Democrats, putting loyalty to the Kennedy clan first and political ideology second.[67]

For example, Tony regularly votes Democrat and occasionally assists with local candidates' campaigns. Tony has done health-related outreach and has been involved in the Portuguese-language media. When I asked him about the most important issue facing the Portuguese community, he answered:

> Family. Because I believe that it is in the house that everything starts. If the family is good, then we get a great foundation, and we can get these people to develop in this country, in the American sense of the word, and be more involved in politics and so forth. . . .
>
> [Portuguese immigrants] come to America, and they think that the government is going to take care of them. . . . There are a lot of services here that help those who don't have a job, who have problems financially. And then they feel, "Hey, this is good." And this is a setback. I'm against this kind of service. I'm not saying that I'm a Republican, but people should be forced to go ahead and succeed.

The implicit link between race and class in the United States further discourages Portuguese Americans from using a discourse of social justice. In

Boston, Portuguese Americans are considered white and grouped with third- and fourth-generation Italians and Irish, but many of their issues are closer to those of newly arriving, nonwhite migrants. Yet since immigrant issues are frequently cast in the language of race, the Portuguese are excluded. These conventions of discourse are reinforced through legislation such as the Voting Rights Act, which fails to guarantee Portuguese-speaking minorities access to the ballot in a manner similar to the Spanish-speaking population.[68] In Toronto, ethnic multiculturalism and the existence of a social democratic party allow Portuguese Canadians to make successful political appeals that incorporate class and ethnicity.[69]

Ideological selection processes are not sufficient to explain the heavy overrepresentation of leftist community leaders in Toronto. Certainly some individuals active in the anti-Salazar opposition migrated to Massachusetts. Rather, the institutional contexts faced by migrants once they arrived in North America reinforce ideological selection. The characteristics of immigrants and their community interact, and become amplified or dampened, by the institutional environment of the adopted country.

DOES REPRESENTATION MATTER?
THE LIMITS AND BENEFITS OF ETHNIC POLITICIANS

So far I have assumed that ethnic representation matters, that newcomers desire coethnic representation or benefit when a member of the community is elected to office. But is this the case? In the American and Canadian political systems, one person is chosen from a particular area to speak for its residents. Since any district, riding, or city ward contains people with diverse interests and policy preferences, representation can never be perfect. An elected official must choose certain policy options over others, making choices based on membership in a particular party, personal values and experiences, or the dominant opinion of the local population. There is no a priori reason that a coethnic must represent an immigrant community.

When asked whether they would prefer to vote for someone from their own ethnic community, the majority of those I interviewed retorted that they would vote for the best candidate, regardless of ethnicity. A Portuguese Canadian pronounced, "I think it makes no difference. Portuguese or not, the important thing is if you are good." A Vietnamese American explained, "Whoever [is] best for the American people, for the country, for the society, then I go for them." Some even harbor a certain prejudice against compatriots who run for office, believing that they do so for personal gain, not out of public mindedness or a desire to further common interests. These people take it as a point of pride that they vote for a candidate's platform, not their last name.

Yet the same individuals, and most others in the community, consistently raise the advantages of coethnic representation.[70] The Portuguese Canadian who feels that ethnicity makes no difference told me later: "I think it is important to have someone from the Portuguese community represented. For the mere fact that you are part of Canada, and that should show. If the point of view is different, then it is important that it be represented. . . . Heart is very important. I think that someone who is Portuguese will push a little harder for issues that are important to the Portuguese, if they are responsible to the community." Indeed, despite initial comments to the contrary, almost everyone favored ethnic representation.[71] Reasoning varied, but three themes arose repeatedly: coethnic politicians better understand the interests of the community and take these interests to heart; ethnic representation offers a point of access into the political system; and having members of the group elected serves an important symbolic function, reflecting mainstream society's willingness to include newcomer communities. I examine each argument in turn, after first weighing the case against coethnic politicians.

Unfit Politicians and the "Ethnic" Vote

A number of those interviewed, especially in the Portuguese community, distrust coethnic politicians. One Portuguese Canadian explained that in downtown Toronto

> What I have witnessed in the last fifteen, sixteen years have been the wrong people getting into politics, representing the community. This is very personal, [but] the wrong people doing it for all of the wrong reasons. For egos, for other economic reasons. And people see through them. They are just not the kind of people that I think that most of the population would embrace and say, "Yes, I would be happy to vote for so-and-so. He's going to serve my interests." No. If I vote for so-and-so, he's going to serve his own interests. So, almost a backlash happens. It's almost as if the vote diminishes. They'll vote for the Italian candidate.

Rivalries also play a role. According to a Portuguese immigrant in Cambridge, Massachusetts, there is a sense that "You can't trust your own. . . . It's a certain jealousy, I think, it's a jealousy that maybe he's going to get ahead and you're not going to. Or, if he's going to go in there, he's not going to do anything for us; he's just going to line his pockets." People outside the community are perceived as more honest and trustworthy.

Others raise an instrumental concern: why vote for an unknown coethnic when you enjoy the support of an experienced politician? In Cambridge, city councilor and state representative Timothy Toomey gets high marks from some Portuguese Americans, as do Edward Kennedy, the state's senior senator to Congress, and Michael Capuano, former mayor of Somerville and current U.S. representative, none of whom are Portuguese. One community leader explained: "There's a couple of legislators who have been here for a long time, very good friends, like Tim Toomey. He's loved by the Portuguese community. He's also been to Portugal. I mean, he's voted for by the Portuguese community. For the most part, they see him as part of the Portuguese community. So . . . they're not going to put in someone [else] just because he's Portuguese. He's been wonderful, and they wanted to thank him for it. People want him there as long as he's doing a good job." Similar arguments are heard in Toronto. Experienced Italian Canadian politicians are considered "good friends" of the Portuguese community. Many see little point in backing challengers when incumbents have a proven track record and occupy positions of power.

Independence from ethnic politics also becomes a source of pride and a subtle way of denigrating other communities, since some link ethnic politics to political manipulation.[72] A few Portuguese explained that in Toronto the Italians vote for anyone with an Italian last name—or the Irish in Boston always support Irish Americans—but the Portuguese assess candidates based on their worth, not their origins. A Portuguese Canadian businessman boasts, "We are very independent-minded in that respect. I think that's a good thing. Other communities, for example, will go to the temple and be told what to vote. Thank God we are not like that. While there is a lack of unity in the Portuguese community, at least they can think for themselves." Ironically, the speaker has been an active participant in ethnic politics, using intraethnic ties to advance a number of political campaigns.

Distaste for ethnic politics is amplified by the perception that such strategies can hurt political candidates more than help and from a fear that being labeled as "ethnic" marginalizes those who succeed in winning office. Reflecting on the failure of Portuguese Americans to get elected in Cambridge and Somerville, one politically active Portuguese American offered the following analysis:

> They ran strictly as Portuguese candidates. I told them, big mistake! You can no longer do this. Nobody does it anymore. Not even the Irish people do it. The Italians don't do that. Nobody does that. . . . I guarantee you, if I went tomorrow, and if I put all my advertising just into "Manuel Azevedo, thirty years in the Portuguese church, fifteen years in the Portuguese Credit Union," and this and that, you know what that does

to me? Sink me more and more and more and more. That's what it will do. It's nice to see someone like Manuel; he's a person who's always involved. He's involved in many aspects of the community; he's hard working, participated in this and participated in that. But start to focus. You have to run as a candidate for the constituents of that area . . . not [as] the Portuguese guy. . . . It happens to be a Portuguese name, that's it.

In these circumstances, when a member of an ethnic minority gets elected, he or she faces the problem of being eternally "ethnic," relegated to portfolios on intercultural and race relations rather than the more powerful ways and means, budget, or intergovernmental affairs. To argue that only insiders can represent the substantive interests of an ethno-racial community carries the danger of being perceived as *only* having competence in this area.[73]

The crux of the problem is determining whether anyone is a "non-ethnic." As one Portuguese Canadian who unsuccessfully ran for office put it, "When do you stop being an 'ethnic'?" Groups with a history of holding political office are implicitly considered mainstream, representing the public good, and are not perceived to have particularistic ethnic backgrounds. If a certain background is celebrated, as with Irish Americans in Boston, it is deemed mainstream, while other groups remain "minority," regardless of their proportion in the general population. To avoid such labels, some immigrants oppose or downplay the desire for ethnic representation.

The Benefits of Ethnic Representation: Taking Ethnic Interests to Heart

Despite these drawbacks and the presence of "good friends" in high places, the great majority of immigrants feel that coethnic politicians better serve group interests.[74] Similar backgrounds and experiences provide a superior understanding of community concerns, according to one Portuguese Canadian:

> I feel that other politicians cannot take our cause equally well. You know, the federal representative [is] very helpful, but . . . [Pause.] How can I put it to you? It's the sense of belonging to a particular group. It has nothing to do with it being a Portuguese Canadian group. It could be the group of the fifty year olds that make quilts. Okay? It's the identification with a particular group, knowing the history, knowing some of the challenges and the issues and so on. Really having the interests of that group at heart. And that's what makes the difference.

A Portuguese American advocate pointed out that when it came time to push legislation dear to immigrants, such as funding for ESL or citizenship education, she and others went to Tony Cabral, the only Portuguese-born representative in the Massachusetts State House.[75]

The Vietnamese express even less certainty, and indeed some skepticism, that those in power can adequately represent the concerns of the community. Lack of representation has a negative effect on issues of particular importance to the Vietnamese community according to Khoi, a first-generation refugee in Boston: "If the Vietnamese population in the country [were] politically active, or did their part, the United States might not normalize relations with Vietnam. . . . I don't think the Clinton administration consulted with the Vietnamese community before he normalized relations with Vietnam because we weren't *there* to consult with." In Toronto, Hai voiced similar frustrations. According to Hai, politicians' impression that "we are not really a big fish" contributed to the failure to establish a Vietnamese Canadian community center. For these individuals, and most Vietnamese or Portuguese immigrants, coethnic representation improves the likelihood of substantive representation.[76]

Points of Access

Beyond the promotion of particular interests, immigrants point to the benefit of having someone from the community serve as a point of access into the political system. A number of elected politicians pointed out that they employ members from their community not only to ensure bilingual and bicultural assistance to their constituents—an important part of their constituency work—but also because they want to provide political experience for ambitious coethnics. In the words of one politically active Vietnamese Canadian, "You can't sit on the sidelines for other people to decide things for you. You have to be in there." A Portuguese American made a similar analogy, "It's a little like a football team. When someone from the outside tries to challenge them, they huddle together and keep others out. Don't listen. But if you are in the inside, part of the team, then they will listen because you are part of the group. They can become sensitive to your issues." This sentiment is echoed in interviews conducted by Stasiulis and Abu-Laban (1991) among non-British, non-French MPs in the Canadian House of Commons. MPs from immigrant communities frequently felt that their presence fostered or strengthened sensitivity to issues of racism, immigration, and human rights within their parties and in the House of Commons.

Ordinary immigrants also feel more comfortable approaching politicians who share the same language and cultural background. Often there is a reasonable chance of meeting a coethnic politician during community events, religious services, or cultural celebrations.[77] Such personal contacts facilitate political incorporation, since most people are drawn into political activity through personal connections. Because the bulk of ordinary immigrants' personal ties are to fellow immigrants, the chances for political mobilization are more limited with few or no coethnics in office.[78]

Of course, people can be mobilized into political activity through friends and acquaintances who are not coethnics, but this process tends to favor privileged individuals. One Vietnamese American explained that she became politically active after a relative attended Harvard University's Kennedy School of Government, "it was his friend who introduced the idea of the Republican Party and how we should participate in it . . . [that] we should take advantage of participating to learn, to know more people, and to get into the system. [These ideas] were first introduced by our Caucasian friend." For those with limited education and English-language skills or occupations that do not provide contact with politically active individuals, having access to a coethnic politician offers an alternative way to connect to the political system.

The Symbolism of Immigrant Electoral Success

Finally, electoral success also becomes a symbol of the community's equality with other groups. Since an immigrant candidate must generate support from individuals of diverse backgrounds to win office, electoral failure can be painted as a rejection of the whole community:

> I think that there needs to be more . . . proportional representation of the various populations. Especially because we become part of this country almost as soon as we come to this country. If the Canadian [government] says, "Well, you are a bona fide Canadian after three years," well, that's wonderful, but then why does it take us fifty or sixty years to put somebody in government? . . . You can't have it both ways. You can't let a quarter of a million people from other countries come into your country every single year and tell them that they can become partners in the full sense of the word, but then that equity kind of stops halfway.

Election results serve as a judgment on the openness and inclusiveness of the host society.

Having one's "own" politician sends a signal announcing the community's importance. Ordinary people's desire for such affirmation can be so strong it trumps other considerations, as one Portuguese Canadian activist explained: "The Portuguese community votes for Mario Silva with pride and pleasure . . . it's that sense of wonderfulness. The interesting thing about the Portuguese community is, [it's] very antisocialist and very family-oriented, the church and the values of family and wife and children. Very homophobic, to a certain extent. [Yet] the first Portuguese that they elect to City Hall is a socialist. The second Portuguese they elect is gay. . . .

Draw your own conclusion." Such symbolism holds inside and outside the ethnic community. After convincing about fifty fellow Vietnamese to attend a local nomination battle that his candidate won, one Vietnamese Canadian remarked, "That shows that it doesn't matter who you are, your vote doesn't have any color. We still can win." Such examples can be particularly powerful for groups such as the Vietnamese and Portuguese, given a history of authoritarian government and limited democratic experience.

The election of a coethnic can spur others to take an interest in politics. Often those elected serve as positive role models to others.[79] Sometimes, however, a coethnic politician throws down a gauntlet for others who disagree with his or her politics or because the person is seen as an unfit representative of the community. Early successes serve as a catalyst: "Knowing the Portuguese psyche, people won't do it [run for office] if no one else is doing it. But, if people do it, then they think, 'I'm better than that person. He has a big accent; I don't.' And thinking that they are better than the other, they will get involved." Whether role model or catalyst, the result is similar: greater interest and activism in the electoral system.

Once in office, coethnic representatives can further promote the community's visibility. In Massachusetts, Azorean-born representative Antonio Cabral was instrumental in instituting an annual Portugal Day in the State House. In Ontario, former member of Provincial Parliament Carl DeFaria had June designated Portuguese History and Heritage Month.[80] Such events tend to be cultural celebrations and social gatherings—the event list for the first Portuguese History and Heritage Month in 2002 included folklore celebrations, singers, and a golf tournament—but having such activities raises the consciousness of fellow elected officials to the concerns of Portuguese immigrants. In addition, it reminds other city residents about the Portuguese presence, enhancing urban citizenship by "laying claim to public space . . . [and] staking out new rights to the city" (Siemiatycki and Isin 1997: 99). Vietnamese complaints over the absence of Vietnamese elected officials stem in part from the lack of such symbols.

Who Represents?

Ethnic representation offers symbolic affirmation, promotes interests, and provides access for newcomer communities. But what constitutes the boundaries of the group? A few immigrants mention the particular concerns of subgroups within the community, such as immigrant women, implying a need to further specify the characteristics of one's representative. Conversely, shared immigrant background, regardless of country of origin, might be sufficient. One Portuguese American active in lobbying the Massachusetts State House regularly contacts Alice Wolf, a Jewish American born in Austria. In Toronto, Portuguese Canadians' willingness to support Italian Canadian politicians stems in part from perceived commonalities that bridge country of origin differences: shared south European origins, Roman Catholic traditions, and employment in manual labor, especially construction.

Among a certain group of young Vietnamese, representation along racial lines—with a primary distinction between whites and people of color—overrides the desire to be represented by a person of Vietnamese decent. Vietnamese Americans educated in American colleges and influenced by discourses of racial justice are particularly apt to question whether whites understand the concerns of minority communities. For these activists, the boundaries of representation become enlarged to encompass all Asian Americans or people of color. Ethnic origin takes second place to common experiences of racial discrimination. In Toronto, a few young activists also identify themselves as Asian rather than Vietnamese.

Nevertheless, most Vietnamese Canadians and older Vietnamese Americans feel that someone of the same ethnic background can best serve the community. These individuals are hesitant to assume that the election of a person of Chinese origin, for example, will ensure strong representation of Vietnamese. The process of building political and financial support for a Vietnamese community center produced disillusionment over pan-ethnic coalitions in both cities. In Toronto, the project never got off the ground. Hai remembers that Chinese Canadians, who successfully engineered a similar project in the metro area, provided little assistance:

> The Chinese community want to build the Chinese community center in Scarborough. Their project cost something like twenty million, or whatever. But the Chinese community only need to spend about ten or fifteen million, and the government would be able to match the rest. . . . They have a lot of connections with the government, three levels of government.
>
> [But] let's say, for us to build one, we call the MP, the MPP. We say, "Look, the Vietnamese want to build, can you match the funding?" When you're at the MP, MPP, or whatever office, they will say, "Well, let me look at that. We [will] respond to you six months later." And nobody say anything.

In a similar manner, Rose recalls that during the successful campaign for a Vietnamese community center in Boston:

> I shouldn't say that I'm upset at my Chinese friends per se . . . [but] they wouldn't come to the community center project. . . . So far

nobody—either Chinese, Filipino—has done anything as yet to advance the cause as far as raising money. You see . . . for me, I make sure that they get the help. . . . But suddenly if I needed help from them, maybe sending fliers out to let them know about the community center project and trying to recruit them, they don't have the time. You know? . . . As far as the linkage, well, to me, yes, but then for them to actually do something, it's not there. So that's something that I feel bitter about.

It is even harder for Rose to imagine a pan-racial coalition. For her, the primary issues for Vietnamese are the obstacles attendant with "foreignness" and being a new community in Boston. Native-born or more established communities of color do not share these concerns.

The desire to use political representation as an affirmation of identity and to mark a group's presence in the urban landscape reinforces the desire for statistical representation on the basis of ethnicity. In Toronto, Chinese Canadians have broken into political circles, but their presence on city council and at other levels of government does not satisfy many Vietnamese Canadians. Being collapsed into the category of *Asian* or, in the words of some of my respondents, *Oriental* runs contrary to centuries of history and cultural pride. As one Vietnamese Canadian explained, recounting his experience with some Chinese Canadians in Toronto: "Political-wise, we do not get along too well with the Chinese community, you know what I'm talking about? Like, we have [a] thousand years of domination, being dominated by the Chinese. . . . So when I told them, 'Hey, I speak only Vietnamese; I don't speak Chinese,' [they said,] 'You've got to learn Chinese, because your blood is Chinese anyways.' I said, *'What?'* " The numerical difference between Chinese and Vietnamese—the former are about ten times more numerous than the latter in the city of Toronto and twice as numerous in Boston—contributes to the fear that one's identity as a person of Vietnamese ethnicity gets lost when the community is represented by other Asians. This is especially true when other Canadians or Americans continuously assume that Vietnamese are Chinese based on cursory physical appearance. Despite arguments that nonethnics can represent the community's concerns, immigrants overwhelmingly hope that coethnics will win office.

In this chapter I have argued that the institutional dynamics outlined earlier—government discourses of citizenship and diversity and state support for ethnic organizations and settlement—culminate to produce divergent patterns of community advocacy and electoral success. A robust newcomer settlement industry facilitates leadership development. It provides a greater number of leadership opportunities, directs individuals to expend time and energy on behalf of the community, and helps to bridge divides within the community and between the community and mainstream society. Since settlement draws significant material and symbolic support from government, state intervention indirectly shapes ethnic leadership and advocacy, and it might also diversify the leadership pool by providing more opportunities for women and those of modest economic backgrounds.

Government's effect on leadership is important because political mobilization requires both interested followers and dedicated leaders. Portuguese living in Toronto have been much more active, and successful, in electoral politics than their compatriots in Boston, a difference that coincides with greater organizational capacity among Portuguese Canadians, more diverse leadership opportunities in the Canadian newcomer settlement industry, and a greater emphasis, within Canadian multiculturalism, on citizenship and ethnicity rather than border control and race. Also important is Canada's more welcoming party system and the dynamics of ideological congruence between elites and each nation's political discourse.

Significantly, the Portuguese difference does not seem to be an isolated case. Immigrant populations have found few openings in the American political structure in the 1980s and 1990s, while in Canada, after being largely shut out in the 1960s and early 1970s, ethno-racial minorities enjoyed an upsurge in political success in the final decades of the twentieth century.[81] The difference is reminiscent of the naturalization gap, which began our investigation into cross-national political incorporation. The answer for both differences lies in a common argument: political integration is facilitated by government policies that promote newcomer settlement and foster ethnic diversity within an overarching discourse of citizenship.

Conclusion

Multicultural Citizenship

The thing that . . . emotionally made me a Canadian was that I got my citizenship . . . and I went to vote for the first time in a provincial election that took place that year in October or November. And I was allowed to vote, with my little Canadian citizenship card. . . . Canada had given me something that was sacred. And my country, the one that had the village where I was born, had not given me. And so that emotional moment was what I finally considered to be the moment when I thought that Canada was my mother country.

NELSON, *Portuguese Canadian, Toronto*

In recent years we have witnessed a retreat from multiculturalism.[1] Countries such as Australia and the Netherlands—previously at the vanguard of the multicultural movement—avoid the language of multiculturalism and draw back from policies that acknowledge ethnic communities as distinct entities worthy of state assistance. Some countries, like Australia, are moving to a model of laissez-faire immigrant integration similar to that of the United States. This model assumes that immigrants' individual choices, within a framework of individual rights and antidiscrimination legislation, will incorporate newcomers into a unified citizenry.[2] Other countries, such as the Netherlands, have shifted toward state-directed assimilation reminiscent of Americanization efforts in the early twentieth century. Immigrants in the Netherlands must now learn Dutch language and culture in classes and through DVDs and then prove their "Dutchness" through examinations. Those who fail might be barred not only from Dutch citizenship but also from permanent residence in the country.

The apparent holdout to this trend is Canada. Although Canadian multiculturalism no longer commands the government resources or bureaucratic centrality that it did during its heyday in the late 1980s, it continues to be the stated policy and ideology of the government of Canada. Indeed, Raymond Chan, Canadian minister of state for multiculturalism, boldly pronounces that "Multiculturalism is at the heart of Canada's fundamental values and Canadian identity. . . . Multiculturalism as ideology, as philosophy, and as government program is for all Canadians" (2005: 5). Canada is staying the multicultural course.

If the American model is one option to which countries are moving and the Canadian one an option from which others are retreating, thoughtful comparison of American and Canadian integration outcomes is imperative. What lessons do Canada and the United States provide for other nations? What are the patterns of immigrant incorporation in these two countries, and how might they be linked to government action? Is multiculturalism— as ideology and policy—something worth embracing? How transferable are the ideas and practices of North America to other traditional immigrant-receiving countries, such as Australia and New Zealand, or to European countries with much stronger ethno-cultural conceptions of membership and belonging? Is there a viable multicultural model?

MULTICULTURAL PHILOSOPHY AND ITS CRITICS

Western liberalism—not in the sense of stances taken by Canadian or American political parties but as political theory—is predicated on a fundamental respect for universalism and equality. Rejecting the hierarchies of the seventeenth and eighteenth centuries, where aristocrats were naturally more "honorable"—and had more privileges—than those of modest birth, liberal thinkers envisioned a society and government in which all individuals were equals, regardless of ethnicity, religion, or birth. To be fair, government and public institutions must be neutral to particularities of background, recognizing people only as free and equal citizens who hold equal rights and entitlements.

The multicultural critique of this view, in some cases advanced by self-defined liberals, starts from the premise that cultural neutrality in public institutions is impossible. Given that democracy is based on government by the majority, minorities face disadvantages in the public sphere. The traditional liberal response is to erect a system of rights, such as freedom of speech and religion, but critics claim that cultural inequality remains pervasive. Not only are institutions of government created by people with specific values and cultural baggage, but seemingly innocuous decisions carry significant cultural bias. Thus, the former Canadian Lord Day's Act, which mandated Sunday closing on stores, could be seen as a neutral day of rest, imposed by the legislature to protect employees from working seven days a week. But it could also be interpreted as forcing a Christian template of work and rest on those with other views.[3]

According to multicultural proponents, true equality demands explicit political recognition of cultural minorities and special accommodations for their needs. If legislatures mandate store closings one day a week, Jewish owners should be able to close on Saturdays but stay open on Sundays. The "politics of recognition" provide concrete benefits, and they provide dignity for groups that otherwise have their particularities ignored and thereby discredited. Paradoxically, as Joppke (2004) notes, while arguments for differentiated citizenship are morally stronger for forcibly incorporated national minorities than largely voluntary migrants, actual multicultural policies have predominantly targeted immigrants.[4]

Multiculturalism is in turn subject to criticism, especially by those concerned with political fragmentation and threats to universalism. Many worry that public recognition and celebration of diversity undermine national unity. Some imagine the introduction of multiculturalism as a cultural big bang: people fly apart like so much atomic dust, regrouping in small galaxies and constellations that move ever farther apart from each other. Such fears lead writers to decry the "disuniting of America" or call for Canadian "nationalism without walls" (Schlesinger 1998; Gwyn 1995).[5]

The big bang metaphor begs the question of whether there ever was a cohesive community in the first place, a dubious proposition for settler societies like the United States and Canada and even questionable for most European nations.[6] Nevertheless, we can legitimately ask whether multiculturalism impedes current and future projects of community building, and in the case of immigration, whether it hinders the integration of diverse peoples into a common citizenry.

The concern over the divisiveness of multiculturalism has at least three variants.[7] One is an almost existential angst about national belonging and shared citizenship. If we all celebrate the distinctions that make us unique and different from one and other, will we not weaken the glue that holds the mosaic together?

A second variant bemoans the loss of shared community not only for itself, but also as the loss of a tool for public action. Under this argument, specific collective endeavors, such as the establishment of the welfare state or support for policies of redistribution, rely on a feeling of shared fate with fellow citizens. When the ties of membership attenuate—as, it is postulated, happens when multiculturalism valorizes other memberships—support for universal social policies or other broad public programs withers. Given persistent economic inequalities that seem to be growing in the twenty-first century, some ask whether recognition of difference does not create false boundaries between similarly situated socioeconomic groups, sapping energies away from redistribution concerns.[8]

A final variant goes even further and worries not only about a lost ability to engage in collective projects, but also about the real possibility that multiculturalism creates or reifies invidious distinctions between people that encourage the perpetuation of policies or practices relegating some to second-class citizenship. Ethnic groups are pigeonholed into categories not of their choosing, ghettoized, or pushed far enough, forced into "an apartheid form of citizenship" (Gwyn 1995: 234). Reflecting on the ethnic clustering he saw around cafeteria tables in York University, Neil Bissoondath crystallizes this concern when he declares: "I learned . . . to keep my distance from the tables that would have welcomed me not as an individual but as an individual of a certain skin colour, with a certain accent, the tables that would have welcomed me not for *who* I was and for what I could do, but for *what* I was and what I represented. I had not come here, I decided, in order to join a ghetto" (1993: 369).[9] When government explicitly recognizes ethnic categories, it takes away individual choice in self-definition and artificially underscores for others a person's cultural or ethnic background. Multiculturalism forces a person to be eternally ethnic, even if he or she just wants to be Canadian or American. At the extreme, "public" policies no longer exist; policies are now tailored to specific groups, undermining standards of universal individual equality.

MULTICULTURAL REALITIES, LESSONS LEARNED

Political theorists and other intellectuals have produced a voluminous literature on multiculturalism. Philosophical arguments over the universalism of rights, the centrality of the individual versus the group, and the relative neutrality of the state in protecting one vision of the "good life" against others abound. Apart from references to court cases and legal codes, most discussions lack grounding in the experiences of ordinary people. I consequently ask, given the evidence collected here and the opinions of the immigrants and refugees I interviewed, what practical promise, if any, does multiculturalism hold for immigrants?

This study can only speak to political incorporation, not to other immigrant outcomes such as learning the language of the host country, income parity, rates of intermarriage, or residential segregation.[10] However, in the cases of citizenship acquisition, political participation, and electoral representation, the results seem clear: on average Canada has been doing better than the United States, in part because multiculturalism provides the symbolic and material resources needed to take out and exercise political membership. Some of the dynamics that facilitate political incorporation in

Canada—support of ethnic organizations and promotion of community leadership—find parallels in U.S. refugee resettlement policy. It is no coincidence that Cuban Americans are one of the most politically successful, and vocal, migrant groups in the United States.

This book has suggested that immigrants' political incorporation must be understood as a process of structured mobilization. First, we must recognize that political integration is a social phenomenon: immigrants rely on fellow immigrants and local institutions such as community organizations to become participatory citizens. Second, and critically, the community's ability and interest in promoting political integration relies heavily on the symbolic and material support of government as provided by policies such as multiculturalism and newcomer settlement.

Relative to much of the world, Canadian and American governments appear quite multicultural. In Banting and Kymlicka's (2005) attempt to distinguish countries with strong and weak immigrant-centered multicultural policies, they evaluate states along eight policy spheres, ranging from official affirmation of multiculturalism in legislation or the constitution to funding for bilingual or mother tongue education.[11] Canada, alone with Australia, scored as a strong multicultural state. The United States came out as a moderate one, less multicultural than Canada but clearly more than countries such as Austria, Denmark, France, Germany, or Japan.

Yet even the modest U.S.-Canada difference carries significant consequences for immigrant citizenship. Evaluating the effects of multiculturalism requires acknowledging the analytically separate influences of symbolic inclusion and instrumental assistance. We can imagine these as two separate axes, with states providing relatively more or less symbolic recognition and more or less material assistance. Canadian multicultural citizenship is very open at a symbolic level; U.S. race-based economic citizenship is moderately open. Public material assistance in Canada is moderately generous to immigrant groups, though a lot of donations and volunteer time still come from the community. The American state offers some support to refugees but little assistance to all other migrants.

The separation of symbolic and instrumental effects is not perfect, since material resources provided by multiculturalism and settlement policies help with the practicalities of participatory citizenship and cement feelings of inclusion and attachment to the country. Also, two countries might recognize diversity, but the categories used to do so might vary, as in Canada and the United States. The former identifies immigrant communities primarily using linguistic and cultural distinctions, with a secondary recognition of "visible minorities," while the latter primarily recognizes racial distinctions in the public sphere but welcomes ethno-cultural diversity in the private sphere. Multicultural policies bring together an emphasis on the symbolic value of a diverse citizenry with concrete support for minorities. What lessons can we carry back to the philosophical debate over multiculturalism?

The Ties That Bind

The simplest fear expressed about multiculturalism is that a country's sense of self will fall apart under the assault of diversity. One of the most prominent recent complaints in this vein comes from the renowned scholar Samuel Huntington, who bemoans how "in the final decades of the 20th century . . . the United States' Anglo-Protestant culture and the creed that it produced came under assault" by, among other things, "the popularity in intellectual and political circles of the doctrines of multiculturalism and diversity" (2004b: 32). He fears, given high Mexican immigration, that "the cultural division between Hispanics and Anglos could replace the racial division between blacks and whites as the most serious cleavage in U.S. society" (2004b: 32). At a certain level, this is a cry of lost bearings and identity. What does being American, or Canadian, mean when people celebrate their background, learn about distinct (rather than shared) histories, and are encouraged to preserve "foreign" cultural and linguistic practices?

The evidence presented here suggests that multiculturalism policies, to the extent that they facilitate immigrants' legal and participatory citizenship, fundamentally *encourage* common bonds of community in multiethnic societies. This is especially true in traditional immigrant settler countries, although it will be increasingly the case for the new immigrant destinations, too. Given multiethnic realities in Canada and the United States, shared national community must rely primarily on civic bonds and a sense of shared political enterprise. This sort of civic nationalism is grounded in political history, government institutions, and common belief in the value of various rights and freedoms. It is sustained through the active practice of citizenship. Virtually all the immigrants and refugees with whom I spoke endorsed such political and civic citizenship.

In this context, immigrants' failure to acquire citizenship or be involved in projects of common governance undermines the political community much more than the means by which they become members. If the United States is having a crisis of immigrant political incorporation—as suggested by Huntington and others—the cause is not recognition of differences but rather the lack of public resources given to immigrant communities. When immigrants are given instrumental assistance, political incorporation follows, and with political incorporation comes effective multicultural democracy.

In other words, the problem is not too much interventionist multiculturalism but too little. When the Massachusetts Alliance of Portuguese Speakers helps to fill out the naturalization form for an elderly Portuguese immigrant or the Vietnamese-American Civic Association encourages a former political detainee to rally on the steps of the legislature, these organizations teach newcomers that being American means citizenship and participation. The very act of citizenship acquisition, even if initially for instrumental reasons not linked to political rights, is a fundamental reaffirmation of the volitional and liberal character of political membership in Canada and the United States. Regardless of birth or background, newcomers *can* become members of the national community. It is in this spirit that Nelson, the immigrant quoted at the start of this chapter, became Canadian.

Ethnic Groups as Political Groups

The second and third criticisms of multiculturalism demand a more complex response. Here critics express reservations over the relationship between group formation and political outcomes. These critics welcome immigrants' political incorporation as a reaffirmation of political community, but they ask why integration must be mediated through government. Newcomers should choose their own associations, not have the state promote the primacy of ethnicity or race over other bonds.

These critics offer two alternatives. The first, which can be called American liberal associationalism, places ethnicity in the private domain, one possible affiliation among many that might be used for political ends.[12] The second, which can be termed French republican assimilationalism, also relegates ethnicity to the private sphere but explicitly makes ethnicity an illegitimate basis for group-centered political action. Both of these nonethnic alternatives have been offered as superior models for dealing with immigrant-generated diversity.

These models hold philosophical appeal, but when it comes to the practicalities of immigrant incorporation, they run a dangerous risk of leaving newcomers out of the political community. This is especially true of first-generation immigrants but potentially true of ensuing generations, too. First, for all of liberal democracy's focus on the individual—as a voter and as a person possessed of rights—politics demands action by groups. In the French republican tradition, the individual citizen is the primary political actor. But in the reality of French politics, groups of individuals—brought together in political parties, unions, or some other collective—work together to influence outcomes.

Critically, the foundations of "groupedness" are not equally compelling.

While immigrants might have various affiliations—to other home buyers, other parents, other soccer enthusiasts—ties based on ethnicity are surely amongst the strongest and most deeply felt. Immigrants might not have had a strong sense of common ethnicity prior to migration, but the reality of moving to a new country certainly increases the salience of ethnic ties. Portuguese immigrants and Vietnamese refugees are clearly cognizant of a sense of coethnic community built on shared origins, migration experiences, cultural habits, dress, food, and language, even if they can also identify important intraethnic differences based on accent, class, region, or religion. Even when an immigrant blends well into his or her new home, the sense of "otherness" generated from having lived in (at least) two distinct countries, each with distinct cultural, social, and political norms, is ever present.[13]

On a practical level, then, ethnicity is a particularly effective way to organize for group ends. Especially in cases where people need others' assistance to become citizens—in both the legal and participatory sense—it is easier to ask fellow immigrants who speak the same language and understand one's background for help. As we saw in chapter 2, the social nature of political incorporation is such that ethnic ties in the form of informal networks, immigrant organizations, or coethnic leaders play a central role. To ignore the ethnic community blinds us to a key mechanism facilitating immigrants' inclusion into the political system. Critiques of multiculturalism as a ghettoizing force overlook the fact that the alternative to coethnic help might be no help at all.

Political Inequalities and Public Intervention

The above argument challenges the French model of political integration but leaves open the American liberal associational model, where ethnicity can be a private source of collective enterprise but should not be legitimized by government largesse. Brian Barry castigates multiculturalism, because "ill-conceived public policies can *make* culture into a problem . . . by gratuitously turning it into a form of pork-barrel politics" (2001: 317). Why give public funding to private identities?

The answer is found in the experience of Portuguese Americans. Although each person in a political system has equality through the allocation of a single vote per person, financial resources, linguistic skills, political experience, and other resources are not similarly distributed. These problems are, of course, not reserved for immigrants, but they can be especially acute for these groups. Those born in Portugal constituted the largest foreign-born population in Massachusetts throughout the 1980s and 1990s, but they have been politically invisible. If we believe that political participation is a good thing—for the United States, because it reinforces the country's civic identity, and for immigrants, because we believe that everyone should have a say in their own government—then we should try to foster newcomers' ability to engage in our political structures. Without public support, we will see significant political inequalities in who participates. A particular danger is the possibility that the political alienation learned by the first generation will be transferred to subsequent, native-born citizens.

State intervention using multiculturalism and settlement policies helps equalize the playing field. It does not have to do this with quotas—as is done for women in some Scandinavian countries, where a certain number of seats are reserved for female candidates—but it can be done by allowing immigrant communities to mobilize themselves.[14] As we have seen, government support for newcomer integration attenuates naturalization differences between the most and least educated immigrants and reduces social inequalities between ordinary immigrants and the leaders who frequently engage in mobilization activities. The effect of government assistance is probably especially powerful for resource-poor migrants such as the Portuguese.[15] If this is indeed the case, the political integration of disadvantaged groups such as Mexican and Central American migrants in the United States requires state support on par to that given to refugees.

One might legitimately ask whether there are other nonethnic community resources that might do the job of political incorporation just as well. Religious bodies, unions, and mainstream civic associations are the most obvious substitutes, and they could surely do some of the work. However, this solution also carries some practical problems. Many religious institutions attended by first-generation immigrants become de facto ethnic organizations because immigrants search out services in their own language. The resource problems of any ethnic organization apply equally to ethnic religious bodies, while religious bridging across ethnic groups—which could pool resources—is rare. Unions facilitate political incorporation, and as we saw in chapter 6, the stronger union movement in Canada played a part in the stories of some Portuguese Canadian community leaders. But union strength and numbers are declining, limiting the effect of unions for the overall immigrant community.

Outreach efforts by mainstream organizations largely composed of the native born—and here I will stretch that definition to include political parties—arguably would be the most helpful in teaching immigrants political skills, transferring knowledge, and fostering nonethnic coalitions. The reality, however, is that immigrants have difficulty joining such groups, in part because of linguistic barriers, but also because mainstream groups do not seem particularly inclined to reach out to newcomer communities. Mainstream civic associations are also arguably increasingly stratified by class, perpetuating economic inequalities in participation. In this context, ethnic organizations offer relatively less class stratification since language and cultural ties span class divisions.[16] These exclusions suggest that not only governments but also civic organizations, including political parties and unions, need to become more multicultural in ideology and practice.

Political Dignity

Multiculturalism goes beyond the provision of resources to also offer state recognition of the special heritages that immigrants bring with them. Newcomers find this invaluable, as it provides legitimacy and dignity. Critics downplay the benefits of recognition. Some find it a hollow promise: you cannot eat recognition if you are living in poverty. But economic indignities are not the only ones suffered, and they are not suffered by all immigrants. In contrast, almost all newcomers will suffer scrutiny because of accent, dress, or some other marker of foreignness. "Where are you from?" they will inevitably be asked. Although many who pose the question do so out of polite interest, the query reinforces the sense of being not quite American or Canadian.

Other critics, such as Australian minister for citizenship and multicultural affairs Peter McGauran, feel that multiculturalism is a mere label, one that has become a distraction. McGauran suggest that "Multiculturalism as a term is in some ways irrelevant—what we need to focus on are the values it represents, such as opportunities for everyone to reach their potential, commitment to the rule of law, freedom of speech and religion and acceptance that everyone has the right to their own beliefs" (McGauran 2005: 6). According to many immigrants and refugees, individual rights guarantees help, but so too does the explicit endorsement, by government, of one's right to be different and still be equal, as articulated by multiculturalism. For most of those I interviewed, being able to assert one's background openly and proudly reduces the sense of second-class citizenship rather than reinforces it. Furthermore, it spurs some mainstream organizations to make special efforts to include immigrants and refugees.

Thus, while American (or, increasingly, Australian) liberal associationalism is a legitimate model for handling immigrant-generated diversity, it is not necessarily the best, at least when we are concerned with newcomers' participatory citizenship. The laissez-faire logic underpinning this model perpetuates inequalities of resources and standing that are particularly acute in most immigrant communities.

CANADIAN EXCEPTIONALISM?

In examining the nature and consequence of government policy for immigrant political incorporation, I have concentrated on a particular variant: Canadian multiculturalism and settlement policy, as compared to the relative lack of similar policies in the United States. Is the Canadian model exportable, or is it too tied to the particular exigencies of that country to be relevant to other nations?

Institutions are always products of their particular society and time, so to a certain extent, Canadian multiculturalism is unique. Will Kymlicka (2005) hypothesizes that popular support for multiculturalism decreases in the face of large-scale illegal immigration, when large numbers of migrants are perceived to be illiberal—in the contemporary period, popularly conceived to be Muslim—and with poor economic times. On each criterion, he says, Canada offers fertile ground for multiculturalism: illegal migration is modest, perceptions of illiberal migration are low, and the economy is healthy.

Canada's history of managing diversity might also make it more amenable to immigrant multiculturalism. Canadians have long learned to use government to mediate cultural concerns due to the presence of a large French Catholic minority in an English-speaking majority. Canadians might be more likely to extend the logic of linguistic and cultural recognition to the foreign born. In contrast, the American legacy of slavery and European countries' histories of colonialism inscribe different power dynamics on majority-minority relations. Although New France became part of the British Empire through conquest, Quebec's political incorporation into Canadian confederation was more one of equals.[17]

Finally, the success of Canadian multiculturalism—or the lack of retreat from it—stems from its integral role in Canadian nation building. The Second World War provided a final, decisive push in a long move away from Canada's old self-conception as a British dominion. The void needed to be filled by a new self-understanding. This crisis of identity was made all the more acute by surging French Canadian nationalism and the attendant Quebec independence movement as well as a perpetual desire to distinguish Canada from the United States, a wish made stronger in the 1960s and 1970s by the perceived social ills besetting the United States and the economic dominance of American companies in Canada. To some extent, multiculturalism was initially defined by what it was not. In response to Quebec nationalism, Canada was not bicultural (though it could be bilingual). Canadians were not Americans, so they did not believe in the melting pot. At a certain level, multiculturalism makes Canadianism possible.

Given these specificities, the Canadian model is probably most exportable to similar Anglo settler nations such as Australia and New Zealand. And indeed, until its recent retrenchment, Australia joined Canada as having developed one of the most extensive immigrant-related multiculturalism policies in the world. At the same time, certain Canadian multicultural practices might be a model for other countries, because other countries will soon face identity crises caused by immigration. European countries with large foreign-born populations need to reconceive of themselves in such a way that immigrants and their children can believe in their common citizenship with tenth-generation Germans, Swedes, Dutch, and Italians. These new identities also need to be embraced by the native-born majority so that public identities of both minorities and majorities are transformed to make multiculturalism not just for "them" but also what defines "us" (Bauböck 2005).

The United States, while not providing much material support for newcomers, provides some symbolic rhetoric of inclusion through its historic self-image as a nation of immigrants. European countries with stronger welfare state traditions are, in contrast, more apt to direct public funding to the foreign born, but they have difficulty on the symbolic side articulating a shared ideal of multicultural citizenship. Indeed, without a common citizenship ideal, state intervention might very well segregate rather than integrate. Thus publicly funded programs for immigrants in Germany might foster little incorporation, given that country's long refusal to consider foreigners as possible citizens. Successful multicultural citizenship demands symbolic *and* material intervention.

Public-Private Partnerships

If Canadian multiculturalism is a model to follow, multiculturalism must be combined with proactive policies of integration, especially around language training and labor market incorporation. The Canadian model does not— unlike the picture painted by some critics or the desires of some radical multiculturalists—promote institutionally separate ethnic blocs. Ideally, immigrant associations and mutual assistance associations should do some of the settlement work, with government grants and contracts fostering organizing within immigrant communities. Howard Duncan argues, correctly I think, that the private-public partnerships idiomatic of Canadian multiculturalism and settlement empower immigrants because newcomers become officially responsible for a portion of their integration. At the same time, such policies give "a signal to the population at large that there is this trust between the government and the newcomer organizations and the newcomers themselves" (2005: 14). The same approach has been successful in refugee integration in the United States.

Universalism, Common Institutions, and Public Benefits

Critics are right that multiculturalism can segregate rather than unite people. Some of those I interviewed raised the specter of ghettoization: multiculturalism might keep multiple generations locked into a self-enclosed ethnic community. The antidote in Canada has been common institutions, especially public schools; reasonable chances for economic mobility; universal public benefits; and a civic nationalism that can include foreigners. Some European countries have probably gone too far when, for example, they set up separate schools for ethnic minorities. Although these certainly preserve difference, they probably do more to segregate than integrate. European multiculturalism will have to ensure that majorities and minorities can come together as equals in schools and the labor market.

In the United States, however, successful multiculturalism might require greater investment in a relatively weak welfare state. In a context of limited public benefits, race and ethnicity take on added salience when a gain for one becomes a loss for another. Newcomers' favorable attitude toward government in Canada is driven not only by multicultural recognition but also by universal social programs such as health care. Universal public benefits teach newcomers that government cares and make multiculturalism less of a threat to native-born Canadians. Debate over immigration and the welfare state in the United States has primarily centered on economic costs. My conversations with newcomers hint that public provision of social benefits might offer political benefits: higher rates of citizenship and a stronger sense of membership.

In this context, lacking political will at the federal level, individual U.S. states could take the lead in combining public benefit provision with multiculturalism and immigrant integration efforts. Large-scale differences in political incorporation are probably most apparent between countries since institutional structures and policies differ much more across countries than within them.[18] Nonetheless, the dynamics of political incorporation might vary in subtle ways for other groups in other states and cities, requiring further research. Boston and Toronto, the sites for my research, are older cities with established traditions of immigrant conflict and accommodation. Places without set norms and patterns of behavior toward newcomers might be able to shape future relations between immigrants and the native born by adopting multicultural and settlement policies. In Canada, immigrants' experiences in Montreal might deviate from the pattern seen in Toronto.

Given competition between Quebec and Ottawa for the hearts and minds of immigrants, newcomers might become more rapidly politicized in Quebec than elsewhere in Canada. The central thrust of this book—that government ideologies, policies, and programs influence immigrant citizenship— remains applicable.

The Cultural Content of Recognition

Canadian multiculturalism also suggests cultural recognition on the basis of ethnicity rather than race. Some of the most powerful criticisms of multiculturalism in the United States turn on the reification of race. Given that racial categories served to enslave, disenfranchise, exclude, and exploit generations of Americans, why legitimize and reinstitutionalize these social constructions through multiculturalism? Aren't minorities better served by the ideal of a color-blind society and equality of rights? Such arguments are not only raised by those on the political Right but also by thoughtful thinkers on the political Left. Attacking what he calls the "ethno-racial pentagon," David Hollinger (2000) argues that the crude categories of black, white, red, yellow, and brown serve white supremacists, not well-meaning Americans of any background.

Many migrants would agree. They acknowledge realities of prejudice and discrimination based on physical appearance, but they see little political, and even less cultural, affinity with others placed into America's predominant racial categorizations. Vietnamese refugees do not feel a natural affinity to other "Asian Americans," and they express resentment at being recast in pan-ethnic terms. Not only does it erase their unique background and heritage, but the historic use of race to ascribe second-class citizenship makes them suspicious of such categorizations. Racialized multicultural citizenship is not particularly appealing. On this point, critics such as Hollinger are correct to argue that the American ethno-racial pentagon cannot be a basis of *cultural* recognition, especially for immigrants.

This does not mean, however, that race cannot be a focus of public policy. If phenotype is used in the United States and Canada to discriminate between individuals, which is undoubtedly the case more often than we would like, solid grounds exist to establish a political category of *people of color* or *visible minority*. As Hollinger writes, "The concept of race, then, serves us reasonably well when we want to be aware of a pattern of behavior: it refers to the lines along which people have been systematically mistreated on the basis of certain physical characteristics" (2000: 35–36). Racialized groups might require added protections and programs of affirmative action to overcome race-based barriers. Beneficiaries of such pro-grams could include immigrants, since phenotype does not distinguish between the foreign and native born. An argument could also be made, however, that in certain countries specific physical features elicit greater discrimination than others due to particular histories of acute exploitation and domination. A number of Vietnamese in Canada told me that First Nations people suffer far more harm than they. A similar case could be made for those labeled black in the United States, as migration scholars increasingly raise the possibility that the American color line will be black/nonblack in the twenty-first century.[19] Deciding who should be assisted by antiracism efforts must be determined by political debate, not current understandings of American multiculturalism policy.

If race-based multiculturalism ill serves immigrants, it does not logically follow that the United States must abandon any form of multiculturalism. Immigrants, and probably many native-born descendents, value recognition of their cultural heritage. Such recognition facilitates a sense of inclusive cit-izenship for all the reasons already enumerated. It is conceivable that such ethnic multiculturalism would, as is largely the case in Canada, promote symbolic ethnicity like we find among many descendants of earlier Euro-pean migrants. Separating the cultural content of ethnicity from the politi-cal content of race might attenuate racialization in the United States.[20]

AMERICAN AND CANADIAN CITIZENSHIP
IN THE TWENTY-FIRST CENTURY

In late-nineteenth- and early-twentieth-century America, scholars, politi-cians, and the general public saw a clear link between immigrants' partici-patory citizenship and larger society. A majority of U.S. states and territo-ries allowed noncitizen suffrage, believing that voting provided a lesson in political socialization for the would-be citizen.[21] Academics and legislators painted a holistic view of Americanization in which citizenship, patriotism, political involvement, and socioeconomic integration conjoined.[22] Many took pains to argue that immigrants who naturalized merely for "practical and material" reasons nonetheless became "truer and stauncher Americans as their citizenship . . . developed" (Fields 1932: 182, 181). Citizenship was not just an individual choice but part of a larger social and political process urged on by political parties, unions, ethnic associations, religious bodies, schools, and other state institutions.[23]

By century's end, the academic literature paints a very different picture, suggesting that political incorporation is less of a social process and more of an individual choice than ever before (DeSipio 2001). American political parties do not seem to reach out to newcomers like they once did. Social pressures around political incorporation, especially citizenship, have declined as discourses of diversity replaced earlier pushes to homogeneity and Americanization.[24] The socioeconomic consequences of citizenship have largely disappeared. Civil, social, and economic rights are largely decoupled from citizenship status, leading legal scholar Peter Schuck (1998) to talk of a "devaluation" of citizenship.[25]

Some worry that the devaluation of citizenship is aggravated by transnationalism. Immigrants use modern communication and transportation technologies to live lives spanning geopolitical boundaries, only sinking weak roots in the country of immigration. In addition, human rights norms and pressures of globalization force states to take more flexible attitudes to citizenship and belonging (Hollifield 1992; Jacobson 1996; Soysal 1994). Reading these accounts, we get the sense that there is little states can do to stem the fading of citizenship in the twenty-first century.

The evidence presented here cautions against a wholehearted adoption of transnational or postnational paradigms of incorporation. Forces of globalization clearly make the world a more interconnected place, and they facilitate the ability of individuals, businesses, and organizations to be active in multiple countries. Yet everyday experiences for many immigrants remain grounded in specific societies that are strongly shaped by particular government policies. As a major exporting country, Canada is more victim to global economic fluctuation than the United States and, as we have seen, it takes a more postnationalist approach to the allocation of rights without regard to citizenship. Yet immigrant citizenship and participation is higher in Canada, suggesting that nation-states continue to influence the fortunes of migrants despite countervailing transnational or supranational forces.

Such influence is not always in the form of assistance. In the 1990s immigrants in the United States were pushed to citizenship via the "stick" of referenda widely perceived as anti-immigrant and by legislation that reemphasizes the legal distinctions between citizens and noncitizens. Such punitive measures probably account, in part, for the modest surge in U.S. citizenship from 1997, when it stood at 35 percent of the foreign born, to 2000, when it was recorded at 40 percent of the foreign born. A number of U.S. states, including Massachusetts, helped immigrants with citizenship, though less out of civic spirit than fiscal concerns.

Those worried about declining levels of citizenship can celebrate the upswing in legal citizenship, but the approach outlined here sounds a note of caution when it comes to broader notions of participatory citizenship. Instrumental naturalization does not necessarily carry over to political involvement, but rather protective or defensive citizenship (Gilbertson and Singer 2003). Indeed, without normative and material support for newcomer communities, it is unlikely that these new citizens will participate actively. Such a scenario raises the possibility that American citizenship will become a legal protection but not an invitation—and obligation—to engage in the governance of the nation. The bonds of citizenship will grow thin; citizens become inhabitants of a physical space or carriers of a passport, but they will not constitute a community. In fact, by 2004 naturalization levels fell again, to 38 percent, despite the increased salience of citizenship following the terrorist attacks of September 11, 2001.

In response to the events of September 11, 2001, the bureaucratic oversight of immigration and naturalization changed dramatically. Under the former INS, the dual functions of the agency—border enforcement on one hand, service delivery on the other— coexisted unhappily, with more focus on control than service. Unflattering stories of poor service, long waits, and difficult officials probably put off some immigrants' decisions to naturalize. More insidiously, negative experiences with the INS affect immigrants' general perceptions of U.S. government and the relationship between citizens and the American state.

On March 1, 2003, the Immigration and Naturalization Service ceased to exist. Its functions were transferred from the Department of Justice to the new Department of Homeland Security and split into three—the Bureau of U.S. Customs and Border Protection (external border control), the Bureau of U.S. Immigration and Customs Enforcement (internal policing), and the Bureau of U.S. Citizenship and Immigration Services (USCIS). This reorganization offers some hope for better incorporation outcomes but also a real danger of further depressing political integration in the United States.

By separating the service function of immigration and naturalization from border control and internal enforcement, the new bureaucratic makeup of Homeland Security provides an opportunity to change the culture and administrative practice of naturalization. Although the U.S. executive branch appears far from adopting Canada's official multiculturalism policy or other policies of explicit government intervention in immigrant incorporation, the refugee resettlement program shows that the country can initiate such efforts. As part of the Homeland Security Act of 2002, Congress mandated a new Office of Citizenship whose chief is charged with "promoting instruction and training on citizenship responsibilities for aliens interested in becoming naturalized citizens of the United States";[26]

fostering partnerships with other government agencies, community groups, faith-based groups, and private organizations that share an interest in civic engagement and integration; and overseeing a staff of community liaison officers who work with local community stakeholders to promote the objectives of the Office of Citizenship. One concrete product of the new focus on integration and outreach has been the development of a "Guide for New Immigrants" in numerous languages that includes sections on rights and responsibilities; settlement information, such as how to get a Social Security number and find work; information on education and childcare; information on emergencies and safety; an overview of U.S. political history and institutions; and information on how to become a citizen.

A new immigration bill introduced by Senators John McCain and Edward Kennedy in the 109th Congress includes an explicit Civics Integration section. Title IX of the bill would establish a United States Citizenship Foundation mandated to accept donations from the general public and receive appropriations from Congress. The foundation would provide monies in the form of grants through the Office of Citizenship to organizations offering civic and English classes. These initiatives carry a strong resemblance to similar promotion and outreach efforts by Citizenship and Immigration Canada.

The question, however, is whether a more proactive and service-friendly atmosphere can be maintained or expanded when naturalization and immigration services are housed within a department dedicated to "homeland security," especially when security is defined largely as against foreign threats. The theme of USCIS's 2005 Strategic Plan, which is also used as a slogan on various customer service publications available to immigrants, is "Securing America's Promise." The promise is one of a "nation of immigrants," but the promise comes second to being "secure."

Service might well become even more subservient to enforcement priorities in Homeland Security than in the former INS. The new USCIS constitutes only a small part of a huge department in which almost all subunits are dedicated to policing functions. In the budget for the 2005 fiscal year, the Bureau of U.S. Immigration and Customs Enforcement (ICE) is slated for a 10 percent increase over the previous fiscal year and will receive an additional $357 million for enforcement efforts, including $100 million for detention and removal of illegal immigrants (U.S. Department of Homeland Security 2004). The proportional increase in ICE's budget is the second largest among all Homeland Security organizational units, only falling behind that of the Transportation Security Administration. In comparison, USCIS will receive an extra $58 million in its allocation, an increase of less than 4 percent. Most of the increase will go to a special program to reduce immigration application waiting times, while the general administrative budgets for immigrant and nonimmigrant services will be cut by 8 and 3 percent, respectively, and the budget for citizenship services will grow a modest 3 percent.[27] If immigrant political incorporation is viewed as a goal, USCIS should remain a separate bureau and it should not be housed in the Department of Homeland Security.

In Canada, relations between government and community organizations have become more strained. Canadian governments have increased administrative reporting requirements for grants, have begun requesting private matching contributions, and have increasingly pushed for competitive bidding in the allocation of public funds. Many in the nonprofit sector feel that these requirements have become excessive. In July 2005 more than two hundred charitable groups in Toronto, many serving immigrants, rallied together to push for changes in the way government structures public-private partnership (Goar 2005).

In the late 1990s and into 2000, Canadian governments also cut funding to multiculturalism programs and scaled back services offered to newcomers. The 2005 federal budget increased funding for integration and settlement services for the first time in five years, with $20 million slated for community organizations in the 2005–06 fiscal year. The budget promised a total of $298 million over five years to community groups, but such promises are tenuous since they were made by a minority government that fell in December 2005. Future governments should consider that any short-term fiscal gains achieved by cutbacks might be undermined by the long-term exclusion of newcomer populations. Reduced public funding to community organizations and government withdrawal from settlement and diversity programs would have a negative effect on political incorporation. Achieving full citizenship cannot be a private effort. It demands public intervention.

The decision to cut multiculturalism programming in Canada or to move USCIS out of Homeland Security is ultimately a political choice, one wrapped in debates that extend beyond immigration and integration to include foreign policy goals, welfare state development, and management of historic ethno-racial tensions in each country. The consequences of such decisions are significant. Robust citizenship is not just an outgrowth of private desires and personal resources nor merely a legal status or passport with which to travel. Democratic governance demands participatory citizenship. This book suggests that political incorporation is better served when governments extend a welcoming hand: offering concrete settlement assistance and recognizing immigrants' diverse identities, ethnicities, and cultures within a framework of *future citizen* rather than *foreigner* or *alien*. The achievement of full citizenship is a mutual process, a relationship between the people who hold citizenship and the state that bestows it. By failing to help others achieve full citizenship, we weaken the democratic foundations upon which common bonds are built.

Interviewees

PORTUGUESE INTERVIEWEES (ORDINARY COMMUNITY MEMBERS)

Boston Area

Name	Sex	Age	Generation	Birth Region	Period Migrated	Education
Amelia	F	54	1	Azores	1970s	None
Antonio	M	68	1	Azores	1960s	None
Cristina	F	18	2	Massachusetts	—	High school diploma
Eddie	M	35	1	Azores	1990s	Grade 11
Fatima	F	52	1	Mainland	1970s	Grade 9
Fernando	M	41	1	Mainland	1980s	University degree
Joe	M	66	2	Madeira	1940s	Grade 9
Jose	M	86	1.5	Mainland	1910s	High school diploma
Ilda	F	46	1.5	Mainland	1960s	Grade 8
Manuel	M	64	1	Azores	1970s	None
Manuela	F	59	1	Azores	1960s	Grade 4
Maria	F	55	1	Azores	1960s	GED
Maria-Paula	F	29	1.5	Mainland	1970s	University degree
Mike	M	30	2	Massachusetts	—	University degree
Steve	M	29	2	Massachusetts	—	University degree
Tina	F	53	1	Azores	1970s	None

The notation "1.5" refers to those who migrated before the age of fourteen.

PORTUGUESE INTERVIEWEES (ORDINARY COMMUNITY MEMBERS)
Toronto Area

Name	Sex	Age	Generation	Birth Region	Period Migrated	Education
Angelina	F	47	1	Mainland	1960s	Post-secondary certificate
Arminda	F	34	1.5	Azores	1970s	Post-secondary certificate
Fernanda	F	47	1	Azores	1960s	Grade 8
F. Sousa	M	45	1.5	Azores	1960s	University degree
George	M	42	1.5	Azores	1970s	Post-secondary certificate
Humberto	M	59	1	Azores	1960s	Grade 4
Ivo	M	64	1	Azores	1960s	None
Jacinto	M	68	1	Mainland	1980s	University degree
Maria Clara	F	44	1.5	Azores	1960s	Grade 10
Mario	M	60	1	Mainland	1960s	Grade 4
Marta	F	76	1	Azores	1960s	None
Noelia	F	38	1.5	Azores	1960s	University degree
Tilla	F	54	1	Azores	1960s	Grade 4
Vasco	M	53	1	Azores	1960s	Grade 8
Victoria	F	54	1	Azores	1960s	None

The notation "1.5" refers to those who migrated before the age of fourteen.

PORTUGUESE INTERVIEWEES (COMMUNITY LEADERS)

Boston Area

Name	*Sex*	*Age*	*Generation*	*Birth Region*	*Period Migrated*	*Education*
Ana	F	44	2	Massachusetts	—	Post-secondary certificate
Armando	M	52	1	Azores	1970s	High school
Father Silva	M	60	2	Massachusetts	—	University degree
Joaquim	M	41	1	Mainland	1970s	University degree
John	M	26	2	Massachusetts	—	University degree
Joseph	M	43	1.5	Azores	1960s	University degree
Judite	F	48	1	Azores	1960s	University degree
Lucia	F	48	1.5	Mainland	1950s	Post-secondary certificate
Marco	M	32	1.5	Mainland	1980s	University degree
Martin	M	43	1	Azores	1980s	High school diploma
Rosana	F	39	1.5	Azores	1960s	University degree
Tony	M	44	1	Azores	1970s	Post-secondary certificate
Victor	M	49	1	Azores	1960s	University degree

PORTUGUESE INTERVIEWEES (COMMUNITY LEADERS)
Toronto Area

Name	Sex	Age	Generation	Birth Region	Period Migrated	Education
Agostinho	M	56	1	Colonies	1980s	University degree
Aldora	F	65	1	Azores	1960s	University degree
Ana Maria	F	49	1	Mainland	1960s	University degree
Artur	M	39	1.5	Mainland	1960s	University degree
Celia	F	42	1.5	Mainland	1970s	University degree
Dan	M	38	2	Ontario	—	University degree
Eduardo	M	49	1	Mainland	1960s	University degree
F. Marques	M	41	1.5	Azores	1960s	University degree
Frank	M	47	1	Mainland	1970s	University degree
Gloria	F	43	1.5	Mainland	1970s	University degree
Jose Manuel	M	56	1	Mainland	1970s	University degree
Michelle	F	30	2	Ontario	—	University degree
Nelson	M	45	1	Mainland	1960s	High school diploma
Rosemary	F	49	1	Azores	1970s	University degree
Teresa	F	49	1	Colonies	1970s	University degree
Tomas	M	32	1.5	Azores	1970s	University degree
Valadao	M	55	1	Mainland	1970s	University degree
Vivaldo	M	60	1	Mainland	1960s	University degree

The notation "1.5" refers to those who migrated before the age of fourteen.

VIETNAMESE INTERVIEWEES (ORDINARY COMMUNITY MEMBERS)

Boston Area

Name	Sex	Age	Generation	Birth Region	Period Migrated	Education
Buu	M	53	1	North	1980s	Post-secondary certificate
Cai	F	56	1	South	1990s	Grade 10
Dam	M	45	1	South	1990s	High school diploma
Ha	F	33	1	South	1990s	Grade 3
Hung	M	53	1	South	1990s	Grade 10
Huynh	F	31	1	South	1980s	High school diploma
Lap	M	43	1	South	1980s	University degree
Ngoc	F	39	1	Central	1990s	Grade 11
Phuoc	M	46	1	South	1980s	Grade 5
Sammy	M	65	1	North	1970s	University degree
Thien	M	41	1	South	1990s	Grade 5
Tong	M	57	1	South	1990s	Post-secondary certificate
Trang	F	60	1	Central	1980s	None
Tri	M	33	1	South	1980s	University degree
Tung	M	38	1	South	1980s	Grade 6
Tuyet	F	50	1	South	1990s	High school diploma

VIETNAMESE INTERVIEWEES (ORDINARY COMMUNITY MEMBERS)
Toronto Area

Name	Sex	Age	Generation	Birth Region	Period Migrated	Education
Ann	F	42	1	South	1980s	Post-secondary certificate
Cong	M	50	1	South	1970s	Grade 11
David	M	28	1	South	1990s	University degree
Doan	F	69	1	North	1990s	Grade 6
Duc	M	60	1	South	1980s	University degree
Duy	M	43	1	South	1980s	Grade 4
Hiep	M	72	1	South	1980s	Grade 8
Hoa	F	71	1	South	1980s	Post-secondary certificate
Jean	F	52	1	South	1970s	University degree
Luong	M	37	1	South	1990s	Grade 6
Mai	F	81	1	South	1980s	Post-secondary certificate
Nghi	M	41	1	South	1980s	Grade 8
Oanh	F	71	1	Central	1980s	High school diploma
Phan	M	25	1.5	South	1970s	Post-secondary certificate
Phuong	M	38	1	South	1980s	High school diploma
Phuongmai	F	61	1	South	1990s	High school diploma
San	M	60	1	South	1980s	University degree
Thuy	F	38	1	South	1970s	University degree
Toan	M	70	1	North	1990s	Grade 8
Tom	M	51	1	South	1980s	University degree
Van	M	32	1.5	South	1980s	University degree

The notation "1.5" refers to those who migrated before the age of fourteen.

VIETNAMESE INTERVIEWEES (COMMUNITY LEADERS)
Boston Area

Name	Sex	Age	Generation	Birth Region	Period Migrated	Education
Becky	F	31	1.5	South	1970s	University degree
Dinh Hao	M	43	1	South	1980s	University degree
F. Tran	M	50	1	South	1970s	University degree
Khoi	M	38	1	South	1980s	University degree
Kim	F	24	1.5	South	1980s	University degree
Lily	F	40	1.5	South	1970s	Post-secondary certificate
Luan	F	40	1	South	1990s	University degree
Moc Van	M	54	1	North	1970s	University degree
Rose	F	50	1	South	1970s	University degree
Sau	M	58	1	South	1980s	University degree
Thanh	M	33	1.5	South	1980s	University degree
Xuan	F	38	1.5	South	1980s	Post-secondary certificate
Yen	M	40	1	South	1980s	University degree

VIETNAMESE INTERVIEWEES (COMMUNITY LEADERS)

Toronto Area

Name	Sex	Age	Generation	Birth Region	Period Migrated	Education
Binh	M	31	1	South	1980s	Post-secondary certificate
Chau	F	46	1	Central	1990s	Post-secondary certificate
Dr. Tran	M	67	1	South	1970s	University degree
F. Nguyen	M	57	1	South	1980s	University degree
Hai	M	48	1	South	1970s	University degree
Jim	M	55	1	South	1970s	University degree
John	M	30	1.5	South	1980s	University degree
Joseph	M	63	1	North	1970s	University degree
Lien	F	59	1	Central	1970s	High school diploma
Long	M	55	1	South	1980s	University degree
My-Khanh	F	64	1	North	1980s	University degree
Quan Van	M	70	1	North	1980s	University degree
Quynh	F	44	1	South	1990s	Post-secondary certificate
Trinh	F	33	1.5	South	1980s	University degree

The notation "1.5" refers to those who migrated before the age of fourteen.

ADDITIONAL INTERVIEWEES

United States

Name	Position	Date Interviewed
Ronald Cruz	President, Portuguese American Leadership Council of the United States	August 24, 2000 (by phone)
Mary Kay Egan	Coordinator, naturalization services, Catholic Charities, Boston	April 20, 1998, Somerville
Westy Egmont	Executive director, International Institute of Boston	June 9, 2000, Boston
Laura Heartquist	Volunteer coordinator, Catholic Charities, Boston	May 13, 1998, Somerville
Doris Meissner	Former commissioner, U.S. Immigration and Naturalization Service	May 2, 2002 (by phone)
Jason Moreira	Office manager, Portuguese American Leadership Council of the United States	August 9, 2000, Washington, D.C.
Anita Nasra	Assistant director, Kit Clark Senior Services, Boston	June 6, 2001, Boston
Nanda Shewmangal	Outreach coordinator, Asian Task Force against Domestic Violence	May 31, 2001, Boston
Barbara Strack	Special assistant, policy and planning, U.S. Immigration and Naturalization Service	November 6, 2001 (by phone)
Reverend Cheng Imm Tan	Director, Office of New Bostonians, Boston	March 1, 2001, Boston
Kimberly Zimmerman	Citizenship coordinator, International Institute of Boston	June 9, 2000, Boston

ADDITIONAL INTERVIEWEES

Canada

Name	Position	Date Interviewed
Frank Alvarez	President, CIRV Multicultural Radio	June 15, 2001, Toronto
Patricia Birkett	Director, citizenship, Citizenship and Immigration Canada	June 13, 2001, Ottawa
Dr. Can Duy Le	President, Vietnamese Canadian Federation	June 23, 2001, Ottawa
Debbie Douglas	Executive director, Ontario Council of Agencies Serving Immigrants	March 30, 2001, Toronto
Maureen Fair	Director of community response and advocacy, St. Christopher House	January 12, 2001, Toronto
Rosaline Frith	Director general, integration, Citizenship and Immigration Canada	June 13, 2001, Ottawa
Loren Grebanier	Community development officer, Toronto	March 30, 2001, Toronto
Rose Lee	Coordinator, access and equity, Toronto	March 19, 2001, Toronto
Anne Mendel	Program officer, integration, Citizenship and Immigration Canada	June 13, 2001, Ottawa
Jennifer Ratansi-Rodriguez	Manager, multiculturalism, Heritage Canada (Ontario division)	January 9, 2001, Toronto
Joe Pantalone	City councilor, Toronto	June 17, 1998, Toronto
Cass Sunderji	Former program officer, multiculturalism, Heritage Canada (Ontario division)	August 1, 2001 (by phone)
Iran Tajbakhsh	Settlement counselor, St. Christopher House	March 28, 2001, Toronto

Notes

1. See, for example, Poston, Camarota, and Baumle (2003).

2. Research on the native born suggests this effect (Miller and Shanks 1996; Verba, Schlozman, and Brady 1995). There is limited research on generational transfers of political behavior and attitudes among immigrants, though Ramakrishnan and Espenshade (2001) offer some cross-sectional data on voting and immigrant generation.

3. Other measures are possible—the decision to cast a ballot being the most obvious—but the three examined here cover a broad spectrum of political activities. At present it is impossible to compare foreign-born citizens' voting patterns in any depth, but as better cross-national data on immigrants' political behaviors and attitudes become available, this framework can be tested on other indicators.

4. By *mainstream* I mean the general political debates and activities of the receiving society, as opposed to the internal politics of the immigrant community.

5. For example, two recent, important overviews of immigrant incorporation in the United States by Alba and Nee (2003) and Bean and Stevens (2003) entirely ignore political incorporation.

6. See, for example, Uhlaner (1996) and Verba, Schlozman, and Brady (1993). Ramakrishnan (2005) levels a similar critique, noting a paucity of research within political science on immigrant political behavior. This situation is slowly changing, as shown in the work by Ramakrishnan (2005), Ramakrishnan and Espenshade (2001), and Wong (2006).

7. See, for example, Kasinitz's (1992) study of West Indians in New York City.

8. See, for example, Cain, Kiewiet, and Uhlaner (1991), Ramakrishnan and Espenshade (2001), and Yang (1994). Behavioralism leads to, and is a product of, a heavy reliance on survey data and other micro-level statistical evidence.

9. There are numerous examples of an individual, behaviorist approach in the United States (Jasso and Rosenzweig 1990; Cho 1999; Portes and Mozo

1985; Uhlaner, Cain, and Kiewiet 1989; Yang 1994) and Canada (Black 1987; Chui, Curtis, and Lambert 1991; Mata 1999).

10. A minority challenges the characterization of decision making as cost/benefit, arguing instead that naturalization flows from assimilation and identification with the host society (Evans 1988; Frideres et al. 1987; Legendre and Shaffir 1984; Wearing 1985). Nevertheless, all these studies share a reliance on statistical methodologies that measure variables at the individual rather than societal level.

11. See also Ireland (1994) and Soysal (1994) for early uses of political opportunity structure arguments to explain migrants' political activities. Favell's (1998) examination of philosophies and policies marks a move by some to examine change in national contexts while still highlighting cross-national differences.

12. See de Rham (1990) and Clarke, van Dam, and Gooster (1998).

13. The U.S. and Canadian figures are my calculation using data published in the corresponding INS yearbooks and CIC statistical reports for naturalizations and U.S. Current Population Survey and Canadian census data for the number of the noncitizen foreign stock.

14. In this tradition, see Brubaker (1989, 1992), de Rham (1990), de Wenden (1987), Favell (1998), and Weil (2001).

15. The exception to this rule is the U.S. presidency, which is restricted to those born on U.S. soil. This stands in contrast to Canada, where a number of foreign-born prime ministers have held office.

16. Laczko (1994) finds that socioeconomic development and cultural and linguistic pluralism tend to be inversely related. The other two noticeable outliers are Belgium and Switzerland.

17. On political mobilization, see Ireland (1994), Jones-Correa (1998b), Ramakrishnan (2005), and Soysal (1994). On comparative U.S.-Canada economic incorporation, see Boyd (2002) and Reitz (1998). On language learning, see Portes and Rumbaut (1996: 207–31). Portes and Rumbaut's emphasis on the *context of reception*—which they define as the intersection between U.S. immigration policy, societal discrimination, ethnic community strength, and immigrants' human capital—aims to understand between-group differences in the United States but could be extended to cross-national research. Similarly, Aihwa Ong's (2003) analysis of how government welfare agencies and government-funded resettlement and medical organizations shape Cambodian refugees' conceptions of American citizenship emphasizes the importance of institutional effects in one national context.

18. There is some indication that future research will treat individual agency more seriously. A recent trend to investigate urban rather than national environments has generated interest in the way immigrant networks and interorganizational ties influence an ethnic community's ability to make political claims and affect local politics. See, for example, Fennema and Tillie (2001).

19. This is in contrast to countries with strong ethnic or cultural notions of

membership such as Japan and Germany, though there are some indications that Germany is moving away from ethnic conceptions of nationhood.

20. For example, over the first half of the twentieth century, U.S. governments passed broad restrictions on noncitizens in certain types of employment (Konvitz 1946). These restrictions remained in force and sometimes grew more widespread through the 1950s and 1960s. Statute books started to change only after a series of Supreme Court decisions in the 1970s struck down state laws that discriminated on the basis of citizenship (Carliner et al. 1977). By 1996 only a few U.S. states had citizenship restrictions on employment (Plascencia, Freeman, and Setzler 2003).

21. See Bauböck (1994), Jacobson (1996), and Soysal (1994).

22. On the contemporary link between citizenship and political rights, see Jones-Correa (1998a), Layton-Henry (1990), and Schuck (1998).

23. I am sensitive to arguments that even with legal citizenship, the foreign born can suffer second-class citizenship when mainstream discourses and dominant cultures define legitimate citizens and legitimate citizenship practices as excluding certain immigrants and minorities (Ong 2003; Rosaldo 1997). I would nonetheless contend that without legal citizenship, the dynamics of marginalization are even more oppressive.

24. On the quantitative and qualitative changes in Americans' political and civic engagement, see Rosenstone and Hansen (1993), Putnam (2000), and Skocpol (2003).

25. Using the "stranger" as an analytical device to generate insight into phenomena close to home has a distinguished history in social science (Honig 2001; Simmel 1972).

26. Overviews of this literature can take the approach of political theory (Kymlicka and Norman 1994), legal scholarship (Aleinikoff 1998; Schuck 1998), or social science (Bloemraad 2000).

27. The lack of attention probably stems from a perception that the two countries are too much alike. Many comparative researchers, interested in exceptional cases or ideal types, contrast radically different manifestations of a similar concept or phenomenon (Ragin 1987). Thus, France and Switzerland offer "polar models of incorporating immigrants" in Ireland's (1994) analysis of political incorporation, while France and Germany represent ideal-typical civic or ethnic visions of citizenship (Brubaker 1992).

28. For example, Joppke (1999) compares the United States, Germany, and Great Britain. He concludes that differences in citizenship and immigrant integration between Western European and traditional immigration countries are even larger than previously theorized. As a result, he finds it difficult to offer general conclusions beyond a statement that national particularities matter and that multiculturalism affects all liberal Western states.

29. In 2000 the Portuguese, most of whom are economic migrants, were the largest immigrant group in Massachusetts, totaling 9 percent of the foreign-born population.

30. It is not always easy to make an objective distinction between economic and political migrants, despite an individual's entry visa. Many Vietnamese had strong economic motivations pushing them from their homeland, and a number of Portuguese I interviewed considered their migration a political act by which they were escaping the Portuguese dictatorship. See chapter 2.

31. Along similar lines, Moreno (1996) argues that in the United States the Cuban model of political incorporation—rapid and effective participation in American politics—cannot be considered a general model for other groups, in part because of the extraordinary help given to Cuban refugees by the U.S. government.

32. The presence of a state/provincial capital is important since it is likely easier for people to become politically engaged in cities where political decisions are made.

33. Troper (2003) says that the UN multicultural designation is actually an urban legend, but it highlights well the change in attitude among Torontonians who perpetuate such a story.

34. Unfortunately, no good comparative quantitative data sources exist on immigrant voting, involvement in public demonstrations, or similar indicators of political participation. The national election studies of both countries have sample sizes too small to include many immigrants, and because they are restricted to citizens, they do not collect information about noncitizens' political behavior. The U.S. Current Population Survey includes, since 1994, a large number of foreign-born respondents in its November Voting Supplements, but no comparable data source exists in Canada.

35. I conducted almost all the interviews between July 1997 and June 2001. I followed a semistructured interview schedule that asked questions about the individual's migration history, experiences living in Portugal or Vietnam and in North America, citizenship and political participation, organizational involvement, and general feelings about the United States or Canada. In particular, I focused on the process by which my respondents became citizens or came to be engaged in political activities. Most interviews lasted ninety minutes, though in a few memorable cases we talked for over five hours. The majority of the interviews were conducted in English, taped, and transcribed. When respondents preferred to speak in their native language, I used a coethnic interpreter. See the appendix for a list of those interviewed.

36. For more on the genesis and evolution of this project's research design and methodology, see Bloemraad (forthcoming).

1. DIVERGING TRAJECTORIES OF POLITICAL INCORPORATION

Epigraphs: Oath of Affirmation of Citizenship, Canada, from the Citizenship Act (R.S. 1985, c. C-29) 1974–75–76, c. 108, Sch.). Oath of Allegiance, United States, from the Immigration and Nationality Act (Sec. 337 [8 U.S.C. 1448]).

1. In July 1997 the Budget Agreement restored Supplemental Security Income to those who had resided in the United States as of August 22, 1996;

food stamps were restored under the Agriculture Research, Extension, and Education Act of 1998 and the Farm Security and Rural Investment Act of 2002. However, eligibility for these programs was not extended to legal immigrants entering the country after August 22, 1996, except in special cases. States may supplement the loss of federal dollars for postenactment immigrants with state monies, but few have done so (Fix and Passel 2002).

2. For more on historic restrictions by citizenship and the elimination of such restrictions , see Rosberg (1977), Raskin (1993), and Plascencia, Freeman, and Setzler (2003). In 1971 the U.S. Supreme Court ruled that states could not deny noncitizens access to social welfare benefits under the Constitution's equal protection clause, because the federal government has jurisdiction over aliens. Because welfare reform was instituted by Congress, and subsequent court decisions restricted the equal protection guarantees, it is unlikely that the 1996 act could be overturned in court based on the legal standards applied in 1971.

3. In general, anyone born on U.S. soil acquires American citizenship at birth, including the children of those who are in the United States on temporary visas or illegally. However, exceptions exist, such as for the children of foreign diplomats, who acquire the citizenship of their parents' country of origin, not the United States. Similarly, there are limits to acquiring U.S. citizenship through blood if one is born abroad. These caveats also hold in Canada.

4. This was clearly established in 1700, when William III decreed that any natural-born subject, whether in the colonies or Great Britain, could inherit even if his father or mother were an alien (Carpenter 1904: 292).

5. Each colony had its own approach and restrictions, especially around religious adherence. For example, Carpenter (1904) reports that seventeenth-century Massachusetts appeared singularly uninterested in allowing broad naturalization.

6. Parliament's Act of Settlement (1700) prohibited naturalized individuals from being members of the Privy Council or Parliament or holding any civil or military office. The general purpose of the legislation was to preserve the Protestant nature of the country and government (Ueda 1982; Kaplan 1991).

7. The most important step in this evolution was an act of Parliament passed in 1740 establishing a general naturalization law. It permitted foreigners in North America to acquire local subjectship (Ueda 1982).

8. In the words of James Madison, it was "a fault in our system . . . laying a foundation for intricate and delicate questions" (Hamilton, Madison, and Jay [1788] 1961: 269).

9. See Ueda (1982) and Bloemraad and Ueda (2006) for further details on this history.

10. The practice of granting citizenship to those born on U.S. soil continued, a holdover of British subjectship. Commenting on the twin influences of ascriptive (birthright) and consensual citizenship, Schuck and Smith underscore that "the American Congress, courts and statesmen had always drawn freely on both traditions, selecting among them largely on grounds of expediency" (1985: 71). American defense of volitional and contractual citizenship was strengthened

during the Napoleonic Wars, when British sea captains would use press gangs on Americans, arguing that they were born English and thus were British subjects for life (Ueda 1982).

11. The Fourteenth Amendment underlined the equality of naturalized and native-born citizens, but legislation passed on July 14, 1870, specified naturalization privileges for aliens of African nativity and of African descent (Smith 1926: 4).

12. Asian-born women remained legally barred from citizenship, and until 1931, non-Asians who married foreign-born Asian men ineligible for citizenship continued to lose their U.S. citizenship (Bredbrenner 1998).

13. Even in 1945, an immigrant who was not a U.S. citizen could not be a teacher in Illinois, a funeral director in Massachusetts, a liquor dealer in Ohio, a barber in Wisconsin, or an attorney in any of the forty-eight contiguous states. Fifty years later, all of these restrictions were gone (Konvitz 1946; Plascencia, Freeman, and Setzler 2003). Alien suffrage was widespread through the later half of the nineteenth century and into the early twentieth century (Aylsworth 1931; Rosberg 1977; Raskin 1993; Harper-Ho 2000).

14. Bureau officials created a standard application form and began to consistently scrutinize documents attesting to immigrants' length of residence in the country. From 1913 to 1933, there existed a separate Bureau of Naturalization and Bureau of Immigration, but for most of the twentieth century, the two were housed together. Since March 1, 2003, the Bureau of U.S. Citizenship and Immigration Services, housed in the Department of Homeland Security, oversees naturalization applications.

15. A number of special provisions can modify these requirements. The most important are a reduced three-year residency requirement for the spouses of U.S. citizens and provisions that allow longtime elderly residents to prove knowledge of U.S. laws and history in their own language. As of January 5, 2006, the processing fee for the N-400 form (for naturalization) was $330. This did not include the extra $70 applicants had to pay to be fingerprinted. These fees are more than triple the amount they were when I started my fieldwork in 1996. Then immigrants paid $95 to file the N-400 form.

16. British subjecthood did not necessarily imply adherence to English language or culture. During the confederation debates, the leading French-Canadian advocate of Canadian confederation, George Etienne Cartier, spoke of political unity and membership rather than ethnic belonging: "When we are united we shall form a political nationality independent of the national origin or the religion of any individual. . . . The idea of unity of races is a utopia; it is an impossibility" (cited in Kaplan 1991: 13).

17. In 1844 Britain passed the first legislation outlining a general process for naturalization in the British Empire (Kaplan 1991: 9).

18. In the area of immigration, federal and provincial governments share authority, with ultimate oversight given to Ottawa (section 95).

19. The residence period was extended to five years in 1914 and brought back to three in 1977.

20. Kelley and Trebilcock (1998) also suggest that the Canadian Conservative government was eager to tighten naturalization requirements since it felt that Liberals encouraged immigrants' naturalization for political gain. This echoes the critiques American Progressives leveled against urban political machines.

21. As in the United States, a married woman's citizenship status was determined by her husband's nationality, even if she was born a British subject. Women regained some control over their citizenship in 1932 and even more in 1946 (Hancock 1937; Brown 1996). The last vestiges of unequal treatment were eliminated in the 1977 Citizenship Act. Canada, unlike the United States, had no racial restrictions on citizenship; Asians and ex-slaves from the United States could become British subjects. However, this status proved hollow since the Canadian system rested on parliamentary supremacy, not a written constitution guaranteeing rights to citizens. Thus, the province of British Columbia could and did deny voting rights to Asians on racial grounds, regardless of citizenship, and the federal government worked to deport Japanese Canadians during World War II (Angus 1937; Kelley and Trebilcock 1998; Galloway 2000).

22. The secretary of state's discretionary power to unilaterally grant or refuse certificates of naturalization was taken away under the Citizenship Act, 1947, but the minister responsible still has the power to order a rehearing and make special grants of citizenship in exceptional circumstances.

23. The term *Canadian citizen* first appeared in the Immigration Act, 1910, and *Canadian national* was defined in the 1921 Canadian Nationals Act as a precondition for participation in the League of Nations (Kaplan 1991: 12–13).

24. An earlier attempt to introduce independent Canadian citizenship occurred following the 1931 Statute of Westminster, an act that transformed the British Empire into a Commonwealth of independent countries and removed most British oversight in Canadian affairs. The secretary of state made an aborted attempt to use Canada's increased sovereignty to introduce a bill on Canadian citizenship in 1931 but it was withdrawn, in large part due to protest over granting Canadian citizenship to Asians in British Columbia (Galloway 2000; Kaplan 1991: 23).

25. The secretary of state responsible for introducing the legislation, Paul Martin, initially championed citizenship legislation because of the fragmented state of Canadian nationality law, but his support solidified following a visit to a war cemetery in Dieppe, France (Martin 1993). Former prime minister and fellow Liberal Wilfred Laurier's vision of a united, dynamic Canada also influenced Martin and then prime minister William Lyon Mackenzie King.

26. Debate in the House of Commons over the proposed citizenship bill attacked the special provisions for British subjects as both being too radical and too miserly (Schwartz 1976; Demirjian, Gray, and Wright 1996). Nationalists, especially those from Quebec, would have been happy to see fewer, or no, concessions to British subjects. The Conservative Party felt that the break with Britain and the rest of the Commonwealth embodied in Canadian citizenship was too much. According to the minister who introduced the bill to the House,

"The reaction of those two extremes proved beyond a doubt that the bill was a careful balance of opinion expressed in terms that accommodated the general wish for a separate Canadian citizenship" (Martin 1993: 74).

27. Canadian citizens still automatically become "citizens of the Commonwealth" upon naturalization. This status has little consequence.

28. Unless otherwise indicated, all statistics were calculated using U.S. Census of Population and Housing microfile data accessed through the Minnesota Population Center Integrated Public Use Microdata Series, which covers 1850 to 2000. Calculations for Canada, unless otherwise indicated, are also mine and come from microfile data for the 1971 to 1996 Canadian Census of Population. These data were made available to me by the Housing, Family and Social Statistics Division of Statistics Canada, to which I am grateful.

29. There are only limited sources of data available on naturalization. The most consistent are the U.S. and Canadian censuses. Unfortunately, year of naturalization, needed to calculate a naturalization rate, only appeared in the U.S. census of 1920. For other decades we must use a proxy that compares the naturalization levels of migrant cohorts, that is, people who migrated at the same time and who therefore have lived in the host society the same amount of time.

30. Given changing citizenship laws, it is hard to interpret women's level of naturalization in the first half of the century and almost impossible to compare with current figures. Data from 1920 suggest that women were more eager to take out citizenship than men: 54.7 percent of foreign-born women held U.S. citizenship compared to 48.8 percent of men. However, if we consider marital status—separating the never married from those married at least once—a different picture emerges. Only 26.5 percent of single women had naturalized, compared to 34.8 percent of single men. The reverse was true for those who were married: 58.0 percent of married women reported American citizenship compared to 49.9 percent of men. The discrepancy is understandable given prevailing laws: foreign-born women marrying Americans automatically became U.S. citizens or acquired citizenship when their immigrant husbands naturalized. The largest gender differences occurred in 1940 and 1950, with more foreign-born men reporting U.S. citizenship than foreign-born women. One implication is that women, finally free to naturalize on their own, were slower to do so than men. The Second World War might also have had an uneven effect on the sexes. Although the United States had not entered World War II in 1940, threat of imminent hostilities probably encouraged naturalization or at least the reporting of American citizenship. Those who served in the U.S. military—overwhelmingly men—were encouraged to become citizens and benefited from less stringent naturalization regulations. In the contemporary period, researchers find that gender is either an insignificant predictor of naturalization or that it correlates weakly with citizenship status (Liang 1994; Yang 1994; Bloemraad 2002).

31. The discrepancy between admissions and census figures is probably due to multiple admissions, mortality once in the United States, census undercounts

of the immigrant population, and return migration. Of these, multiple admissions and return migration are probably the most important.

32. The year 1991 stands out as the peak of post-1965 migration. In that year alone, more than 1.8 million people acquired legal immigrant status in the United States, more than in the entire period of 1931–50 combined (U.S. Immigration and Naturalization Service 2000: 18).

33. Until 1950 the U.S. census did not have a separate identification for the foreign-born children of American parents. Estimates of naturalization levels in earlier decades consequently have a slight upward bias, but since the number of people who fit into this category appears small in the early twentieth century, the bias is negligible. For example, in the first year the Census Bureau distinguishes citizens born abroad to American parents from foreign-born migrants (1950), foreign-born citizens represented approximately 1 percent of all foreign-born residents and 1.6 percent of those naturalized if they were to be included in that category. Today the number of foreign-born citizens is significantly higher.

34. Starting in 1991 the Canadian census began to distinguish the permanent immigrant population from nonpermanent residents, such as those on temporary visas. The U.S. census makes no distinction regarding one's immigration status; thus, the U.S. foreign-born population includes illegal immigrants, those who are in the United States on student visas, and those who are on temporary work visas. The different definitions should not substantially affect the central findings of the chapter since undercounts for these populations are very high and, where possible, the Canadian figures are adjusted to include nonpermanent residents.

35. *Open door* refers exclusively to numbers. Canada, like the United States, had clear national origin preferences, even if it never instituted a national origins quota. Initial efforts to attract settlers to the new Dominion of Canada in the second half of the nineteenth century met with little success—poor economic conditions in Canada and the lure of the United States sent migrants southward (Knowles 1992). The appointment in 1896 of a new minister of the interior, Clifford Sifton, heralded a significant change. Immigration rose from a record low that year of 16,835 newcomers to 141,465 the year Sifton resigned from the Cabinet in 1905 (Citizenship and Immigration Canada 2002). Sifton established an aggressive promotion campaign in Europe and the United States. Immigrant admissions also swelled with the closing of the American West, a strong economic upswing, new demand for Canadian wheat, and overpopulation in Europe (Knowles 1992).

36. The substantial jump in the percent immigrant from 1941 to 1951, from 9 to 15 percent, is due to the inclusion of United Kingdom migrants in the latter year. If we look at the proportion of the Canadian population that was foreign born over this decade, the percentage actually dropped, from 17.5 percent to 14.7 percent. It is best not to place too much emphasis on the 1951 numbers, given the newness of Canadian citizenship and the change in the "immigrant" base category.

37. The dip in naturalization levels from 1981 to 1991 probably stems in large part from a change in the population enumerated by Statistics Canada. In 1991 the census included for the first time temporary residents as well as foreign-born permanent residents (immigrants). The graph is based on the total foreign-born population in order to make it comparable to U.S. data. If we consider just the immigrant population, the proportion of naturalized Canadian citizens rises constantly over this period, from 69 percent in 1981 to 70 percent in 1991 and 75 percent in 2001.

38. Looking at those who migrated five to nine years prior to the census, we find a similar pattern. In the United States, naturalization levels are 34 percent, 28 percent, and 24 percent for 1970, 1980, and 1990, respectively, while in Canada the figures are 36 percent, 58 percent, and 72 percent. Considering the cohort with fifteen to nineteen years of residence, in the United States naturalization again decreases—75 percent, 57 percent, and 50 percent—while in Canada it remains relatively constant: 79 percent, 73 percent, and 79 percent.

39. For the United States, see Liang (1994), Portes and Rumbaut (1996), and Yang (1994). On citizenship among immigrants in Canada, see Mata (1999).

40. See, for example, the work by Jasso and Rosenzweig (1986; 1990), Neice (1978), and Yang (1994).

41. Of course, some foreign-born individuals might still be ineligible for naturalization even if they satisfy the length of residence requirement. I discuss the regulations governing naturalization further below.

42. Michael Fix, Jeffrey Passel, and Kenneth Sucher of the Urban Institute (2003) have calculated naturalization levels in the United States using demographic techniques that try to distinguish the legal immigrant population from the undocumented population. According to them, citizenship levels plummeted from 64 percent of legal immigrants in 1970 to 39 percent in 1996. However, they estimate that the naturalization level in 2002 stood at 49 percent of legal residents, thanks to large numbers of immigrant naturalization in the late 1990s. Rapid growth in the undocumented population kept the aggregate citizenship low, however. Although the problem of immigrant citizenship ameliorates somewhat in this scenario, the figure remains far below that found in Canada.

43. Country of origin is equated to an individual's reported place of birth. In rare cases the two might not overlap, but it is the best measure available from census data.

44. The U.S. census asks respondents, "When did this person come to the United States to stay?" The Canadian census asks, "In what year did this person first become a landed immigrant in Canada?"

45. To see whether the citizenship gaps in table 3 are stable across the 1990s, I also compared immigrants with eleven to thirteen years of residence who reported Canadian citizenship in the 1996 Canadian census to those with American citizenship and ten to fifteen years of residence in the 2000 U.S. census. The size of the U.S.-Canada gap remained substantially the same for most groups. Larger changes were recorded for individuals born in Iran, Haiti, and Jamaica,

with the naturalization gap diminishing over the course of the decade by twenty-six, fifteen, and thirteen percentage points, respectively. In contrast, the U.S.-Canada difference increased by thirteen and ten percentage points for El Salvadorans and Koreans, respectively. In all cases, level of citizenship was always higher in Canada, and the size of origin group gaps fluctuated between twelve and seventy-one percentage points.

46. In this tradition, see Jasso and Rosenzweig (1986, 1990) and Yang (1994).

47. A third psychological/identity explanation has generated little empirical support. The psychological approach posits naturalization to be a final step in psycho-social adjustment to the new host country. Once an immigrant feels that he or she enjoys a good quality of life and develops a sense of attachment to the new country (Wearing 1985) or switches his or her identification from the old to new (Legendre and Shaffir 1984; Frideres et al. 1987), citizenship acquisition will follow. However, studies repeatedly find that immigrants can have multiple attachments and identifications rather than face a zero-sum psychological tradeoff.

48. See, for example, Borjas (1999), Duleep and Regets (1992, 1996), and Reitz (1998).

49. U.S. policy establishes annual quotas across a selection of "preference" categories, but some individuals, such as the spouse of a U.S. citizen, fall outside of the quota and can gain admission regardless of the number of visas already disbursed in a given year.

50. In the original point system, which went into effect in October 1967, those who wished to enter Canada based on their entrepreneurship and ability to engage in capital investment were accorded extra points toward their total score. Separate Entrepreneur and Investment categories of immigrants were established later in 1978 and in the 1980s. While formally separate, they function under the same logic as the Independent category by choosing migrants without personal ties to Canada but who are considered admissible based on their potential contribution to the Canadian economy.

51. Special admissions include humanitarian cases not falling under the refugee category, home caregiver admissions, and other specialized programs.

52. For example, Camarota (2001) notes a decline in the educational attainment of immigrants relative to the American native born and suggests that this accounts for contemporary immigrants' increased poverty, lower rates of home ownership, and decreased propensity to naturalize. There might also be indirect effects on political participation and civic engagement according to Camarota, since home owners "are more likely to take an active interest in the long-term condition of their neighborhood, the quality of the local schools, and their community in general" (2001: 8).

53. The new Immigration and Refugee Protection Act, which went into effect June 28, 2002, ceased assigning different points for specific occupations and now assigns points for years of education and work experience, as long as the job is not on the restricted occupations list.

54. Exceptions include Mexico and some Latin American countries.

55. All national data reported here are from the 2000 U.S. census and 2001 Canadian census.

56. The political science literature tells us that those with higher incomes and who own homes tend to be more interested in politics, yet the naturalization literature finds no relationship between income and citizenship (Evans 1988; Neice 1978; Portes and Curtis 1987) or only a weak correlation (Barkan and Khokhlov 1980; Yang 1994).

57. Unlike in the United States, the Canadian federal government and some provinces subsidize a range of English and French language training programs. I discuss this further in later chapters.

58. On Portuguese migration, especially to the Toronto and Boston areas, see Anderson (1983), Ito-Alder (1980 [1972, 1978]), and Teixeira and Lavigne (1992).

59. According to the 1991 Canadian census (20 percent sample), 96 percent of Portuguese-born adults in Ontario reported being Catholic. The U.S. census does not include a question on religious affiliation, but a survey in southeastern Massachusetts in 1999–2000 found that 95 percent of Portuguese American respondents reported being Roman Catholic (Barrow 2002).

60. Even in the late 1960s, about 40 percent of the population in Portugal was illiterate (Pap 1981). In both Canada and the United States, almost half of all Portuguese immigrants have only an elementary education or less. Whereas 15 percent of all immigrants in Canada and 18 percent of the foreign born in the United States hold a university degree, the percentage for the Portuguese is 2 and 5 percent, respectively.

61. A more detailed examination of Portuguese immigration to North America is provided in chapter 2.

62. Because language ability is a requirement for naturalization, greater English skills in the United States should boost citizenship levels, yet this is not the case. However, the two censuses' language questions are not strictly comparable, so conclusions on relative language skills are at best tentative. Interviews with local Portuguese leaders in Toronto and Boston did not reveal any perceived differences in language ability.

63. Liang's (1994) work on naturalization for six immigrant groups demonstrates that the effect of some independent variables vary by national origin. Others have found a curvilinear relationship between education and naturalization such that the very highly educated are somewhat less likely to naturalize than those with some postsecondary schooling (Neice 1978; Portes and Curtis 1987; Yang 1994).

64. The statistical analysis uses logistic regression analysis because the dependent variable—citizenship—is dichotomous with only two possible outcomes, citizenship or no citizenship. Unlike multiple regression using Ordinary Least Squares, the substantive effect of an explanatory variable varies, depending on the other independent variables. To make effects more understandable, we can calculate predicted probabilities and evaluate first differences, that is, the change in probability that occurs from varying one of the independent variables.

In this example, the "average" Portuguese immigrant has the median income and years of residence of all individuals and the mean value on the other variables.

65. Estimation uncertainty is inherent to statistical sampling; thus outcome measures should report a distribution of expected values in the same way standard errors describe a band of possible coefficient values (King, Tomz, and Wittenberg 2000). By employing statistical simulation techniques, we can calculate the effect of place of residence on citizenship, and we can estimate 95 percent confidence intervals around the predicted probabilities. I used Monte Carlo simulations based on the vector of parameter estimates and the variance/covariance matrix (Tomz, Wittenberg, and King 2001).

66. Imagine, for example, that religious affiliation is correlated with naturalization—some religions might encourage, directly or indirectly, secular citizenship more than others (Verba, Schlozman, and Brady 1995; Levitt 2003). Many immigrants groups include more religious diversity than the overwhelmingly Roman Catholic Portuguese. The U.S. census, however, does not include a question about religious affiliation, so we cannot evaluate cross-national differences in religious affiliation.

67. Indeed, the U.S. Coast Guard sent boats carrying Haitian migrants back to Haiti, arguing that these people are economic migrants who should apply for residency using regular channels.

68. Most of this group had, by 1990–91, been in North America for many years, attenuating cross-national differences. Also, many are of Jewish background. Since the Jewish community is institutionally complete (Breton 1964), the benefit of state intervention might matter less for this community than others.

69. While not comparative, this is the argument implicit in work by Jasso and Rosenzweig (1986, 1990), Jones-Correa (1998a), and Yang (1994).

70. For the application of this argument in Europe, see Brubaker (1992), de Rham (1990), and Clarke, van Dam, and Gooster (1998).

71. Soysal (1994) advances the personhood argument most forcefully. See also Joppke (1999), Schuck (1998), and Plascencia, Freeman, and Setzler (2003).

72. The distinction made between Americans and noncitizens in the Welfare Reform Act reverses a trend toward the elimination of such differences. Such distinctions have also become more salient since the terrorist attacks of September 11, 2001: some courts have denied noncitizens rights accorded to citizens.

73. The eventual 1967 regulations did not restrict the sponsorship of certain relatives to citizens, as is the case in the United States, but they did give slightly more points to the nominated relatives of citizens. "Nominated relatives" applied for entry on a combination of personal characteristics (education, age, etc.) and family ties. Later changes dropped the distinction between citizens and noncitizens.

74. The fact that Canada allowed immigrants to hold de facto dual citizenship prior to 1977 also undermines the contention that the upsurge in natural-

ization in Canada since 1970 is purely a function of legal changes. For the naturalized immigrant, nothing really changed. However, the attitude of the Canadian government toward dual citizenship has changed since the 1970s. Today Citizenship and Immigration Canada openly advertises that Canadian law does not prevent dual citizenship, a move in line with the country's multiculturalism policy. As I argue below, dual citizenship and official multiculturalism *together* might carry important symbolic repercussions for citizenship.

75. Former Commissioner Doris Meissner made similar comments to me during an interview on May 2, 2002.

76. There is no indication that the new U.S. Citizenship and Immigration Services in the Department of Homeland Security is reversing the stance of the old INS.

77. Quoted in the newsletter "Cidadão 2000 Citizen" 1, no. 1 (March 1998): 3 (author's translation). The original quotation is "A melhor maneira de ser um bom cidadão protuguês nos Estados Unidos, é ser um bom cidadão americano." This newsletter was produced by the Boston Citizenship 2000 campaign. The priest at St. Anthony's Catholic Church in Cambridge, a Portuguese-language church, also quoted Dr. Soares in speeches encouraging Portuguese immigrants to naturalize on March 8, 1998.

78. Doris Meissner, interview on May 2, 2002.

79. A slightly different issue is the *symbolic* importance of allowing—or forbidding—dual citizenship. As Jones-Correa (1998a: 104–105) documents, some Latino immigrants have the impression that applicants for citizenship are required to step or spit on their homeland flag in order to become a naturalized American. In Canada, dual citizenship appears to reinforce the message of multiculturalism: one can be both Canadian and another ethnicity or nationality. In following chapters I further consider the impact of such symbols for political participation.

80. In the United States, except for a very few local or school elections, only citizens have the right to vote (Harper-Ho 2000). In Canada, voting is also restricted to citizens.

81. Macdonald came to Canada at the age of five, making him a "1.5-generation" immigrant, although, as I outline earlier in the chapter, his status in Canada would have been that of a British subject, equal to those born on what is considered today Canadian territory. Other foreign-born prime ministers include Mackenzie Bowell and Alexander Mackenzie, both of whom served in the nineteenth century. The most recent has been John Turner, who held office for two and a half months in 1984. He was born in England to a British father and Canadian mother, making him a Canadian citizen by birth. He migrated to Canada as a young child following the death of his father.

82. A third form of representation, often associated with Edmund Burke, views the representative as an enlightened decision maker. The elected representative should use his or her superior knowledge and judgment to make the best decision for the collective, regardless of personal interests or the particularistic desires of his or her constituents. I leave this view of representation aside.

83. I take up these issues in more detail in chapter 6.

84. The assumption here is that there is no innate, or biological, predisposition to office seeking, though there might very well be social, cultural, or economic dynamics that generate greater interest among some than others. Finding intergroup differences would then point to some form of inequality in the political system. A similar logic drives many academics' study of politicians' ethno-racial origins. Black and Lakhani, for example, justify their analysis of Canada's 35th Parliament by noting that "social composition may index the equality of access the system provides into the corridors of power. . . . Considerations of access, in turn, are bound up with issues touching on the importance of symbolism and public acknowledgement of the group, the possibility that lack of access leads to exclusionary discourse and behavior within Parliament, and, most concretely, whether this all may translate into indifference to the group's public policy preoccupations" (1997: 1).

85. Theoretically, the Queen (or her representative, the governor general) can refuse to approve a Senate appointment, but this has never been done.

86. Direct election versus selection by the prime minister is the most important difference between the Canadian and American Senates, but there is also a difference in areas represented. Each American state sends two senators to Washington, D.C. In Canada, Senate seats are divided into regional blocks. Ontario and Quebec each have twenty-four seats, the West (British Columbia, Alberta, Saskatchewan, and Manitoba) has twenty-four, the Atlantic Provinces have thirty, reflecting the late addition of Newfoundland and Labrador into the confederation, and each of the territories—the Yukon, Northwest Territories, and Nunavut—have one senator.

87. Information about those elected to Canadian and U.S. legislatures, including information about place of birth, come from the Canadian Parliamentary Library, the ICPSR-archived database Roster of United States Congressional Officeholders and Biographical Characteristics of Members of the United States Congress, 1789–1996: Merged Data, the Congressional Research Office, and various *Who's Who* guides of prominent individuals.

88. Indeed, even after the establishment of Canadian citizenship, British immigrants were able to vote even if they had not naturalized. This policy was set in a spirit of reciprocity, since Canadians enjoyed the same access to the ballot box if they moved to the United Kingdom. Legislation in 1970 removed this privilege but allowed British subjects eligible to vote on June 25, 1968, suffrage without citizenship until 1975. Today only Canadian citizens may vote in national elections, but the province of Nova Scotia still allows British subjects to vote, and Saskatchewan allows British subjects to vote if they qualified as voters on June 23, 1971.

89. Since 1941 the difference in representation indices for all foreign born versus non-British foreign born is negligible. Indeed, in 2001 migrants born in countries other than the United Kingdom were better represented in the House of Commons than those of British birth.

90. Even this measure raises problems. Voting has not been perfectly linked

to citizenship over the twentieth century. Women were denied the franchise in both countries' national elections for the first two decades of the century, as were Canadian citizens of certain Asian origins who were residents in British Columbia and Saskatchewan. Conversely, some U.S. states allowed noncitizen immigrants to vote in elections early in the century as long as they declared their intention to naturalize. The presence of foreign-born politicians in an elected body is a useful way to gain insight into immigrants' political incorporation, but the construction and interpretation of a measure to evaluate this presence raises a host of issues.

91. Since I consider the foreign-born composition per Congress, in some cases we are talking about the same individuals, reelected numerous times, in two different periods.

92. Again, place of birth does not necessarily reflect ethnic or cultural origins. While the cultural origins of MPs born in India, China, the Philippines, and the Middle East appear to reflect their place of birth, two of the four Africans are of Indian background. Among those from the Caribbean or South America—that is, born in Trinidad, Grenada, Guyana, the Dominican Republic, and Paraguay—two probably grew up in families of European cultural background.

2. THE SOCIAL NATURE OF CITIZENSHIP AND PARTICIPATION

1. See Verba, Schlozman, and Brady (1995) and Putnam (2000).

2. Social ties are important for electoral politics (Rosenstone and Hansen 1993; Verba, Schlozman, and Brady 1995) and social movements (Gould 1995; McAdam, McCarthy, and Zald 1996; Munson 2002; Oberschall 1973; Useem 1980).

3. For a historical perspective, see Park and Burgess (1921) and Warner and Srole (1945). Contemporary accounts on the benefits of social ties and social organizations include Massey (1990), Zhou and Bankston (1998), Portes (1995), and Sanders, Nee, and Sernau (2002). Scholars suggest that in-group cohesion can be an especially important resource for nonwhite immigrants facing possible downward mobility into America's poor urban core (Portes and Zhou 1993; Portes 1995; Zhou and Bankston 1998; Waters 1999).

4. For the most part, I have retained the speech patterns of immigrant interviewees in quotations.

5. In the United States, a small number also entered as refugees. Regarding illegal migration, "there was a fairly substantial illegal immigration to both the United States and Canada throughout the 1960s and 1970s. It was not uncommon for Portuguese citizens . . . to visit the United States or Canada on a tourist visa, find a job through the efforts of friends or relatives, and simply neglect to return to their homeland. . . . It is impossible to determine precisely how many Portuguese availed themselves of this shortcut, but apparently many did" (Williams 1982: 110, 112; see also Anderson 1974).

6. The Portuguese first came to what is today called Canada in the sixteenth century, fishing cod in the Grand Banks off the coast of Newfoundland

(Andrieux 2000). A few historical documents indicate that some of the colonists in New France were of Portuguese origin (Higgs 1990: 16). However, unlike the United States, Canada was not home to a significant Portuguese community in the nineteenth and early twentieth century. Bulletins from the Portuguese Geographical Society claim perhaps a few hundred Portuguese, most likely seamen, lived in Canada around 1870; by 1939 there were scarcely any in the country, just a few immigrants who came by way of the United States (Anderson 1974: 6, 8).

7. The result was clandestine emigration from the Azores and across Portugal's northern border. One interviewee recalls that her father would smuggle people through the mountains into Spain to make some extra money. Sometimes men would leave without telling their wives and families so that those left behind could honestly claim no knowledge of the illegal departure when interrogated by authorities (Serpa et al. [1975?]; Black 1993; Brettell 2003).

8. In the Azores, population pressures reached a point that in 1960 there were 368 inhabitants per square mile of land, not all of it arable (Williams 1982). See also Pap (1981).

9. On the myth of return among Portuguese and *saudade*, see Brettell (1977; 2003), Feldman-Bianco (1992), Halpern Pereira (1980), and Klimt (1989).

10. Initially capped at 1,200 visas, the Azorean Refugee Act was extended in 1960 and 1962 to cover 2,000 household heads, ultimately providing entry to 4,811 individuals (Ito-Alder 1980 [1972, 1978]; Pap 1981). Unlike the vast majority of officially designated refugees to the United States, these people were primarily fleeing natural disaster, not political persecution.

11. Early arrivals often used family connections to individuals who arrived during the first substantial wave of Portuguese migration that occurred prior to 1924. In the decade 1911–20 alone, the INS records the entry of 89,732 Portuguese nationals; the census of 1930 reports 118,242 Portuguese-born individuals in the United States. Starting in the nineteenth century, whaling vessels would go through the Azores to pick up ship hands before embarking on a trajectory that brought them to the American northeast, California, and Hawaii. The first Portuguese communities in the United States grew around these whaling centers, latter augmented by the pull of textile mills in New England, farming and fishing in California, and plantation work in Hawaii (Baganha 1990, 1991; Bohme 1956; Geschwender, Carroll-Seguin, and Brill 1988; Pap 1981; Williams 1982).

12. These individuals had been active in student demonstrations against the regime or had been members of the Communist Party, the only organized opposition to the dictatorship. See chapter 6 for more on this group.

13. After Salazar suffered a stroke in 1968, Marcello José das Neves Caetano became prime minister. Political repression loosened somewhat after Salazar's death in 1969, but democracy wasn't restored until 1975.

14. Some political dissenters undoubtedly moved to the United States, but they were not among those I interviewed and apparently were not active as community leaders. There might also have been a certain preference for Canada among dissenters since the United States was avidly anticommunist. For exam-

ple, past membership in the Communist Party constitutes grounds to be refused U.S. citizenship.

15. Canada signed the convention and the protocol in 1969, although it admitted refugees through the postwar period. In 1968 the United States chose to only accede to the protocol; it has not signed the convention. The text of the convention is available at http://unhchr.ch/html/menu3/b/o_c_ref.htm. Accessed January 5, 2006.

16. For example, the seventh preference of the 1965 Immigration Act reserved 6 percent of Eastern hemisphere visas to refugees from "communist-dominated countries," but Central Americans fleeing bloodshed in regimes supported by the American government were not considered refugees or asylees (Loescher and Scanlan 1986; Zucker and Zucker 1989).

17. Before 1975 barely 13,000 Indochinese immigrants and 4,342 American citizens of Vietnamese ethnicity called the United States home (Hein 1993: 31). The majority were the wives of U.S. servicemen or had come to the United States for military training, for postsecondary education, or as part of the diplomatic corps. In Canada, the numbers were even smaller, about 1,500, mostly students or graduates of Canadian universities living in Quebec City, Montreal, and Toronto (Dorais 2000). Vietnamese students had first come to Canada in the 1950s as recipients of scholarships under the Colombo Plan for development aid to Asian countries. Numbers increased in the mid-1960s—especially at Francophone universities—after diplomatic relations between France and South Vietnam were severed (Dorais 2000).

18. The 2000 U.S. census reports that 988,174 U.S. residents were born in Vietnam. If we instead consider claims of Vietnamese ethnicity as measured by the race question on the U.S. census, 1,223,736 individuals reported some Vietnamese background.

19. Only 4.9 percent of those in U.S. resettlement camps came from farming or fishing backgrounds, while 60 percent of the population in Vietnam worked in agriculture (Kelly 1977: 53).

20. According to Kelly's analysis of those in the U.S. reception camps in 1975, only 13.9 percent of the refugees spoke English well enough to function effectively in an English-only work environment, and 64.7 percent spoke no English at all (1977: 56). Those who settled in Francophone Canada were better off: about 25 percent of all those admitted to U.S. resettlement camps were fluent in French, and this percentage was likely higher among those who chose to move to Quebec (Kelly 1977: 51). French-language competency reflects Vietnam's history as a French colony (1867–1954) and the continued use of French in elite schools after independence.

21. Michael Jones-Correa finds the same among middle-class Latino migrants (1998a, 1998b).

22. In the period between the 1975 exodus and the 1979 explosion in refugee departures, about 37,000 Indochinese were resettled in the United States and another 7,000 in Canada (Hawkins 1991; Hein 1993).

23. Worried about the continuing exodus, governments agreed to a compre-

hensive plan of action at the 1989 International Conference on Indochinese Refugees. The purpose was to discourage continued emigration from Vietnam, since many of the migrants were assumed to be leaving because of economic reasons rather than political persecution. As a result, the Canadian government in 1990 amended its "Indochinese" designated class of refugees to only include those who left Vietnam before June 16, 1988, for those in refugee camps in Hong Kong, or before March 14, 1989, for those in another Southeast Asian country of first asylum. Those who fled after those dates would need to demonstrate eligibility as a convention refugee rather than under the more liberal definition of humanitarian refugee (Kelley and Trebilcock 1998).

24. Because of relaxed immigration procedures for Amerasians, these formerly shunned individuals became "golden children," with people claiming family connections to them in order to migrate to the United States (Zhou and Bankston 1998).

25. One of the earliest claims of invisibility comes from Taft (1923). These complaints continue through the twentieth century (Smith 1974; Pap 1981; Valdés 1995; Almeida 1999) and are found in Canada (Anderson and Higgs 1976; Alpalhão and da Rosa 1980; Almeida 2000).

26. The first three explanations probably do help to explain differences between the Portuguese and other ethnic groups. The fourth carries a certain cultural determinism that seems suspect. Almeida suggests that the political failings of the Portuguese probably stem from a general mindset characterized by "a high degree of emotion [sic] life strongly connected to and affecting their intellectual domain" (Almeida 1999: 237). Almeida believes that the Portuguese share such a cultural orientation with other Mediterranean cultures, but this explanation flies in the face of Italians' overrepresentation in Toronto at all levels of government (Siemiatycki and Isin 1997). Almeida (2000) also argues that those in Massachusetts and Ontario share the Portuguese psyche, yet we find important cross-national difference in electoral success.

27. In the 1994 *Los Angeles Times* poll, only 49 percent of Vietnamese respondents reported American citizenship. Of those with citizenship, 59 percent said they were registered voters. Nonvoters in the 2000–01 Pilot Study of the National Asian American Political Survey were asked why they did not vote. Lack of citizenship was named by 55 percent of nonvoters (about a third of the total sample), and lack of voter registration by 39 percent. The pilot study, although encompassing a broader geographic area than the *Los Angeles Times* poll, only counted 137 Vietnamese respondents.

28. Of course, the groups also differ along racial lines, a critical factor explored in subsequent chapters.

29. In interviews with Vietnamese leaders in Montreal and Toronto, Simard (1991) heard similar comments from those she and her researchers interviewed.

30. Few academic studies examine whether immigrants' prior experience with an authoritarian system depresses political activity in a new political context. Black (1987) finds that among recent migrants to Canada, past activity and interest in politics appears readily transferred to the adopted country, regardless

of the political system in the home country. If, however, authoritarian countries provide fewer chances for such activity, immigrants from authoritarian countries might have fewer political experiences from which to draw. An alternative hypothesis would be that refugees or those leaving authoritarian regimes might be *more* motivated to make use of political freedoms once settled in a democratic country.

31. No surveys exist that measure the political attitudes of Vietnamese Canadians or Portuguese Americans in the Boston area. A study of Portuguese Americans in southeastern Massachusetts found relatively low levels of political interest in affairs outside the local community. Thus, whereas no significant differences existed between the political knowledge or activity of Portuguese Americans and non-Portuguese in Taunton, Massachusetts, Portuguese Americans were significantly less likely to know the name of the Massachusetts governor or to express interest in national affairs than non-Portuguese (Barrow 2002). The small number of people sampled (depending on the question, between 53 and 403 individuals) means that these results should be treated with caution.

32. Based on interviews with community leaders from six minority groups (Chinese, Haitians, Arabs, Indians, Jamaicans, and Vietnamese) in three major cities (Vancouver, Toronto, and Montreal), Simard (1991: 226) also concludes that Vietnamese are amongst the least knowledgeable and interested in Canadian politics.

33. These figures come from the 1996 Canadian census and are based on ethno-racial origins, not place of birth. Only 6 percent of Toronto residents reported no ability in English or French, compared to 18 percent of Vietnamese and 20 percent of Portuguese. According to Richard and Dorais (2003: 3), nationally 15 percent of ethnic Vietnamese claimed to speak neither English nor French in 1996, a number which dropped to 12 percent in 2001. The decline might be because of the effectiveness of language classes run by government and ethnic associations, as suggested by the authors, but also might result from a greater number of Canadian-born Vietnamese relative to the total ethnic Vietnamese population.

34. Higher levels of education correlate with greater participation among the native born (Miller and Shanks 1996; Rosenstone and Hansen 1993; Verba, Schlozman, and Brady 1995) and greater likelihood of naturalization among immigrants (Bloemraad 2002; Jones-Correa 2001b; Yang 1994). A slight exception seems to be that in some immigrant groups, very high levels of education (holding a four-year college degree or more) decrease the likelihood of citizenship slightly, compared to those with a high school diploma or some secondary training.

35. These numbers are based on the 2000 U.S. census 5 percent Public Use Microdata Sample, whereas Ornstein's numbers are from the 20 percent 1996 Canadian census sample (Ornstein 2000). In order to increase the sample size of Portuguese for the U.S. case—and thus reduce margins of error in the estimates for education—I consider all Portuguese in Massachusetts. The statewide numbers are in line for what we would expect to find for the metro Boston area. I

focus on the immigrant generation in Massachusetts because the longer history of Portuguese migration to the United States results in a more significant proportion of Portuguese Americans who are second, third, or even fourth generation as compared to Canada. With access to the U.S. education system, American-born individuals of Portuguese background are much less likely to have only completed elementary school. Nationally, for example, 11 percent of U.S.-born Portuguese Americans have a grade eight education or less, compared to 47 percent of the foreign born (U.S. Bureau of the Census 1993: 265). Looking at those lacking a high school diploma, the rates are 27 and 63 percent, respectively.

36. In Toronto, former metro councilor Martin Silva, a Portuguese Canadian, attributes his electoral loss in part to comments he made on Portuguese radio describing illiteracy as a significant problem for the community.

37. But see Gold (1992) on diversity with the Vietnamese community. A distinction must be made regarding people born in the north who moved south in 1954 following the victory of communist forces. These people, mostly Catholics, share the mindset of other southerners. The northerners referred to in these quotes are people who stayed in North Vietnam following 1954.

38. According to most in the Vietnamese community, other potential lines of conflict around religion (Catholic versus Buddhist) or ethnicity (ethnic Vietnamese versus Sino-Vietnamese) that were significant in Vietnam cause fewer problems in North America, although some friction remains. In contrast, Gold (1992) notes that the Vietnamese community in Southern California is really three separate communities: those who came in 1975 and earlier, ethnic Vietnamese who came later, and Sino-Vietnamese.

39. In a related vein, Chan and Lam report that recently arrived Sino-Vietnamese refugees in Montreal express only a rudimentary and somewhat stereotyped understanding of Canadian politics given the sociopsychological demands of resettlement (1983).

40. Based on a survey of Portuguese in Taunton, Massachusetts, Clyde Barrow draws a similar conclusion, "a vast majority of the Portuguese interviewed . . . express a desire to become U.S. citizens, but they simply do not know how to do so or even know how to initiate an application. . . . It is a problem of political information and immigrant assistance" (2002: 33).

41. Immigrants are not alone in their reliance on social relations. Research shows that localized interpersonal ties generate and facilitate civic and political engagement among the native born (Putnam 2000; Useem 1980), and various scholars claim that civic and community organizations act as crucibles of democracy for all citizens (Salamon 1999; Van Til 2000; Verba, Schlozman, and Brady 1995). Organizations and mobilization by leaders also appear to play a critical role in augmenting participation among politically inactive Americans (Rosenstone and Hansen 1993).

42. See, for example, Parenti (1967) and Marwell (2004).

43. Although Maria did not say so explicitly, her brother was likely in the country illegally, having overstayed a visitor's visa. Becoming a citizen would help Maria sponsor her brother for legal residence.

44. A long-standing requirement of naturalization in the United States was the presence of two witnesses who could swear to an applicant's good moral standing. Today this is no longer necessary.

45. See, for example, Menjívar's (2000) study of networks among Salvadoran immigrants. She does not focus on political incorporation, but she shows clearly how intraethnic ties can fail, especially in contexts of extreme poverty, illegal status, and significant internal divisions.

46. On the relationship between informal ties and formal institutions, see Breton (1964) and Verba, Scholzman, and Brady (1995).

47. In the Vietnamese community, news from the homeland tends to come from a California-based wire service, while in the Portuguese community, because travel is much easier, the larger Toronto papers occasionally send one of their staff to Portugal to cover important events.

48. The Vietnamese also have a tradition of using community newspapers to publish fiction, poems, and other literary pieces written by members of the community.

49. Most ethnic newspapers are free to readers; they seek to make a profit based on paid advertisements.

50. In part this reliance stems from a lack of alternative options; there are relatively few Vietnamese-language radio or TV programs. Compared to the Portuguese, Vietnamese immigrants' more frequent use of newspapers also stems from their relatively greater literacy.

51. Ethnographic research in the Toronto Portuguese community during the 1970s confirms Beatriz's recollection of the role played by travel agents, but Brettell (1977, 2003) argues that the economic rewards are secondary to the desire for standing in the community and to competition between travel agencies.

52. Indeed, in 2002 the Canadian government created the Advisory Committee on Regulating Immigration Consultants to investigate and report on those collecting fees in exchange for helping with petitions for citizenship, immigration, and refugee status. The report, submitted in May 2003, eventually led to the formation of a new professional oversight body, the Canadian Society of Immigration Consultants, and new government regulations delineating who may act as an immigrant's representative. As of April 13, 2004, CIC and the Immigration and Refugee Board will only allow members of the Canadian Society of Immigration Consultants, individuals accredited with a provincial or territorial bar association, or notaries public accredited with Quebec's Chambre des notaires du Québec to act as an individual's paid representative.

53. Community agencies, especially smaller and newer organizations, are not immune to the charges of abuse and exploitation leveled at certain ethnic businesses. One Portuguese immigrant claims that the Somerville Portuguese American League, a forerunner of the large and professional MAPS, wanted to charge his mother $1,500 to fill out and file immigration paperwork that eventually cost $180 once he dealt directly with the INS. In Toronto, a number of individuals criticized the former nonprofit agency Portuguese Social Services

for financial mismanagement. In general, however, because such organizations rely on public funding, foundation grants, and private donations, greater oversight makes abuse more difficult than with less regulated private businesses.

54. On the advantages and disadvantages of interacting with government through an immigrant organization, see Breton (1991), Indra (1987), and Martiniello (1993). On the media's preference for established organizations, see Gitlin (1981).

55. Such services and classes were supposed to be targeted to individuals on state public assistance, but they also benefited other noncitizens.

56. The program was retained beyond the initial three-year period but with an allocation of only $750,000. In 2002 Governor Jane Swift vetoed the budgeted allocation of $750,000 in a general push to balance the state budget.

57. Interview with VACA's executive director, May 9, 2001.

58. Field notes, April 13, 2000.

59. See Stockman and Dedman (2002). Based on data from the Massachusetts secretary of the Commonwealth, the number of eligible voters in Boston rose by only 1.8 percent from 1990 to 2000 while the number of registered voters increased by almost 50 percent, going from 49.1 percent of those eligible in 1990 to 72.2 percent in 2000 (Massachusetts Area Planning Council 2002: 20). The substantial increase is not only due to the efforts of grassroots groups but also to the effects of Massachusetts's implementation of the National Voter Registration Act (the "Motor Voter" law) in 1993.

60. Toan has also learned a lot about Canadian political history, understanding the role that former prime minister Pierre Elliot Trudeau played in the Liberal Party, even though Trudeau's leadership predated his arrival to the country. At times, however, he and other veterans reinterpret the Canadian political system along American lines: "As you know the Vietnamese in Canada [and] the U.S.A. usually vote for the Democracy or Republic."

61. In both Toronto and Boston, veterans' associations and other groups organize an annual demonstration on April 30 to commemorate the fall of South Vietnam. In Boston this event, organized by the Vietnamese Community of Massachusetts, a voluntary organization largely composed of former combatants, regularly draws one hundred to two hundred people. Activities include a wreath-laying ceremony at the Vietnamese War Memorial on Morrissey Boulevard, a march to Boston City Hall, where the city holds a ceremonial flag raising using the flag of the former Republic of South Vietnam, and a march to the Massachusetts State House. Each stop is accompanied by numerous speeches in Vietnamese and English by members of the community and non-Vietnamese veterans of the Vietnam conflict. Passersby are given information sheets highlighting atrocities committed by the communist regime, and paper flags of South Vietnam are distributed to those attending. Such public demonstrations and displays serve an important symbolic function, reminding decision makers that the community exists and showing community members that it is acceptable to organize in defense of community interests (fieldnotes, April 30, 2001; Aguilar–San Juan 2005; Siemiatycki and Isin 1997).

62. PEN Canada, an affiliate of PEN International, works on behalf of writers who are censored, imprisoned, or otherwise silenced because of their writing.

63. When the first waves of post–World War II Portuguese immigrants arrived in North America in the 1950s, only a few elites evidenced interest in homeland politics (Rogers 1974; Anderson and Higgs 1976). Discussion, and in some cases activism, centered on Portugal's efforts to preserve its colonial empire and, to a lesser extent, on attempts to overthrow the authoritarian regime of the Estado Novo. During Portugal's transition to democracy in the mid-1970s, some Azoreans in Toronto, Cambridge, and Somerville embraced calls for Azorean independence. The numbers agitating for a separatist movement were very small, and proponents cited widely divergent rationales: those on the Left considered Azorean independence a logical outgrowth of anticolonial movements, while those on the Right saw separation as a way to avoid political rule by communists and socialists on the mainland (Anderson and Higgs 1976; Dreyer 1978; Ito-Alder 1980 [1972, 1978]).

64. For example, one issue taken up by representatives of the overseas communities is the duty-free importation of foreign cars for use by emigrants who spend part of the year in Portugal. Other concerns are equally technical.

65. I further consider differences in organizational capacity in chapter 5.

66. The discussion that follows is based on fieldwork and interviews.

67. The campaign in Toronto focused exclusively on those with origins in Portugal. The Boston campaign cast a wider net, targeting all Portuguese-speaking people, including Brazilians and Cape Verdeans, the other two significant Lusophone populations in the Boston area. Based on my own observations and interviews, Portuguese immigrants were the main audience of the campaign. The overlap in names appears to be a coincidence. Planning for the Boston Citizenship 2000 drive started in late 1997, and the official launch occurred on March 8, 1998. The first meeting of what would become the Toronto Citizenship 2000 campaign was held on February 28, 1998, though it would only be later in the summer that the group decided to focus on naturalization. The two campaigns were run independently of one another.

68. The Boston campaign had more ambitious goals for the state as a whole: organizer Fatima Martins told the crowd at the launch of the Citizenship 2000 campaign that she hoped twenty-five thousand Portuguese immigrants statewide would take up the challenge to become naturalized by 2000.

69. It is difficult to verify these estimates, but they seem fair. In Boston, the campaign was informational, directing people to local organizations. The primary social service organization offering naturalization assistance in Boston is MAPS. Its 1998 annual report claims that the agency provided citizenship classes for sixty-four individuals and helped nearly two hundred in citizenship drives and through in-office assistance. MAPS might debate, however, what proportion of its clients responded to its own outreach efforts and how many were influenced by Citizenship 2000. In Toronto, one organizer claimed to have counted roughly twenty-four hundred applications filled out during the four processing days.

70. The words of former president Mário Soares promoting dual citizenship

featured prominently on campaign posters, in the campaign's newsletter, and in speeches by those attending the March 8 event. See the discussion in chapter 1 on dual citizenship. The presence of the local consul general of Portugal further underscored the organizers' message that American citizenship was not a betrayal of Portuguese nationality.

71. He also formed part of an "ethnic bloc" during the 1984 Liberal leadership convention, to which he was a delegate along with two Italians and one person of Sikh origin (Stasiulis and Abu-Laban 1991). The group's stated desire was to push an agenda prioritizing ethnic issues and promoting ethnic candidates in local ridings.

72. I am thus a bit skeptical of respondents' claims, such as those reported in Verba, Schlozman, and Brady (1995: 136–39), that their political activity stemmed from spontaneous engagement rather than mobilization by others. In my interviews, a respondent's initial claim that he or she "just got involved" usually hid a more complicated story that included personal ties or institutional affiliations. These more complex stories became clear after in-depth questioning regarding the circumstances of a particular incident. Munson (2002) reports a similar interview experience with anti-abortion activists.

3. STRUCTURED MOBILIZATION

1. Lipset's argument is informed by the other central debate over U.S.-Canada cross-national differences in political culture, which focuses on the presence of socialism in North America. According to Hartz and his students (Hartz 1955; Hartz et al. 1964), the United States failed to develop socialism because the original settlers carried a "liberal fragment" to the New World but not feudalism. The lack of feudalism arrested the dialectic between collectivist orientations and liberalism necessary for socialism's development. Horowitz (1966), however, maintains that feudalism in New France and a significant Loyalist (Tory) element provided the conservatism needed to counterbalance liberalism, which ultimately produced Canadian socialism.

2. Joppke (1999), for example, suggests that Brubaker's characterization of German nationalism and citizenship overstates ideological and institutional durability. Multiple centers of policy making in Germany—federal versus local, parliament versus the courts—muddies the ethnocentric portrait most scholars paint. German citizenship law was relatively restrictive, but its asylum policies were amongst the most generous in the world.

3. One could also argue the reverse: hostility—as long as it is not too strong—would encourage political integration as a means to "fight back" against anti-immigrant voices while acceptance would decrease the need or importance of political participation.

4. Gallup poll data come from http://brain.gallup.com.

5. Data supplied by Ipsos–Public Affairs to the author.

6. The "very good" percentages in Canada and the United States were by far the highest of all the countries polled. The next highest percentage was 8 percent

in Mexico; in Europe, the range was from 3 percent in France to 6 percent in Italy, Spain, and the United Kingdom. Adding in the proportion of respondents who thought immigrants had a "somewhat good" influence made Canada stand out as the most open to immigrants, while the United States fell to third place after Japan. (Forty-one percent of Japanese respondents thought that immigrants were having a "somewhat good" influence, compared to 28 percent in the United States.) Given, however, that Japanese immigration is a fraction of that found in North America, it is unclear how comparable these responses are. A 2005 Gallup poll, conducted only in the United States, found that 61 percent of Americans felt that, on the whole, immigration is a good thing for the country, compared to only 34 percent who thought it was a bad thing.

7. While funding Social Security in the United States will become a critical problem once the baby boom generation begins to retire, the birth rate in the United States is higher than in Canada, perhaps attenuating the perceived need for immigrant workers.

8. For example, the Immigration Reform and Control Act of 1986 made it possible for approximately three million illegal migrants to legalize their status in the United States, and the 1990 Immigration Act raised the overall immigration cap to a flexible cap of 675,000 per year. Even the 1996 Welfare Reform Act, one of the clearest legislative measures hurtful to immigrants, has seen clawbacks of many of its immigrant-related provisions.

9. In 2000 the Reform Party became the Canadian Alliance Party, and in 2003 it merged with the historic right-of-center Progressive Conservative Party to become the new Conservative Party. This party became the elected minority government following the elections of 2006. It is important to note that even in its earliest days, the Reform Party could not be considered like anti-immigrant parties in Europe since its main strength came from voicing regional discontent with the distribution of political power and espousing a neoconservative economic agenda. Furthermore, a number of foreign-born individuals, including visible minorities, have campaigned and won office under Reform, Alliance, or Conservative banners.

10. See, for example, Pierson (1993, 1994).

11. Thus from an institutional perspective, a policy orientation provides room for change: contradictory policies may clash and provide openings for mutation or disruption of the institutional order, or new policies can change access points and players (Clemens and Cook 1999; Thelen and Steinmo 1992). For an empirical example looking at British and French policies of integration, see Favell (1998).

12. I focus on the INS since my field research and interviews were conducted before 2003. In the conclusion I consider how the new organization of immigration and naturalization services might affect future immigrant political incorporation.

13. Similarly, results from the National Latino Political Survey reveal that the majority of respondents felt very or somewhat satisfied with the naturalization process (Pachon and DeSipio 1994).

14. There was very little regulation of immigration for much of the first one hundred years following U.S. independence. Federal customs officials started collecting passenger lists of incoming ships in 1820, and some states had local oversight bodies. In 1875 the U.S. Supreme Court judged immigration to be a federal responsibility, but immigration laws continued to be enforced primarily by state boards or commissions. The Immigration Act of 1891 created the first Office of the Superintendent of Immigration within the Treasury Department, and U.S. immigrant inspectors were stationed at principal ports of entry, assuming responsibility for inspecting, admitting, or rejecting all immigrants to the United States. In 1895 the office was upgraded to the Bureau of Immigration; in 1903 the bureau was transferred from the Treasury Department to the newly established Department of Commerce and Labor; and in 1906, when naturalization procedures were standardized nationwide, the bureau expanded its mandate to encompass immigration and naturalization (Smith 1998).

15. According to INS historian Marian Smith, "Because most immigration laws of the time sought to protect American workers and wages, an Act of February 14, 1903, transferred the Bureau of Immigration from the Treasury Department to the newly created Department of Commerce and Labor" (1998). Prior to its location in the Department of Justice, the Bureau of Immigration engaged in some police functions. During World War I the bureau was given responsibility for the internment of enemy aliens, mostly seamen working on captured enemy ships. In 1924 Congress created the Border Patrol to prevent illegal immigration and placed it in the Bureau of Immigration. Subsequently, "The strict new immigration policy coupled with Border Patrol successes shifted more agency staff and resources to deportation activity" (Smith 1998).

16. CIC, the contemporary department in charge of naturalization, mirrors the INS in its dual functions. These functions were also joined from 1949 to 1966 in the Department of Citizenship and Immigration. At other points, immigration has been placed with employment planning, and citizenship has been housed with the Department of the Secretary of State. Only once, during the last months of the Conservative government in 1993, was immigration linked to security issues in the Department of Public Security. This move led to "strong objection from many quarters that immigration policy was now likely to be perceived as a law-enforcement function" (Kelley and Trebilcock 1998: 387). After winning office, the new Liberal government established the current department of citizenship and immigration in the fall of 1993. Following the terrorist attacks in the United States in 2001, CIC reemphasized its control functions, such as screening immigrants for terrorist backgrounds, but there was no move to transfer immigration services to a new internal security department as was done in the United States.

17. Interview with Doris Meissner, May 2, 2002. See also Magaña (2003).

18. King also specified that Canada's absorptive capacity did not extend to "large-scale immigration from the Orient" and defended Canada's absolute right to choose potential immigrants. Aliens had no "fundamental human right" to enter Canada (cited in Knowles 2000: 68).

19. Interview with Doris Meissner, May 2, 2002.

20. Ellen Fairclough, reflecting on her four years as minister of the department, commented that cabinet and senior public servants generally regarded immigration as a necessary evil but an exceedingly touchy political issue and thus of relatively less interest (Hawkins 1988: 136).

21. In total, government provided community groups with $250,000 in funds that year. The other monies went to native groups, women's groups, French linguistic minorities outside of Quebec, and "human relations" groups.

22. COSTI historically stood for "Centro Organizzativo Scuole Tecniche Italiane," but it no longer uses this since its services are much broader in scope and its clientele includes immigrants from dozens of countries. This organization, which later merged with the older Italian Immigrant Aid Society, still exists today. COSTI now serves thirty linguistic communities and is one of the largest community social service providers in greater Toronto.

23. In 1966 the immigration functions of the Department of Citizenship and Immigration were integrated into a new Department of Manpower and Immigration. The citizenship branch, in charge of all citizenship and integration efforts outside of employment preparation programs, was moved to the Department of the Secretary of State.

24. The INS employee later revealed that he was a Vietnam War veteran and behaved in a sympathetic manner to the applicant. However, the change in attitude only came after his adversarial style of interviewing.

25. This is not to say that anti-immigrant attitudes and problems with racism do not exist in both bureaucracies. I interviewed immigrants who had previous work experience with the INS or CIC, and I heard reports of fellow employees making disparaging remarks about immigrant newcomers in both the United States and Canada.

26. The main difference in the two tests appears to be the subjects covered. In the United States, questions focus on American history and government. In Canada, there are also questions on geography and economy, for example, "Which products from Southern Ontario are some of Canada's key exports?" According to North (1985), the level of knowledge required by Canadian citizenship judges is comparable to what the INS demands.

27. From "100 Typical Questions," available on the USCIS website, http://uscis.gov/graphics/services/natz/100q.pdf (last accessed January 5, 2006).

28. From questions provided by the Toronto Public Library, based on the booklet *A Look at Canada*, http://www.tpl.toronto.on.ca/mul_ser_citizenship _test.jsp (last accessed January 5, 2006). The booklet *A Look at Canada* is available on the CIC webpage: http://www.cic.gc.ca/english/pdf/pub/look.pdf (last accessed January 5, 2006).

29. Information provided by the CIC to the author.

30. The booklet is free in that immigrants are not asked to submit additional payment for it. However, CIC likely incorporates the price of the booklet into applicants' administrative fee.

31. The INS did introduce a new reader-friendly pamphlet in the late 1990s to help applicants determine their eligibility for citizenship. This guide is mostly an explanation of legal requirements. It includes sample civics questions.

32. The federal government does fund language instruction for refugee groups and can contribute indirectly to ESL instruction through block grants made to cities that then use these funds for language instruction. An estimate of ESL demand in Massachusetts in 2002 found that those on waiting lists, approximately 15,500 people, exceeded the total annual number enrolled in ESL classes (about 14,000 per year) (Lawrence K. Fish, "Mastering English for Economic Reasons," *Boston Globe*, November 23, 2002, A15).

33. While less personal, the call center approach does provide benefits of accessibility, especially for immigrants living further from local CIC offices. An internal audit of the call center system in 1999 concluded that accessibility increased from 30 to 70 percent and that employees were better able to answer specific questions about an individual's file due to improved access to CIC information systems. Conversely, the major problem from the users' perspective was access problems due to busy signals or dropped calls, while CIC had problems retaining employees to staff the call center (Citizenship and Immigration Canada 1999a).

34. The choice of citizenship judge, made by the government in power, is also a source of patronage appointments.

35. Using data from 1984 to 1985, North reports that median wait times in the United States were eleven months between filing the application and being sworn in as a citizen; in Canada it was six and a half months (1985: 54). The 1990 report of the auditor general of Canada criticizes the citizenship program in the Department of the Secretary of State for letting wait times that were thirty weeks in 1986 balloon to forty and sometimes sixty-four weeks in 1989 (Auditor General of Canada 1990: 28, 36).

36. In 1973 Manpower and Immigration set up a small settlement branch within the department that took on wider settlement activities beyond employment. The branch developed two important programs: the Immigrant Settlement and Adaptation Program, which gave fee-for-services grants to voluntary agencies that provided reception, information, orientation, counseling, interpretation, and referral services to immigrants, and the Adjustment Assistance Program, which allocated grants to immigrants and refugees needing food, clothing, shelter, and other necessities (Hawkins 1991: 82; Indra 1987). These policies, with various modifications, still exist today.

37. For example, Indra notes that "local CEIC [Canadian Employment and Immigration Commission] officers were highly constrained to address primarily employment issues, even though . . . refugee psychological and other non-employment needs were as great and extremely pressing" (1987: 153).

38. Thus, one of the explicit objectives of the Immigration and Refugee Protection Act is "to promote the successful integration of permanent residents into Canada, while recognizing that integration involves mutual obligations for new

immigrants and Canadian society" (3[l][e]). This is one of ten immigration objectives. The text of the act is available at http://laws.justice.gc.ca/en/i-2.5/143444.html (last accessed February 8, 2006).

39. A major sticking point for Ontario was a perceived inequality in how federal immigration and settlement monies are disbursed. The province long claimed, with some justification, that it did not receive funding commensurate to the number of newcomers it attracts. The federal-provincial agreement promises that the federal government will provide Ontario with $920 million in new funding for immigrant settlement over a five-year period.

40. It is worth noting that the Ontario government consistently linked citizenship with community. The first citizenship branch was housed in the Community Services Division of the Department of the Provincial Secretary and Citizenship, moving in 1971 to the Ministry of Community and Social Services and in 1982 to the Ministry of Citizenship and Culture (Hawkins 1988: 392, 445 n. 1). In 2003 the new provincial Liberal government created a Ministry of Citizenship and Immigration "committed to the full participation of all people living in Ontario" (Ministry of Citizenship and Immigration website: http://www.citizenship.gov.on.ca/english/index.html [last accessed January 5, 2006]). The ministry oversees programs related to immigration and settlement, volunteerism, honors and awards, the Ontario Women's Directorate, and the Ontario Seniors' Directorate. It thus continues the tradition of combining immigrant citizenship with other social and diversity issues.

41. This amount does not include the $164 million transferred to the government of Quebec in a block grant under the 1991 federal-provincial settlement agreement, nor an additional $45 million allocated to additional service support in British Columbia and Manitoba. Although Quebec only receives about 15 percent of newcomers to Canada, its funding is almost equivalent to the total given to all other provinces. This creates resentment, notably in Ontario. (See n. 39, above.)

42. A 2003 report by the House of Commons Standing Committee on Citizenship and Immigration recommended that the amount be increased to $3,000 per immigrant. While making twenty-eight specific recommendations for changes to the settlement program, the Standing Committee did report that, overall, settlement provision in Canada appears "fundamentally sound."

43. Hawkins reports little interest in immigration by provinces prior to the 1970s, perhaps due to a perception that immigration is a federal matter, limited provincial funds, and a philosophy among key federal Liberals and civil servants of "intelligent and sophisticated management of affairs from the center" (1988: 179). Lack of coordination led to inclusion in the 1976 Immigration Act of a directive to the federal government "to encourage and facilitate the adaptation of persons who have been granted admission as permanent residents to Canadian society by promoting cooperation between the Government of Canada and other levels of government and non-governmental agencies in Canada" (cited in Hawkins 1988: 403).

44. Multiculturalism thus exhibits two key features promoting institution-

alization: the use of state power to set up bureaucracies, make laws, and direct funding and the elite endorsement of a normative structure (DiMaggio and Powell 1991).

45. On the symbolic importance of multiculturalism, also see Breton (1986) and Fleras and Elliott (1992).

46. Estimates of the number of African slaves in Canada vary but likely did not exceed a few thousand. As part of the British Empire, Canada automatically adopted British emancipation laws, culminating in the abolition of slavery throughout the empire on July 31, 1834. Prior to the 1960s, the largest group of blacks in Canada came from the United States; it is estimated that thirty thousand Southern slaves arrived through the Underground Railway, but many moved back to the United States following the American Civil War. While the northern British colonies offered freedom to American blacks during the War of Independence and War of 1812 and Canada was a prime destination for slaves fleeing the South along the Underground Railway, black immigrants generally suffered a poor reception. They were seldom granted the same land holdings or other benefits given to white migrants. In 1911 Canada came close to officially excluding black immigrants purely on racial grounds. It did not, but informal administrative practices of exclusion made black migration almost impossible (Knowles 1992: 23–24, 85–86).

47. As was typical of the time, Durham saw this as a racial conflict: "I found a struggle, not of principles, but of races" (in Lucas [1912] 1970).

48. Some Francophone separatists drew an explicit link between the two, calling French Canadians the "white niggers" of North America (Vallières 1968), and they also tried to draw parallels between Quebec independence and anticolonial movements in the third world.

49. Commentators and scholars debate Trudeau's motivations for embracing multiculturalism over biculturalism. Some argue that the goal of multiculturalism was to undermine Quebec's unique place in confederation (Labelle, Rocher, and Rocher 1995); others suggest it was an electoral ploy aimed at building support for the Liberal Party among new ethnic voters (Hawkins 1991).

50. I thus disagree with Ujimoto's assessment that "Canadian citizenship was never emphasized in the concept of multiculturalism" (1999: 280). Ideologically and administratively, multiculturalism has everything to do with building a uniquely "Canadian" citizenship, as contrasted to a British identity or Quebec nationalism.

51. Other agencies involved included the Canadian Radio-Television and Telecommunications Commission, the National Film Board, the National Library and Archives, and the National Museum of Man. The Canadian Consultative Council on Multiculturalism was also established, which aimed to provide the government with feedback and access to Canada's multiple ethnic communities. Established in 1973, the CCCM was disbanded in the early 1980s, as it was widely seen as ineffective due to its large size (about one hundred representatives) and its patronage appointments. See Hawkins (1991: 219–21).

52. In 1983 the minister of state responsible for multiculturalism, Jim Flem-

ing, reported that ninety thousand children across Canada attended heritage language schools (Hawkins 1991: 225). In the 1990s the federal government largely stopped funding heritage language classes, passing the responsibility on to local school boards and lower levels of government.

53. In 2001 less than half of the foreign born claimed birthplaces in the United States or Europe.

54. The three programs that received the remainder of the funding were Institutional Change, Heritage Enhancement, and Heritage Language Education.

55. The text of the Multiculturalism Act is available at http://laws.justice.gc .ca/en/C-18.7/32217.html (last accessed January 5, 2006). The Constitution Act of 1982 also enshrined the concept of multiculturalism into the Canadian Charter of Rights and Freedoms. Section 27 directs judges to interpret the charter "in a manner consistent with the preservation and enhancement of the multicultural heritage of Canadians."

56. All financial data come from Canadian Heritage *Department Performance Reports*, 1996–2004.

57. On the federal government's relative neglect of multiculturalism, see Hawkins (1991: 217–28), McRoberts (1997: 127–28), Stasiulis (1988), and Pal (1993).

58. There are some small signs that this might be changing. In the fall of 2004 the two-year-old Office of Citizenship, a unit within the Department of Homeland Security's U.S. Citizenship and Immigration Services, announced the launch of the web-based *Welcome to the United States: A Guide for New Immigrants*. This guide offers information on initial settlement, such as getting a Social Security number and a driver's license, and some general information on health care, employment, education, and childcare. It also includes information on how to become a U.S. citizen.

59. Before 1962 the only federal assistance offered were grants of $40 per person given to voluntary agencies to transport refugees from their port of entry to their final U.S. destination (Holman 1996). The 1962 act significantly expanded this commitment, allocating funds for such things as health services, the operating costs of local public schools, ESL and job training, basic maintenance requirements of needy Cubans, and increased grants to voluntary agencies.

60. Although the support offered to refugees was relatively generous given past U.S. nonintervention in newcomer settlement, some critics contend that it was not enough. For example, while approximately $5 million went to adult education, the equivalent of $150 per person, an internal HEW memo estimated that $325 per adult was necessary just to teach adequate English skills (Kelly 1977: 186).

61. It was estimated in 1977 that without the provision waiving family composition requirements, 45 percent of all Indochinese refugees would have lost their benefits (Hein 1993: 49). A 1976 amendment extended the act to Laotians as well.

62. In the words of the act, it would provide "a permanent and systematic procedure for the admission to this country of refugees of special humanitarian

concern to the U.S. and to provide comprehensive and uniform provisions for the effective resettlement and adsorption of those refugees that are admitted" (Refugee Act of 1980, Public Law no. 96–212). It also incorporated the United Nations definition of refugees into U.S. law and removed the previous requirement that a refugee must have fled from a communist or communist-dominated country.

63. Eligibility periods for Refugee Cash Assistance have fluctuated wildly. Initially set for two years, it was increased to thirty-six months, and then, when the Refugee Act came up for reauthorization in 1982, it was dropped back to twenty-four months and later to eighteen months. In the 1990s it would fall further to eight months.

64. While prorefugee forces succeeded in establishing these institutions, state administration of refugee resettlement relied on the governor's executive orders, interagency agreements, and the existence of federal regulations. Legislation which would have given statutory existence to the Massachusetts Office for Refugees and Immigrants died in the state legislature (Pho 1991).

65. The nine VOLAGs were the United States Catholic Conference, the Lutheran Immigration and Refugee Service, the International Rescue Committee, the United Hebrew Immigration and Assistance Service, the Church World Service, the Tolstoy Foundation, the American Fund for Czechoslovak Refugees, the American Council for Nationalities Services, and Travelers' Aid–International Social Services. The U.S. Catholic Conference resettled about half of the refugees (Kelly 1977: 151–52).

66. Kelly (1977) contends that the $500 per person offered to voluntary agencies was not enough to cover the actual costs.

67. Originally the U.S. government directed the VOLAGs to disperse the Southeast Asian refugees throughout the country; officials were anxious to avoid "another Miami," where the Vietnamese might repeat the Cubans' overwhelming concentration in one city (Rumbaut 1995). Scattering the newcomers produced its own problems, including loneliness and isolation from coethnic support networks. Many Vietnamese subsequently engaged in secondary migration, producing a number of sizeable Vietnamese communities in the United States (Zhou and Bankston 1998).

68. All the financial figures cited here and throughout the chapter come from the annual reports of the U.S. Office of Refugee Resettlement.

69. ORR did not explicitly declare the end of the incentive grant program in 1994, but it ceased to report a specific expenditure for the program in subsequent years.

70. In a fascinating study, anthropologist Sarah Horton (2004) uses Cuban refugees and Mexican migrants' experiences with the U.S. health care system to draw out the civic implications of differential government treatment. Cubans who have government-paid health coverage under the Cuban Refugee Program can access medical services and are subsequently seen as more deserving by medical staff and treated as citizens who can make demands. Mexicans, both legal and undocumented, receive no state support and must pay for services, but

sometimes they do not have the resources to pay fees. They are perceived as being a drain on society and discouraged from pressing demands on American institutions. See also Pedraza-Bailey (1985).

71. Before then, refugees were admitted as special admissions at the behest of the minister in charge of immigration using a cabinet order-in-council, somewhat analogous to the American use of presidential parolee power.

72. Canada became a signatory to the 1951 Convention on the Status of Refugees in 1969, and in 1970 the Department of Manpower and Immigration incorporated the UN convention definition of a refugee into its new guidelines for refugee admissions (Adelman 1991: 193). The 1976 Immigration Act made these guidelines law.

73. For example, refugees might be met at the airport by employees from the Canada Employment Centres, by workers at a community-based organization, or by a volunteer from the ethnic community or a mainstream resettlement organization. They would receive orientation training and were expected to find housing and employment with assistance from the Canada Employment Centres, a nonprofit agency, or on their own initiative.

74. Refugees accepted from overseas receive permanent residency upon arriving in Canada. Those who make in-land refugee claims (asylum claims) can apply for permanent residency once they are accepted as protected refugees. Some groups, such as the Canadian Council for Refugees, have criticized this process for being at times too slow or, in some cases, insurmountable, since permanent residency generally requires individuals to have some identity documents, to pay a hefty "landing" fee, and to pass security clearances.

75. For example, American asylum policy was roiled in political controversy during the 1980s over the ideological determination of status, such that Cubans were accepted but those fleeing civil war in El Salvador were not. During this period, the Canadian government designated Salvadorians a special humanitarian class of refugees and admitted some who, after having made failed asylum claims in the United States, faced deportation back to El Salvador.

76. See also Smith (1997) on "ascriptive" American citizenship and Loury (2002) on racial stigma.

77. Over the course of U.S. history, other groups have also been racialized, that is, typified and treated as if origins, biology, and culture naturally come together to determine one's abilities and life chances. The Irish, Jews, Chinese, Japanese, and Mexicans all, at various times, faced the label of "inferior race" and the reality of group discrimination. At the same time, identification of distinct races has always been contested and in flux. Thus in the early twentieth century Indian Asian and Mexican migrants sought inclusion into the mainstream "white" majority through court challenges of citizenship restrictions and through pressure by their foreign governments. Over the twentieth century, various European groups became progressively "whiter." Blacks have found the least room to maneuver. See, for example, the limited ethnic options of black immigrants and their descendents described by Mary Waters (1999).

78. *Latino* or *Hispanic* is officially an ethnic category. For example, on the

U.S. census, respondents who indicate that they are Hispanic also provide a separate racial classification. In reality, however, the salient political categories in the United States are racialized into separate *Latino* (or *Hispanic*) and *non-Hispanic white* groupings.

79. See chapter 4 for more on the internal Portuguese community debate over minority status.

80. In addition, the group must show a level of illiteracy above the national average.

81. Department of Justice website, http://www.usdoj.gov/crt/voting/28cfr/ 55/28cfr55.htm#anchor55_1, accessed January 5, 2006. These provisions were renewed in 1982 and extended an additional fifteen years in 1992. In 2002, 296 municipalities and counties across the United States were required to make special linguistic accommodations (Kong 2002).

82. Following the 2000 U.S. census, the town of Southbridge in Worcester County was added (*Federal Register* 67 [144] [July 26, 2002]: 48874).

83. The same is true in Canada.

84. This is true both for critics of these government policies, such as those against affirmative action, as well as supporters who wish to channel government assistance to certain groups.

4. THE MEANING OF CITIZENSHIP

1. There are parallels between the argument here and some anthropologists' concept of *cultural citizenship* (Horton 2004; Ong 1996, 2003; Rosaldo 1997). The concept highlights how the state's subjectification of immigrants divides them into more and less deserving citizens using norms of worth and acceptable middle-class behavior. For some, such as Horton and Ong, this process is fundamentally structured by the prevailing global, capitalist economic system. I place more emphasis on the state as an independent actor, I raise the possibility that certain white immigrants such as the Portuguese in the United States might be as badly served as some nonwhite groups, and I am more optimistic that state action is not always negative, though it certainly can be.

2. For a more general discussion of cognitive maps and schemas, see Clemens and Cook (1999) and Zucker (1991).

3. See, for example, the contributions on framing in McAdam, McCarthy, and Zald 1996. See also the writings by Benford and Snow (2000), Snow and Benford (1992), and Snow et al. (1986).

4. Throughout the 1990s, between 77 to 83 percent of Canadians agreed with the statement "the multicultural make-up is one of the best things in Canada" (Multiculturalism Program 2001: 3).

5. Of course, both ethnicity and race are socially constructed terms. In the nineteenth and early twentieth centuries, groups today considered ethnic, such as the Italians or Poles, were regarded as separate races. The distinction I draw is between a large category, primarily defined by phenotype or broad cultural or geographical origin (i.e., black, white, Asian, or Hispanic/Latino), compared to a

more specific ethnic category highlighting particular cultural traits (e.g., Haitian, Irish, Chinese, or Mexican). Social discourse in the United States recognizes hyphenated ethnic Americanism, but policy invariably considers race.

6. See, for example, Joppke (1999) and Skerry (1993).

7. I am not saying that race is irrelevant to the immigrant experience for those seen as racially "other" in the United States. I am, however, arguing that immigrant integration demands considerations beyond race and that policies meant to redress important structural and attitudinal barriers to blacks' full participation in American society might follow logics that are, at best, awkwardly applied to migrants.

8. While the Ontario government fully funds a separate Catholic school system as part of Canada's historic French Catholic/English Protestant compromise, it has refused to support other religious or ethnic educational institutions with public monies.

9. On white Americans' symbolic ethnicity see Gans (1979), Alba (1990), and Waters (1990).

10. See Li (1999) and, for a similar argument in the United States, Waters (1990).

11. The disjuncture between public perceptions and official policy is not reserved to Portuguese and Vietnamese Canadians. One staff member at Canadian Heritage, the ministry overseeing the multiculturalism program, noted, "We still get calls asking for funding for a folklore event. A group will phone us because they are holding a cultural festival. But, we don't do that anymore."

12. The question asked, "What do you think is better for [Canada/the United States], for new immigrants to be encouraged to maintain their distinct culture and ways, or to change their distinct culture and ways to blend with the larger society?" (Reitz and Breton 1994: 27).

13. This is not to say that Vietnamese do not experience multiple instances of prejudice and discrimination based on their nationality, accent, or race. However, none report having been told to "become American" and completely give up their prior identities and culture. Perhaps in part this is because of race; native-born Americans might not consider them able to become American (Tuan 1999). However, it also seems to be because many Americans accept hyphenated Americanism.

14. Portuguese levels of education are low in metro Boston and metro Toronto, due in part to many traditional Portuguese parents' belief that work carries more value than education. It is not clear that either Joe or Ilda would have finished school if they had met with less hostility and more understanding, yet I was struck, and disconcerted, by how raw and exposed their feelings remained forty years later.

15. For both men, openness to sociocultural differences translates into dual political citizenship. Such attitudes can be contrasted to the Latinos Jones-Correa (1998a) interviewed in Queens; these individuals felt that U.S. citizenship laws forced an either-or choice between the nationality of the home country and that of the receiving society. The difference might stem from Latinos' closer

contact to their homeland but might also be a function of refugee status. Vietnamese, through their flight, reject the political citizenship of Vietnam, although they embrace being Vietnamese in a cultural sense. They also might feel more welcomed by government because of the greater resettlement assistance they received.

16. Indeed, some well-educated Vietnamese perceive more commonalties between themselves and the French—former colonizers who had a substantial impact on education in Vietnam—than to South Asians or even some Southeast Asians.

17. As Joppke notes, "a colour-conscious civil-rights law and discourse has provided incentives for ethnic leaders to conceive of their immigrant constituencies in terms of racial minorities" (1999: 13). See also Skerry (1993).

18. Other Vietnamese Americans reported similar experiences.

19. See, for example, Moc Van's comment about racism in Congress. Post-1965 U.S. immigration is largely nonwhite, but it is not always evident whether Americans' anti-immigrant sentiments stem from racism, nativism, or some combination. I do not want to downplay the extra barriers faced by nonwhite immigrants, but I do want to highlight how economically disadvantaged groups such as the Portuguese become marginalized when little distinction is made between racial minorities and the foreign born.

20. Census reports divided Caucasians into *Portuguese* and *other Caucasians*. According to Geschwender, Carroll-Seguin, and Brill (1988), the separate classification of Portuguese stems from class hierarchies that put the Portuguese closer to local laborers than capitalist European landowners.

21. See Dreyer (1978) and Moniz (2001). According to Moniz, who was not a participant at the conference, the vote by leaders, intellectuals, and other members of the Portuguese American community was five hundred to three in favor of having Portuguese included within the Hispanic category as a minority ethnic group.

22. *Congressional Record* 121 (February 25, 1975): 4339.

23. One young, native-born Portuguese American with whom I spoke readily admitted marking *Hispanic/Latino* on a college application form because he felt he should receive the same benefits as native-born Hispanics. Portuguese names, some of which are similar to Spanish names, makes "passing" as a Latino easy.

24. Suzanne Mettler offers a similar conclusion drawn from a very different context. Examining the special boost in political and civic engagement provided by the GI Bill to veterans of modest backgrounds, Mettler concludes, "the interpretive effects of the G.I. Bill were especially powerful for such veterans, conveying to them a sense of an elevated status in the polity. As a result, they gained a sharper sense of civic duty, feeling that they owed something back to American society" (2002: 361).

25. In the United States, development of the welfare state and access to public benefits have been often intertwined with politics of race (Lieberman 1998; Quadagno 1994). See also Ong (2003) on how prior black-white racialization of

the American welfare state's "citizen-subjects" carries over to Cambodian refugees.

26. Opportunities for political coalitions are also hurt by the persistent racial hierarchies carried by white Bostonians. Contradicting the earlier assessment of racial harmony in Dorchester, another community member describes what he sees as understandable black hostility to the influx of Vietnamese refugees, given that the newcomers displace natives in the housing market and drive up rents: "So [white] landlords kick the African Americans out of the house [in order to] to rent to us [Vietnamese], jack the price up. So what would you feel if you see your relative is kicked out or your friend is kicked out and then some yellow faces come in? [Our] cars were slashed; windows were broken."

27. As noted in the previous chapter, settlement programs have eligibility guidelines. In the past, these included gendered notions of employment. Today, many programs funded by Citizenship and Immigration Canada are restricted to noncitizens or to newcomers' with three years of residency or less. Some groups are challenging such limits since, according to one activist, "service should be based on need, not on immigration status." Importantly, however, there are no ethno-racial distinctions in service eligibility.

28. The closest respondents in Toronto came to espousing a similar zero-sum view of intergroup relations was when they linked refugee status to social assistance benefits.

29. On the intersection of American citizenship and notions of work and economic independence, see also Shklar (1991) and Ong (2003).

30. When it came to negative qualities, the respondent felt "people [in Canada] pay too many taxes. There are too many social programs; some should be cut. They are a burden on the citizens of Canada. I would tell Quebec, this wonderful province, to shut up." As for the United States, "Well, I love the United States, but Medicare. And, they are not very sensitive, generally, to immigrants, to ethnic groups, not very open or receptive. It is still, in many ways, a very close-minded society."

5. COMMUNITY ORGANIZATIONS AND POLITICAL MOBILIZATION

1. Research on the social organization of the Vietnamese thus concentrates on the role of the family in Vietnamese life, the impact of informal social networks for psychological support, material assistance and educational success, and the establishment of religious institutions. In the Portuguese case, scholars also concentrate on the family and religious organizing. On Vietnamese and Portuguese families, see Caplan, Whimore, and Choy (1989), Chan and Dorais (1998), Kibria (1993), Woon (1986), and Noivo (1997). On religious organizing, see Pfeifer (1999), Dorais (1991), Bankston and Zhou (2000), and Cabral (1989). On the role of social networks, see Buchignani (1988) and Zhou and Bankston (1998). One notable exception to the lack of attention to immigrant associations is Hein's study (1997) of Indochinese mutual assistance associations.

2. The importance of organizations in promoting collective action is well established for other groups usually excluded from the corridors of power, including African Americans (McAdam 1982; Morris 1984; Andrews 2001) and women (Staggenborg 1991). We should not be surprised that immigrants benefit from mobilization around group membership, given obstacles that might prevent them from directly accessing the political system on their own.

3. Institutional completeness encompasses the total social organization of the immigrant community, and it reflects the degree to which immigrants and their children can live their lives within the ethnic community. The term is thus a broader measure of immigrant social cohesion than alternative concepts such as the ethnic business enclave (restricted to for-profit activity) or social capital (focused on interpersonal ties).

4. See, for example, de Tocqueville ([1835] 1945), Habermas (1989), Olasky (1992), Joyce and Schambra (1996), and Barnett (1999).

5. For example, Hein (1997) finds that a major determinant of the number of Indochinese MAAs in U.S. states in 1984 is the size of the Indochinese population in the state. The relationship between population and organizations is likely curvilinear: a small community that doubles in size will double the number of organizations, but beyond a certain population threshold, organizations likely expand their membership or clientele rather than generate new organizations.

6. The figures are from the 1996 Canadian and 2000 U.S. censuses. The data for Toronto reflect the new political unit that came into being on January 1, 1998, following the merger of the former municipalities of Toronto, York, East York, North York, Scarborough, and Etobicoke.

7. These areas are west downtown Toronto for the Portuguese and Vietnamese, Somerville/Cambridge for the Portuguese in Boston, and the Dorchester area in Boston for the Vietnamese. These areas are historically the site of first settlement and contain the primary ethnic business district and most community organizations. For a more detailed discussion of the methodology behind the organizational count, see Bloemraad (2005).

8. I focus on organizations highlighted by Breton (1964) as central to an institutionally complete community: churches, social service organizations, and the ethnic media. In addition, I include political and advocacy organizations that speak out on behalf of the community, and in the Portuguese case, I include social clubs organized along regional lines. Organizations that fill several roles are categorized according to their primary purpose as reflected in a mission statement or the group's predominant activities.

9. For example, I classify the Vietnamese Seniors of Metropolitan Boston as an advocacy organization but the Vietnamese American Voters' League of Greater Boston as a political group. I have excluded from this category, and from the fraternal/social category, regiment-specific veterans associations which are found in the Vietnamese community. It was almost impossible to get an accurate count of these groups since most are quite informal and somewhat secretive. (See, for example, Pfeifer's [1999] similar problems in gaining access to these groups.) I do, however, include groups such as the Free Vietnam

Alliance of Canada or the Vietnamese Community of Massachusetts, both of which are largely made up of veterans.

10. The count of temples includes a few that do not possess a formal site of worship but which organize regular religious rites in a private residence. A number of non-Catholic Christian churches offer services in Portuguese or Vietnamese, but they serve an extremely small minority in both communities and are not included.

11. There are about 45,000 individuals of Portuguese ethnicity living in the area which constituted the old city of Toronto (population 646,480) and 13,500 in the traditional Portuguese settlement area of Arlington, Belmont, Boston, Cambridge, Medford, and Somerville in metropolitan Boston (population 890,322).

12. See, for example, Marwell (2004), Salamon (1999), and Smith and Lipsky (1993). Salamon (1995) calls this pattern of contracted social service delivery a system of third-party government.

13. Catholics comprised a large proportion of the Vietnamese who fled immediately following the fall of Saigon in 1975. Since the United States welcomed many more individuals from this first wave, their proportion in the overall refugee pool will be larger than in Canada.

14. At minimum, we might expect parity between Portuguese and Vietnamese organizations, based on only counting the smaller number of Portuguese and Vietnamese who live in the traditional core settlement area rather than the larger metropolitan region. See n. 11, above.

15. For example, Vietnamese Catholics found a sympathetic friend in former Boston cardinal Bernard Law.

16. The financial data are for the 1997 fiscal year. Revenue sources fluctuate from year to year, but the percentage of monies from municipal, provincial/state, and federal governments in 1997 accurately reflects each organization's dependence on public funding in the late 1990s.

17. Groups with nonprofit status in the United States do not need to file tax forms if their revenues are below $25,000. Many local civic associations probably fall under this threshold, so this figure only refers to relatively large and important civic associations. Salamon's categorization includes groups focused on community improvement, social change, neighborhood development, and consumer education as well as essentially social groups such as fraternities and singing societies. It also includes the United Way and social welfare agencies that oversee social service planning. Among the native born, public funding helps groups as diverse as community development corporations (Grønbjerg 1993), civic associations (Skocpol et al. 2002), social service agencies (Grønbjerg 1993; Smith and Lipsky 1993), and advocacy organizations (Pal 1993).

18. Groups that primarily serve refugees also tend to belong to refugee-specific organizations such as the Canadian Council for Refugees.

19. Smith and Lipsky note this positive potential but also caution, "Former workers in the voluntary sector, now employed in the public sector, come to recognize the imperatives of government as they assume the burden of distribut-

ing resources over the entire service area," and they can work to "persuade their former colleagues in the private sector of the need for government priorities (sometimes they are regarded as traitors to the cause)" (1993: 15).

20. Viet-AID was established with three primary goals: fostering home ownership among Vietnamese Americans; promoting economic development by working with small business owners, including training women to run home-based daycare centers; and promoting community organizing by building what Viet-AID claims is the first nonprofit Vietnamese community center in the United States.

21. Under Canada's parliamentary system, civil servants usually formulate drafts of proposed policy and legislation. Senior civil servants make executive decisions by narrowing down the range of policy options and presenting these to the minister and his or her political staff. Many of the senior managers I met in Ottawa cautioned that they have little say over eventual policy, which is essentially a political decision. However, compared to bureaucrats in the United States, they exercise much greater discretion in shaping options and outcomes. INS policy, for example, was formulated by its Policy and Planning Office or vetted through its legal bureau, but members of Congress frequently proposed detailed legislation formulated by their political staff, not by career civil servants.

22. A related model, labeled by Andrews (2001) as the persuasion model of movement outcomes, agrees with the thesis that only acts of protest can cause political change, but the mechanism is slightly different. According to this view, protest convinces more powerful actors to take on a cause.

23. All budgetary information comes from the organization's audited financial statements, 1964–2000, made accessible to the author by St. Christopher House.

24. Portuguese Canadian activists have engaged in a series of campaigns to improve the work conditions of office cleaners (many of whom are Portuguese immigrants) both in- and outside St. Christopher House. Portuguese Americans in Boston have been much less active in this area, despite a similar socio-economic status and occupations.

25. The Boston Portuguese Continental Union of the United States and the Toronto Federation of Portuguese Canadian Businesses and Professionals offer some college scholarships. Although helpful, such initiatives do not address the prior problem of encouraging high school completion.

26. Until September 2002, Cambridge's "controlled choice" education system assigned students to schools primarily according to race. Yet class is arguably the more important issue in this city, one that hurts Portuguese children in particular. One of the city's worst performing schools, Harrington School, is largely white and has traditionally taught a significant population of Portuguese American children. It is the school with the highest rate of poverty, as judged by eligibility for federal school lunch programs. In 2001, 72 percent of the student body was eligible (Scott S. Greenberger, "Cambridge Eyes Income, Not Race, for Desegregation," *Boston Globe*, December 16, 2001, 1; Mary Hurley and Scott S. Greenberger, "Income Level Eyed on School Selection," *Boston*

Globe, December 19, 2001, 1). Since September 2002, assignment to schools is made primarily through socioeconomic criteria.

27. Poor educational outcomes are a point of particular sensitivity in the Portuguese community. Immigrants who are illiterate or semiliterate because they could not access schooling in Portugal are embarrassed by their inability to read and write, and educated community leaders do not want to promote the perception in mainstream society that their community is ignorant. In Toronto, for example, researchers who document poor educational outcomes regularly get criticized for only focusing on the problems of the community rather than the successes.

28. This is a problem for nonprofits since, as one executive director explained, many public and private sources of funding "have now gone to specific projects. They want to feel like they're servicing people. And they don't [give money for] general operating costs. . . . It's just kind of sad, because an organization, in order to be able to service the community, needs to operate, needs to have administration. You need a building; you need space; you need a director; you need people." There are some hints that the situation in Canada eased in the early years of the twenty-first century. In the United States, little has changed.

29. Vietnamese communities in both Toronto and Boston have distinct AIDS organizations, built on the large influx of government monies directed at HIV/AIDS that flowed to community groups in the late 1980s and throughout the 1990s. Toronto's Asian Community AIDS Service, a fusion of three separate initiatives, receives funding from the federal Ministry of Health, the Ontario AIDS Bureau, and the city of Toronto's Office of Public Health in addition to private donations and fees. The parallel organization in Boston, the Massachusetts Asian AIDS Prevention Project, receives significant funding from the Office for Minority Health in the Massachusetts Department of Public Health.

30. The IRS has the power to interpret "substantial" as it sees fit, though it has been taken to mean 20 percent of an organization's expenditures. This understanding derives from a little-known option that nonprofits may exercise when they file their income forms with the IRS. If they take the "H" option, organizations may use 20 percent of their first $500,000 in revenues and a declining percentage of further revenues, to a maximum of $1 million, for lobbying activities (Salamon 1995; Berry 2003). Not all nonprofit organizations hold 501(c)3 status. The IRS recognizes twenty-nine different categories of tax-exempt entities, most of which are mutual benefit associations that provide goods or services exclusively to their members. The "501(c)3s" are, however, most commonly associated with nonprofit status, and in addition to being exempt from taxes on revenues, they can provide tax deductions for donations.

31. Advocacy also carries a more positive connotation than lobbying, although occasionally an advocate is branded as one of the "white sneaker people," do-gooders who prowl the halls of the legislature, drumming up support for one cause or another.

32. The Canadian tax code restricts advocacy to 10 to 20 percent of total resources, depending on the size of annual revenues.

33. This is not to say that significant internal conflicts do not arise about the

direction of public policy. Biles reports significant tension in the 1980s among federal bureaucrats who favored policies directed at cultural retention and those who supported greater emphasis on race relations (1997: 82).

34. Interview with the executive director of OCASI, Debbie Douglas, March 30, 2001.

35. In the United States, there is greater reliance on political appointees to head departments of the executive branch, and there is therefore a stronger sense that elected officials can control program administration. In Canada, the parliamentary tradition supports a strong, independent civil service; administration of government programs is not supposed to be tied to political considerations.

36. They can also choose to surrender their 501(c)3 status and register as 501(c)4 organizations. The latter have no restrictions on lobbying and are nonprofit, but unlike 501(c)3s, donors cannot receive a tax deduction for their contributions.

37. Indeed, one Portuguese Canadian group, Portuguese Women 55+, received money from an American foundation in honor of its innovative "theater of the oppressed" (first developed in Brazil) in which seniors discuss conceptual issues and problems through mime. That program got its initial seed grant from one of the few large foundations in Ontario, the Trillium Foundation. Ironically, the Trillium Foundation is publicly funded—it receives $100 million annually from provincial casino revenues—although its administration and decisions are supposed to be nonpartisan and at arm's length from government.

38. The bulk of the public monies went to administering the state's Citizenship Assistance Program. In 1998 the figure was 14 percent. Financial information is from the organization's 990 federal tax forms.

39. It is possible that there are diminishing returns to having more organizations. Some in the Toronto Portuguese community complain that there are too many social clubs, fracturing the community and rendering it incapable of collective action.

6. LEARNING TO LEAD AND WINNING POLITICAL OFFICE

1. The importance of leadership is not restricted to immigrant communities. Leaders' mobilization efforts promote electoral participation among native-born Americans (Rosenstone and Hansen 1993), strengthen communities' civic life (Verba, Schlozman, and Brady 1995), and encourage protest behavior among disadvantaged populations (Ganz 2000; McAdam 1982; Morris 1984).

2. See, for example, Breton (1991), Higham (1982), Indra (1987), and Martiniello (1993).

3. Given its importance, the dearth of contemporary scholarship on ethnic leadership is surprising. Yet Higham's comment twenty-eight years ago that the subject is neglected due to a "general distrust of elites and [scholars'] desire to look at history from the bottom up" continues to hold true (1978: 1).

4. For an extensive and varied list of leadership definitions, see Bass (1990: 14–18).

5. I focus primarily on domestic Canadian or American politics, except to the extent that political agitation around homeland concerns leads to domestic activism.

6. Although the term *industry* might project a negative connotation when used to include nonprofit organizations, it best describes the constellation of interdependent organizations and services available to immigrants.

7. Not all successful entrepreneurs become community leaders, but if a businessperson has political motivations, material resources help buy standing and influence (Aguilar–San Juan 1998; Brettell 1977). Describing the early days of the Portuguese Canadian community in Toronto, Anderson and Higgs explain, "The first shopkeepers, travel agents, and real estate salesmen found their prosperity deriving from their ability to provide a bridge between newer arrivals and Canadian society. This favoured position gave them a prominence which made them de facto community spokesmen" (1976: 154). Business owners and professionals can build networks with coethnic clients and employees, and they can donate resources to community projects or community events. The most successful can also leverage their money in the mainstream through political donations.

8. Organizations within newcomer settlement are usually public or nonprofit, running programs such as ESL classes, job-placement services, or family counseling, but some for-profit businesses also assist immigrants by filling out government paperwork and offering translation services. It has become commonplace to make distinctions between the public sector, private "civil society," and the world of for-profit organizations. Whereas businesses are guided by the profit motive and government holds coercive power in deciding and implementing the "public good," civil society supposedly promotes voluntary action toward communally defined interests. Proponents of the tripartite division recognize that reality often fails to match neat theoretical boundaries, but they promote the distinction as meaningful (Salamon 1999). I accept a certain distinction between organizations run by government, voluntary boards, or profit-seeking owners, but an arbitrary division between organizational forms impedes our understanding of how individuals in these different organizations are unified by the services they provide.

9. Hai refers to the English-language classes offered by the federal government.

10. For example, as reported in the public tax records of Viet-AID, the executive director—an experienced lawyer in his forties—earned a salary of $37,000 in 1998, a salary far below the amount he might have made in the private sector. I borrow the term *clean jobs* from Giles's (1993) analysis of the higher prestige accorded to low-paid clerical work done by second-generation Portuguese women as compared to the lower prestige (but sometimes higher paying) janitorial work done by their first-generation mothers.

11. In the Portuguese and Vietnamese communities, high levels of education command respect. A survey of ethnic groups conducted in Toronto found that three-quarters of Portuguese respondents agreed that education was one of the

two most important characteristics of a leader (Breton 1991). Education also provides skills for effective leadership, what Morris and Staggenborg (2003) label the "science of human action," including the creative manipulation of language and improvisation of political strategies and tactics. Every community leader I interviewed had completed at least a high school education, and most held a university degree, a level of schooling far above the average for their communities. The disjuncture between the characteristics and background of leaders and followers is not restricted to immigrant communities and appears whether we consider electoral politics, social movements, or even revolutionary activities (Verba, Schlozman, and Brady 1995; Ganz 2000; Morris and Staggenborg 2003; Wickham-Crowley 1992).

12. Portugal possessed a number of colonies in Africa, notably Angola and Mozambique. A significant community of Portuguese-born individuals lived and worked in these colonies, but most left following decolonization. Such was the case for Agostinho.

13. Differences in American and Canadian government administration come into play here. In the United States, top public officials are often political appointees, making politics an integral part of some public sector jobs. In Canada, with its tradition of an independent civil service, I heard almost no stories of political recruiting from the public service sector.

14. Dusenberry (1981) notes, for example, that the individuals instrumental in the creation of the pan-ethnic National Association of Canadians of Origins in India, an ethno-political advocacy group, had prior experience dealing with Canadian government through private or governmental employment and/or leadership in Sikh/Punjabi community organizations.

15. Marco Martiniello (1993) makes a useful distinction between ethnic elites and ethnic leaders. Elites achieve success—whether economic, political, cultural, or in some other domain—to a greater degree than the community average. Leaders exert some degree of influence on members of the community with the aim of pursuing certain community interests.

16. The Vietnamese hold those in positions of authority in high regard, but a similar though more subtle problem can arise. Those who founded and initially ran important Vietnamese community organizations often occupied high-status positions in Vietnam as doctors, engineers, lawyers, government officials, and senior military officers. Some community members, especially more recent arrivals and those of more modest backgrounds, express resentment toward these self-appointed spokespeople. At its most benign, individuals with less schooling who come from farming or fishing backgrounds perceive an almost insurmountable status gap between themselves and these elites. A less benign form of resentment, rarely expressed openly, stems from divergent experiences following South Vietnam's fall. For those who were unable to leave Vietnam in 1975, leadership by individuals who got out (often using money and connections) and who never experienced reeducation camps or economic destitution under the communists generates bitterness and hostility. Such antipathy can be exacerbated when someone of modest origins achieves a measure of success in

North America but remains shut out of elite circles because of his or her family background.

17. Civic and political skills can be learned in school, from family, or through participation in voluntary associations or other community institutions, but if we consider key civic skills that can be transferred into the political system, we find that the workplace is a primary institution, allowing individuals to practice and perfect such skills. Using indicators such as writing a letter, attending a meeting where decisions are made, organizing such a meeting, or giving a presentation or speech, Verba, Schlozman, and Brady found that twice as many of those employed engaged in such activities as compared to those who participated in nonpolitical organizations or attended a religious institution (1995: 312). See also Burns, Schlozman, and Verba (2001).

18. There is a larger, mostly anthropological literature on middlemen minorities under colonialism. In these cases, the colonial power selects a certain minority group for special privileges, such as filling local government positions. Through this strategy, Europeans were able to divide the subject population and direct anger over colonial administration away from themselves and toward another ethnic group.

19. Jerome Black suggests that this route might be particularly important for women. Based on interviews with Canadian members of Parliament, he notes "the greater importance for minority women of organizational work and office-holding at the community level. . . . There is at least a first-blush sense from the evidence that their access experiences . . . relied more on active community involvement and formal positions as stepping stones towards parliamentary office" (1997: 22).

20. Success can be measured in a variety of ways, from merely having one's voice heard to substantially shaping a particular government policy (Andrews 2001). I concentrate on the ability of immigrants to win elected office at all levels of government, from school boards to federal legislature.

21. See chapter 2 for a detailed discussion of these barriers.

22. I concentrate on these two decades since the bulk of my interview material comes from people active during this period and because it appears to be the turning point in Portuguese Canadians' political fortunes. In Toronto in the 1950s and '60s, the Portuguese were a new immigrant group and did not participate actively in Canadian politics. The exceptions to this were a few prominent individuals—mostly real estate brokers, travel agents, and a few priests—who established links to local political parties and became, in the words of one informant, "political brokers and political interpreters." (See also Brettell 1977.) In the late 1960s and 1970s there was a nascent movement to run Portuguese electoral candidates, but these campaigns invariably ended in failure.

23. Mario Silva is the first Portuguese-born person to serve in federal Parliament. Some members of the community point to John Rodriguez, an MP from 1972 to 1980 and 1984 to 1993 for the riding of Nickle Belt, Ontario, as the first MP of Portuguese ethnicity. Rodriguez was born in Georgetown, Guyana. The two MPPs, Carl DeFaria and Peter Fonesca, were elected in the riding of

Mississauga East, just east of Toronto proper. As the Portuguese move to the suburbs, many find homes in Mississauga (Teixeira 1999). Portuguese is the third most spoken non-English language in Mississauga East. As reflected in table 8, school board elections in Toronto are held for the English Public School Board, the English Separate (Catholic) School Board, the French Public School Board, and the French Separate (Catholic) School Board. The right of French and Catholic minorities to their own schools is enshrined in the Canadian Constitution. Unlike in the United States, Catholic schools receive public funding. They are consequently held accountable to the public through elections run by the city of Toronto.

24. The one exception is Christine Ferreira, a second-generation Portuguese Canadian elected to the Public School Board in November 1997.

25. These figures refer to the new city of Toronto, roughly the old metropolitan Toronto area. Before amalgamation, there was one Portuguese Canadian on the Toronto City Council and one on the Metropolitan Toronto Council.

26. One Portuguese immigrant, Antonio Cabral, sits in the Massachusetts State House, representing an area of New Bedford estimated to be about 50–60 percent Portuguese. A few other state representatives and senators claim some Portuguese ancestry but do not speak Portuguese; all are from southeastern Massachusetts. In the post–World War II period, no one of Portuguese origin has been elected to federal office from Massachusetts, although prior to World War II a number of U.S.-born individuals of Portuguese heritage represented Massachusetts in the U.S. Congress (Pap 1981). At the national level, former senator Ben Nighthorse Campbell (1993–2005) claims partial Portuguese ancestry through his Portuguese-born mother. In California there are a few representatives with some Portuguese ancestry. The longest serving is Representative Richard Pombo, a fourth-generation Portuguese American first elected in 1992. Significantly, none are foreign born.

27. These figures refer to first ancestry reported and are from the 1990 census, the midway point for the period under consideration (1980–2000). The 2000 census shows a slight decline in the percent Portuguese in the two cities: just over 3 percent in Cambridge and 7.5 percent in Somerville. The proportion of an ethnic group in a district or riding generally but imperfectly correlates with electoral success (Pelletier 1991).

28. *British origin* includes those reporting English, Scottish, and Irish heritage. They are often not considered an ethnic community, given their traditional dominance, but it is useful to distinguish those of British origins as an ethnic group separate from other communities. *Black* is the term used by Siemiatycki and Isin. Most black politicians in the Toronto area, at all levels of government, are Afro-Caribbean. Those of Jewish background can come from many different countries, but I follow Siemiatycki and Isin's separate categorization.

29. These figures are the proportion of each ethnicity among single ancestry responses. If we include multiple ancestry responses—of which British origins figure prominently—the percentage of the Toronto city population with

some British roots increases to 33 percent. The percentage of Italians stays about the same at 8 percent, and the percentage of Chinese rises to 11 percent.

30. Figures are from the 2000 U.S. census. The race statistics exclude those of multiple racial backgrounds.

31. Almost a quarter of the Asian American population is Vietnamese. The first Latino to ever serve on Boston City Council, Felix Arroyo, took his seat in January 2003. Arroyo was born in Puerto Rico and moved to Boston as a young man to attend college. The first Asian American elected to city council, Sam Yoon, took his seat in January 2006. Yoon was born in South Korea but moved to the United States when he was just ten months old.

32. In 2003 one person with a Vietnamese last name ran unsuccessfully for Toronto Municipal Council, Nha Le. Le was apparently born in Vietnam but appears to be of Chinese ethnicity. Le received a meager 234 of 11,250 votes.

33. I come to these conclusions after extensive interviews with key community leaders. It is possible, however, that there are additional people of Vietnamese origin, unknown to these leaders, who are active in party politics. Interviews by Simard in 1990–91 with Vietnamese community leaders in Montreal and Toronto similarly found little interest in party politics (Simard 1991: 221). In contrast, Vietnamese Canadians have had successful runs for provincial office in Alberta. Given the larger Toronto community, the difference in political interest and success demands further study.

34. He had a brief show from 1972 to 1973.

35. Members of the New Democratic, Liberal, and Conservative Parties discussed ways to reduce vote splitting—the tactic of running a candidate with a Portuguese name merely to siphon off votes from an opposing party—in order to help a Portuguese Canadian get elected.

36. This pattern was also evident among some Portuguese Canadian activists. In the words of one: "I joke around with friends sometimes that the only reason we started [the association] was to meet girls, but it's true. On a certain level it's true. It's because we wanted to have people, to be around people to whom we did not have to explain what our home life was like. That's the important thing about belonging to an ethnic enclave. You don't have to explain to these people what you are like at home."

37. There are some exceptions to local control of party nominations. In some parties, such as the Liberal Party, the national leader can "parachute in" a candidate of his or her choice for a federal election. The practice is quite unpopular at the local level but defended as a way of increasing diversity in the candidate pool. Black (1997) notes that in the 1993 Canadian parliamentary elections, three of the eleven female MPs who came from an ethno-racial minority background had been appointed as a candidate by the leader of the federal Liberal Party, Jean Chrétien.

38. Unlike in the United States, Canadian electors are not asked to register a party affiliation when put on a voting roll. Would-be party members must apply separately and pay a small fee, which means that joining requires more effort in

Canada than it does in the United States. The pool of "registered" party members is consequently much smaller in Canada than in the United States.

39. Although it can also, according to various respondents, make such nomination battles particularly nasty affairs, with some question about the legality of various mobilization techniques.

40. A corollary to greater electoral uncertainty in Toronto is that incumbency appears to hold less power than in the Boston area. Frequent political turnover increases the chance that a newcomer can make a successful bid for political office.

41. Candidates for the Toronto council are, for example, not allowed to accept campaign contributions from federal or provincial party committees (Watkiss 2002). This is a stricter requirement than in Massachusetts, where a party's state committee may donate up to $3,000 and a city or ward committee can donate up to $1,000 (Office of Campaign and Political Finance 2001).

42. As in Toronto, partisanship did not have to be formalized on the ballot but did need to involve the selection of a party ticket. More generally, Pelletier (1991) argues that partisan support is the most decisive factor in explaining the success or failure of ethnic minorities in the 1988 Canadian federal election.

43. Somerville and Boston do not use proportional representation, but the Boston City Council contains a mix of local district and at-large representatives.

44. On the system and its history, see http://www.cambridgema.gov./Election/prop-voting.html (last accessed January 5, 2006).

45. For Mario Silva, a 1.5-generation Portuguese Canadian who represented a heavily Portuguese downtown ward in 2003, this funding formula worked out to a spending limit of about $25,000–30,000.

46. In 1998 Massachusetts voters approved a Clean Elections Act that allows candidates to voluntary accept a spending limit in return for public monies. Few candidates have run under the act, and it is the subject of considerable controversy.

47. These figures come from reports on file at the Cambridge Election Commission. Candidates for Cambridge City Council are required to maintain special accounts that are reported directly to the state's Office of Campaign and Political Finance. Reports are not always forwarded to local election officials, so this number could be higher.

48. DeFaria is a lawyer with a private practice, and Pedro was a successful real estate agent before she moved into television.

49. Interestingly, a number of those who failed in their bid for office probably possess much greater wealth than people like Martin Silva and Mario Silva. Unsuccessful candidates include the owners of prosperous insurance, travel, and real estate agencies.

50. Beyond the initial flow of Loyalists, I am not entirely convinced that Lipset's observation about historical migration is accurate either, but it is worth further investigation.

51. Swift and sometimes deadly opposition meets support for communism. In the 1980s and into the '90s, up to a dozen Vietnamese were murdered or dis-

appeared mysteriously due to their political views, mostly in Southern California (Zhou and Bankston 1998: 64–65).

52. The 2000–01 Pilot Study used a different question wording and found a much higher percentage of people unwilling to declare a party affiliation (Lien et al. 2001). Fifteen percent reported being Republican, 12 percent Democrat, and 46 percent answered Independent or no party affiliation. Another 27 percent said they were "unsure" about their party preference.

53. In Massachusetts, the state Democratic convention reserves some delegate spots for minorities in order to encourage their involvement. The state Republican Party has no comparable policy but is sensitive to increasing the presence of minority delegates, according to a number of Vietnamese American respondents.

54. For a small group of Vietnamese, disinterest in U.S. politics stems from an overriding concern about homeland politics. In the words of one journalist, "Most of us, we leave the country for here because we didn't agree with the government back home. We are more or less not interested in [U.S.] politics." A larger group blames the horrors of war and flight on "politics"; they consequently avoid political activities.

55. By 2000 the situation seemed to changing slightly. Neither party appeared extremely active, but various grassroots initiatives to get people registered and interested in voting occurred in Dorchester. At least two Vietnamese organizations took part in such voting campaigns, one on its own initiative and one in conjunction with a campaign organized by the city of Boston's Office of New Bostonians. Some also suggest that Sam Yoon's successful bid for a city council seat in 2005 was aided by increased voting among Vietnamese and Chinese Americans (Michael Jonas, "In Yoon Win, a Show of Unity," *Boston Globe,* January 1, 2006, p. 8). Yoon is the first Asian American to be elected to Boston City Council. Conversely, the U.S. Department of Justice launched a lawsuit against the city of Boston on July 29, 2005, alleging that the city has infringed the rights of Hispanics and Asian Americans by failing to provide adequate translation services (Yvonne Abraham, "Justice Dept. Accuses City of Voting Rights Violations," *Boston Globe,* July 30, 2005, A1).

56. This has also increasingly been the discourse used in the United States, starting in the 1990s. As one Vietnamese American put it, "back in the early '80's or mid-80s, the term *human rights* wasn't there yet. Because Vietnam [was] still pretty much a communist country and people [were] still trying to get out and then coming here in that way. Human rights is more of the '90s."

57. Some younger community members are attracted to the social democratic NDP, while in western Canada the Conservative Party has attracted some politically active Vietnamese Canadians.

58. The engagement by non-Vietnamese Americans in the Vietnam War provides additional bridges of political contact that are missing in Canada. For example, in the yearly April 30 commemoration of Saigon's fall held before Boston City Hall and the Massachusetts State House, non-Vietnamese representatives from U.S. veterans' associations come to show their support for the South Vietnamese cause.

59. As Black and Lakhani (1997) document, following the 1993 federal election, the percentage of non-British, non-French members of Parliament was highest among the New Democratic and (right of center) Reform Parties, but this was mostly due to the participation of European-origin ethnics and immigrants. Of the thirteen visible minorities elected to office, who were of Armenian, black/Caribbean, Chinese, Filipino, Lebanese, and South Asian origins, twelve were elected under the Liberal banner. (In Canada those from the Middle East are considered an ethno-racial minority. Among those from South America, people from Argentina and Chile are not considered visible minorities according to Statistics Canada definitions. One MP in the 35th Parliament was Chilean Canadian. Others from South America are counted as visible.)

60. The idea of making one's fortune was especially strong during the dictatorship. Since 1974 Portugal's economic situation has steadily improved, especially after Portugal's entry into the European Union in 1986.

61. In metro Boston, relatives sponsored the families of ten of thirteen community leaders, two arrived on work visas or had fathers holding a work visa, and a third was the child of parents who migrated before the United States established visa requirements. Of the eighteen community leaders I interviewed in Toronto, the families of ten were sponsored, four came through the independent class, three were illegal immigrants who later legalized their situation, and one man's father arrived on a work visa.

62. Two others who labeled themselves as political migrants are ethnic Portuguese who spent most of their lives in Portugal's African colonies. They left Africa after the colonies gained independence and eventually moved to Canada. They came to Canada with conservative political instincts. As one explained, "I think it's . . . that when we came, we had the feeling of being left [behind]. Like, for me, the Tories would be the ones that would give you that protection if you were afraid." One remains affiliated with the political Right; the other has become centrist.

63. This perception has some basis in reality. In the United States, an individual must formally declare past communist affiliation on applications for permanent residency and citizenship. Past membership in the Communist Party constitutes grounds upon which American officials can refuse to grant U.S. citizenship. There is no similar question on Canadian citizenship forms.

64. These people were largely outside the traditional power structures of the Portuguese Canadian community. According to Anderson and Higgs, the majority of Portuguese community leaders in the late 1960s and early 1970s, especially the most economically successful, "either favoured or were not openly hostile to the Lisbon government." The left-wing dissidents fell "outside this somewhat traditional hierarchy," constituting a "generally younger group of community leaders, some of whom were acknowledged opponents of the Portuguese government prior to 1974 and some who see themselves as . . . more modern and progressive in their outlook" (1976: 170, 154).

65. For example, an important if controversial community leader, Father Cunha, has repeatedly attacked those perceived to be communist sympathizers

in his writings and speeches. In the words of one left-wing dissident, Cunha "see[s] communists under his bed."

66. The Democratic Association has moderated its politics, although it remains a meeting place for left-wing activists. The group also sponsors various intellectual events, occasionally bringing in a writer, politician, or artist from Portugal.

67. In California, more Portuguese appear to support the Republican Party than in Massachusetts.

68. See chapters 3 and 4 for a fuller discussion of these dynamics.

69. Despite Canadians' perception of their greater multicultural sensitivity, the formal guarantees of the U.S. Voting Rights Act go further than anything found in the Canadian Elections Act. Under the Voting Rights Act, the city of Los Angeles provided election information in Spanish, Tagalog, Vietnamese, Chinese, Japanese, and Korean in 2002. In comparison, the Canadian city with the most immigrants, Toronto, does not guarantee multilingual staff, although it does make informal efforts to have assistance on hand. Municipal elections are governed by the Ontario Municipal Elections Act and Regulations, which states that ballots and election materials are in English only, except for elections to the French School Board or where a municipality has passed a bylaw providing other linguistic services. Electors who face language difficulties are encouraged to bring an interpreter. This person, once sworn in, can translate for the voter.

70. Just as a political district or riding contains a diversity of opinion and interests, so does the immigrant community. It is consequently somewhat misleading to talk about the preferences of the community as a whole. However, the solution to the first problem also serves to answer the second: liberal democracy demands that the desire of the majority is followed, with protection and support for the needs of minorities.

71. A study of Portuguese Americans in southeastern Massachusetts found a similar disjuncture. Only 20 percent of those surveyed felt strongly that being of the same ethnicity made a difference in an elected official's ability to represent a particular group, yet 70 percent reported the need for a particularized or parochial contact when dealing with government (Barrow 2002). Among Vietnamese respondents in the Pilot Study of the National Asian American Political Survey (Lien et al. 2001), 75 percent said that they would vote for an Asian American candidate if presented with two candidates of equal ability, compared to a survey average of 60 percent. If the Asian American candidate were less qualified, only 10 percent would prefer this individual, compared to a survey average of 24 percent.

72. In the 1980s Toronto newspapers carried a series of articles reporting on the efforts by ethnic minorities, from Portuguese to Sikhs, to capture party nominations for federal office by signing up hundreds of fellow ethnics—some of whom lacked Canadian citizenship, since this status is not required for party membership—as "instant" party members shortly before riding association elections (Stasiulis and Abu-Laban 1991).

73. The problem of tokenism might be particularly acute for immigrant women since, in politics, they are a double minority. They might not only be rel-

egated to "ethnic" portfolios but also to those focused on gender issues; placing a minority woman in such a post is attractive to decision makers since it deals with two minority issues at once. Political success, once in office, might also be discounted on the same grounds—advances are due to demographic attributes, not hard work or merit. Such charges can come from majority colleagues or male politicians from the same minority community (Black 1997).

74. Siemiatycki and Isin reached the same conclusion after interviewing minority community leaders in Toronto, although they raise questions about the link between ethno-cultural representation and tangible returns (1997: 96).

75. There are a few other legislators with some Portuguese ancestry, but Cabral is the only immigrant. He represents the Thirteenth Bristol District, a heavily Portuguese district in New Bedford.

76. Scholarly research supports this belief in the case of women (Bashevkin 1993).

77. When elected officials are not of the same ethnic group, individuals try to draw similarities, sometimes in imaginative ways. Thus, the Portuguese American who supports Tim Toomey in Cambridge notes that Toomey has been to Portugal, while the Kennedy family "has been very close to the Portuguese family for a long, long time. Just because they are, and because of their direct linkage in Cape Cod and southeastern Massachusetts," where so many Portuguese Americans live. Similarly, other Portuguese Americans told me about their special connection with John Kerry, the state's junior senator, due to the Portuguese ancestry of his wife, Teresa Heinz. Heinz was born Teresa Simões-Ferreira in Portuguese-controlled Mozambique.

78. Indeed, while the American political machines of the nineteenth and early twentieth century were widely criticized as corrupt, they have also been lauded as providing an entry for immigrant newcomers, or at least for certain groups of newcomers such as the Irish (Merton 1957; Erie 1988).

79. Desire to serve as a role model also leads some ethnic minorities in Toronto to run for a party's "unwinnable seats," that is, those ridings where the party has historically done very poorly (Stasiulis and Abu-Laban 1991: 22).

80. DeFaria was also the minister of citizenship at the time he first inaugurated Portuguese History and Heritage Month in June 2002.

81. The most striking exception to this general tendency has been the experience of Cubans in Florida (Moreno 1996). Canadian parties still have a way to go, as they have a history of cultural and organizational exclusion that hinders equitable representation (Stasiulis and Abu-Laban 1991), but the upsurge is marked (Black and Lakhani 1997; Black 2000; Canada. Royal Commission on Bilingualism and Biculturalism 1970; Pelletier 1991).

CONCLUSION

1. See recent articles by Brubaker (2001) and Joppke (2004) as well as the winter 2005 issue of *Canadian Diversity,* entitled *Multicultural Futures? International Approaches to Pluralism.*

2. This model can also be found in Alba and Nee's (2003) recent conceptualization of social and economic assimilation in the United States. While they argue that government has a role to play in the integration process, that role is largely restricted to passing antidiscrimination legislation and upholding equal rights.

3. In 1964, before Canada had its Charter of Rights and Freedoms, which includes a section on multiculturalism (Section 27), the Canadian Supreme Court ruled in *Robertson v. Regina* that forced Sunday closing was not an infringement of freedom of religion since the goal of the legislation was secular, and thus it did not take away from someone's right to have his or her own religious beliefs. In 1985, under the new charter, the Supreme Court struck down the Lord's Day Act in the landmark case *Regina v. Big Drug Mart Ltd.* It was the first major decision in which the Supreme Court referred to Section 27 of the Charter of Rights and Freedoms. Explicitly stating that one must look to both the purpose and the effect of legislation, the court found that freedom of belief was not sufficient in assuring freedom of religion. The absence of constraint must also be taken into account, especially where that constraint is based on religious views not held by all. This decision sent a signal down the entire court system that religious rights were to be upheld in a much more generous manner than had previously been the case. Multiculturalism did not, however, help a similar case heard before the court a year later. The legislation in question, the Ontario Retail Business Holidays Act, did not make explicit mention of religion and allowed small businesses to open on Sunday if they were closed another day. The court upheld the law for large businesses in *Regina v. Edwards Books and Art Ltd.*

4. Multicultural theorists identify various groups worthy of special recognition. Kymlicka distinguishes between national minorities—previously self-governing, territorially concentrated communities such as indigenous peoples, the Quebecois, or Catalans—and ethnic groups created from migration (1995). Kymlicka thus rejects the inclusion of marginalized groups such as women and gays/lesbians in the definition of multiculturalism, a practice more common in the United States (cf. Young 1990). He notes that the case of African Americans is particularly difficult given forced migration through slavery and the lack of territorial concentration.

5. Key texts in the debate between proponents and opponents of multiculturalism include Young (1990), Taylor (1994), Kymlicka (1995, 2001), Barry (2001), and Parekh (2002).

6. The United States and Canada never had a cohesive ethnic core around which to build nationalism. According to the first federal U.S. census of 1790, more than two out of five whites in the United States were of non-English background, and the English were a minority in all the colonies south of New England (McDonald and McDonald 1980). Further north, the 1763 Treaty of Paris ensured that the British colonies, which would come together to form the Canadian confederation, would unite two distinct cultural and religious groups, those with British Protestant roots and those with French Catholic origins. Even

in the case of European nations, the research on nationalism suggests that elite cultures, the national media, and state institutions such as schools and the army were needed to impose a sense of ethnic nationalism on diverse populations (Gellner 1983; Anderson 1991; Weber 1976). The concern that multiculturalism undermines a shared national core certainly romanticizes past bonds of community.

7. This list is not exhaustive, but it captures the central critiques of the disunity argument.

8. Thus Richard Gwyn argues, "It cannot be coincidence that the higher the various cultural walls have gone up inside Canada, the stronger popular resistance to paying taxes has become" (1995: 8). In the United States, see especially Gitlin (1995) and also Hollinger (2000: 201–202) and Barry (2001).

9. Bissoondath's use of the term *ghetto* refers more to a bounded, self-enclosed group than the usual American use of the term, which refers to an inner city neighborhood of severe poverty and (usually) minority segregation.

10. To my knowledge, there is no comparative empirical research measuring the effect of multiculturalism policies on concrete indicators of integration such as those listed. My sense, however, is that multiculturalism might help with some and, at worst, be neutral toward others.

11. The other six areas are explanation/celebration of multiculturalism in school curricula; ethnic representation in public media or licensing; cultural exemptions from public regulations or laws, for example, regarding dress code or Sunday-closing legislation; acceptance of dual citizenship; funding of ethnic cultural activities; and affirmative action for disadvantaged immigrant groups.

12. Thus, Hollinger advocates that "ethno-racial cultures ought to look after themselves much the way religious cultures have been expected to do [in the United States]. Both are sustained by voluntary affiliations. The products of both are to be welcomed as contributions to the richness of the nation's cultural life and thus as part of the environment for its politics. But both partake more of the private than the public sphere, and neither is to be the beneficiary of outright public subsidies" (2000: 124).

13. It is this sense of "other" that drives even Canadian immigrants in the United States to feel nationalistic bonds with other Canadians. In this case, the civic nationalism of Canada—like that of the United States—becomes ethnic in feeling following migration. Fellow Canadians comment on linguistic differences in the two countries' use and spelling of English; the availability of specific food products, such as Smarties; and the puzzling designation of Canadian universal healthcare as socialized medicine. While in a certain sense it seems ridiculous to call this Canadian ethnicity, there is a sense of cultural community. The fact that this occurs for a group so similar to the residents of the host country underscores the powerful ethnicizing force of migration.

14. These lessons might also be transferable to those born in North America. An important theme running throughout this book is the role government can play in helping communities build their own organizational capacity and internal leadership. Such communities do not need to be defined by ethnicity or

race. We know that those who are economically disadvantaged are less likely to participate politically. Low-income communities usually have limited internal resources, so they would derive particular benefits from external support. Such groups also need to feel valued and to believe that they have standing in the polity as citizens with the right and responsibility to participate.

15. Both of the groups I studied are, on average, resource poor. Government policies probably help such groups the most, providing seed monies and encouragement where personal resources are lacking. However, the opposite possibility also deserves consideration: communities and individuals that already possess political skills and interests might be best poised to take advantage of public support. The relationship between internal resources and external assistance could also be curvilinear, affecting the most and least endowed communities less while serving as an important catalyst to groups with internal potential but which face some obstacles to political incorporation. All of these scenarios demand further comparative research.

16. I do not want to downplay class dynamics in ethnic communities or ethnic organizations since these clearly exist. However, if Skocpol (2003) is right that American associational life is increasingly stratified by professional status, organizing around shared origins attenuates this tendency. On parties' failure to reach out to immigrants, see Jones-Correa (1998a), Wong (2006), and DeSipio (2001).

17. In contrast, European Canadians' relations with native peoples can be compared to colonialism and to American treatment of indigenous populations.

18. Countries usually have nationally specific discourses on immigrant integration, and jurisdictions tend to borrow or imitate policies across regions and cities. For example, work by Koopmans (2004) shows that migrant mobilization in British, Dutch, and German cities cluster together in distinct national patterns: greater migrant mobilization in the United Kingdom, moderate mobilization in the Netherlands, and relatively limited mobilization in Germany. This raises questions about the tendency among some students of European immigration to compare cities rather than countries.

19. See, for example, Waters (1999) and Bean and Stevens (2003).

20. This might be difficult for the descendants of black immigrants in the United States but is conceivable for immigrants from Asia and Latin America. Some suggest a parallel with the experiences of earlier European migrants (Foner 2000). It would probably have been inconceivable for those of the Italian and Slavic "races" in late-nineteenth-century America to envision that their descendants a hundred years later could voluntarily celebrate—or ignore—ethnic markers with little consequence for their lives (Alba 1990; Waters 1990).

21. See Keyssar (2000) and Raskin (1993).

22. For example, see Gosnell (1928), Gavit (1922), and the U.S. Commission on Naturalization (1905).

23. On political parties, see Erie (1988). See Sterne (2001) on religious and civic institutions.

24. See Foner (1997), Glazer (1997), and Gleason (2001). The events of Sep-

tember 11, 2001, have changed this dynamic somewhat, placing increased pressure on immigrants to display their loyalty and patriotism to the United States. It is unclear whether this trend is transitory or will usher in a new period of pressure for political integration

25. On the legal decoupling of rights and citizenship in the United States, see Carliner and colleagues (1977) and Plascencia, Freeman, and Setzler (2003).

26. See http://uscis.gov/graphics/citizenship/officeofcitizenship.pdf, last accessed April 19, 2006.

27. In President Bush's budget proposal for the 2007 fiscal year, the president requested about $6.5 billion for Customs and Border Protection and $4.4 billion for Immigration and Customs Enforcement. These are the two agencies primarily responsible for border security. At those levels, the budget for Customs and Border Protection would increase by 12 percent and ICE's budget would increase by 22 percent over fiscal 2006 funding enacted by Congress (Chris Strohm, "DHS Budget Emphasizes Immigration Reform, Border Security," *GovExec.com*, February 6, 2006, http://www.govexec.com/story_page .cfm?articleid=33312&dcn=e_gvet [last accessed February 8, 2006]). Congress might well change these allocations, but they symbolize the strong message that the Bush White House wants to send about the importance of border enforcement.

References

Abella, Irving, and Harold Troper. 1983. *None Is Too Many: Canada and the Jews of Europe, 1933–1948*. Toronto: Lester & Orphen Dennys.

Abu-Laban, Yasmeen. 1994. "The Politics of Race and Ethnicity: Multiculturalism as a Contested Arena." Pages 242–63 in *Canadian Politics*, 2nd ed., ed. James P. Bickerton and Alain-G. Gagnon. Peterborough, ON: Broadview Press.

———, and Daiva K. Stasiulis. 1992. "Ethnic Pluralism under Siege: Popular and Partisan Opposition to Multiculturalism." *Canadian Public Policy* 18 (4): 365–86.

Adelman, Howard. 1991. "Canadian Refugee Policy in the Postwar Period." Pages 172–223 in *Refugee Policy: Canada and the United States*, ed. Howard Adelman. Toronto: York Lanes Press.

Aguilar–San Juan, Karin. 1998. "Gazing/Colonial: Looking at the Vietnamese American Community in Boston and Orange County." *Critical Mass: A Journal of Asian American Culture* 5: 89–106.

———. 2005. "Staying Vietnamese: Community and Place in Orange County and Boston." *City and Community* 4 (1): 37–65.

Alba, Richard. 1990. *Ethnic Identity: The Transformation of White America*. New Haven, CT: Yale University Press.

———, and Victor Nee. 2003. *Remaking the American Mainstream: Assimilation and Contemporary Immigration*. Cambridge, MA: Harvard University Press.

Aleinikoff, T. Alexander. 1998. *Between Principles and Politics: The Direction of U.S. Citizenship Policy*. Washington, D.C.: Carnegie Endowment for International Peace.

Almeida, Onésimo T. 1999. "The Portuguese-American Communities and Politics—A Look at the Cultural Roots of a Distant Relationship." *Gavea-Brown: A Bilingual Journal of Portuguese-American Letters and Studies* 19–20: 229–43.

———. 2000. "Value Conflicts and Cultural Adjustments in North America."

Pages 112–24 in *The Portuguese in Canada: From the Sea to the City*, ed. Carlos Teixeira and Victor M. P. da Rosa. Toronto: University of Toronto.

Alpalhão, J. A., and Victor M. P. da Rosa. 1980. *A Minority in a Changing Society: The Portuguese Communities of Quebec*. Ottawa: University of Ottawa Press.

Alvarez, Robert R. 1987. "A Profile of the Citizenship Process among Hispanics in the United States." *International Migration Review* 21 (2): 327–51.

Anderson, Benedict. 1991. *Imagined Communities: Reflections on the Origins and Spread of Nationalism*. London: Verso.

Anderson, Grace M. 1974. *Networks of Contact: The Portuguese in Toronto*. Waterloo, ON: Wilfred Laurier University Press.

———. 1983. "Azoreans in Anglophone Canada." *Canadian Ethnic Studies* 15 (1): 73–82.

———, and David Higgs. 1976. *A Future to Inherit: The Portuguese Communities of Canada*. Toronto: McCelland and Stewart.

Andreas, Peter. 2000. *Border Games: Policing the U.S.-Mexican Divide*. Ithaca, NY: Cornell University Press.

Andrews, Kenneth T. 2001. "Social Movements and Policy Implementation: The Mississippi Civil Rights Movement and the War on Poverty, 1965 to 1971." *American Sociological Review* 66 (1): 71–95.

Andrieux, Jean-Pierre. 2000. "Portuguese Fishermen in Newfoundland." Pages 53–67 in *The Portuguese in Canada*, ed. Carlos Teixeira and Victor M. P. da Rosa. Toronto: University of Toronto Press.

Angus, H. F. 1937. "The Legal Status in British Columbia of Residents of Oriental Race and Their Descendants." Pages 58–72 in *The Legal Status of Aliens in Pacific Countries*, ed. Norman MacKenzie. London: Oxford University Press.

Aubry, Jack. 2002. "Government Can't Win on Immigration." *National Post*, June 24, A4.

Auditor General of Canada. 1990. *1990 Report of the Auditor General of Canada*. Ottawa: Minister of Supply and Services Canada.

Aylsworth, Leon E. 1931. "The Passing of Alien Suffrage." *American Political Science Review* 25 (1): 114–16.

Baganha, Maria Ioannis Benis. 1990. *Portuguese Emigration to the United States, 1820–1930*. New York: Garland Press.

———. 1991. "The Social Mobility of Portuguese Immigrants in the United States at the Turn of the Nineteenth Century." *International Migration Review* 25 (2): 277–302.

Bankston, Carl L., III, and Min Zhou. 2000. "De Facto Congregationalism and Socioeconomic Mobility in Laotian and Vietnamese Immigrant Communities: A Study of Religious Institutions and Economic Change." *Review of Religious Research* 41 (4): 453–70.

Banting, Keith, and Will Kymlicka. 2005. "Multiculturalism and the Welfare State: An Emering Debate." *Canadian Diversity* 4, no. 1 (Winter): 103–106.

Barkan, Elliott Robert, and Nikolai Khokhlov. 1980. "Socioeconomic Data as

Indices of Naturalization Patterns in the United States: A Theory Revisited." *Ethnicity* 7: 159–90.

Barnett, Don. 1999. *Show Me the Money: How Government Funding Has Corrupted Refugee Resettlement*. Brief in Backgrounder Series. Washington, D.C.: Center for Immigration Studies.

Barrow, Clyde W., ed. 2002. *Portuguese-Americans and Contemporary Civic Culture in Massachusetts*. North Dartmouth: Center for Portuguese Studies and Culture and the Center for Policy Analysis, University of Massachusetts, Dartmouth.

Barry, Brian. 2001. *Culture and Equality: An Egalitarian Critique of Multiculturalism*. Cambridge, MA: Harvard University Press.

Basch, Linda, Nina Glick Schiller, and Cristina Szanton Blanc. 1994. *Nations Unbound: Transnational Projects, Postcolonial Predicaments and Deterritorialized Nation-States*. Langhorne, PA: Gordon and Breach.

Bashevkin, Sylvia B. 1993. *Toeing the Lines: Women and Party Politics in English Canada*. 2nd ed. Toronto: Oxford University Press.

Bass, Bernard M. 1990. *Bass and Stogdil's Handbook of Leadership: Theory, Research, and Managerial Applications*. 3rd ed. New York: Free Press.

Bauböck, Rainer. 1994. *Transnational Citizenship: Membership and Rights in International Migration*. Aldershot, England: Edward Elgar.

———. 2005. "If You Say Multiculturalism Is the Wrong Answer, Then What Was the Question You Asked?" *Canadian Diversity* 4, no. 1 (Winter): 90–93.

Bean, Frank D., and Gillian Stevens. 2003. *America's Newcomers and the Dynamics of Diversity*. New York: Russell Sage Foundation.

Benford, Robert D., and David A. Snow. 2000. "Framing Processes and Social Movements: An Overview and Assessment." *Annual Review of Sociology* 26: 611–39.

Berry, Jeffrey M. 2003. *A Voice for Nonprofits*. Washington, D.C.: Brookings Institution.

Biles, John. 1997. "It Is All a Matter of Priority: Multiculturalism under Mulroney (1984–1988)." Master's degree research essay, School of Canadian Studies, Carleton University.

Bissoondath, Neil. 1993. "A Question of Belonging: Multiculturalism and Citizenship." Pages 368–87 in *Belonging: The Meaning and Future of Canadian Citizenship*, ed. William Kaplan. Montreal: McGill-Queen's University Press.

———. 1994. *Selling Illusions: The Cult of Multiculturalism in Canada*. Toronto: Penguin.

Black, Jerome H. 1987. "The Practice of Politics in Two Settings: Political Transferability among Recent Immigrants to Canada." *Canadian Journal of Political Science* 20 (4): 731–53.

———. 1997. "Minority Women in the 35th Parliament." *Canadian Parliamentary Review* (Spring): 17–22.

———. 2000. "Ethnoracial Minorities in the Canadian House of Commons: The Case of the 36th Parliament." *Canadian Ethnic Studies* 32 (2): 105–14.

———, and Aleem Lakhani. 1997. "Ethnoracial Diversity in the House of Com-

mons: An Analysis of Numerical Representation in the 35th Parliament."
Canadian Ethnic Studies 29 (1): 1–21.

———, and Christian Leithner. 1988. "Immigrants and Political Involvement in
Canada: The Role of the Ethnic Media." *Canadian Ethnic Studies* 20 (1): 1–
20.

Black, Richard. 1993. "Migration, Return, and Agricultural Development in the
Serra Do Alvão, Northern Portugal." *Economic Development and Cultural
Change* 41 (3): 563–85.

Bloemraad, Irene. 2000. "Citizenship and Immigration: A Current Review."
Journal of International Migration and Integration 1 (1): 9–37.

———. 2002. "The North American Naturalization Gap: An Institutional
Approach to Citizenship Acquisition in the United States and Canada." *International Migration Review* 36 (1): 193–228.

———. 2003. "The New Face of Greater Boston: Meeting the Needs of Immigrants." Pages 71–105 in *Governing Greater Boston: Meeting the Needs of
the Region's People,* ed. C. C. Euchner. Boston: Rappaport Institute for
Greater Boston.

———. 2005. "The Limits of de Tocqueville: How Government Facilitates
Organisational Capacity in Newcomer Communities." *Journal of Ethnic and
Migration Studies* 31 (5): 865–87.

———. Forthcoming. "Of Puzzles and Serendipity: Doing Research with Cross-
national Comparisons and Mixed Methods." In *Research Methods Choices
in Interdisciplinary Contexts: War Stories of New Scholars,* ed. Louis DeSipio, Sherrie Kossoudji, and Manuel Garcia y Griego.

———, and Reed Ueda. 2006. "Naturalization and Nationality." In *A Companion to American Immigration,* ed. Reed Ueda. Oxford, U.K.: Blackwell.

Bluestone, Barry, and Mary Huff Stevenson. 2000. *The Boston Renaissance:
Race, Space, and Economic Change in an American Metropolis.* New York:
Russell Sage Foundation.

Bohme, Frederick G. 1956. "The Portuguese in California." *California Historical Society Quarterly* 35 (3): 233–52.

Borjas, George J. 1999. *Heaven's Door: Immigration Policy and the American
Economy.* Princeton, NJ: Princeton University Press.

Borowski, Allan, Anthony Richmond, Jing Shu, and Alan B. Simmons. 1994.
"The International Movement of People." Pages 31–62 in *Immigration and
Refugee Policy: Australia and Canada Compared,* ed. Howard Adelman,
Allan Borowski, Meyer Burstein, and Lois Foster. Toronto: University of
Toronto Press.

Boyd, Monica. 2002. "Educational Attainment of Immigrant Offspring: Success
or Segmented Assimilation?" *International Migration Review* 36 (4): 1037–
60.

———, John DeVries, and Keith Simkin. 1994. "Language, Economic Status and
Integration." Pages 549–77 in *Immigration and Refugee Policy: Australia
and Canada Compared,* ed. Howard Adelman, Allan Borowski, Meyer
Burstein, and Lois Foster. Toronto: University of Toronto Press.

Bredbrenner, Candice Lewis. 1998. *A Nationality of Her Own: Women, Marriage, and the Law of Citizenship.* Berkeley: University of California Press.

Breton, Raymond. 1964. "Institutional Completeness of Ethnic Communities and the Personal Relations of Immigrants." *American Journal of Sociology* 70 (2): 193–205.

———. 1986. "Multiculturalism and Canadian Nation-Building." Pages 27–63 in *The Politics of Gender, Ethnicity and Language in Canada,* ed. Alan C. Cairns. Toronto: University of Toronto Press.

———. 1991. *The Governance of Ethnic Communities: Political Structures and Processes in Canada.* Westport, CT: Greenwood Press.

———, Wsevolod W. Isajiw, Warren E. Kalbach, and Jeffrey G. Reitz. 1990. *Ethnic Identity and Equality: Varieties of Experience in a Canadian City.* Toronto: University of Toronto Press.

Brettell, Caroline B. 1977. "Ethnicity and Entrepreneurs: Portuguese Immigrants in a Canadian City." Pages 168–80 in *Ethnic Encounters: Identities and Contexts,* ed. George L. Hicks and Philip E. Leis. North Scituate, MA: Duxbury.

———. 2003. *Anthropology and Migration: Essays on Transnationalism, Ethnicity, and Identity.* Walnut Creek, CA: AltaMira Press.

Brotz, Howard. 1981. "Multiculturalism in Canada: A Muddle." *Canadian Public Policy* 6 (1): 41–46.

Brown, Robert Craig. 1996. "Full Partnership in the Fortunes and in the Future of the Nation." Pages 9–25 in *Ethnicity and Citizenship: The Canadian Case,* ed. Jean A. Laponce and William Safran. London: Frank Cass.

Brubaker, William Rogers. 1989. "Citizenship and Naturalization: Policies and Politics." Pages 99–127 in *Immigration and the Politics of Citizenship in Europe and North America,* ed. William Rogers Brubaker. Lanham, MD: University Press of America.

———. 1992. *Citizenship and Nationhood in France and Germany.* Cambridge, MA: Harvard University Press.

———. 2001. "The Return of Assimilation? Changing Perspectives on Immigration and Its Sequels in France, Germany, and the United States." *Ethnic and Racial Studies* 24 (4): 531–48.

———, ed. 1989. *Immigration and the Politics of Citizenship in Europe and North America.* Lanham, MD: University Press of America.

Buchignani, Norman. 1988. "Towards a Sociology of Indochinese Canadian Social Organization: A Preliminary Statement." Pages 13–36 in *Ten Years Later: Indochinese Communities in Canada,* ed. Louis-Jacques Dorais, Kwok B. Chan, and Doreen Marie Indra. Montreal: Canadian Asian Studies Association.

Bui, Diana D. 1980. *The Indochinese Mutual Assistance Association.* Washington, D.C.: Indochina Refugee Action Center.

Burns, Nancy, Kay Lehman Schlozman, and Sidney Verba. 2001. *The Private Roots of Public Action: Gender, Equality and Political Participation.* Cambridge, MA: Harvard University Press.

Cabral, Stephen L. 1989. *Tradition and Transformation: Portuguese Feasting in New Bedford*. New York: AMS Press.

Cain, Bruce E., D. Roderick Kiewiet, and Carole J. Uhlaner. 1991. "The Acquisition of Partisanship by Latinos and Asian Americans." *American Journal of Political Science* 35 (2): 390–422.

Camarota, Steven A. 2001. *The Slowing Progress of Immigrants: An Examination of Income, Home Ownership, and Citizenship, 1970–2000*. Brief in Backgrounder Series. Washington, D.C.: Center for Immigration Studies.

Canada. 1971. *House of Commons Debates*. Ottawa: Queen's Printer.

———. Department of Manpower and Immigration. 1967. *Immigration Statistics, 1966*. Ottawa: Queen's Printer and Controller of Stationery.

———. House of Commons. 1984. *Equality Now!* Report of the Special Committee on   Visible Minorities in Canadian Society. Ottawa: Supply and Services Canada.

———. House of Commons. 2003. *Settlement and Integration: A Sense of Belonging, "Feeling at Home."* Report of the Standing Committee on Citizenship and Immigration. Ottawa: Communication Canada.

———. Royal Commission on Bilingualism and Biculturalism. 1970. *Report, Book 4*. Ottawa: Queen's Printer.

Canadian Heritage, Department of. 2002. *Annual Report on the Operation of the Canadian Multiculturalism Act, 2000–2001*. Ottawa: Minister of Public Works and Government Services Canada.

Caplan, N., J. K. Whimore, and M. H. Choy. 1989. *The Boat People and Achievement in America: A Study of Family Life, Hard Work and Cultural Values*. Ann Arbor: University of Michigan Press.

Carens, Joseph H. 1987. "Aliens and Citizens: The Case for Open Borders." *The Review of Politics* 49 (2): 251–73.

Carliner, David, Lucas Guttentag, Arthur C. Helton, and Wade J. Henderson. 1977. *The Rights of Aliens and Refugees: The Basic ACLU Guide to Alien and Refugee Rights*. Carbondale: Southern Illinois University Press.

Carpenter, A. H. 1904. "Naturalization in England and the American Colonies." *American Historical Review* 9 (2): 288–303.

Chan, Kwok B., and Louis-Jacques Dorais. 1998. "Family, Identity, and the Vietnamese Diaspora: The Quebec Experience." *Sojourn* 13 (2): 285–308.

Chan, Kwok B., and Lawrence Lam. 1983. "Resettlement of Vietnamese-Chinese Refugees in Montreal, Canada: Some Socio-psychological Problems and Dilemmas." *Canadian Ethnic Studies* 15 (1): 2–15.

Chan, Raymond. 2005. "Interview with Minister Raymond Chan, Canadian Minister of State (Multiculturalism)." *Canadian Diversity* 4, no. 1 (Winter): 3–5.

Chaves, Mark, Laura Stephens, and Joseph Galaskiewicz. 2004. "Does Government Funding Suppress Nonprofits' Political Activity?" *American Sociological Review* 69 (2): 292–316.

Cho, Wendy K. Tam. 1999. "Naturalization, Socialization, Participation: Immigrants and (Non-)Voting." *Journal of Politics* 61 (4): 1140–55.

Chui, Tina W. L., James Curtis, and R. D. Lambert. 1991. "Immigrant Background and Political Participation: Examining Generational Patterns." *Canadian Journal of Sociology* 16 (4): 375–97.

Chung, Angie Y. 2002. "Negotiating the Political Dimensions of Community Work Among Ethnic Non-profits in Koreatown." Paper presented at the annual meeting of the Association for Asian American Studies, Salt Lake City, Utah, April 24–28.

Citizenship and Immigration Canada. 1995. *Audit of Settlement Contributions Programs*. Ottawa: Citizenship and Immigration Canada.

———. 1999a. *National Review of Call Centres*. Ottawa: Citizenship and Immigration Canada.

———. 1999b. *Operational Review of the Citizenship Processing Centre, Sydney*. Ottawa: Citizenship and Immigration Canada.

———. 2001. *Facts and Figures, Immigration Overview, 2000*. Ottawa: Minister of Public Works and Government Services Canada.

———. 2002. *Facts and Figures, Immigration Overview, 2001*. Ottawa: Minister of Public Works and Government Services Canada.

———. 2005. *Facts and Figures, Immigration Overview, Permanent and Temporary Residents, 2004*. Ottawa: Minister of Public Works and Government Services Canada.

Clarke, James, Elsbeth van Dam, and Liz Gooster. 1998. "New Europeans: Naturalization and Citizenship in Europe." *Citizenship Studies* 2 (1): 43–67.

Clemens, Elisabeth S., and James M. Cook. 1999. "Politics and Institutionalism: Explaining Durability and Change." *Annual Review of Sociology* 25: 441–66.

Cordero-Guzmán, Héctor R. 2005. "Community Based Organisations and Migration in New York City." *Journal of Ethnic and Migration Studies* 31 (5): 889–909.

Cornwell, Elmer E., Jr. 1980. "Ethnic Group Representation: The Case of the Portuguese." *Polity* 13 (1): 5–20.

de la Garza, Rodolfo, Angelo Falcon, F. Chris Garcia, and John A. Garcia. 1992. *Latino Voices: Mexican, Puerto Rican and Cuban Perspectives on American Politics*. Boulder, CO: Westview Press.

de Rham, Gérard. 1990. "Naturalisation: The Politics of Citizenship Acquisition." Pages 158–85 in *The Political Rights of Migrant Workers in Western Europe*, ed. Zig Layton-Henry. London: Sage Publications.

de Wenden, Catherine. 1987. *Citoyenneté, Nationalité et Immigration*. Paris: Arcantère Editions.

Demirjian, Annie, Douglas Gray, and David Wright. 1996. *The 1947 Canadian Citizenship Act: Issues and Significance*. Report prepared for Citizenship and Immigration Canada. Ottawa: Consulting and Audit Canada.

DeSipio, Louis. 2001. "Building America, One Person at a Time: Naturalization and the Political Behavior of the Naturalized in Contemporary American Politics." Pages 67–106 in *E Pluribus Unum? Contemporary and Historical*

Perspectives on Immigrant Political Incorporation, ed. Gary Gerstle and John Mollenkopf. New York: Russell Sage Foundation.

DiMaggio, Paul J., and Walter W. Powell. 1991. "The Iron Cage Revisited: Institutional Isomorphism and Collective Rationality in Organizational Fields." Pages 41–82 in *The New Institutionalism in Organizational Analysis*, ed. Walter W. Powell and Paul J. DiMaggio. Chicago: University of Chicago Press.

Dorais, Louis-Jacques. 1991. "Refugee Adaptation and Community Structure: The Indochinese in Quebec City, Canada." *International Migration Review* 25 (3): 551–73.

———. 2000. *The Cambodians, Laotians and Vietnamese in Canada*. Ottawa: Canadian Historical Association.

Dreyer, John R. 1978. "A Study of the Portuguese Immigrants of Somerville, Massachusetts, with a View toward Developing a Community-Responsive English Language Program for Adults." PhD diss., Columbia University.

Duleep, Harriet Orcutt, and Mark C. Regets. 1992. "Some Evidence on the Effect of Admission Criteria on Immigrant Assimilation." Pages 410–39 in *Immigration, Language and Ethnic Issues: Canada and the United States*, ed. Bruce Chiswick. Washington, D.C.: American Enterprise Institute.

———. 1996. "Admission Criteria and Immigrant Earnings Profiles." *International Migration Review* 30 (2): 571–90.

Duncan, Howard. 2005. "Multiculturalism: Still a Viable Concept for Integration." *Canadian Diversity* 4, no. 1 (Winter): 12–14.

Dusenberry, Verne A. 1981. "Canadian Ideology and Public Policy: The Impact on Vancouver Sikh Ethnic and Religious Adaptation." *Canadian Ethnic Studies* 13 (3): 101–19.

Edmonston, Barry, Joshua Goldstein, and Juanita Tamayo Lott, eds. 1996. *Spotlight on Heterogeneity: The Federal Standards for Racial and Ethnic Classification, Summary of a Workshop*. Washington, D.C.: National Academic Press.

Erie, Steven P. 1988. *Rainbow's End: Irish-Americans and the Dilemmas of Urban Machine Politics, 1840–1985*. Berkeley: University of California Press.

Esping-Andersen, Gøsta. 1990. *The Three Worlds of Welfare Capitalism*. Princeton, NJ: Princeton University Press.

Evans, M. D. R. 1988. "Choosing to Be a Citizen: The Time-Path of Citizenship in Australia." *International Migration Review* 22 (2): 243–64.

Favell, Adrian. 1998. *Philosophies of Integration: Immigration and the Idea of Citizenship in France and Britain*. New York: St. Martin's Press.

Feldman-Bianco, Bela. 1992. "Multiple Layers of Time and Space: The Construction of Class, Ethnicity, and Nationalism among Portuguese Immigrants." Pages 145–74 in *Towards a Transnational Perspective on Migration*, ed. N. G. Schiller, Linda Basch, and C. Blanc-Szanton. New York: New York Academy of Sciences.

Fennema, Meindert, and Jean Tillie. 2001. "Civic Community, Political Participation and Political Trust of Ethnic Groups." *Connections* 24 (1): 26–41.

Fields, Harold. 1932. "Why Aliens Seek Citizenship." *The Commonweal*, June 15, 180–82.

Finifter, Ada W., and Bernard M. Finifter. 1995. "Pledging Allegiance to a New Flag: Citizenship Change and Its Psychological Aftermath among American Migrants in Australia." *Canadian Review of Studies in Nationalism* 22 (1–2): 1–21.

Fix, Michael, and Jeffrey Passel. 2002. *The Scope and Impact of Welfare Reform's Immigrant Provisions.* Discussion paper no. 02–03 from Assessing the New Federalism Project. 02–03. Washington, D.C.: Urban Institute.

———, and Kenneth Sucher. 2003. "Trends in Naturalization." In *Immigrant Families and Workers: Facts and Perspectives Series.* Brief No. 3, September 17. http://www.urban.org/url.cfm?ID = 310847, Washington, D.C. (accessed September 16, 2005).

Fleras, Augie, and Jean Leonard Elliott. 1992. *Multiculturalism in Canada: The Challenge of Diversity.* Scarborough, ON: Nelson.

Foner, Nancy. 1997. "What's New about Transnationalism? New York Immigrants Today and at the Turn of the Century." *Diaspora* 6 (3): 355–75.

———. 2000. *From Ellis Island to JFK: New York's Two Great Waves of Immigration.* New Haven, CT: Yale University Press and Russell Sage Foundation.

Frideres, J. S., S. Goldenburg, J. Disanto, and J. Horna. 1987. "Becoming Canadian: Citizen Acquisition and National Identity." *Canadian Review of Studies in Nationalism* 14 (1): 105–21.

Galloway, Donald. 2000. "The Dilemmas of Canadian Citizenship Law." Pages 82–118 in *From Migrants to Citizens: Membership in a Changing World,* ed. T. Alexander Aleinikoff and Douglas Klusmeyer. Washington, D.C.: Carnegie Endowment for International Peace.

Gans, Herbert. 1979. "Symbolic Ethnicity: The Future of Ethnic Groups and Cultures in America." *Ethnic and Racial Studies* 2 (1): 1–19.

Ganz, Marshall. 2000. "Resources and Resourcefulness: Strategic Capacity in the Unionization of California Agriculture: 1959–1966." *American Journal of Sociology* 105 (4): 1003–62.

Gavit, John Palmer. 1922. *Americans by Choice.* New York: Harper and Brothers.

Gellner, Ernest. 1983. *Nations and Nationalism.* Ithaca, NY: Cornell University Press.

Gerstle, Gary, and John Mollenkopf. 2001. "The Political Incorporation of Immigrants, Then and Now." Pages 1–30 in *E Pluribus Unum? Contemporary and Historical Perspectives on Immigrant Political Incorporation,* ed. Gary Gerstle and John Mollenkopf. New York: Russell Sage Foundation.

Geschwender, James A., Rita Carroll-Seguin, and Howard Brill. 1988. "The Portuguese and Haoles of Hawaii: Implications for the Origin of Ethnicity." *American Sociological Review* 53 (4): 515–27.

Gibson, Campbell, and Emily Lennon. 1999. *Historical Census Statistics on the*

Foreign-Born Population of the United States: 1850–1990. U.S. Census Bureau working paper 29. Washington, D.C.: Government Printing Office.

Gilbertson, Greta, and Audrey Singer. 2003. "The Emergence of Protective Citizenship in the USA: Naturalization among Dominican Immigrants in the Post-1996 Welfare Reform Era." *Ethnic and Racial Studies* 26 (1): 25–51.

Giles, Wenona. 1993. "Clean Jobs, Dirty Jobs: Ethnicity, Social Reproduction and Gendered Identity." *Culture* 8 (2): 37–44.

Gitlin, Todd. 1981. *The Whole World Is Watching: Mass Media in the Making and Unmaking of the New Left.* Berkeley: University of California Press.

———. 1995. *The Twilight of Common Dreams: Why America Is Wracked by Culture Wars.* New York: Metropolitan Books.

Glazer, Nathan. 1997. *We Are All Multiculturalists Now.* Cambridge, MA: Harvard University Press.

———. 1998. "Governmental and Nongovernmental Roles in the Absorption of Immigrants in the United States." Pages 59–82 in *Paths to Inclusion: The Integration of Migrants in the United States and Germany,* ed. Peter H. Schuck and Rainer Münz. New York: Berghahn Books.

Gleason, Philip. 2001. "Sea Change in the Civic Culture in the 1960s." Pages 109–42 in *E Pluribus Unum? Contemporary and Historical Perspectives on Immigrant Political Incorporation,* ed. Gary Gerstle and John Mollenkopf. New York: Russell Sage Foundation.

Goar, Carol. 2005. "Red Tape Throttles Charities." *Toronto Star,* July 25, A18.

Gold, Steven J. 1992. *Refugee Communities: A Comparative Field Study.* Newbury Park, CA: Sage Publications.

Goldfarb Consultants. 1999. *Toronto Star Community Study.* A research report prepared for the *Toronto Star.* Toronto: Goldfarb Consultants.

Gosnell, H. F. 1928. "Non-naturalization: A Study in Political Assimilation." *American Journal of Sociology* 33: 930–39.

Graham, Hugh Davis. 2002. "The Origins of Official Minority Designation." Pages 288–99 in *The New Race Question,* ed. Joel Perlmann and Mary C. Waters. New York: Russell Sage Foundation.

Greeley, Andrew M., and William C. McCready. 1975. "The Transmission of Cultural Heritages: The Case of the Irish and Italians." Pages 210–30 in *Ethnicity: Theory and Experience,* ed. Nathan Glazer and Daniel Patrick Moynihan. Cambridge, MA: Harvard University Press.

Grønbjerg, Kirsten. 1993. *Understanding Nonprofit Funding: Managing Revenues in Social Services and Community Development Organizations.* San Francisco: Jossey-Bass.

Gualtieri, Sarah. 2001. "Becoming 'White': Race, Religion, and the Foundations of Syrian/Lebanese Ethnicity in the United States." *Journal of American Ethnic History* 20: 29–58.

Gwyn, Richard. 1995. *Nationalism without Walls: The Unbearable Lightness of Being Canadian.* Toronto: McClelland and Steward.

Habermas, Jürgen. 1989. *The Structural Transformation of the Public Sphere:*

An Inquiry into a Category of Bourgeois Society. Cambridge, MA: MIT Press.

Hall, Michael H., et al. 2003. *The Capacity to Serve: A Qualitative Study of the Challenges Facing Canada's Nonprofit and Voluntary Organizations.* Toronto: Canadian Center for Philanthropy.

Hall, Michael H., Cathy W. Barr, M. Easwaramoorthy, et al. 2005. *The Canadian Nonprofit and Voluntary Sector in Comparative Perspective.* Toronto: Imagine Canada.

Halpern Pereira, Miriam. 1980. "Fondements de la Politique d'Émigration Portugaise (1850–1930)." *Peuples méditerranéens* 12: 51–73.

Hamilton, Alexander, James Madison, and John Jay. [1788] 1961. *The Federalist Papers.* Ed. Clinton Rossiter. New York: Penguin.

Hammar, Tomas. 1990. *Democracy and the Nation State: Aliens, Denizens, and Citizens.* Aldershot, England: Gower.

Hancock, M. 1937. "Naturalization in Canada." Pages 88–100 in *The Legal Status of Aliens in Pacific Countries,* ed. Norman MacKenzie. London: Oxford University Press.

Haney López, Ian F. 1996. *White by Law: The Legal Construction of Race.* New York: New York University Press.

Harper-Ho, Virginia. 2000. "Noncitizen Voting Rights: The History, the Law, and Current Prospects for Change." *Law and Inequality Journal* 18: 271–322.

Hartz, Louis. 1955. *The Liberal Tradition in America.* New York: Harcourt, Brace and World.

———, et al. 1964. *The Founding of New Societies.* New York: Harcourt, Brace and World.

Hawkins, Freda. 1988. *Canada and Immigration: Public Policy and Public Concern.* 2nd ed. Kingston and Montreal: McGill-Queen's University Press.

———. 1991. *Critical Years in Immigration: Canada and Australia Compared.* 2nd ed. Montreal and Kingston: McGill-Queen's University Press.

Hein, Jeremy. 1993. *States and International Migrants: The Incorporation of Indochinese Refugees in the United States and France.* Boulder, CO: Westview Press.

———. 1997. "Ethnic Organizations and the Welfare State: The Impact of Social Welfare Programs on the Formation of Indochinese Refugee Associations." *Sociological Forum* 12 (2): 279–95.

Higgs, David, ed. 1990. *Portuguese Migration in Global Perspective.* Toronto: Multicultural History Society of Ontario.

Higham, John. 1978. "Introduction: The Forms of Ethnic Leadership." Pages 1–18 in *Ethnic Leadership in America,* ed. John Higham. Baltimore: Johns Hopkins University Press.

———. 1982. "Leadership." Pages 69–92 in *The Politics of Ethnicity,* ed. Michael Walzer, Edward T. Kantowicz, John Higham, and Mona Harrington. Cambridge, MA: Belknap/Harvard University Press.

Hollifield, James F. 1992. *Immigrants, Markets, and States: The Political Economy of Postwar Europe.* Cambridge, MA: Harvard University Press.

Hollinger, David A. 2000. *Postethnic America: Beyond Multiculturalism.* New York: Basic Books.

Holman, Philip A. 1996. "Refugee Resettlement in the United States." Pages 3–27 in *Refugees in America in the 1990s,* ed. David W. Haines. Westport, CT: Greenwood Press.

Honig, Bonnie. 2001. *Democracy and the Foreigner.* Princeton, NJ: Princeton University Press.

Horowitz, Gad. 1966. "Conservatism, Liberalism and Socialism in Canada: An Interpretation." *Canadian Journal of Economics and Political Science* 32: 143–71.

Horton, Sarah. 2004. "Different Subjects: The Health Care System's Participation in the Different Construction of Cultural Citizenship of Cuban Refugees and Mexican Immigrants." *Medical Anthropology Quarterly* 18 (4): 472–89.

Huntington, Samuel P. 2004a. "The Hispanic Challenge." *Foreign Policy* (March/April): 30–45.

———. 2004b. *Who Are We? The Challenges to America's National Identity.* New York: Simon and Schuster.

Indra, Doreen Marie. 1987. "Bureaucratic Constraints, Middlemen and Community Organization: Aspects of the Political Incorporation of Southeast Asians in Canada." Pages 147–70 in *Uprooting, Loss and Adaptation: The Resettlement of Indochinese Refugees in Canada,* ed. Doreen Marie Indra and Kwok B. Chan. Ottawa: Canadian Public Health Association.

Inter-university Consortium for Political and Social Research (ICPSR) and Carroll McKibbin. 1997. "Roster of United States Congressional Officeholders and Biographical Characteristics of Members of the United States Congress, 1789–1996: Merged Data" [computer file]. 10th ICPSR ed. Ann Arbor, MI: ICPSR [producer and distributor].

Ireland, Patrick R. 1994. *The Policy Challenge of Ethnic Diversity: Immigrant Politics in France and Switzerland.* Cambridge, MA: Harvard University Press.

Ito-Alder, James P. 1980 [1972, 1978]. *The Portuguese in Cambridge and Somerville (Combined Edition).* Cambridge, MA: Cambridge Department of Community Development.

Jacobson, David. 1996. *Rights across Borders: Immigration and the Decline of Citizenship.* Baltimore: Johns Hopkins University Press.

Jasso, Guillermina, and Mark R. Rosenzweig. 1986. "Family Reunification and the Immigrant Multiplier: U.S. Immigration Law, Origin-Country Conditions, and the Reproduction of Immigrants." *Demography* 23 (3): 291–311.

———. 1990. *The New Chosen People: Immigrants in the United States.* New York: Russell Sage Foundation.

Jedwab, Jack. 2005. "Neither Finding nor Losing Our Way: The Debate over Canadian Multiculturalism." *Canadian Diversity* 4, no. 1 (Winter): 95–102.

Jenkins, J. Craig. 1987. "Nonprofit Organizations and Policy Advocacy." Pages 296–318 in *The Nonprofit Sector: A Research Handbook,* ed. Walter W. Powell. New Haven, CT: Yale University Press.

Jimenez, Marina. 2003. "200,000 Illegal Immigrants Toiling in Canada's Underground Economy." *The Globe and Mail,* November 15, A1, A9.

Jones-Correa, Michael. 1998a. *Between Two Nations: The Political Predicament of Latinos in New York City.* Ithaca, NY: Cornell University Press.

———. 1998b. "Different Paths: Gender, Immigration and Political Participation." *International Migration Review* 32 (2): 326–49.

———. 2001. "Under Two Flags: Dual Nationality in Latin America and Its Consequences for Naturalization in the United States." *International Migration Review* 35 (4): 997–1029.

———. 2001b. "Institutional and Contextual Factors in Immigrant Naturalization and Voting." *Citizenship Studies* 5 (1): 41–56.

Joppke, Christian. 1999. *Immigration and the Nation-State: The United States, Germany, and Great Britain.* Oxford: Oxford University Press.

———. 2004. "The Retreat of Multiculturalism in the Liberal State: Theory and Policy." *British Journal of Sociology* 55 (2): 237–57.

Joyce, Michael S., and William A. Schambra. 1996. "A New Civic Life." Pages 11–29 in *To Empower People: From State to Civil Society,* 2nd ed, ed. Michael Novak. Washington, D.C.: AEI Press.

Kallen, Evelyn. 1982. "Multiculturalism: Ideology, Policy and Reality." *Journal of Canadian Studies* 17 (1): 51–63.

Kaplan, William. 1991. *The Evolution of Citizenship Legislation in Canada.* Ottawa: Multiculturalism and Citizenship Canada.

Kasinitz, Philip. 1992. *Caribbean New York: Black Immigrants and the Politics of Race.* Ithaca, NY: Cornell University Press.

Katznelson, Ira. 1981. *City Trenches: Urban Politics and the Patterning of Class in the United States.* Chicago: University of Chicago Press.

Kaufman, Jason. 1999. "Three Views of Associationalism in 19th Century America: An Empirical Examination." *American Journal of Sociology* 104 (5): 1296–345.

Kelley, Ninette, and Michael Trebilcock. 1998. *The Making of the Mosaic: A History of Canadian Immigration Policy.* Toronto: University of Toronto Press.

Kelly, Gail Paradise. 1977. *From Vietnam to America: A Chronicle of Vietnamese Immigration to the United States.* Boulder, CO: Westview Press.

Kettner, James H. 1978. *The Development of American Citizenship.* Chapel Hill: University of North Carolina Press.

Keyssar, Alexander. 2000. *The Right to Vote: The Contested History of Democracy in the United States.* New York: Basic Books.

Kibria, N. 1993. *Family Tightrope: The Changing Lives of Vietnamese Americans.* Princeton, NJ: Princeton University Press.

King, Gary, Michael Tomz, and Jason Wittenberg. 2000. "Making the Most of Statistical Analyses: Improving Interpretation and Presentation." *American Journal of Political Science* 44 (2): 341–55.

Klimt, Andrea C. 1989. "Returning 'Home': Portuguese Migrant Notions of Temporariness, Permanence, and Commitment." *New German Critique* 46 (Winter): 47–70.

Knowles, Valerie. 1992. *Strangers at Our Gates: Canadian Immigration and Immigration Policy, 1540–1990.* Toronto: Dundurn Press.

———. 2000. *Forging Our Legacy: Canadian Citizenship and Immigration, 1900–1977.* Ottawa: Citizenship and Immigration Canada.

Kong, Deborah. 2002. "30 States Have Multilingual Ballots." *Washington Post*, September 25, 1.

Konvitz, Milton R. 1946. *The Alien and the Asiatic in American Law.* Ithaca, NY: Cornell University Press.

Koopmans, Ruud. 2004. "Migrant Mobilisation and Political Opportunities: Variation among German Cities and a Comparison with the United Kingdom and the Netherlands." *Journal of Ethnic and Migration Studies* 30 (3): 449–70.

———, and Paul Statham. 1999. "Challenging the Liberal Nation-State? Postnationalism, Multiculturalism, and the Collective Claims Making of Migrants and Ethnic Minorities in Britain and Germany." *American Journal of Sociology* 105 (3): 652–96.

Kramer, Ralph M., and Bart Grossman. 1987. "Contracting for Social Services: Process Management and Resource Dependencies." *Social Service Review* 61 (1): 32–55.

Kymlicka, Will. 1995. *Multicultural Citizenship: A Liberal Theory of Minority Rights.* Oxford, England: Clarendon Press.

———. 2001. *Politics in the Vernacular: Nationalism, Multiculturalism and Citizenship.* Oxford, England: Oxford University Press.

———. 2005. "The Uncertain Futures of Multiculturalism." *Canadian Diversity* 4, no. 1 (Winter): 82–85.

———, and Wayne Norman. 1994. "Return of the Citizen: A Survey of Recent Work on Citizenship Theory." *Ethics* 104: 352–81.

Labelle, Micheline, François Rocher, and Guy Rocher. 1995. "Pluriethnicité, Citoyenneté et Intégration: De la Souveraineté pour Lever les Obstacles et les Ambiguités." *Cahiers de recherche sociologique* 25: 213–45.

Laczko, Leslie S. 1994. "Canada's Pluralism in Comparative Perspective." *Ethnic and Racial Studies* 17 (1): 20–41.

Lanphier, Michael, and Oleh Lukomskyj. 1994. "Settlement Policy in Australia and Canada." Pages 337–71 in *Immigration and Refugee Policy: Australia and Canada Compared,* ed. Howard Adelman, Allan Borowski, Meyer Burstein, and Lois Foster. Toronto: University of Toronto Press.

Layton-Henry, Zig. 1990. "The Challenge of Political Rights." Pages 1–26 in *The Political Rights of Migrant Workers in Western Europe,* ed. Zig Layton-Henry. London: Sage Publications.

Leacy, F. H., ed. *Historical Statistics of Canada.* 2nd. ed. Ottawa: Statistics Canada.

Legendre, Camille, and William Shaffir. 1984. "Altering Citizenship Status:

Some Preliminary Thoughts." *Canadian Review of Studies in Nationalism* 11 (2): 257–70.

Levitt, Peggy. 2001. *The Transnational Villagers*. Berkeley: University of California Press.

———. 2003. " 'You Know, Abraham Was Really the First Immigrant': Religion and Transnational Migration." *International Migration Review* 37 (4): 847–74.

Li, Peter S. 1999. "The Multiculturalism Debate." Pages 148–77 in *Race and Ethnic Relations in Canada*, 2nd ed, ed. Peter S. Li. Toronto: Oxford University Press.

Liang, Zai. 1994. "Social Contact, Social Capital, and the Naturalization Process: Evidence from Six Immigrant Groups." *Social Science Research* 23: 407–37.

Lieberman, Robert. 1998. *Shifting the Color Line: Race and the American Welfare State*. Cambridge, MA: Harvard University Press.

Lien, Pei-te. 2001. *The Making of Asian American through Political Participation*. Philadelphia: Temple University Press.

———, M. Margaret Conway, Taeku Lee, and Janelle Wong. 2001. "Summary Report of the Pilot Study of the National Asian American Political Survey," March 2. http://www.apa-politics.org/ (accessed January 21, 2002).

Lipset, Seymour Martin. 1986. "Historical Conditions and National Characteristics: A Comparative Analysis of Canada and the United States." *Canadian Journal of Sociology* 11 (2): 113–35.

———. 1990. *Continental Divide: The Values and Institutions of the United States and Canada*. New York: Routledge.

Loescher, Gil, and John A. Scanlan. 1986. *Calculated Kindness: Refugees and America's Half-Open Door, 1945 to the Present*. New York: Free Press.

Lucas, C. P. [1912] 1970. *Lord Durham's Report on the Affairs of British North America*. 3 vols. Oxford: Clarendon Press.

Loury, Glenn C. 2002. *The Anatomy of Racial Inequality*. Cambridge: Harvard University Press.

Magaña, Lisa. 2003. *Straddling the Border: Immigration Policy and the INS*. Austin: University of Texas Press.

Marques, Domingos, and Manuela Marujo. 1993. *With Hardened Hands: A Pictorial History of Portuguese Immigrants to Canada in the 1950s*. Etobicoke: New Leaf.

Marques, Domingos, and Joao Medeiros. 1984. "Portuguese Immigrants in Toronto." *Polyphony* (Summer): 154–58.

Martin, Paul. 1993. "Citizenship and the People's World." Pages 64–78 in *Belonging: The Meaning and Future of Canadian Citizenship*, ed. William Kaplan. Montreal: McGill-Queen's University Press.

Martiniello, Marco. 1993. "Ethnic Leadership, Ethnic Communities' Political Powerlessness and the State in Belgium." *Ethnic and Racial Studies* 16 (2): 236–55.

Marwell, Nicole P. 2004. "Privatizing the Welfare State: Nonprofit Community Organizations." *American Sociological Journal* 69 (2): 265–91.

Massachusetts Area Planning Council. 2002. *A Decade of Change. Community Profiles: Growth Trends in Greater Boston's 101 Communities—1990 to 2000.* Boston: Massachusetts Area Planning Council.

Massey, Douglas S. 1990. "The Social and Economic Origins of Immigration." *Annals of the American Academy of Political and Social Science* 510: 60–72.

———, Joaquin Arango, Graeme Hugo, et al. 1998. *World's in Motion: Understanding International Migration at the End of the Millennium.* New York: Oxford University Press.

Mata, Fernando. 1999. "Patterns of Acquiring Citizenship." Pages 163–82 in *Immigrant Canada: Demographic, Economic and Social Challenges,* ed. Shiva S. Halli and Leo Driedger. Toronto: University of Toronto Press.

McAdam, Doug. 1982. *Political Process and the Development of Black Insurgency, 1930–1970.* Chicago: University of Chicago Press.

———, John D. McCarthy, and Mayer N. Zald. 1996. *Comparative Perspectives on Social Movements: Political Opportunities, Mobilizing Structures and Cultural Framings.* New York: Cambridge University Press.

McDonald, Forrest, and Ellen McDonald. 1980. "The Ethnic Origins of the American People, 1790." *The William and Mary Quarterly* 37 (2): 179–99.

McGauran, Peter. 2005. "Interview with the Australian Government Minister for Citizenship and Multicultural Affairs, the Hon. Peter McGauran, MP." *Canadian Diversity* 4, no. 1 (Winter): 6–8.

McRoberts, Kenneth. 1997. *Misconceiving Canada: The Struggle for National Unity.* Toronto: Oxford University Press.

Meissner, Doris. 2001. *After the Attacks: Protecting Border and Liberties.* Policy Brief No. 8. Washington, D.C.: Carnegie Endowment for International Peace.

Menjívar, Cecilia. 2000. *Fragmented Ties: Salvadoran Immigrant Networks in America.* Berkeley: University of California Press.

Merton, Robert K. 1957. *Social Theory and Social Structure.* Rev. ed. Glencoe, IL: Free Press.

Metropolitan Area Planning Council. 2002. *Boston Community Profile.* Boston: Metropolitan Area Planning Council.

Mettler, Suzanne. 2002. "Bringing the State Back In to Civic Engagement: Policy Feedback Effects of the G.I. Bill for World War II Veterans." *American Political Science Review* 96: 351–65.

Miller, Warren E., and J. Merrill Shanks. 1996. *The New American Voter.* Cambridge, MA: Harvard University Press.

Minkoff, Debra C. 1994. "From Service Provision to Institutional Advocacy: The Shifting Legitimacy of Organizational Forms." *Social Forces* 72 (4): 943–69.

Moniz, Miguel. 2001. "The Conflicted Minority: Pan Luso–Latin Identity Undone." Paper presented at the conference Race, Culture, Nation: Arguments across the Portuguese-Speaking World, Providence, RI, April 6–8.

Moreno, Dario. 1996. "Cuban Americans in Miami Politics: Understanding the Cuban Model." Pages 145–62 in *The Politics of Minority Coalitions: Race, Ethnicity and Shared Uncertainties,* ed. Wilbur Rich. Westport, CT: Praeger.

Morris, Aldon D. 1984. *The Origins of the Civil Rights Movement: Black Communities Organizing for Change*. New York: Free Press.

———, and Suzanne Staggenborg. 2003. "Leadership in Social Movements." Pages 171–96 in *The Blackwell Companion to Social Movements*, ed. David A. Snow, Sarah A. Soule, and Hanspeter Kriesi. Oxford: Blackwell.

Multiculturalism Program, Department of Canadian Heritage. 2001. *Annual Report on the Operation of the Canadian Multiculturalism Act, 1999–2000*. Ottawa: Minister of Public Works and Government Services Canada.

Munson, Ziad. 2002. "Becoming an Activist: Believers, Sympathizers, and Mobilization in the American Pro-life Movement." PhD diss., Harvard University.

Neice, David. 1978. *Ethnicity and Canadian Citizenship: A Metropolitan Study*. Ottawa: Citizenship Registration Branch, Department of the Secretary of State.

Noivo, Edite. 1997. *Inside Ethnic Families: Three Generations of Portuguese-Canadians*. Montreal: McGill-Queen's University Press.

North, David S. 1985. *The Long Grey Welcome: A Study of the American Naturalization Process*. Washington, D.C.: National Association of Latino Elected and Appointed Officials Education Fund.

———. 1987. "The Long Grey Welcome: A Study of the American Naturalization Program." *International Migration Review* 21 (2): 311–26.

Nowland-Foreman, Garth. 1998. "Purchase-of-Service Contracting, Voluntary Organizations and Civil Society." *American Behavioral Scientist* 42: 108–23.

Nunes, Fernando. 1998. *Portuguese-Canadians from Sea to Sea: A National Needs Assessment*. Toronto: Portuguese-Canadian National Congress.

O'Connor, Patricia J. 1986. *The Story of St. Christopher House, 1912–1984*. Toronto: Toronto Association of Neighbourhood Services.

Oberschall, Anthony. 1973. *Social Conflict and Social Movements*. Englewood Cliffs, NJ: Prentice-Hall.

Office of Campaign and Political Finance. 2001. *Campaign Finance Guide: Candidates for Municipal Office*. Boston: Office of Campaign and Political Finance, commonwealth of Massachusetts.

Olasky, Marvin N. 1992. *The Tragedy of American Compassion*. Washington, D.C.: Regnery Gateway.

Oliveira, Manuel Armando. 2000. "Immigrants Forever? The Migratory Saga of Azoreans in Canada." Pages 83–96 in *The Portuguese in Canada: From the Sea to the City*, ed. Carlos Teixeira and Victor M. P. da Rosa. Toronto: University of Toronto Press.

Ong, Aihwa. 1996. "Cultural Citizenship as Subject-Making: Immigrants Negotiate Racial and Cultural Boundaries in the United States." *Current Anthropology* 37 (5): 737–62.

———. 2003. *Buddha Is Hiding: Refugees, Citizenship, the New America*. Berkeley: University of California Press.

Ornstein, Michael. 2000. *Ethno-racial Inequality in the City of Toronto: An Analysis of the 1996 Census*. Report prepared for the Access and Equity Unit, City of Toronto. Toronto: City of Toronto.

Pachon, Harry, and Louis DeSipio. 1994. *New Americans by Choice: Political Perspectives of Latino Immigrants.* Boulder, CO: Westview Press.

Pal, Leslie. 1993. *Interests of State: The Politics of Language, Multiculturalism, and Feminism in Canada.* Montreal and Kingston, ON: McGill-Queen's University Press.

Palmer, Douglas L. 1999. *Canadian Attitudes and Perceptions Regarding Immigration: Relations with Regional Per Capita Immigration and Other Contextual Factors.* Ottawa: Minister of Public Works and Government Services Canada.

Pap, Leo. 1981. *The Portuguese-Americans.* Boston: Twayne Publishers.

Parekh, Bhikhu. 2002. *Rethinking Multiculturalism: Cultural Diversity and Political Theory.* Cambridge, MA: Harvard University Press.

Parenti, Michael. 1967. "Ethnic Politics and the Persistence of Ethnic Identification." *American Political Science Review* 61 (3): 717–26.

Park, Robert E., and Ernest W. Burgess. 1921. *Introduction to the Science of Sociology.* Chicago: Chicago University Press.

Pedraza-Bailey, Silvia. 1985. *Political and Economic Migrants in America: Cubans and Mexicans.* Austin: University of Texas Press.

Pelletier, Alain. 1991. "Politics and Ethnicity: Representation of Ethnic and Visible-Minority Groups in the House of Commons." Pages 101–59 in *Ethnocultural Groups and Visible Minorities in Canadian Politics: The Question of Access,* ed. Kathy Megyery. Vol. 7 of *Research Studies of the Royal Commission on Electoral Reform and Party Financing.* Toronto: Dundurn Press.

Pfeifer, Mark E. 1999. "'Community,' Adaptation, and the Vietnamese in Toronto." PhD diss., University of Toronto.

Pho, Hai B. 1991. "The Politics of Refugee Resettlement in Massachusetts." *Migration World* 19 (4): 4–10.

Pierson, Paul. 1993. "When Effect Becomes Cause: Policy Feedback and Political Change." *World Politics* 45 (4): 595–628.

———. 1994. *Dismantling the Welfare State? Reagan, Thatcher, and the Politics of Retrenchment.* New York: Cambridge University Press.

Piven, Frances Fox, and Richard Cloward. 1977. *Poor People's Movements.* New York: Pantheon.

Plascencia, Luis F. B., Gary P. Freeman, and Mark Setzler. 2003. "The Decline of Barriers to Immigrant Economic and Political Rights in the American States, 1977–2001." *International Migration Review* 37 (1): 5–23.

Porter, John. 1965. *The Vertical Mosaic.* Toronto: University of Toronto Press.

Portes, Alejandro. 1995. "Children of Immigrants: Segmented Assimilation and Its Determinants." Pages 248–79 in *The Economic Sociology of Immigration,* ed. Alejandro Portes. New York: Russell Sage Foundation.

———, and John W. Curtis. 1987. "Changing Flags: Naturalization and Its Determinants among Mexican Immigrants." *International Migration Review* 21 (2): 352–71.

Portes, Alejandro, and Rafael Mozo. 1985. "The Political Adaptation Process of

Cubans and Other Ethnic Minorities in the United States: A Preliminary Analysis." *International Migration Review* 19 (1): 35–63.

Portes, Alejandro, and Rubén G. Rumbaut. 1996. *Immigrant America: A Portrait.* Berkeley: University of California Press.

Portes, Alejandro, and Min Zhou. 1993. "The New Second Generation: Segmented Assimilation and Its Variants." *Annals of the American Academy of Political and Social Science* 530: 74–96.

Poston, Dudley L., Steven A. Camarota, and Amanda K. Baumle. 2003. *Remaking the Political Landscape: The Impact of Illegal and Legal Immigration on Congressional Apportionment.* Brief in Backgrounder Series. Washington, D.C.: Center for Immigration Studies.

Putnam, Robert D. 2000. *Bowling Alone: The Collapse and Revival of American Community.* New York: Simon & Schuster.

Quadagno, Jill. 1994. *The Color of Welfare: How Racism Undermined the War on Poverty.* New York: Oxford University Press.

Ragin, Charles C. 1987. *The Comparative Method: Moving beyond Qualitative and Quantitative Strategies.* Berkeley: University of California Press.

Ramakrishnan, S. Karthick. 2005. *Democracy in Immigrant America: Changing Demographics and Political Participation.* Palo Alto, CA: Stanford University Press.

———, and Thomas J. Espenshade. 2001. "Immigrant Incorporation and Political Participation in the United States." *International Migration Review* 35 (3): 870–907.

Raskin, Jamin B. 1993. "Legal Aliens, Local Citizens: The Historical, Constitutional, and Theoretical Meanings of Alien Suffrage." *University of Pennsylvania Law Review* 141: 1391–470.

Reitz, Jeffrey G. 1998. *Warmth of the Welcome: The Social Causes of Economic Success for Immigrants in Different Nations and Cities.* Boulder, CO: Westview Press.

———, and Raymond Breton. 1994. *The Illusion of Difference: Realities of Ethnicity in Canada and the United States.* Toronto: C. D. Howe Institute.

Richard, Eric, and Louis-Jacques Dorais. 2003. "Statistical Profile of Immigrants of Vietnamese Origin in Quebec and in Canada: Comparison of 1991, 1996 and 2001 Data." *Review of Vietnamese Studies* 3 (1): 1–9.

Rogers, Francis M. 1974. *Americans of Portuguese Descent: A Lesson in Differentiation.* Beverly Hills, CA: Sage Publications.

Rosaldo, Renato. 1997. "Cultural Citizenship, Inequality, and Multiculturalism." Pages 27–38 in *Latino Cultural Citizenship: Claiming Identity, Space and Politics*, ed. William V. Flores and Rina Benmayor. Boston: Beacon Press.

Rosberg, Gerald M. 1977. "Aliens and Equal Protection: Why Not the Right to Vote?" *Michigan Law Review* 75: 1092–136.

Rosenstone, Steven J., and John Mark Hansen. 1993. *Mobilization, Participation, and Democracy in America.* New York: Macmillian.

Ruggles, Steven, et al. 2004. *Integrated Public Use Microdata Series: Version*

3.0. [Machine-readable database.] Minneapolis: Minnesota Population Center [producer and distributor].

Rumbaut, Rubén G. 1995. "Vietnamese, Laotians, and Cambodian Americans." Pages 232–70 in *Asian Americans: Contemporary Trends and Issues,* ed. Pyung Gap Min. Thousand Oaks, CA: Sage Publications.

Salamon, Lester M. 1995. *Partners in Public Service: Government-Nonprofit Relations in the Modern Welfare State.* Baltimore: Johns Hopkins University Press.

———. 1999. *America's Nonprofit Sector: A Primer.* 2nd ed. New York: Foundation Center.

Sanders, Jimy, Victor Nee, and Scott Sernau. 2002. "Asian Immigrants' Reliance on Social Ties in a Multiethnic Labor Market." *Social Forces* 81 (1): 281–314.

Sapiro, Virginia. 1984. "Women, Citizenship, and Nationality: Immigration and Naturalization Policies in the United States." *Politics and Society* 13: 1–26.

Schlesinger, Arthur M., Jr. 1998. *The Disuniting of America: Reflections on a Multicultural Society.* New York: W. W. Norton.

Schmidley, A. Dianne, and Campbell Gibson. 1999. *Profile of the Foreign-Born Population in the United States: 1997.* U.S. Census Bureau Current Population Reports, series P23–195. Washington, D.C.: Government Printing Office.

Schuck, Peter H. 1998. *Citizens, Strangers, and In-betweens: Essays on Immigration and Citizenship.* Boulder, CO: Westview Press.

———, and Rogers M. Smith. 1985. *Citizenship without Consent: Illegal Aliens in the American Polity.* New Haven, CT: Yale University Press.

Schwartz, Mildred A. 1976. "Citizenship in Canada and the United States." *Transactions of the Royal Society of Canada* 4 (14): 83–96.

Serpa, Margaret C., Jeremias Botelho, Anne S. Katzeff, et al. [1975?]. *Portuguese Resource Directory, 1975–76.* n.p.

Shklar, Judith. 1991. *American Citizenship: The Quest for Inclusion.* Cambridge, MA: Harvard University Press.

Siemiatycki, Myer, and Engin Isin. 1997. "Immigration, Diversity and Urban Citizenship in Toronto." *Canadian Journal of Regional Sciences* 20 (1–2): 73–102.

Siemiatycki, Myer, Tim Rees, Roxana Ng, and Khan Rahi. 2003. "Integrating Community Diversity in Toronto: On Whose Terms?" Pages 373–456 in *The World in a City,* ed. Paul Anisef and Michael Lanphier. Toronto: University of Toronto Press.

Simard, Carolle. 1991. "Visible Minorities and the Canadian Political System." Pages 161–261 in *Ethno-cultural Groups and Visible Minorities in Canadian Politics: The Question of Access,* ed. Kathy Megyery. Vol. 7 of *Research Studies of the Royal Commission on Electoral Reform and Party Financing.* Toronto: Dundurn Press.

Simmel, Georg. 1972. *On Individuality and Social Forms.* Ed. Donald N. Levine. Chicago: University of Chicago Press.

Simmons, Alan B., and Kieran Keohane. 1992. "Canadian Immigration Policy:

State Strategies and the Quest for Legitimacy." *Canadian Review of Sociology and Anthropology* 29 (4): 421–52.

Skerry, Peter. 1993. *Mexican Americans: The Ambivalent Minority.* Cambridge, MA: Harvard University Press.

Skocpol, Theda. 1999. "Advocates without Members: The Recent Transformation of American Civic Life." Pages 461–509 in *Civic Engagement in American Democracy*, ed. Theda Skocpol and Morris P. Fiorina. Washington, D.C.: Brookings Institution Press.

———. 2003. *Diminished Democracy: From Membership to Management in American Civic Life.* Norman: University of Oklahoma Press.

———, Ziad Munson, Andrew Karch, and Bayliss Camp. 2002. "Why Great Wars Nourished American Civic Voluntarism." Pages 134–80 in *Shaped by War and Trade: International Influences on American Political Development*, ed. Ira Katznelson and Martin Shefter. Princeton, NJ: Princeton University Press.

Skrentny, John D. 2002. *The Minority Rights Revolution.* Cambridge, MA: Harvard University Press.

Smith, Darrell Hevenor. 1926. *The Bureau of Naturalization: Its History, Activities, and Organization.* Baltimore: Johns Hopkins University Press.

Smith, Estellie M. 1974. "Portuguese Enclaves: The Invisible Minority." In *Social and Cultural Identity: Problems of Persistence and Change*, ed. T. K. Fitzgerald. Athens: University of Georgia, Southern Anthropological Society Proceedings.

Smith, Marian L. 1998. "Overview of INS History." U.S. Citizenship and Immigration Services website, http://uscis.gov/graphics/aboutus/history/articles/oview.htm.

Smith, Rogers M. 1997. *Civic Ideals: Conflicting Visions of Citizenship in U.S. History.* New Haven, CT: Yale University Press.

Smith, Steven Rathgeb. 1999. "Government Financing of Nonprofit Activity." Pages 177–211 in *Nonprofits and Government: Collaboration and Conflict*, ed. Elizabeth T. Boris and C. Eugene Steuerle. Washington, D.C.: Urban Institute Press.

———, and Michael Lipsky. 1993. *Nonprofits for Hire: The Welfare State in the Age of Contracting.* Cambridge, MA: Harvard University Press.

Snow, David A., and Robert D. Benford. 1992. "Master Frames and Cycles of Protest." Pages 133–55 in *Frontiers in Social Movement Theory*, ed. Aldon D. Morris and Carol M. Mueller. New Haven, CT: Yale University Press.

Snow, David A., E. B. Rochford, S. K. Worden, and Robert D. Benford. 1986. "Frame Alignment Processes, Micromobilization, and Movement Participation." *American Sociological Review* 51: 464–81.

Soss, Joe. 1999. "Lessons of Welfare: Policy Design, Political Learning and Political Action." *American Political Science Review* 93: 363–80.

Soysal, Yasemin Nuhoglu. 1994. *Limits of Citizenship: Migrants and Postnational Membership in Europe.* Chicago: University of Chicago Press.

St. Christopher House. 2000. *Annual Report, 1999–2000.* Toronto.

Staggenborg, Suzanne. 1988. "The Consequences of Professionalization and Formalization in the Pro-choice Movement." *American Sociological Review* 53 (4): 585–605.

———. 1991. *The Pro-choice Movement: Organization and Activism in the Abortion Conflict.* New York: Oxford University Press.

Stasiulis, Daiva K. 1988. "The Symbolic Mosaic Reaffirmed: Multiculturalism Policy." Pages 81–111 in *How Ottawa Spends 1988/89: The Conservatives into the Stretch,* ed. Katherine A. Graham. Ottawa: Carleton University Press.

———. 1997. "Participation by Immigrants, Ethnocultural/Visible Minorities in the Canadian Political Process." Discussion paper. Prepared for the research domain seminar "Immigrants and Civic Participation: Contemporary Policy and Research Issues," convened by Heritage Canada. Montreal, November 23.

———, and Yasmeen Abu-Laban. 1991. "The House the Parties Built: (Re)Constructing Ethnic Representation in Canadian Politics." Pages 3–99 in *Ethnocultural Groups and Visible Minorities in Canadian Politics: The Question of Access,* ed. Kathy Megyery. Vol. 7 of *Research Studies of the Royal Commission on Electoral Reform and Party Financing.* Toronto: Dundurn Press.

Statistics Canada. 1995. 1991 Census Public Use Microfile [computer file]. Ottawa: Statistics Canada.

———. 2001. "Total Population by Citizenship Status and Sex, for Canada, 1996 Census, 20% Sample." In the Nation Series, December 18, http://www.statcan.ca/english/census96/nov4/imm3.htm (accessed February 11, 2002).

———. 2004. 2001 Census of Population. "Immigrant Status and Period of Immigration (10A) and Place of Birth of Respondent (260) for Immigrants and Non-permanent Residents, for Canada, Provinces, Territories, Census Metropolitan Areas and Census Agglomerations, 20% Sample Data." Available at www12.statcan.ca/english/census01/Products/standard/themes/DataProducts.cfm?5=1&T=43&ALEVEL=2&FREE=O (last accessed January 5, 2006).

Sterne, Evelyn Savidge. 2001. "Beyond the Boss: Immigration and American Political Culture from 1880 to 1940." Pages 33–66 in *E Pluribus Unum? Contemporary and Historical Perspectives on Immigrant Political Incorporation,* ed. Gary Gerstle and John Mollenkopf. New York: Russell Sage Foundation.

Stockman, Farah, and Bill Dedman. 2002. "Hub Records Show Boost in Minority Voting Rates." *Boston Globe,* August 10, A1.

Taft, Donald R. 1923. *Two Portuguese Communities in New England, 1910–1920.* New York: Columbia University.

Tarrow, Sidney. 1994. *Power in Movement: Social Movements, Collective Action and Politics.* New York: Cambridge University Press.

Taylor, Charles. 1994. "The Politics of Recognition." Pages 25–73 in *Multiculturalism,* ed. Amy Gutmann. Princeton, NJ: Princeton University Press.

Teixeira, Carlos. 1999. *Portugeses Em Toronto: Uma Comunidade Em Mudança.*

Azores: Direcção Regional das Comunidades, Regional Autonomous Government of the Azores.

———, and Gilles Lavigne. 1992. *The Portuguese in Canada: A Bibliography*. Toronto: Institute for Social Research, York University.

Thelen, Kathleen, and Sven Steinmo. 1992. "Historic Institutionalism in Comparative Politics." Pages 1–32 in *Structuring Politics: Historical Institutionalism in Comparative Analysis*, ed. Sven Steinmo, Kathleen Thelen, and Frank Longstreth. New York: Cambridge University Press.

Thompson, Richard. 1979. "Ethnicity versus Class: An Analysis of Conflict in a North American Chinese Community." *Ethnicity* 6: 306–26.

Tichenor, Daniel J. 2002. *Dividing Lines: The Politics of Immigration Control in America*. Princeton, NJ: Princeton University Press.

Tocqueville, Alexis de. [1835] 1945. *Democracy in America*. New York: A. A. Knopf.

Tomz, Michael, Jason Wittenberg, and Gary King. 2001. "CLARIFY: Software for Interpreting and Presenting Statistical Results. Version 2.0." Cambridge, MA: Harvard University. http://gking.harvard.edu.

Troper, Harold. 2003. "Becoming an Immigrant City: A History of Immigration into Toronto since the Second World War." Pages 19–62 in *The World in a City*, ed. Paul Anisef and Michael Lanphier. Toronto: University of Toronto Press.

Tuan, Mia. 1999. *Forever Foreigners or Honorary Whites? The Asian Ethnic Experience Today*. Piscataway, NJ: Rutgers University Press.

Ueda, Reed. 1982. "Naturalization and Citizenship." Pages 106–54 in *Immigration*, ed. Richard A. Easterlin, David Ward, William S. Bernard, and Reed Ueda. Cambridge, MA: Belknap/Harvard University Press.

———. 2001. "Historical Patterns of Immigrant Status and Incorporation in the United States." Pages 292–327 in *E Pluribus Unum? Contemporary and Historical Perspectives on Immigrant Political Incorporation*, ed. Gary Gerstle and John Mollenkopf. New York: Russell Sage Foundation.

Uhlaner, Carole J. 1996. "Latinos and Ethnic Politics in California: Participation and Preference." Pages 33–72 in *Latino Politics in California*, ed. Aníbal Yáñchez-Chávez. San Diego: Center for U.S.-Mexican Studies, University of California, San Diego.

———, Bruce E. Cain, and D. Roderick Kiewiet. 1989. "Political Participation of Ethnic Minorities in the 1980s." *Political Behavior* 11 (3): 195–231.

Ujimoto, K. Victor. 1999. "Studies of Ethnic Identity, Ethnic Relations and Citizenship." Pages 253–90 in *Race and Ethnic Relations in Canada*, 2nd ed., ed. Peter S. Li. Toronto: Oxford University Press.

United Nations, Department of Economic and Social Affairs. 2002. *International Migration Report 2002*. New York: United Nations.

U.S. Census Bureau. 1993. *Ancestry of the Population in the United States*. Vol. 1990 CP-3–2. 1990 Census of Population. Washington, D.C.: Government Printing Office.

———. 2002. 2000 Census of Population and Housing, Summary File 3 (SF

3)—Sample Data, http://factfinder.census.gov/servlet/DatasetMainPage-Servlet?_ds_name=DEC_2000_SF3_U&_program=DEC&_lang=en.

U.S. Commission on Naturalization. 1905. *Report to the President.* Washington, D.C.: Government Printing Office.

U.S. Department of Homeland Security. 2004. *Budget in Brief: Fiscal Year 2005.* Washington, D.C.: Department of Homeland Security.

U.S. General Accounting Office. 2001. *Immigration Benefits: Several Factors Impede Timeliness of Application Processing.* GAO-01–488. Washington, D.C.: General Accounting Office.

U.S. Immigration and Naturalization Service. 2000. "INS Achieves 2-Year Naturalization Program Goals." In *News Release from Media Services, Office of Public Affairs,* www.ins.gov/graphics/publicaffairs/newsreels/NatzGoal.htm (accessed April 25, 2000).

———. 2002. *Statistical Yearbook of the Immigration and Naturalization Service, 2000.* Washington, D.C.: Government Printing Office.

U.S. Office of Refugee Resettlement. 1981. *Report to Congress: Refugee Resettlement Program.* Washington, D.C.: U.S. Office of Refugee Resettlement.

———. 1985. *Report to Congress: Refugee Resettlement Program.* Washington, D.C.: U.S. Office of Refugee Resettlement.

Usdansky, Margaret L., and Thomas J. Espenshade. 2001. "The Evolution of U.S. Policy toward Employment-Based Immigrants and Temporary Workers: The H-1B Debate in Historic Perspective." Pages 23–53 in *The International Migration of the Highly Skilled: Demand, Supply, and Development Consequences in Sending and Receiving Countries,* ed. Wayne A. Cornelius, Thomas J. Espenshade, and Idean Salehyan. La Jolla: Center for Comparative Immigration Studies, University of California, San Diego.

Useem, Bert. 1980. "Solidarity Model, Breakdown Model, and the Boston Anti-busing Movement." *American Sociological Review* 45: 357–69.

Valdés, Alisa. 1995. "In Mass., Potential Clout." *Boston Globe,* April 20, 61, 64.

Vallières, Pierre. 1968. *Negres Blancs d'Amérique: Autobiographie Précoce d'un "Terroriste" Québécois.* Montreal: Editions Parti pris.

Van Til, Jon. 2000. *Growing Civil Society: From Nonprofit Sector to Third Space.* Bloomington: Indiana University Press.

Verba, Sidney, Kay Lehman Schlozman, and Henry E. Brady. 1995. *Voice and Equality: Civic Voluntarism in American Politics.* Cambridge, MA: Harvard University Press.

Verba, Sidney, et al. 1993. "Race, Ethnicity and Political Resources: Participation in the United States." *British Journal of Political Science* 23: 453–97.

Vietnamese Association of Toronto. 1979. *A Profile of the Vietnamese Community in Toronto.* Mimeograph. Toronto Public Library.

Warner, Lloyd, and Leo Srole. 1945. *The Social Systems of American Ethnic Groups.* New Haven, CT: Yale University Press.

Waters, Mary C. 1990. *Ethnic Options: Choosing Identities in America.* Berkeley: University of California Press.

———. 1999. *Black Identities: West Indian Immigrant Dreams and American Realities.* Cambridge: Harvard University Press.

Watkiss, Ulli. 2002. *Toronto Votes 2003: Candidate's Guide.* Toronto: Toronto City Council.

Wearing, Rosemary J. 1985. "Some Correlates of Choosing Australian Citizenship." *Australian and New Zealand Journal of Sociology* 21 (3): 395–413.

Weber, Eugen. 1976. *Peasants into Frenchmen: The Modernization of Rural France, 1870–1914.* Stanford, CA: Stanford University Press.

Weil, Patrick. 2001. "Access to Citizenship: A Comparison of Twenty-five Nationality Laws." Pages 17–35 in *Citizenship Today: Global Perspectives and Practices,* ed. T. Alexander Aleinikoff and Douglas Klusmeyer. Washington, D.C.: Carnegie Endowment for International Peace.

Whitaker, Reg. 1987. *Double Standard: The Secret History of Canadian Immigration.* Toronto: Lester and Orpen Dennys.

Wickham-Crowley, Timothy P. 1992. *Guerrillas and Revolution in Latin America: A Comparative Study of Insurgents and Regimes since 1956.* Princeton, NJ: Princeton University Press.

Williams, Jerry. 1982. *And Yet They Come: Portuguese Immigration from the Azores to the United States.* New York: Center for Migration Studies.

Wilson, Warwick. 1997. "Ethnic Associations and Immigrant Integration: The Vietnamese in Toronto, Canada." Unpublished paper.

With, Tatiana M. 1996. "A Friendship and Culture Club; Elderly Vietnamese Find a Way to Combat Isolation." *Boston Globe,* November 17, 10.

Wolforth, Sandra. 1978. *The Portuguese in America.* San Francisco: R. & E. Research Associates.

Wong, Janelle. 2006. *Democracy's Promise: Immigrants and American Civic Institutions.* Ann Arbor: University of Michigan Press.

Woon, F. W. 1986. "Some Adjustment Aspects of Vietnamese and Sino-Vietnamese Families in Victoria, Canada." *Journal of Comparative Family Studies* 17 (3): 349–70.

Yang, Philip Q. 1994. "Explaining Immigrant Naturalization." *International Migration Review* 28 (3): 449–77.

Young, Iris Marion. 1990. *Justice and the Politics of Difference.* Princeton, NJ: Princeton University Press.

Zhou, Min, and Carl L. Bankston III. 1998. *Growing Up American: How Vietnamese Children Adapt to Life in the United States.* New York: Russell Sage Foundation.

Zolberg, Aristide R. 1992. "Response to Crisis: Refugee Policy in the United States and Canada." Pages 55–112, in *Immigration, Language and Ethnicity: Canada and the United States,* ed. Barry Chiswick. Washington, D.C.: American Enterprise Institute Press.

Zucker, Lynne G. 1991. "The Role of Institutionalization in Cultural Persistence." Pages 83–107 in *The New Institutionalism in Organizational Analysis,* ed. Walter W. Powell and Paul J. DiMaggio. Chicago: University of Chicago Press.

Zucker, Norman L., and Naomi F. Zucker. 1989. "The Uneasy Troika in US Refugee Policy: Foreign Policy, Pressure Groups, and Resettlement Costs." *Journal of Refugee Studies* 3: 359–72.

———. 1992. "From Immigration to Refugee Redefinition: A History of Refugee and Asylum Policy in the United States." *Journal of Policy History* 4 (1): 54–70.

Index

Cunha, Father, 313–14n65
Curtis, John W., 44
Czechoslovakia, 63

DeFaria, Carl, 214, 229, 308–9n23,
311n48, 315n80
DeGette, Diane, 63
Democratic Party (U.S.): INS and, 110;
outreach efforts by, 312n53; party
competition and political incorporation, 210; Vietnamese affiliation
with, 205, 216–17, 312n52
DeSipio, Louis, 64
diversity/diversity policies: citizenship
and, 139; government-sponsored,
106; official categorization of, 140;
U.S. vs. Canadian views of, 145. *See
also* multiculturalism *entries*
Dorais, Louis-Jacques, 282n33
dual citizenship: Canadian multiculturalism policy and, 275–76n74,
276n79; political, 298–99n15;
Portuguese extension of, 94–95,
286–87n70; relationship to naturalization, 7; symbolic value of, 276n79;
U.S. vs. Canadian regulations on, 25,
49–53
Duncan, Howard, 244–45
Durham, Lord, 123, 293n47
Dusenberry, Verne A., 307n14

education: community leadership and,
195, 306–7n11; immigrant community organizations and, 303n25; naturalization likelihood and, 282n34;
political activism and, 205; political
incorporation and, 6, 76–77; of Portuguese Americans, 282–83n35,
298n14; religious/ethnic, government funding of, 298n7; social class
and, 303–4n26; U.S.-Canada naturalization gap and, 42–43, 44, 45–
47, 273n47, 274nn60, 63
electoral success: definition of, 202,
308n20; ideological congruence and,
214–15; immigrant community
organizations and, 207–10; political

system and, 54–56, 210–14; symbolic value of, 228–29; U.S. vs.
Canada, 54, 56–63, 202–7, 204 table
8. *See also* politicians, foreign-born
electoral system: campaign finance
regulations, 213–14; primaries, 211
elite, immigrant: community leadership vs., 200, 307n15; homeland
politics and, 286n63; mobilization
of, 217; private donations/grants
and, 187
Elnyiak, Wasyl, 25
El Salvadoran immigrants, 273n45,
284n45, 296n75
employment: assistance with, 119–20,
121, 244, 300n27; immigration policy and, 10, 40–41, 265n20
Employment and Immigration
Canada, 132
England, 57–58, 63, 318n18
ESL classes: Canadian settlement programs for, 119; ethnic media as
information source for, 85; government funding of, 116, 291n32;
immigrant community organizations and, 91, 92–93; naturalization
assistance in, 3116, 119
Estado Novo, 69, 286n63
ethnic brokers, 202
ethnic businesses: abuses committed
by, 284–85n53; community leadership and, 306n7; political incorporation facilitated by, 66, 85–87
ethnic ghettoization, 155, 159, 236,
245, 317n9
ethnicity, 140–41; Canadian, 317n13;
cultural recognition and, 246–47;
group formation and, 239–40;
nationalism and, 316–17n6; as
socially constructed term, 297–
98n5; symbolic, 141–43, 149, 153–
54, 159, 247; Vietnamese American
conflict and, 283n38
ethnic media: community functions of,
284nn47–48; literacy and, 284n50;
organizational capacity and, 164–66,
167; political incorporation and, 84–

Text: 10/13 Aldus
Display: Aldus
Compositor and illustrator: BookMatters, Berkeley
Indexer: Kevin Millham
Printer and binder: Sheridan Books, Inc.